Business Data Systems

G000123644

Business Data Systems

A practical guide to systems analysis and data processing

4th Edition

H. D. Clifton

Prentice Hall

New York • London • Toronto • Sydney • Tokyo • Singapore

First published 1990 by
Prentice Hall International (UK) Ltd,
66 Wood Lane End, Hemel Hempstead.
Hertfordshire, HP2 4RG
A division of
Simon & Schuster International Group

© 1990, 1986, 1983 & 1978
Prentice Hall International (UK) Ltd

Text designed by Lesley Stuart
Typeset in 10/12pt Plantin
by MHL Typesetting Ltd, Coventry, UK
Printed and bound in Great Britain at
the University Press, Cambridge

Library of Congress Cataloging-in-Publication Data

Clifton, H. D. (Harold Dennis), 1927–
    Business data systems: a practical guide to systems
analysis and data processing/H. D. Clifton. – 4th ed.
        p.   cm.
    Includes bibliographical references.
    ISBN 0-13-091695-1
    1. Business—Data processing.   2. System analysis.
    I. Title.
HF5548.2.C5427   1990
658'.05—dc20   89-28502
                                                           CIP

British Library Cataloguing in Publication Data

Clifton, H. D. (Harold Dennis), 1927–
    Business data systems. — 4th ed.
    1. Business data systems a practical guide to systems
analysis and data processing H. D. Clifton
    I. Title
    658'.05

ISBN 0-13-091695-1

1 2 3 4 5   94 93 92 91 90

Contents

Preface

This edition, as in the case of the three previous editions, is tuned to the needs of readers in the broadest sense, being based upon suggestions and comments from a survey of adopting tutors. The text is of a practical orientation and is aimed towards students and practitioners in the fields of systems development, data processing, accounting and other business activities. It is of especial interest to business studies and computer science students in higher education, and to those studying for professional qualifications in accountancy and computing. This is evidenced by the exercises and solutions at the end of each chapter, most of which are drawn from the examination papers of professional institutions. These exercises are intended both as supplementary learning material and as practice questions for prospective examinees.

This, fourth, edition includes information covering the newer areas of systems development and data processing, and so provides the reader with a comprehensive overview of the latest methodologies, software and hardware. Extensive bibliographies enable readers to acquire further information on topics of particular interest.

The case study (Chapter 9) is intended to integrate the contents of the preceding chapters by setting them against practical business operations. It is based on an actual business and has been chosen in order to emphasize problems, methods and procedures against a background understandable to all readers.

The glossary has been enhanced by incorporating the most recent terminology. The entries therein were selected from a larger range, many of which were too transient or too vague to be of real value. This reflects the unfortunate but perhaps unavoidable tendency of the data processing industry to coin an unending stream of acronyms and jargon to the mystification of many computer users.

The author and the publisher are pleased to receive suggestions and observations regarding this book's contents and usage.

Acknowledgements

The author acknowledges with gratitude the assistance of all persons who provided suggestions for this edition. In particular, the help of my former colleague, Mr T. P. Moore, is gratefully appreciated.

The exercises include questions drawn from the examination papers of the professional institutions listed below; their respective permissions are acknowledged with thanks.

The British Computer Society
The Chartered Association of Certified Accountants
The Chartered Institute of Management Accountants
The Institute of Chartered Accountants in England and Wales
The Institute of Chartered Secretaries and Administrators

It should be pointed out that the solutions to the exercises are attributable entirely to the author and do not necessarily reflect those of the respective professional institutions.

H.D.C.

Business and management information

1.1 Business organizations

All concerns that are in some ways constrained by money and resources can be regarded as business organizations. These include manufacturing and commercial companies, central and local government departments, administrative organizations, financial institutions, and service agencies. All of these organizations are referred to hereafter by the generic terms 'organization' or 'company'.

The organizations involved with data systems, i.e. data processing (DP) and systems analysis, vary considerably in size, from huge international corporations and government departments down to small 'back street' companies and private individuals. The factors common to all of these should be a clear understanding of the purpose and aims of the organization, and a systems approach to the solution of problems.

We tend nowadays to talk of 'solving' business problems as if they are mathematical equations that have unique and absolute solutions. What is really meant by a solution is a method of alleviating the burden of a task or of avoiding a calamity that might ensue from difficulties encountered. There are no immediate solutions to most business problems; it is more likely that effective results derive from a well-organized system carefully planned and assiduously operated. Business problems are usually associated with the need for information to control the business's activities.

What are the aims of business organizations? Why do businesses exist and for what purposes? There are, no doubt, many metaphysical answers to these questions but in the pragmatic sense they are related to the control over money, people and resources. A company financed by privately owned share capital aims to maintain or increase its profitability and thereby maximize the long-term value of its shares. The vagaries of the stock market are beyond the scope of this text but profitability is a prime aim if a company is to continue in existence. Other long-term aims of companies are expansion, diversification, and monopolization of products and markets.

Organizations that are publicly owned, i.e. government controlled, are usually regulated by the need to keep within their operating budgets. Their objectives may be decided as a result of political, social or economic considerations but, in the end, they are operated within monetary constraints. This calls for the provision of adequate information about their activities and environment.

Readers unfamiliar with business organizations are advised to read References 1.1–1.4.

Business work areas

The need for information and the consequent requirement for a means of processing raw data rapidly and accurately applies to a wide range of work areas in business. From Figure 1.1 can be seen in broad outline the way in which work areas connect together and contribute to the financial and management accounting systems of a 'typical' manufacturing company.

Perhaps the most obviously needed information is a company's financial position as derived from its business transactions. Closely associated with financial accounting is management accounting, i.e. the control over a company's manufacturing costs in relation to its productive output.

Accounting information stems from book-keeping procedures, each and every financial transaction contributing to some extent to the financial position of a company. There are numerous items of expenditure and income that have to be accounted for in arriving at a company's annual balance sheet and profit/loss statement. We are therefore, in DP systems, aiming for a means of gathering all the financial transactions, and processing them accurately and economically in order to provide not only the statutory information required of an organization but also further information to improve its efficiency and profitability. References 1.5–1.8 provide useful knowledge for readers unacquainted with accounting principles.

The major work areas inherent to most companies and organizations are:

wages accounting
sales control and accounting
purchases control and accounting
management (cost) accounting
stock control
production control.

These areas are described below in outline mainly with the intention of providing readers who are unfamiliar with business with some basic understanding of the procedures and problems therein.

Wages accounting

A paramount feature of all business enterprises is the necessity to employ and remunerate a workforce. The workforce usually comprises people of a wide range

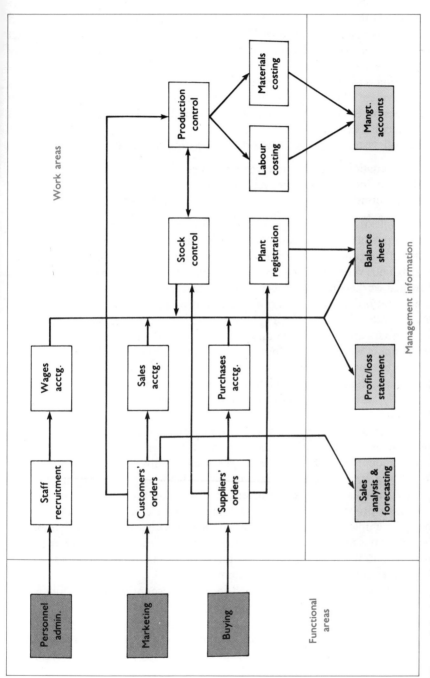

Figure 1.1 Interrelationships of work areas and management information

of skills — manual, technical and managerial. The factor common to all the workforce is that they must be paid and hence the organization must be geared to doing this in a precise manner. This necessitates the existence of a personnel administration system, however rudimentary it may be, allied to a properly organized payroll system. The former exists, among other things, to provide information regarding the employees' personal attributes, capabilities and terms of employment. The payroll system is the means of knowing how much to pay employees on each occasion, and of accounting for the monies thus disbursed and otherwise expended.

Payroll systems can be regarded as consisting of the following parts:

Computation of each employee's gross earnings, wage or salary.
Computation of the employee's net payment based on gross earnings.
Accounting for amounts deducted from earnings.

The complexity of the first part varies and is dependent upon the employee's terms of payment. In the case of staff, their monthly salary is usually simply a twelfth of their annual salary plus commission or bonus to which they are entitled (if any). Thus very little computation is entailed. On the other hand, certain types of manual workers have complicated wage structures and so several calculations are necessary. For instance, earnings may depend upon hours worked in various time periods with a different hourly rate for each period (dayworkers). Pieceworkers are so called because all or some of their earnings depend upon the amount of work done, i.e. output achieved, either individually or collectively.

The computation of net payments is more standardized than that of gross wages, being mainly the calculation of deductions such as income tax (PAYE in the UK), national insurance contributions, superannuation (pension) payments, and so on.

The accounting aspects of wages are mainly (1) the distribution of monies to employees as either cash, cheques or credit transfers, and (2) the entry of the correct amounts into the nominal ledger to cover subsequent payments (in the UK) to the Inland Revenue (income tax deductions), Department of Social Security (national insurance contributions), pension funds, and so on.

Another problem of net wage distribution is note/coin analysis. This applies where the employees are paid in cash rather than cheques or credit transfers. The problem is in determining the precise number of each denomination of bank note and coin needed to make up all the pay packets (wage envelopes) so that each packet contains the exact net amount.

The principal documents involved in wages accounting are the following:

Pay advice

A small document (payslip) for each employee on which are the precise details of the pay for the period. Typically, the pay advice shows the gross earnings, and in some cases how this is composed, each amount deducted and the net amount. Also shown is indicative information such as the employee's number and name, department number, tax code, national insurance number, week number and/or the date.

Payroll
A list containing for each employee substantially the same information as on the pay advice but perhaps amplified to include the amounts-to-date, e.g. the gross wage paid up to and including this period since the start of the tax year. The payroll is usually listed in some sequence such as employee number within department number to facilitate reference to it subsequently.

Bank direct credit list
Since most salaried employees have their net pay transferred directly into their bank accounts, it is necessary to send a list to the company's bank detailing the amounts to be transferred to the employees' accounts.

Cheques and Giro credits
In cases where an employee is not paid in cash nor by credit transfer, a cheque or Giro credit has to be drawn.

Note and coin analysis
As explained above, the total and probably the individual person's amount of each denomination of note and coin is shown in this analysis. In larger organizations the analysis is subdivided into departmental totals for ease of handling. The analysis is sent to the bank so that the cash can be made up for insertion into pay packets.

Deductions analysis
This shows the total amount of each deduction made from wages for the period and to date. It may also be split into departmental totals.

Cost analyses
These are less standardized than the other payroll documents. As they are for the purposes of cost accounting, their contents depend entirely upon the nature of the company's activities. There is likely to be a number of cost analyses but typically in a manufacturing company a cost analysis contains the period and year-to-date gross amounts paid to each labour group for each current job in the factory.

End-of-year documents
These are statutory documents required by the Inland Revenue in order for them to check that the correct amount of income tax has been deducted. There is one document, known as a P60, per employer of which he or she receives a copy. Similar documents (P45s) are prepared for employees leaving the company.

Audit and control documents

Payrolls need to be carefully controlled and checked as large amounts of money are involved. The various documents described above need to be supplemented by sets of totals so that if a discrepancy arises, it is not too difficult to trace. This is particularly important where cash is involved.

Wages records

It is necessary to maintain a record for each employee containing full and absolutely accurate details of pay items. This record must be kept up-to-date in terms of amendments as well as the updating of the totals-to-date. Amendments include changes to an employee's gross wage, tax code, department, bank, and so on. The wages records have also to be amended to incorporate details of new employees (starters) and remove details pertaining to leavers. The wages records are connected with the personnel records in that the personnel department informs the wages department of changes in personnel.

Sales control and accounting

Customer order control entails procedures for ensuring that orders from customers/clients are received, recorded and acknowledged in an efficient and organized manner. This applies no matter whether the orders are received through the post, by telephone, via sales representatives, by means of electronic mail or through other communication systems.

At a later stage, order control is necessary to ensure that orders are actually fulfilled, i.e. customers receive the correct goods on time and at the right destination.

Particular features of order control include:

- Dealing with enquiries from prospective purchasers *re* prices, availabilities and delivery dates.
- Checking in conjunction with the accounts department the credit ratings of customers who place large orders on credit.
- Comparison of orders received against quotations given prevously (if any) in terms of price and availability.
- Checking that goods ordered are valid, i.e. exist, and querying dubious orders with customers.
- Handling customer complaints and queries regarding price and delivery; these may be passed on to the sales representatives in certain cases.
- Checking the fulfilment of orders via the dispatch department.

Sales accounting is a function of the accounts department involving the monetary side of customers' orders. In this respect customers fall into two main types: (1) companies or persons who have accounts with the company; and (2) customers who pay CWO, COD or against pro-forma invoices. Note that we are not concerned here with over-the-counter sales in shops and supermarkets. Some firms' customers are all type (1) e.g. government departments, local authorities, accredited companies and persons. Other firms deal with all type (2) customers, e.g. mail-order customers. A number of firms have both types of customers.

The main documents connected with sales accounting are:

Customer orders
These must hold all the information needed to identify the customer, the goods ordered, the delivery address and, perhaps, the price and date of delivery. Identification is likely to entail catalogue numbers, commodity codes, account numbers, etc.

Goods dispatched notes
These are records of goods sent and perhaps acknowledged as received by customers. Often they are copies of the sales invoices (see below).

Sales invoices
A sales invoice is sent to a customer after he or she has received the goods as a request for payment. Copies are often used as dispatch notes and packing notes. An invoice needs to contain sufficient information to clearly identify the goods, their prices and values, discounts, packing and carriage charges and VAT (sales tax).

Sales statements
Statements are sent to customers at regular intervals, e.g. monthly, in order to show their indebtedness or credit position. Each statement lists the sales and payments transacted since the previous statement, and shows the current financial position, i.e. the amount owing or in credit. The contents of statements are derived from the sales ledger records, usually held on computer files.

Sales analysis reports
A very wide variety of sales analyses are created within the totality of company marketing. Essentially they show sales quantities and values summarized into various groupings. The purpose of sales analysis is to find what has been sold, where, when and to whom. This information can then be used to forecast future sales demands and to plan marketing activities.

Typical groupings are commodities, commodity groups, sales areas, regions, zones, sales periods and customer categories. These are combined together in numerous ways to suit the needs of sales manager, e.g. commodity groups within sales areas for each of the past twelve months.

Purchases control and accounting

Purchasing involves the procedures for ensuring that all the materials, components, tools, equipment and other items needed by the company are made available at the right time, right place and right price. The precise nature of the purchasing function depends upon the type of items purchased, but generally the following procedures apply:

- Obtaining quotations of price, delivery date and quality from prospective suppliers.
- Placing orders with suppliers, monitoring delivery and chasing overdue orders.
- Checking goods received (by goods receiving department) for correct type, quality and quantity.
- Passing details of accepted goods to the accounts department for subsequent payment of suppliers.
- Checking suppliers' invoices and statements for accuracy before actually making payment.
- Accumulating various statistical data pertaining to prices, delivery achievements and quality for the purpose of improving decisions regarding the placement of purchase orders.

The main documents associated with purchases accounting are:

Purchase orders   These must contain sufficient information for the supplier to be able to supply the correct item(s) to the right location or person at the appropriate date. Absolute identification of the required item depends to some extent on the supplier. If he has a clear catalogue showing all his goods clearly labelled and coded, then there should be no problem. On the other hand if the requirement is non-standard or made-to-specification, great care is necessary to ensure that the correct item is ordered and received.

Goods Received Notes (GRNs)   A GRN is a record of receipt of a certain quantity of an item. It is made out at the time of receipt and then validated after the goods have been inspected.

Purchase invoices   These are received from suppliers after the goods have been received. They must contain sufficient detail to relate to the goods supplied and to the purchase order. Known discrepancies between the order and the invoice should be noted on the invoice, e.g. items omitted or short.

Remittance advices   These are documents sent to the suppliers advising that payment is being made to them. The information thereon is primarily the amounts, date and method of payment, and any reference numbers that apply to the remittance.

Cheques   A cheque to accompany the remittance advice has to be drawn unless payment is by bank credit transfer.

Credit transfers   A list is sent to the company's bank instructing them to transfer monies to the accounts of the suppliers listed.

Purchases analyses   In some cases it is beneficial to analyse the company's purchases in various ways. There are several reasons for this, the main ones are (a) in order to measure the efficiency of suppliers, and (b) to cost the purchases of the departments and those pertaining to the jobs being done.

The possible range of purchase analysis information is wide but nevertheless some companies have no such requirement.

Purchase records   A record must be kept for each supplier to show the details of his account, i.e. the purchase ledger. The main information in each record is the supplier's account number, name, the current balance and the transactions (invoices and remittances) outstanding for the period in question, e.g. for the current month.

Another, or perhaps the same record, holds details of the supplier such as the method of payment, terms of trade and discount structure(s).

Management (cost) accounting

Management accounting, often referred to as costing, is a complex subject and so only a superficial explanation is given here. The general idea is that costing ensures that the organization's activities are accomplished at acceptable costs and that all cost discrepancies are accounted for. Thus cost expenditures are compared with standards and the differences between actual and standard costs are analysed.

Standard costing entails the setting of predetermined estimated costs, i.e. standards, and the regular comparison of these standards with the actual costs incurred. The difference between standard and actual costs is termed a 'variance' and it is the analysis of variances that can provide management with valuable information for control and planning.

Variance analysis is a complex subject owing to the different ways in which the variances may be broken down. A profit variance, for instance, may be split into a sales variance and a cost variance.

The sales variance is then broken down further into volume variance, i.e. the difference between the standard sales quantity and the actual quantity sold, and the price variance, i.e. the difference between the standard price and the actual price. Similarly, the cost variance is broken down into materials and labour, which in turn are broken down into finer detail such as materials prices and usages, wage rates, and labour efficiency. Further information on standard costing is available in Reference 1.7.

Costing applies particularly to production, in which small rises in costs can reduce or completely eliminate profitability. The two major production costs are labour and materials, and nowadays the former is so high that automation is more economic in developed countries for many types of production. Similarly, certain materials have risen in cost to such an extent that other materials have to be used.

The processing of cost data provides information that helps management to take decisions regarding methods of production and materials to use. One of the complexities of costing is the apportionment of overheads, for instance, the allocation of overhead costs such as rates, rent, heating, management, etc., to production jobs or output so that their realistic cost and hence their selling price can be determined.

Other aspects of costing include marginal costing, break-even analysis, and budgeting. Marginal costing is the determination of the extra cost involved in producing an item above a certain level of production. Thus if the fixed overheads have been apportioned, a marginal cost would tend to be less than the standard cost — but by how much?

Break-even analysis relates turnover to costs so that it is possible to decide at what level of turnover the operation becomes profitable and, above this level, what profit is made.

Budgeting or budgetary control is a means of controlling expenditure and other monies by making forecasts of future expenditure, income, sales, etc. This enables provisional accounts and costs to be devised so that an advance estimate of the financial situation is available. Departments are then expected to conform to their budgets or otherwise to justify deviations.

The aforementioned costing procedures all demand considerable processing of data in order that suitable reports can be presented to management, and hence there is a need for computer power to be available for most costing applications.

Stock control

Stock (inventory) control is closely connected in practice with stores control. The former is the monitoring and decisions regarding the actual items held in the stores, the latter is the methods of operating the warehouse or stores.

Items are held in stock as a buffer between supply and demand. The supply may be either from the company's production or from external supplies, or both. The demand may derive from customers or from internal sources. In any event it is important that when a demand arises, there is sufficient stock to meet it with a minimum of delay. The exception to this philosophy is when an item is so expensive or so unmanageable that it is simply not economic or practical to stock it, and it therefore must be purchased or manufactured as and when required.

Inventory theory (modelling) takes us into the realms of operations research, introducing mathematical and statistical principles. In a nutshell, inventory theory covers the methods of minimizing the overall cost of stockholding. It takes into consideration the costs of storage, reordering, capital tied up in stock, stock depreciation and deterioration, and the loss of profit caused by out-of-stock situations.

More mundanely, stock control involves the maintenance of records relating to stock levels, issues, outstanding orders, reorder levels, and so on. These figures apply to various categories of stock such as raw materials, bought-out and made-in components, subassemblies, finished and part-finished products, tools, jigs, machines, and consumable materials (lubricants, fuels, etc.). It is apparent from the diversity of items on this list that the methodologies of stock and stores control vary widely. As an example, the methods of recording and holding a volatile and flammable chemical, such as acetone, differ from those for a precious metal, such as platinum, and again from a bulky inert substance, such as house bricks.

The factors entering into stores control are the size and weight of stock items, also their value, flammability, stability (chemical and physical), and identification. These factors determine the need for handling equipment, security, packaging, labelling and space (both indoors and outside).

From the information aspect an important requirement is stock valuation, i.e. the book value of all stock-in-hand at a certain time. This valuation often follows a physical stock check carried out annually but may also stem from computer-held records – or from a combination of both. In any event, the figures should be accurate, and allow for stock losses, deterioration and enhanced value since these contribute to the firm's annual balance sheet.

From the DP aspect much depends upon the number of stock items, their turnover and dispersal. If there is a large number of items being issued from and received into several dispersed stores, there is obviously a significant problem both as regards capture of the data and its subsequent processing.

Production control

This subject encompasses a truly immense area of knowledge since there are so many different manufactured products and methods of production. Essentially, production planning covers what to make and how to make; production control ensures that the planning is achieved.

From the DP aspect, the engineering industry poses the need for most information. This is particularly so for industries that purchase materials, make and/or buy components, and assemble products through various levels of subassembly. Examples are the car, machine tool, domestic appliance, aircraft, and entertainment equipment industries.

The information required for production control purposes includes:

- material requirements for each time period;
- quantities of components and subassemblies to be made by each period;
- the amounts of equipment, machines, tools, jigs, etc., needed for each stage;
- the amount of each labour category needed during each period;
- the loading of each production unit in each period;
- the progress of each job and reasons for delays.

If the products and production processes are complex, as is usually the case, the above information may be difficult to acquire.

In order to determine the quantities of materials, components and subassemblies needed each period, a huge amount of computation may be necessary. There could be a large range of products each comprising several levels of assembly. Each level entails determining the precise quantities of all items at a lower level, resulting in perhaps tens of thousands of components and materials being needed at the lowest level.

Similarly, the components may be made through a series of manufacturing operations involving different machines and types of labour. In view of the high cost of labour and of most machines, it is advantageous to keep these facilities fully occupied. This again involves very considerable computation so that machine and labour resources can be assigned to tasks in the correct production sequence and to tie in with the availability of materials and components, etc.

Although this is an abbreviated explanation of a big subject, it should give the reader some notion of production control problems.

It is evident from the above descriptions of the work areas that they generate a great amount of raw data, and that their control requires a considerable amount of information. The comparison of data and information is discussed in the next section, for the present we are concerned with the interrelationship of work areas through their common use of data and information. Every work area has links with some or all of the others, e.g. stock control receives data from the purchasing department concerning materials and passes information to production control about components required.

The interrelationships between work areas give rise to the concept of 'integration' of activities and information. This concept is especially pertinent to the sharing of data held in file records, e.g. stock data is of use in purchasing, sales and production control. Data systems designers are well aware of this common use of data and consequently they attempt to create systems that allow every application to have access to the data in an up-to-date condition.

The above requirements mean that in practice it is necessary to use a computer-based system which has the capability of storing all the records. Such an arrangement is termed a 'database'; this concept is explained in more detail in Section 4.4. These aims have proved difficult to realize for many organizations, and, in recent years, there has been an acceptance of the fact that centralized computer systems are not always the answer. This has led to the growth of more autonomous systems but with some degree of interconnection. These are known as distributed processing systems (Section 2.5).

Similarly, the departments of a company are nowadays likely to have their own microcomputers, probably connected to other computers by means of a network system (Section 2.5).

1.2 Business information

Before discussing business information it is worthwhile considering what is meant by 'data' and by 'information' in this context.

Data is the raw figures appertaining to the routine activities of the organization. These figures in themselves do not enable decisions of any consequence to be taken, and in order for data to be more useful it needs to be 'processed' to provide information.

Processing is a broad term but essentially can be taken as meaning the conversion of data into information, that is to say turning not very useful figures into useful facts and figures. This generally means a reduction in amount; a lot of data is 'distilled' into a smaller amount of information. For example, the data might stem from the huge number of transactions of a bank, and the resultant information is the bank's balance sheet.

Levels of information

Information can be regarded as being of several levels, the number of which depends upon the framework within which the information is used. It is also true to say that one man's information is another man's data. In other words, the difference between information and data is only meaningful in relation to the level under consideration.

For instance, the population statistics submitted by local government authorities to national government is information at the local government level and data at national government level. By combining and processing the statistics from local authorities, national government is able to produce national-level information.

The five levels of information described below are sensible for most business situations.

- *International information*, e.g. projected world food resources over the next few years based upon land usage and the availability of seed and fertilizer, also information regarding world natural resources, weather patterns, currency exchange rates, population statistics and energy demands.
- *National information*, e.g. a country's balance-of-payments statistics derived from import/export figures and invisible earnings, industrial output, employment statistics and population trends.
- *Corporate information*, e.g. a company's balance sheet derived from summaries of the various accounts, stock evaluation and plant register; also sales analyses, productive output and market trends.
- *Departmental information*, e.g. a department's expenditure analysis derived from its individual expenses, a branch's turnover based upon its sales transactions.
- *Individual information*, e.g. a worker's take-home pay derived from his rate of pay, hours worked, tax liability and social security deductions, also a sales representative's sales total for a certain period.

Categories of information

There are three main categories of business information, and these are related to the purpose for which the information is utilized. These categories also tend to relate to the levels of information described above. Higher levels of information tend to be associated with strategic information and lower levels with operational information.

Strategic information

This relates to long-term planning policies and is therefore of most interest to top management. Government-wise, strategic information includes factors such as population studies, national resource availabilities, foreign investments and balance-of-payment statistics. Company-wise, it includes market availability and penetration figures, projected raw material costs, product developments, manpower changes and new technologies. The meaning of 'long-term' depends very much on the level of the strategic information. At international level long-term could mean twenty years or more, at corporate level it is likely to be closer to five years.

The nature of strategic information should obviously be such as to facilitate long-term planning and is therefore likely to include projections and forecasts. It is improbable that an organization's strategic information is entirely computer-produced. Most strategic information stems from events and sources whose data is not amenable to computer processing.

Tactical information

This is of use in shorter-term planning, i.e. months rather than years, and is of more interest at departmental level. Included in tactical information are sales analyses and forecasts, cashflow projections, production resource requirements, and the annual financial statements.

These types of information are generally based on data arising from current activities. There is thus an obvious need for a means of rapidly processing this data. It is also probable that some tactical information stems directly from external sources with little or no need for processing. As an example, a change to a competitive company's product range could have a definite effect on future sales that would not show up in a computer-prepared sales forecast. In tactical planning it is therefore wise to combine information from several sources before making decisions.

Operational information

This applies to the short-term, perhaps hourly, running of a department. It includes current stocks-in-hand, outstanding and overdue purchase orders, work-in-progress levels, and customers' to-follow orders. Operational information is of such a nature that it can generally be derived quickly from current activity data. It is often connected with the need for emergency action and so demands rapid preparation. Operational information is usually of direct interest to a fewer number of people than is tactical information but is more specific to those persons. This implies that operational information must be closely geared to the needs of its recipients.

Quality of information

When considering the desirability of providing information, the following points should be taken into account.

Brevity

Too much detail can result in the overlooking of vital facts. Each recipient of information should therefore be provided only with his or her needs. This suggests that a large amount of information should, wherever possible, be split into smaller packets tailored to meet requirements of individual recipients.

The need for brevity also indicates a need for specificity — the information should go straight to the heart of the matter, especially if immediate actions are called for.

Accuracy

The degree of accuracy of information relates to its usages. There is no point in striving for great accuracy if this is of no consequence, e.g. the marketing director is not interested in the value of sales accurate to within a penny — the nearest hundred pounds will probably suffice; the financial accountant, however, is concerned with accuracy to the exact penny.

Generally, the degree of accuracy of information is known to its recipient; where any doubt might exist, the degree of accuracy should be stated on the report. In computer terms the calculations upon which the information is based are exact; it is during or after output from the computer that the information is adjusted to the most suitable level of accuracy, e.g. £5,193,748.63 becomes £5.2 million.

Timeliness and up-to-dateness

Information should be as timely and up-to-date as is necessary for the use made of it. Speed in creating information increases its cost and so it is unwise to prepare it unnecessarily quickly. On the other hand, information that arrives too late or is out of date is entirely useless, and so the time, effort and cost is wasted.

Timeliness and up-to-dateness are allied. Timeliness implies that the information is delivered punctually after its preparation. Up-to-date means that it is accurate at a certain moment in time.

In some situations timeliness takes priority over up-to-dateness, e.g. the sales manager wants the previous day's sales figures first thing next morning, even though they do not include the last hour's sales. On the other hand up-to-dateness might be paramount, so for instance a financial report needs to be fully up-to-date as at the exact end of the financial year but it need not appear until several days afterwards.

Action

Information calling for action must be directed to the person(s) who can initiate the appropriate action. It is important that it goes directly to that person and not via a chain of disinterested managers. Such a communication chain tends to devalue the information by making it less timely and it erodes the time available for performing the necessary actions.

The information should comprise sufficient facts and figures to enable effective and immediate action to be taken, e.g. an out-of-stock report must contain the data needed to enable a reorder to be rushed through. Where all the required information cannot be included in the report itself, reference to its whereabouts could well be made.

Rarity

The value of a piece of information depends upon its unusualness. 'Man bites dog' has news value but not vice versa. Thus information reports should emphasize the unusual, as described in the following section under exception reports.

1.3 Management information

The term 'management information system' has become synonymous with computer-based DP systems. This is misleading, however, since it is quite possible to operate an efficient DP system that does not provide true management information. An example of this situation is a payroll system that provides all the necessary figures for paying the employees, and the tax and social security deductions, but no real information for managerial purposes.

Management information arises, among other places, from the routine data processed regularly in the organization. This is illustrated in Figure 1.1, and although this is a simplification of a company's operations, the contributions of the work areas to management information can be seen. Management information, in turn, contributes to policy-making by managers. The other significant factor is environmental information; this is often of a diverse and subjective nature and the manager combines it with the information he receives as a result of the company's activities before making a decision of any consequence.

An example of this combining of information is the sales director's decisions in regard to future marketing policy. These decisions cannot be based entirely upon internal information derived from customers' orders because, although sales of a product range may be increasing, it is evident from intelligence of competitive developments that this situation is unlikely to continue. And so a subjective judgement is made by the sales director as to what market share the company's product range can continue to enjoy. This judgement, together with the actual sales figures, enables a reasonable forecast to be made of future sales.

Developments in microcomputers have brought many managers closer to the means of obtaining information. And although there is much conflict of opinion as to the efficiency of personal computers, they have undoubtedly created an awareness of what might be done. Managers are becoming increasingly specific in their demands for computer-produced information, and will be less inclined to accept 'information' based on the DP staff's judgement of what is required. Younger managers, brought up with a more technological background, combined with the introduction of more friendly software (Section 3.8) have induced a happier relationship.

There is nowadays widespread practical usage of graphical representation of information. Computer software is readily available for displaying coloured charts, graphs, histograms, etc., including those giving a three-dimensional effect. Graphical presentation is a rapid means for managers to detect information that is of particular interest or calls for further investigation. Discriminating and sensible employment of colours and shapes (icons) makes a strong impact on the user and enables him rapidly to assess the information represented.

Management reports

The information passed to managers and the use made of it varies considerably from one organization to another. Nevertheless, management reports can be categorized into the following general groups.

Analyses

An analysis is a grouping together of data in order to provide a summarized picture of results within the various groupings of the analysis. A typical example is the analysis of sales quantities and values under group headings such as commodity group, sales area, customer classification and period; in other words, what, where, who and when?

Because of the vast amount of information available from analysing data under various headings, it is advisable to be selective in its preparation. Selection may be in terms of either (a) the headings included in the analyses, or (b) the items included within those headings. For instance, the four headings mentioned above can give rise to many different analyses if we include various combinations of headings. It is unlikley that this number of analyses could be effectively made use of. The other means of selection is to include only certain items within each heading, e.g. only selected sales areas.

It is beneficial if the selection of analyses and/or items can be varied on request so that no unnecessary information is prepared and presented. This might entail variations from week to week and from one recipient to another, but these requirements need not prove insurmountable. Although the aim of providing variable and selectable analytical information might seem overambitious, this is not so if a suitable approach is adopted right from the start. In other words, the system is designed to be capable of providing all possible combinations of analytical heads and the requirements selected by entering parameters immediately prior to the preparation of the analysis.

Generally, managers at a higher level require more highly summarized information than those under them. The marketing director, for instance, may want sales values for the whole country analysed into commodity groups, whereas a sales manager needs the sales figures for his area only analysed by individual commodities. In a situation like this, there is obviously scope for processing the two analyses simultaneously and then printing only the information of interest for each recipient.

Analyses can be thought of as being multi-dimensional. The simplest, a one-dimensional analysis, is a straightforward list of summarized items, e.g. the sales values in each sales area. A two-dimensional analysis could be sales of each commodity group within each sales area. Next by adding the periods we get a three-dimensional analysis, and so on. There is of course no theoretical limit to the extent of analyses but practical considerations usually restrict them to not more than three or four dimensions.

Predictions and forecasts

A prediction is information based upon previous figures projected into the future. A forecast is based upon conjectural information, i.e. subjective judgements as to the effect of various factors. So-called sales forecasting is usually based upon past sales figures and strictly speaking ought therefore to be called sales prediction.

It is important with predictions and forecasts that managers understand what is involved in their preparation. The danger is otherwise that they come to rely too much on mathematical techniques and not enough on judgements based on other information.

The fact of the matter is that in business there are few situations that lend themselves to mathematical forecasting techniques. The unpredictability of business often clouds the meaning of forecasted information. Nevertheless there are situations that can benefit from forecasting and, when this is the case, forecasting software proves valuable.

The presentation of forecasted information should incorporate a means of showing its decreasing accuracy as it goes further into the future. This is important otherwise the manager may think that next year's forecast is no less valid than tomorrow's.

Optimizations

It is often the case that many alternatives are possible within a situation, only one or a few of which are the best. An optimization technique is applied to the raw data in order to select mathematically the optimum arrangement.

The question then arises as to what is meant by the 'best' or optimum and the answer is 'it depends what you want'. That is to say, the manager who will be making use of an optimization report must decide what he wants bearing in mind the conflicting constraints. If the least-cost arrangement is required this must be evaluated against the longer time and lower quality that might well be incurred. Nothing comes free and so it is usually a case of selecting from a small number of alternatives, perhaps taking other factors into account as well as those employed in the techniques. Typical of such techniques are linear programming, inventory modelling, assignment and allocation. These techniques form part of operational research (OR) methodology, also known as management science.

Linear programming Methods for determining the optimum amalgamation of several variables of known characteristics to obtain results subject to predecided constraints. For example, the blending of foodstuffs of known dietary characteristics and costs in order to produce a diet meeting certain nutritional standards at minimum cost.

Inventory modelling Determines the stockholding levels and reorder quantities that give minimum overall stockholding costs. Taken into account are the separate costs such as capital invested, reordering and space occupied, and also the pattern of the item (see Stock Control, Section 1.1).

Assignment and allocation techniques For planning the optimum utilization of resources, taking into consideration the characteristics of the resources and the requirements of the project, e.g. allocating skilled workers to tasks.

Other OR methodologies include the following:

Queuing theory The study (analysis) of times spent waiting for service taking into account the number of service points and the amount of traffic (persons or things needing service). An example is the analysis of queuing in a large supermarket in order to decide the number of tills needed. Another example is the analysis of queues of data messages awaiting transmission through a computer network.

Simulation (modelling) The modelling of a process or situation mathematically so as to determine the outcome of various combinations of influential factors, e.g. vehicle flow patterns are simulated by the use of random numbers in order to facilitate road network planning.

Decision theory The application of statistical probability theory in deciding the best policy to adopt to achieve an objective, e.g. a number of methods have various probabilities of success and lead to other tasks. Which is the best set of methods to adopt in order to maximize success?

Game theory   The application of statistical logic to competitive situations such as bidding for contracts.

Replacement theory   Deciding the best point of time to replace equipment subject to wear and tear in order to minimize the probability of sudden failure and also to minimize replacement costs.

The reader is reminded that References 1.9 and 1.10 contain more facts on OR.

Management reports can also be categorized into other groupings as described below, these groups are complementary to those above.

Regular reports

These are prepared automatically at regular cycles, e.g. every week, and are usually associated with a cycle of activities, e.g. a payroll. Some people question the genuine need for ongoing regular reporting. This is discussed in Chapter 7, so for the moment we will accept that a genuine need exists in most cases.

The recipient of a regular report becomes completely familiar with its contents and layout. Nevertheless, even a regular report must be clearly headed and annotated in accordance with the recipients' understanding of the information thereon.

It is important that some arrangement exists for the feedback of ideas, complaints and other comments about regular reports. Otherwise a situation may arise in which all the recipients of the report believe that everyone else is entirely satisfied and so no attempt is made to improve or modernize it. Feedback also covers cessation of the need for a report, otherwise a manager may continue receiving it needlessly.

Regular reports are satisfactory provided there is a continuing need, but otherwise the recipient may be swamped by too frequent information. This could lead to the overlooking of valuable details. It is more effective to supply information only when it is actually needed by the manager, and with the precise content that he or she requires at that point of time.

Exception reports

The principle of exception reporting is based upon the idea that 'no news is good news'. In other words, if no decisions or actions are necessary, then the situation goes unreported. This philosophy also applies to 'management by exception', i.e. managers should direct their attention to exceptional items and situations as the means of maintaining control.

The problem is in deciding what is exceptional. This needs to be carefully studied and the resultant informational requirements fully determined before exception reporting is implemented. A fundamental aspect of exception reporting is the capability of altering the exception parameters. With inflation, for instance, exceptionally high cost values may become normal. An alternative method is to use relative parameters instead of absolute values. For example, the exception level would be that which is twice the average level and therefore immune from the effect of inflation.

Exception reports, perhaps more than other types, should contain sufficient information for the recipient to be able to deal with the problem. It is likely that an exception report induces a request for further information regarding the exceptional situation.

Decision support systems

An extension of the exception concept is decision support systems (DSSs). These are intended to enable managers to retrieve information *ad hoc* and as straightforwardly as possible in order to facilitate current decision-making. The goal of a DSS is to support the decision-making process and not necessarily to provide sufficient information to make the decision a *fait accompli*. In fact, by the nature of many business decision situations, it is unlikely that the DSS could do that in any case.

DSSs are most effective in risk, i.e. probability, situations where the manager is faced with a number of alternative actions. Ideally the DSS, if given estimates of relevant costs, times, workloads, etc., is capable of assessing all or some of the outcomes of the alternatives. If, for instance, the situation was such that OR techniques could be applied, this would be done automatically by the DSS and the optimum result presented to the manager. In a straightforward case, which would be exceptional, the need for management decision might be eliminated as the OR technique had made the decision for him.

There are usually too many factors, however, for the DSS to be able to come up with *the* answer. Consequently it is necessary for the DSS to have access to a wide range of software and a Database Management System (Section 4.4) so that facilities needed to support a particular type of decision can be utilized.

Examples of such facilities include the following:

- OR methodologies such as those explained in the previous paragraph.
- Network analysis (PERT) for decisions calling for project planning and cost estimations.
- Statistical techniques such as trend analysis, correlation analysis and sampling techniques.
- Database searching and analysis in order to extract relevant information and analyse or summarize it. For this purpose a structured query language (SQL) might be built into the DSS.

A DSS is interactive to a much greater extent than most management information systems. This is a vital characteristic owing to the wide nature of user's requirements. The DSS should be capable of routeing the user towards his requirements without the need for command words, code numbers and so on.

DSSs are fertile ground for the use of WIMPs (see glossary), and in particular pull-down menus and touch-screens.

Ideally a DSS is evolutionary in that it can adapt itself to the needs of a user this is bordering on expert systems methodology. A more realistic arrangement is for the DSS to record the user's requirements and subsequently to analyse and measure the degree of success. The DSS could then be adapted manually to improve its efficacy.

The presentation of the output from a DSS is of importance since it must convey the user's requirements in an easily assimilable way. This means that a variety of methods have to be available, especially in visual form. A wide range of graphics software is available enabling the presentation of information in the form of graphs, histograms and so on in a variety of colours (see Sections 3.8 and 8.5). Graphical presentation gives the user the chance to see results quickly and to get the general idea. This can be backed up by printouts giving the same information in tabular and/or graphical form.

Examples of business scenarios calling for the employment of DSSs include the following:

- The allocation of sales offices and representatives to areas taking into account the market potentials of the areas, the representatives' past performances (track records), predicted changes in markets and products, costs of premises and staff redeployment costs.
- Production planning taking into account factors such as existent factory/plant loads, new orders, availabilities of raw materials, and machine capabilities and reliabilities.
- Stock (inventory) planning of expensive goods giving consideration to present stocks, likely future demands, availability of space in the stores, capital tied-up, price history of the goods and restocking lead times.

1.4 Systems theory

Before proceeding to the practical aspects of business DP systems, which is the main subject of this book, it is worthwhile to consider briefly the theoretical aspects of systems in general and business systems in particular. The term 'system' is used extensively, and sometimes rather loosely, in connection with many facets of life and existence. We talk of business systems, computer systems, information systems, solar systems, biological systems, and so on. What do all of these have in common? The main point is that they are all composed of parts that interact to achieve a purpose or result — although the purpose of a solar system is debatable!

Every system has a boundary within which it lies and outside of which is its 'environment'. The environment of a business system includes any human, business or political activity that impinges upon the business's operation. The environment of an information system is any activity, person or entity that gives rise to data or responds to information from the system.

The boundary of a system is often defined arbitrarily by the person studying it in order to limit its extent. This approach is correct and acceptable provided the system's limits are not imposed too narrowly. Every system consists of other systems (subsystems) that interface with each other, and this hierarchy often applies through several levels. Some of the subsystems interface with the system's environment and hence take the form of input or output sensors, e.g. the skin nerves of an animal (biological system), the canvassers of a political system, the salesmen of a business system, the input/output peripherals of a computer system.

Deterministic and probabilistic systems

A deterministic system operates according to a predetermined set of rules. Its future behaviour can therefore be predicted exactly if its present state and operating characteristics are accurately known. Examples of deterministic systems are a computer program and a planet in orbit. Business systems are not deterministic owing to the fact that they interface with a number of indeterminate factors such as customer and supplier behaviour, national and international situations, and climatic and political conditions.

A probabilistic system is controlled by chance events and so its future behaviour is a matter of probability rather than certainty. This is true of all social systems, particularly business enterprises. Information systems are deterministic in the sense that a preknown type and content of information emerges as a result of the input of a given set of data. This assumes that the information system operates according to predecided and formulated rules — which it generally would do. In a broader sense, information systems can be regarded as probabilistic because the wide variability in the nature of their input introduces many indeterminates, and so their future behaviour, i.e. output, is not absolutely certain.

Closed and open systems

A closed system is one that does not interface with its environment, i.e. it has no input or output. This concept is more relevant to scientific systems than to social systems. The nearest we can get to a closed social system would be a completely self-contained community that provides all its own food, materials and power, and that does not trade, communicate or come into contact with other communities.

Open systems, on the other hand, have many interfaces with their environments, and so need to be capable of adapting their behaviour in order to continue to exist in changing environments. An information system falls into this category since it needs to adapt to the changing demands for information.

Similarly a business system must be capable of reorganization in order to cope with a changing world, e.g. markets wax and wane, products become obsolete and social attitudes change. If an open system does not continually reorganize itself to meet the conditions of its environment, as detected from its input, it will move rapidly towards a state of disorganization.

When functioning properly an open system reaches a state of dynamic equilibrium. This is a steady-state condition in which the system readily adapts to environmental factors by reorganizing itself according to the internal forces of its subsystems. With a manufacturing company, for instance, the steady state can be thought of as the purchasing of materials and productive means, and the manufacturing and selling of products. An environmental factor could be an increase in the costs of materials, the internal force of its subsystem would then cause a rise in manufacturing costs, and the consequent reorganization would be an increase in the selling prices of its products.

The term *entropy* is used as a measure of disorganization, thus we can regard open systems as tending to increase their entropy unless they receive 'negative entropy' in the form of information from their environment. In the above example, if the increased costs of materials were ignored, the products would become unprofitable and so the company would move into insolvency, i.e. into a state of disorganization.

Regulation (control) in systems

An information system has inputs, outputs and processes; and if its environment is not in some way forced to respond to the system's output by modifying the data that it subsequently inputs to the system, the system becomes disorganized. The process whereby a system is regulated is called 'negative feedback'. In order to obtain negative feedback, a system's output must be compared with a standard, and the result of the comparison fed back as an input control signal into the system, i.e. a closed-loop system.

An example of this is shown in Figure 1.2 wherein each customer's balance is regularly compared with a standard, i.e. a credit limit; those above the limit are caused to give rise to an input control signal that temporarily restricts the customer's future trading with the company. It is apparent that without negative feedback, the accounting systems tend to become disorganized because debts increase and more bad debts are incurred.

Positive, as opposed to negative, feedback is where the control signal tends to increase the difference between the output and the standard. In the above case, positive feedback would result in customers above their credit limit being permitted to increase their indebtedness, thus encouraging bad debts, i.e. disorganization of the system. Another instance of positive feedback, this time of a social nature, is where a city council deems it necessary to increase the price of school meals as a consequence of reduced demand. If no financial subsidies are available, there is obviously only one final outcome of such a policy, i.e. the collapse of the meals service.

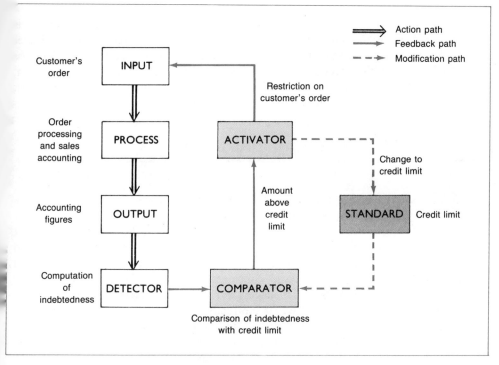

Figure 1.2 Feedback control in an accounting system

Oscillatory situations

A negative feedback system can be regarded as target-seeking in that it attempts to maintain a state of stability, i.e. keep close to the target. In a previous example the target is keeping each customer within his credit limit and thus minimizing the chance of bad debts occurring. This process is also known as 'homeostasis' and is in some ways similar to the mechanism by which the human body is kept at a constant temperature. If there is a time delay (lag), however, in either the feedback loop or the system's response to the feedback, this can result in an oscillatory situation arising. This is also termed 'hunting', and takes the form of an over-reaction in the input and consequent over-reaction by the system itself.

EXAMPLE

Delay in the feedback of accounting information in a sales orders application allows a customer's debts to rise well above his credit limit. When the feedback information eventually arrives, stringent controls are imposed but by then the customer is likely to have paid his debts. This means that his orders are now refused and by the time the information pertaining to his payments is fed back, orders have been lost.

Oscillatory situations are generally not too damaging provided the oscillation is damped, i.e. reduced in magnitude, fairly quickly. A bad state of affairs is where the oscillations continue unabated or, even worse, increase as time goes by. Both of these situations, and particularly the latter, result in complete loss of control with consequent disorganization and eventual failure of the system.

There are many types of feedback delay and resultant oscillatory patterns, but, in general, the shorter the delay the better the control achieved.

1.5 Data systems and users

This section brings together a number of factors impinging upon users as a consequence of their becoming involved with data systems. By user, or end-user as they sometimes are known, is meant anyone who, in the course of his or her work, receives information from or supplies data to a DP system. All users should be able to exert some measure of control or influence over the DP system, and certain users must be allowed considerable influence and control. This is tantamount to saying that all managers and most other clerical and administrative staff are, in fact, users, however indirectly.

Data processing is merely a service to its users: the preparation of information achieves little on its own, it is its subsequent use that brings about benefits. These facts should be borne in mind by the user and more so by the DP professional.

How can users, and in particular managers, relate more effectively to data systems and, in so doing, improve the efficiency of the organization and the quality of their jobs?

User requirements

Users should give on-going thought as to how DP can help them to meet their responsibilities and hence contribute to achieving corporate objectives. By being positive in this respect they have nothing to lose and something to gain personally. The thoughts in each person's mind must be, 'Can this work be done more effectively and/or economically by using a different method?', 'Does the work as done at present entail repetitive drudgery or duplication of effort that could be alleviated by using a machine?', 'Is the existing computer system friendly enough, i.e. easy to operate and communicate with?'

These questions inevitably propel people's minds towards thinking about new methods. There has been a tendency in the past for DP methodology to be dictated by the limitations of technology and by the DP department's interpretation of what was required. This led to a machine-orientated approach in which the user was largely the outsider.

Those days are now gone as indicated by the ready acceptance of micro-computers and the increased use of terminals and office automation. Users are more determined to participate at all stages and thus obtain information that really meets their needs. Participation is encouraged by the growing use of prototyping, i.e. users being allowed to see and discuss what they will be required to do and what they will receive in the way of information (see Section 6.9).

User/DP staff co-operation

Assignment briefs are discussed in some detail in Section 7.1, but for the moment we can say that an assignment brief is a request for certain things to be done. The danger with formal requests is that they engender a formal atmosphere and this is the opposite of what is really needed. The user and the DP specialist should 'sit at the same side of the table'. By co-operating and if necessary admitting to lack of knowledge on certain points, the parties move towards a strong position to create an efficient and comprehensive system.

Co-operation includes a willingness to explain the technicalities of one's trade. It has sometimes been the case that a systems analyst and an accountant, when discussing a problem, each had no understanding of the other person's job and indeed in a few cases they were determined not to impart any information about their respective trades. The attitude, sometimes subconscious, was 'Why allow someone to pick my brain and take away my hard-earned knowledge and experience?'

Another attitude was to keep quiet and so avoid exposing one's ignorance. 'Keep quiet and let people think you a fool rather than speak and prove you are.' The danger with this attitude is that each party, unaware of the other's lack of understanding, proceeds on the basis that the problems are understood, only to discover later that this was not so.

User knowledge and training

It goes without saying that a professional person must have in-depth knowledge of his or her profession. It is perhaps less obvious that a professional needs some knowledge of others' expertise. Returning to the systems analyst and the accountant, the former needs to understand the broad principles and the terminology of accountancy. Even though the accountant may be willing to explain carefully the accountancy aspects of the problem, he or she cannot be expected to give the systems analyst an accountancy course. Similarly, the accountant needs to understand the general concepts of DP and the more common terminology.

In regard to DP terminology, it is difficult even for the professionals to keep up to date. The plethora of buzzwords, i.e. jargon, terms, acronyms and names, is overwhelming if one attempts to remember them all. Fortunately this is not really necessary as much of the jargon passes quite quickly into disuse.

Returning to the users' need for knowledge, it is fairly easy to acquire information about computers but perhaps not so easy to learn about methods. There are many books available at an introductory level, e.g. Reference 2.20, and also numerous training courses. The difficulty with certain courses is their orientation towards one make of computing equipment (hardware) or one method of using it (software). This does not matter too much as long as the user does not allow himself to be indoctrinated.

The main topics of a user training course should be:

- The general capabilities and limitations of computers and data communication systems.
- The broad approach to handling business applications by DP methods.
- The capabilities and *modus operandi* of some of the readily available application packages (Section 5.4).

Additionally, if the user is a go-it-alone microcomputer user:

- The capabilities of and practice with specific application packages, preferably those that the user will be using and on the same model of microcomputer.
- The methods of capturing, organizing and editing source data.

Personnel

Users of data systems must accept that some changes will occur to their work patterns and they must be willing to face up to these. New methods involve the need for retraining, as described above, and user personnel may find themselves learning something entirely different from their present work. In an organization in which there is some choice, managers must judge who are the most suitable persons to retrain. It frequently turns out that middle-aged staff, who have perhaps been doing a satisfactory job with the present system for many years, are unfortunately the least eligible for retraining. They often cannot cope with the radical changes necessitated by a new system, and with the reorientation of thinking that goes with it.

These are problems for managers to handle and, by knowing their staff's and their own capabilities, the best decisions can be made. Such decisions may entail early retirement, transfers, retraining and occasionally recruitment of staff. The decisions are most poignant in small companies in which there are few staff members from whom to choose.

Steering committees

Steering committees tend to be associated with larger organizations and so their membership calls for careful selection from amongst the numerous staff. Like any other committee a steering committee is not an end in itself — its attitude requires flexibility and its meetings should be based on a definite agenda.

In a smaller firm, the steering committee is likely to be less formalized and could consist of just a few managers or representatives of the departments most affected by the introduction of a new system.

The purposes of a steering committee are as follows:

- To decide and maintain an overall policy with regard to DP systems.
- To represent the views of individual departments but also to bear in mind the interests of the organization as a whole.
- To promulgate systems development by setting up study groups and initiating systems work, to maintain thereafter a watch over the work of the project teams and systems department, and to receive and evaluate their reports.
- To maintain a watch over the DP department as regards its cost, efficiency and, most importantly, its service to the end users.
- To act as the official negotiating body with suppliers of expensive hardware and software.
- To report to the board of directors or top management with recommendations for systems developments.
- To appoint senior systems and DP personnel.

Constitution of the steering committee

A typical constitution consists of the following:

a senior manager as chairman;
managers of the user departments;
the senior member of the systems team;
the senior member of the DP department;
a representative from any external organization involved, e.g. consultants;
co-opted members as and when necessary.

1.6 Exercises

Exercise 1.1 Interrelationships of work areas and management information

Consider the functional areas, work areas and management information appertaining to a self-financing college, and redraw Figure 1.1 so as to show their interrelationships. If you are in doubt, use your imagination based on the contents of Figure 1.1. Remember that the college is self-supporting and therefore operates on a profit-making basis.

Exercise 1.2 Information categories

Suggest three lots each of strategic, tactical and operational information which might be of use to (a) an electricity company, (b) a supermarket and (c) a government education department.

Exercise 1.3 Systems categorization

Categorize the following systems according to whether they are (a)
deterministic or probabilistic, and (b) closed or open.
1. A space vehicle in orbit under ground control.
2. A bank cash-dispensing terminal.
3. A factory inventory control system.
4. A chemical reaction in a sealed and insulated container.
5. A shop.
6. ERNIE (machine for automatically generating the winning numbers of
    premium bonds by self-contained electronics).

Exercise 1.4 Information and data

'What is information to one manager will simply be data to another.'
Consider, in the light of your own definitions of data and information, what
you feel is meant by this statement.
(ICSA part 4, Man. of sys., June 1987)

Exercise 1.5 Quality of information

'Relevance, timeliness and accuracy are the main ingredients of information,
and without them information is of limited value to the administrator.'
Discuss, with particular reference to organizational support systems.
(ICSA part 2, Inf. sys., Dec. 1986)

Exercise 1.6 Management information

Outline the nature and purpose of information likely to be used at each of
the following levels of a business enterprise:

(a) top management;
(b) middle management;
(c) supervisory management.
(CACA level 2, Sys. an. & des., June 1988)

Exercise 1.7 Steering committees

Critically assess the role which a steering committee normally plays in
determining priorities for computerization.
(ICSA part 4, Man. of sys., Dec. 1988)

Exercise 1.8 Control in activities

The traditional management control cycle has elements generally termed
activator, detector and comparator. Explain, by reference to a control

ctivity with which you are familiar, the role of each of these three
elements.

(ICSA part 4, Man. of sys., Dec. 1988)

Exercise 1.9 Sales order entry system

Describe the main activities which would normally form part of a sales
order entry system. (Flow charts and procedural diagrams can be used in
your answer. Please state clearly the conventions which you use.)

(ICSA part 4, Man. of sys., Dec. 1988)

1.7 Outline solutions to exercises

Solution 1.1

Figure 1.3 shows the basic interrelationships. Do not be perturbed if your answer is
somewhat different from this: the important thing is that you have understood the
principle behind the exercise, i.e. the fact that work areas are interrelated and
connect with management information.

Solution 1.2

Figure 1.4 shows examples of information categories, illustrating solution 1.2.

Solution 1.3

Table 1.1 shows the solution.

Table 1.1

System	(a)	(b)
(1)	D	O
(2)	D	O
(3)	P	O
(4)	D	C
(5)	P	O
(6)	P	C

D = deterministic, P = probabilistic, C = closed, O = open

Solution 1.4

Refer to Sections 1.2 and 1.3.

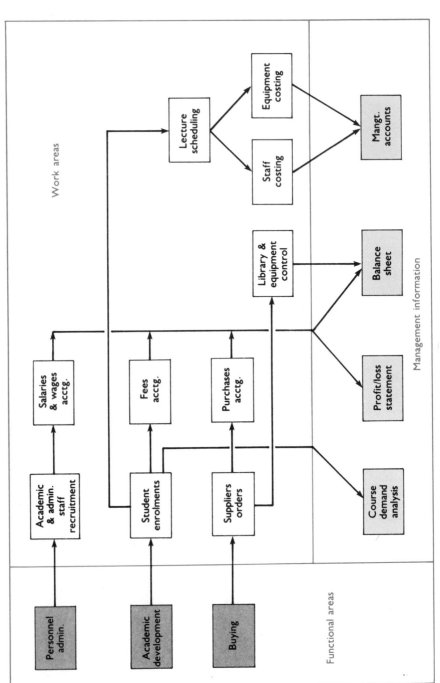

Figure 1.3 Interrelationships of work areas and management information in a college

	Electricity co.	Supermarket	Education dept.
Strategic information	1. Long-term fuel costs and availability 2. Technical developments in generating plant 3. Long-term demand forecasts based on population and industry	1. Consumer attitudes to products based on standards of living 2. Long-term availability of foodstuffs 3. Effect of town planning developments	1. Actual and predicted birth rates 2. Teacher training resources 3. School building needs based on demand and legislation
Tactical information	1. Seasonal fluctuations in demand for electricity 2. Changes in fuel costs 3. Maintenance and replacement of equipment	1. Seasonal variations in demand 2. Seasonal variations in supplies 3. Shortage of items due to industrial action	1. Current age-group populations of children 2. Requirements of books and equipment 3. Teacher availability and requirements
Operational information	1. Equipment breakdown 2. Labour disputes 3. Power generation demand and balancing	1. Out-of-stock items 2. Immediate price increases 3. Staff absenteeism	1. Staff illness 2. Pupil transportation problems 3. Pupil absenteeism

Figure 1.4 Examples of information categories

Data, in so far as it can be defined, is the raw facts and figures appertaining to activities and items. It does not, *per se*, enable decisions to be made or planning to be arranged. Information is the presentation of figures in such a way as to facilitate planning and decision-making. It derives from the processing of the data acquired as a result of the organization's activities. An example of data is the labour times spent on the various jobs in a factory. These do not, in themselves, provide true information but, when converted into monetary terms and summarized for each job, they provide valuable labour cost variation figures for use in management accounting, i.e. information.

Information at one level of management is often data to the level above. To emphasize the statement in the question one could take a sales example. Each sales representative's weekly sales total is information as far as he or she is concerned, particularly if this determines the commission earned. To the branch manager these totals are data because they accumulate to form the branch sales, i.e. the manager's information. Similarly, branch sales are data forming the company sales information for the sales manager.

Even this simple example is confounded by the branch manager seeing certain representative's sales as information also. This arises when it is necessary to make a decision regarding a particular representative's efforts.

Solution 1.5

Refer to 'Quality of information' in Section 1.2.

Relevance:
- Information contents should facilitate decision-making for immediate actions or future activities.
- Certain information may be of lesser relevance but of general interest.
- Totally irrelevant information, if not recognized as such, can obscure the facts and confuse a situation.
- It should be fully apparent exactly what the information refers to, i.e. indicative references such as dates, code numbers and precise names must be included.

Timeliness:
- Information needs to arrive early enough for decisions to take effect.
- Long-term decisions generally call for less urgent information.
- Immediate decisions demand early information.
- Information must be completely up-to-date at the time/date stated in it.

Accuracy:
- Information must always be a faithful representation of the situation it covers.
- Omissions should not be such as to cause people to be misled.
- Computational results need only be as accurate as their purpose demands but the degree of accuracy should be apparent.

Solution 1.6

(a) Information for top management:
- Must facilitate decisions in regard to strategic long-term planning.
- Needs to relate to the objectives of the organization as a whole.
- In broad terms in the first instance, supported by further, more detailed information if required.
- Overall position quickly assimilable.
- Important points highlighted, and backed up by extra detail.
- Graphic presentation can be effective.

(b) Information for middle management:
- Related to shorter-term tactical planning.
- Relevant only to the manager's own sphere of responsibility.
- Sufficient detail for comparison with other results.
- Important points highlighted.
- Graphics useful but should be also available in numeric form.

(c) Information for supervisory management:
- Applicable to short-term decisions.
- Immediate-action information clearly distinguishable from more general information.
- Formatted in a standard layout for rapid assimilation.
- Contains suggestions for necessary actions.

Solution 1.7

Refer to 'Steering committees' in Sections 1.5 and 9.5.

Solution 1.8

Refer to 'Regulation in systems' in Section 1.4. Three examples of control are shown in Figure 1.5.

Activity	Detector	Comparator	Activator
Customer credit control	Records of accounts payable	Outstanding debt versus credit limit	Restrictions on further orders
Stock replenishment	Records of stocks in hand	Stock level versus reorder level	Order more stock
Materials costing	Materials costing system	Actual cost versus standard cost	Reduce cost of materials

Figure 1.5 Examples of control activities

Solution 1.9

Refer to 'Sales control and accounting' in Section 1.1.

It is assumed that the question applies strictly to order entry and so no mention is made of invoicing, etc.

The main points are as follows:

- Method of order data capture — mail, phone, sales reps., electronic mail, etc.
- Method of input — keyboard, OMR, data transmission, bar codes, WIMPS.
- Check customer for validity and credit worthiness.
- Check goods ordered for validity and reasonableness in terms of quantity ordered, price (if included in order), date for delivery, existence of options (colours, sizes etc.).
- Check stock in hand, allocate stock to order, record sales order.
- Query any discrepancies with customer.
- Arrange for to-follow items, i.e. outstanding orders.

Figure 1.6 depicts these procedures in the form of a structure chart.

1.8 References and further reading

1.1   Lewis, D., *The Basics of Business* (Pitman, 1988).
1.2   Pitfield, R.R., *Business Organisation* (Pitman, 1982).
1.3   Gray, J., *Business Organisation* (NCC, 1987).
1.4   Jackson, J.H. and Musselman, V.A., *Business: Contemporary Concepts and Practices* (Prentice Hall, 1987).

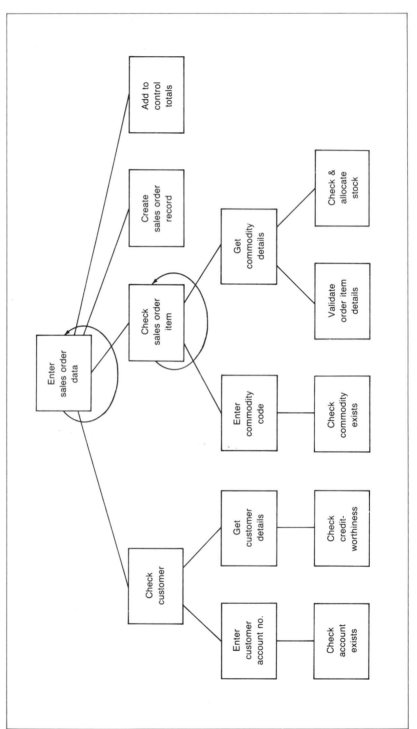

Figure 1.6 Simplified structure chart of sales order entry procedure (Exercise 1.9)

1.5   Dyson, J.R., *Accounting for Non-accounting Students* (Pitman, 1987).

1.6   Hitching, C. and Stone, D., *Understand Accounting* (Pitman, 1984).

1.7   Mearns, I.J., *Fundamentals of Cost and Management Accounting* (Pitman, 1981).

1.8   Page, J. and Hooper, P., *Accounting and Information Systems* (Prentice Hall, 1987).

1.9   Eppen, G.D., Gould, F.J. and Schmidt, C.P., *Introductory Management Science* (Prentice Hall, 1987).

1.10 Moore, P.G., *Operational Research* (Pitman, 1986).

1.11 Rosenberg, R.S., *Computers and the Information Society* (John Wiley, 1986).

1.12 Martin, J., *An Information Systems Manifesto* (Prentice Hall, 1984).

1.13 Earl, M.J., *Management Strategies for Information Technology* (Prentice Hall, 1988).

1.14 Beddie, L. and Raeburn, S., *An Introduction to Computer Integrated Business* (Prentice Hall, 1989).

1.15 Bassett, P.H., *Computerised Accounting* (NCC, 1987).

1.16 Clare, C.P. and Loucopoulos, P., *Data Processing: Current Theories and Practices* (Abacus Press, 1987).

1.17 Davis, M.W., *Applied Decision Support* (Prentice Hall, 1988).

1.18 Sprague, R. and Watson, H. (eds), *Decision Support Systems: Putting Theory into Practice* (Prentice Hall, 1989).

2 Computers in business

2.1 Development of business information systems

Prior to the early 1950s, computers were made individually and used for scientific, technical and military purposes only.

By the mid 1950s the first business computers were available. The first model to make a substantial impact on business was the IBM 650 with over 1,000 machines installed, mostly in the USA.

The early 1960s saw the introduction of the 'second-generation' computers. These models used cold transistors instead of the hot valves (vacuum tubes) of the first-generation models, and so avoided the cooling problems of their predecessors.

The third-generation computers arrived in the mid 1960s and were a significant step forward from the second-generation machines owing to three main factors:

- Integrated circuits (several circuit elements in one monolithic chip) giving much cheaper and faster processing power.
- Modularity (building block principle of constructing a computer of the required specification) giving greater flexibility and economy, especially as regards expansion by adding further modules.
- Multiprogramming (several programs running simultaneously) providing a more rapid throughput of jobs and higher efficiency in computer system usage.

Concurrently with the development of these aspects, the peripheral units of computers also improved. Faster input and output devices, and larger amounts of magnetic storage, also became available to match the greater electronic capabilities of the central processing units (CPUs, i.e. processors — the calculating, logic and control unit of a computer). At about this time computers and their associated equipment became known as 'hardware', mainly in order to differentiate the electronic and electromechanical aspects from the systems and programming aspects (software).

Following the third-generation computers, manufacturers have attempted to designate their new models as fourth or later generations. Although there have been immense developments in terms of the speed, memory and power of processors, there has not really been a quantum jump to justify these designations. Computers are no longer capable of being segregated into clearly defined generations.

Data transmission and real-time DP

A significant development in the late 1960s was the ability to transmit data over long distances between a computer and terminals. The possibility of a large number of users being able to use a computer from a long distance away became a reality. The users are said to be 'on-line', and this development not only caused an explosive increase in computer availability but also introduced a new concept in DP.

The new concept was 'real-time DP'. This implies the use of a distant computer to give instantaneous control over widespread business activities. The most prominent users of real-time systems are the airline companies with their seat reservation systems and the banks and building societies for customer account updating.

Minicomputers

During the early 1970s the cost of integrated circuits fell dramatically and their speeds of operation increased. These developments caused some swing away from the larger (mainframe) computers towards smaller computers, called minicomputers. These compact and less expensive machines are capable of meeting the DP needs of most middle-size companies. As is explained in Section 2.3, minicomputers facilitate the adoption of distributed (data) processing; they are also useful for other purposes, especially in regard to data communications.

Microcomputers

More recent developments engendered by the reduced cost and greater miniaturization of electronics, are microprocessors and microcomputers. The former are, broadly speaking, microprogrammed devices capable of being incorporated into or attached to other equipment for purposes of control. Microcomputers, as the reader is no doubt aware, are desk-top computers available in many walks of life, from primary schools to advanced research laboratories. They have a wide range of sizes, capabilities and costs, and can be incorporated into microcomputer systems along with a variety of peripherals and storage devices. They are playing an increasingly significant role in education and business, sales now being measured in hundreds of thousands of units per annum. Microcomputers are described in more detail in Section 2.4.

Software

In parallel with the huge increase in the computer (hardware) manufacturing industry over the past twenty years has been the expansion of the 'software' industry. Software is a broad term covering the methods of using and controlling computers. It includes programs, systems and other facilities, and the software industry is now a governing factor in the development of computer methodologies. This is particularly the case as regards microcomputers for which many software companies are supplying programs and systems.

See Chapter 5 for some further details of software.

Networks

The late 1970s saw a swing away from centralized computers towards the notion of distributed DP. That is to say processing power being more accessible to users with the hardware available in their actual workplaces. The low price of computers, and particularly microcomputers, together with their increasing power and sophistication has resulted in these devices not only being more widely used but also being linked, forming wide area networks. The main advantage of networking is that a user is no longer working in isolation but is plugged into a powerful and perhaps extensive grid of computing facilities.

Thus data and programs can be shared between users and intercommunication becomes possible through the sending of messages over the network (Section 2.5).

Office automation

The advent of networks and the parallel introduction of word processing were the principal spearheads of office automation (Section 2.6). The nature of office work means that it will never be entirely automated in the sense that people will be eliminated from offices, there are too many discrepancies and variations for that to happen. Nevertheless the present generation of office workers are far more technology-orientated than those of previous generations.

Expert systems (ESs)

Long-term developments that could be of immense importance are in the areas of ESs and, in particular, the so-called fifth-generation project. ESs are progeny of the research into artificial intelligence that has been conducted since the early 1960s. Up to now artificial intelligence has had little or no effect on the conduct of business. Being largely carried out by academics, artificial intelligence has contented itself with providing solutions and methods associated with problems and situations of interest to the researchers rather than matters of a practical business nature.

An ES purports to be knowledge-based rather than data-based. In other words, it is far less reliant on human instruction in the form of system design and computer programming, and is capable of making its own judgements and forming its own solutions within a given field of knowledge. When presented with a problem, an ES does not follow a predetermined set of instructions, as does a conventionally programmed computer, but utilizes sets of rules derived from its own knowledge, i.e. it is told *what* to solve but not *how* to solve.

This 'expertise' is achieved by breaking problems and requirements down into smaller and smaller subproblems until a situation is reached where a direct solution is applicable. An ES also builds up its own fund of knowledge based on experience gained from the problems presented to it. This knowledge enables logical inferences to be made in a similar manner to those of human beings.

ESs are the embodiment within a computer of knowledged-based processes deriving from the skills and experience of human experts. Such a system should also be capable of justifying its line of reasoning in a way that is understandable to the user.

Thus an ES is informed about a particular problem or situation and it responds by providing relevant advice. Furthermore, if required, it can give an explanation as to how it arrived at that advice. The input to the ES generally takes the form of answers to questions posed by the ES. This method of accepting a problem is necessary since no computer program is, or ever will be, capable of accepting completely unstructured information. The ES's questions are obviously geared to the particular application and the user's responses must fall within a limited range of acceptable and understandable answers.

An important aspect of an ES is that it 'learns' from the feedback provided by its users after they have acted upon its advice. That is to say, advice that results in a satisfactory outcome for the user is strengthened, whereas unsatisfactory results cause the advice to be weakened or deleted.

The working of an ES is of course determined by a computer program and in this respect it does not differ from any other computer application. The difference lies in the fact that an ES follows rules and guidelines rather than strict instructions. The rules are sophisticated, however, and are related to the probability of the advice being correct or valuable.

EXAMPLE OF AN ES

A simple example of a potential ES might be the purchasing of materials over an extended period from a range of alternative worldwide suppliers. Some suppliers keep their delivery promises, others deliver late, others not at all. This situation could be made more complicated by fluctuating costs and world shortages of some of the materials.

The question arising is which supplier to place each new order with so as to optimize cost and delivery. From the buying department's past experience of these matters – perhaps largely subjective – there should be a basis for initiating the ES.

Factors entering into this scenario are as follows:

- the prospective supplier's cost quotation or estimate for the order;
- the promised delivery date(s);
- the supplier's history of costs and deliveries (where known);
- the size of the order;
- the size of the supplying company;
- the current rate of exchange with supplier's country;
- the political situation in supplier's country;
- the time of the year.

Thereafter the feedback to the ES would be measures of the actual outcome – time and cost-wise – of each order. The ES would then be able to qualify its recommendations for future order-placing. As well as feedback of past orders, it would be necessary to inform the ES regarding changeable factors such as the last two points above.

Beyond all this, there is the distinct possibility of completely new factors entering into the scenario, i.e. those not apparent initially. An instance of this could be the sudden emergence of a competitive buyer for scarce materials.

These factors are obviously based on human knowledge through experience and intuition, and this information needs to be put into the ES at the outset. The persons who do this are termed 'knowledge engineers'; they translate their experience and expertise relating to a particular problem, application or situation into the rules and strategies followed by the ES.

In order to achieve this, special computer languages, such as Prolog and Lisp, are used. These are for general ES applications but particular applications have their own dedicated languages. At present most ESs are directed towards scientific, medical and military problems. This is understandable as these areas have clearer objectives than in many business situations.

An aspect of ESs is the 'shell' concept. A shell, as the name suggests, is an ES that has general inference capabilities but no specific domain knowledge. The intent is that users of a shell must first enter into it their own rules and knowledge. This is an ambitious concept and it remains to be seen to what extent it will actually work.

It is quite possible, however, that ESs will be applicable to particular aspects of business such as financial planning, marketing strategies and portfolio management.

As far as most business is concerned, ESs at the moment are potential solutions looking for suitable problems. In other words their theoretical capabilities are way ahead of the business users' abilities to exploit them. As has been only too apparent over the past thirty years or so, the business user has only slowly and hesitatingly come to grips with computer systems. Now that there is a degree of acceptance of computers, it could be counterproductive — if not disastrous — if ESs turn out to be difficult to use and misleading.

The main problem will be the difficulty for the user to translate his or her expertise into computer-acceptable logic. It must be the experienced business manager or executive who becomes the so-called knowledge engineer, for a time at least. There would be no point in him having to explain the problems and past results to an 'instant expert' as has sometimes happened with conventional systems.

In some companies the situation is so fluid that by the time the ES has been set up, and sufficient feedback entered into it, the problems will have altered so radically that the knowledge in the ES would be irrelevant.

Fifth-generation projects

The fifth-generation project was instigated by the Japanese government in 1981 as a ten-year project to completely revolutionize the use of computers. It is not a project concerned essentially with the development of computer hardware itself but with much more sophisticated methods of utilizing computational power. These include not only ESs in the widest sense but also other concepts, in particular, intelligent interfacing. The latter means the ability to accept, understand and convey information in the form of written and spoken natural languages, and as visual images. Thus, in theory, a fifth-generation system will be able to read books, write text, listen and speak to people, look at pictures and create diagrams, as ways of interfacing with the world.

These objectives demand extensive understanding of subjects such as the semantics and syntax of languages, pattern recognition, harmonic analysis and fuzzy theory.

Fifth-generation systems will also be equipped with very high-level enquiry language facilities so that users will be able to make complex enquiries calling for the information and knowledge acquired by the system. These enquiries will include 'what if' types of questions necessitating the creation of sophisticated simulations of technical, business and social situations in order to forecast the effect of making important decisions.

These are indeed very ambitious aims: only time and a massive amount of effort and capital will prove or disprove their feasibility.

Up to the time of writing the Japanese fifth-generation project has shown no evidence of real progress in spite of eight years of development. This can also be said of the more recent European and US projects, Esprit and Alvey respectively.

It is becoming increasingly evident that attempts to mimic the human brain are not just a matter of faster processors and larger memories. There is the far more fundamental problem of how the brain works and how we can make a machine to imitate it. Until we truly know the answer to the first question, we cannot hope to tackle the second problem.

2.2 Structure of a computer

Digital computers represent numbers, and data in general, as electrical pulses and as magnetic spots. This means that number representation is exact, as are also the instructions that are executed in processing the data. 'Processing' is a wide term meaning any series of calculations, aggregations, tests and rearrangements applied to data in order to extract useful information from it. The instructions (program) are stored in magnetic form in the computer's main store (memory), which consists of metal-oxide semiconductor chips. As shown in Figure 2.1, the instructions are transferred one at a time from the main store to the control unit. Here they are decoded and the control unit then sends control signals to all the other units. The peripheral units have their own control units that 'interface' with the main control unit situated in the central processing unit

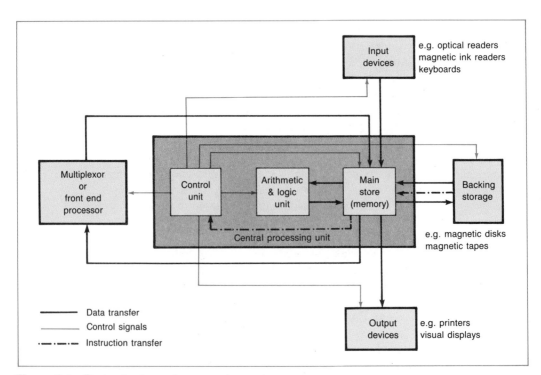

Figure 2.1 Basic structure of a computer system

(CPU). The CPU comprises the main control unit, the arithmetic unit and the main store.

The arithmetic unit not only does calculations, but also executes logical functions such as testing the signs (+ or −) of numbers, shifting parts of numbers about, and moving them between storage locations. It is also employed to modify the program itself by altering the instructions held in the main store. Program modification is the kernel of a computer's flexibility and hence its broad applicability. Without the ability to change its own instructions, a computer would be impotent.

Data and instructions can also be transferred between the main store and backing storage. The main store normally consists of hundreds of thousands of storage elements, each of which is capable of representing a 'nought' or a 'one' (a bit) according to its state. By suitably grouping bits together they are able to represent digits, letters, complete numbers, signs or instructions for the computer itself.

There are three methods by which a computer is capable of decoding ('understanding') and executing a program instruction − circuitry, micro-programming or software. Circuitry, also known as hard-wiring, means that permanent and fixed electronics is used. Microprogramming, means that the read-only microinstructions needed to execute a program instruction are permanently held in the form of pluggable, i.e. removable, boards holding the relevant chips (integrated microcircuitry). Thus, if necessary, these boards can be easily replaced. Software is the storage of sets of program instructions capable of doing the same as one programmable function, e.g. the division function could be achieved by a series of subtraction and shift functions. Processing capability (intelligence) is becoming more dispersed among the other units apart from the CPU. This makes these units more autonomous and has become practicable owing to the reduced size and cost of microelectronics. Thus an intelligent peripheral, e.g. certain printers, can operate for relatively long periods without need for the CPU to be involved.

Multiprocessing

A way of achieving higher processing speeds is an array of processors operating in parallel, this is termed parallel processing, multiprocessing or array processing. Thus each processor plays its part, at the same time as the others, towards arriving at the final result. In scientific and technical applications it is often feasible to compute the various parts of the problem concurrently, e.g. evaluating different parts of a complex equation independently and then bringing the results together for the final evaluation. In business, the computations are relatively simple; it is the large amount of data and its inherent need to be organized that bring about the demand for powerful computers in big companies. In this case each of the processors in the array does the same processing but with different data.

In a multiprocessing computer there are an input/output processor, a control processor and an array of work processors — perhaps several thousands. The input/output processor handles all data transfers between the input/output ports and the main store, thus relieving other processors of this time-consuming task. The control processor's function is to allocate tasks to the work processors; this is done dynamically according to the requirements at any instant of time. Thus if a work processor is held up by the need for more data, its program and current data are put into backing storage and it is reallocated to another task. When the data arrives, the program and data are retrieved and allocated to any free work processor for continuation of the processing.

The aforementioned procedures are possible because work processors can use replicas of the same program and share a common pool of cache memory into which the program instructions are transferred for execution. The work processors can also perform different tasks, i.e. multiprogramming, under the control of an operating system.

The principle of multiprocessing engenders an exceptionally high level of reliability because the large number of work processors can be used at will. Thus those that are faulty or need testing or maintenance are merely disconnected from the array, and apart from a slight reduction in speed of operation, no effect is apparent. Similarly, it is possible to split the work processors into two or more separate systems and to use these effectively as individual computers.

Backing storage

The principal backing storage of a computer is nowadays mostly magnetic disks but magnetic tapes are still also used, especially for archival data and for back-up purposes. Backing storage is less expensive for holding large amounts of data than are main store media but is much slower in operation and can only work via the main store. These devices are described more fully in Sections 2.4 and 4.2.

Terminals and peripheral devices

Many computers have terminals linked to them, in which case the CPU is usually assisted by a front end processor. These are virtually CPUs in their own right and control the terminals after the style in which the CPU controls the peripherals. More is written about data communications in Section 2.5.

Peripherals are diverse both in their nature and their capabilities. A peripheral differs from a terminal in that it is sited fairly close to the CPU, and generally fulfils only one function, i.e. input, output or backing storage. Chapters 3 and 4 provide more facts and figures regarding input/output and storage.

Terminals are a computer's interface with environmental activities, and they come in a wide variety of forms. Terminals fall into two main categories. The first is the batch terminal intended for remote job entry (RJE), and consequently needing high input/output speeds to cope with the large volume of data. A batch terminal could include any type of fast operation input and/or output device such as an optical reader, a magnetic tape drive (holding large amounts of input data) or a line printer. These devices operate autonomously to a large extent once set up by the operator.

The second category is the interactive terminal intended for manual input and low-volume output, such as for file enquiries, seat booking and on-line programming. An interactive terminal normally consists of a keyboard together with a visual display unit (VDU) and a serial printer. It is also possible to have a cluster of VDU terminals sharing one printer. This type of terminal is nowadays in extensive use for a wide range of applications such as business DP, engineering design, education, and file interrogation by police forces and similar organizations.

Another way of categorizing terminals is as general-purpose and dedicated.

General-purpose terminals usually comprise a keyboard for input and a serial printer and VDU for output; this enables them to be employed for a wide variety of applications.

Dedicated terminals often incorporate hardware devices specifically designed for a particular application.

EXAMPLES OF DEDICATED TERMINALS

- Real-time banking terminals with a passbook printer and cash dispenser.
- Cash-receipting terminals comprising a rent-book printer and a locked audit tally roll printer.
- Retail store terminals with a cash register and a bar code reader.

A more flexible terminal is one with a stored program and its own built-in processor, i.e. it is intelligent. These terminals can hold several thousand instructions and so are effectively a small computer in their own right. They are programmed to reduce the mainframe's processing load, and they may also be employed to control the data of a group of non-intelligent terminals.

Acoustic couplers

An acoustic coupler is a soundproof box into which the handset of an ordinary telephone is placed. The box is connected to a keyboard and printer, and the operation of the keys is converted from electrical pulses to acoustic signals. These are picked up by the telephone's microphone and transmitted as signals to the computer. Similarly the signals from the computer are emitted acoustically by the telephone's earpiece and converted into electrical pulses by the acoustic coupler in order to operate the printer.

An acoustic coupler provides a high level of portability in communicating with a computer since it can be used anywhere that a telephone is available, including vehicles equipped with radio telephones. See also Section 3.12.

Data representation

It is not the intention of this text to explain the technicalities of data representation in any depth but some explanation at this juncture is not out of place. As stated earlier, the only basic way in which data can be represented in a computer is in the form of bits. A few examples of the more common bit combinations used to represent data are explained below.

Byte
A byte consists of eight bits and represents either one character or two digits. Since eight bits can represent 2^8, i.e. 256, different characters, there is ample capacity for all the numeric digits, alphabetical letters and a host of symbols. Either the Extended Binary Coded Decimal Interchange Code (EBCDIC) or the American Standard Code for Information Interchange (ASCII) coding system is usable within the eight bits of a byte. The former utilizes all eight bits to represent the full range of characters, whereas the latter takes only seven bits.

The eight bits in a byte may also be split into two groups of four bits, each of which can represent a numeric digit since four bits covers from 0 to 15. Thus with this arrangement a byte can hold two digits.

Word
A word is a group of bits that can represent a number in binary form, a computer instruction, or one or more characters. Thus a 24-bit word, if used in binary form, is capable of representing any decimal number up to $2^{24}-1$, i.e. 16,777,215. In practice the word may also hold a parity bit and a sign, and so the remaining 22 bits represent up to $2^{22}-1$, i.e. 4,194,303. The various computer models have different numbers of bits per word, e.g. 16, 32 or 64.

A word may be split into groups of bits each of which represents a digit, letter or symbol, e.g. a 24-bit word split into three bytes.

Instructions
As stated above, a group of bits is also used to represent a computer instruction. There are many ways in which this is done; suffice to say that the longer the word (and so the more bits available for an instruction), the more powerful the instruction. More is said about computer instructions in Chapter 5.

Addressable locations
A group of bits or bit combinations that the computer's logic is capable of locating in storage by means of the group's address is referred to as an addressable location or simply as an address.

2.3 Minicomputers

Characteristics of minicomputers

The first point to make is that minicomputers have the same basic structure as the larger (mainframe) computers, as shown in Figure 2.1. They do not introduce any fundamentally new concepts in terms of their logic, storage media and mode of control. As with mainframes, the technology changes with time, but a minicomputer still has input/output, employs magnetic media and is controlled by a stored program of instructions. In many cases the distinction between a minicomputer and a mainframe is somewhat blurred, this is especially true of the so-called superminis, and, in the long term, the distinction will undoubtedly disappear entirely.

Physical size
Minicomputers are more compact than mainframes, the CPU occupies less space as it is not so powerful and has a smaller amount of memory.

Environment
The smallness, ruggedness and lower heat emission of a minicomputer enable it to be installed in a less protected environment. There is no need for air-conditioning, and it can be installed close to its end-user, such as in a factory or a vehicle. This favours decentralization of the DP functions in an organization by facilitating distributed DP (Section 2.5).

These advantages, however, are of lesser value with the larger models of minicomputer, which, if fitted with a hard disk drive, require some degree of air-conditioning.

Cost
The lower development costs combined with high sales and mass production result in minicomputers' CPUs being less expensive than the larger CPUs. This is less true of the peripheral units however unless they are of lower speed or capacity. The prices of basic minicomputers are in thousands as against the tens of thousands of pounds for mainframes.

Modular construction
The compactness of a minicomputer's circuitry results in easy expansion of its CPU. A minicomputer is upgraded by merely inserting different circuit boards instead of replacing the complete CPU as with a mainframe computer.

Simplicity
The employment of smaller word sizes and fewer logical features in the smaller minicomputers makes them simpler to manufacture and maintain. This makes them more cost effective provided the workload is not too demanding. It is also true that the capabilities of mainframes, in terms of computation and logic, are greatly underemployed in most DP applications and so minicomputers are able to cope with the processing.

Word length
The majority of minicomputers have words of either 16 or 32 bits. A 16-bit word does not carry much information in computer terms. This means that the

minicomputer has some difficulty in addressing its main store because there are
not enough bits to address each and every storage location; remember that 2,000
locations need 11 bits for complete identification.

Another weakness of 16-bit words is that two words are needed for certain
instructions and quantities. If one bit is used as a sign bit and another for parity,
the remaining 14 bits represent a maximum quantity of only 16,383. This is small
by any standards and far too small for monetary transactions.

These drawbacks result in a need for more words of main storage, and in more
time taken for program execution.

Main store sizes

For the most part minicomputers have main stores (memories) of a few million
words. It should be remembered that a minicomputer's small words (16 bits)
make the instructions of low power, and therefore a large number are needed
even for modest programs.

Another factor is the storage occupied by the software, especially the operating
system. If this results in a shortage of main store, the application program(s) will
need to be transferred in segments from the backing storage, thus increasing the
time taken for the job in hand.

Input/output interrupts

With all types of computers, when an input or output peripheral is ready to
transfer or accept data, it interrupts the normal processing so that the CPU can
initiate a data transfer under program control. A minicomputer transfers only
one word at a time, as compared with a block of data with a mainframe, and
therefore interrupts the CPU more often. This may cause delay in the peripheral
units obtaining service and, in effect, limits the number of peripherals that the
CPU can handle.

Direct memory access

This facility allows data to be transferred directly between the main store and
the peripheral units. It is particularly advantageous for the higher speed
peripherals such as magnetic tape. The CPU initiates the data transfer which then
proceeds autonomously while the CPU continues with the processing; this
technique is known as 'cycle stealing'.

Minicomputer peripherals

In general, the peripheral units and storage devices attachable to minicomputers
are similar to those for mainframes. This means that a wide range is available
(Chapters 3 and 4) but nevertheless, in practice, fewer different peripherals are
used with one minicomputer. The main difference between minicomputers and
mainframes in this respect is the emphasis on direct data entry (DDE) with
minicomputers.

One of the prime means of input with a minicomputer is the DDE station;
this usually consists of a keyboard and a VDU. Its main advantage is its ability

ɔ carry out immediate checks on the input data in a similar manner to those ᴚsed with key-to-disk systems. The input data is held in a store in the DDE ᴚtation, and then entered into the CPU as a block rather than byte by byte.

A minicomputer's peripheral units, although conceptually the same as for ᴚainframes, are generally slower in operation. In round terms, their speeds are ᴚetween a quarter and a half of those of mainframe peripherals. Similarly, a ᴚinicomputer's backing storage is usually of lower capacity. These characteristics ᴚre only to be expected with minicomputers since they are of lower processing ᴚower and are considerably less expensive.

2.4 Microcomputers

Decreased cost and the miniaturization of electronics has led to the insertion of microprocessors into a wide range of equipment. It has also allowed the development of a large range of microcomputers, and these have by now entered many faces of business, technology, education and domestic life. The available range of microcomputers and the number of manufacturers and suppliers are greater than for larger computers. This has brought about differences in the marketing methods, and microcomputers are often sold by mail order or over the counter.

A point to be borne in mind regarding the wide range is that the microprocessors used in the microcomputers are drawn from a much more limited range. This need not, of course, be of great concern to a business user since other factors such as software availability, backing storage and output devices are usually of more interest.

As things stand at present, a typical business microcomputer is defined essentially by the following attributes:

- It is a small desk-top computer, occupying little more space than a typewriter, and is moveable.
- The cost is relatively low — a few thousand pounds or less for a viable small business system.
- It is a transaction processing device, i.e. one transaction is keyed-in at a time via a keyboard similar to that of a typewriter.
- The main components are a keyboard, a microprocessor, a visual display unit, one or two floppy disk drives, a serial printer, and, perhaps, a hard disk unit.
- A good range of packaged software is available combined with simplicity of programming in the form of high-level languages.
- It can be linked quite simply into a network system.

The above characteristics make microcomputers amenable to most small businesses. This is particularly true as regards size and cost, i.e. they are manageable and economic, and so sales are now millions worldwide. A similar point is that they are approachable by the non-computer person, that is to say they are straightforward and interesting to use. This is demonstrated by their extensive adoption by computer amateurs and for school tuition.

Microcomputers have spawned their own characteristics and terminology, some of which are shared with larger computers.

Memory (main storage)

This falls into two main types — RAM and ROM.

RAM (random access memory) holds the application programs and data in current use, it may also be occupied by software such as operating systems and interpreters (Section 5.2). RAM is usually between 500 kilobytes and several megabytes in a business microcomputer.

ROM (read-only memory) is for the purpose of holding software such as the microcomputer's operating system, interpreters and compilers (Chapter 5). It is programmed and inserted by the manufacturer and cannot be altered by the user. The amount of ROM usually lies between 16 and 40 kilobytes.

An extension of ROM is PROM (programmable read-only memory). This allows the user to program his own software for permanent and unalterable use. The danger with PROM is the possibility of errors and consequent cost of correction.

EPROM (erasable programmable read-only memory) is erasable by means of ultraviolet light so that correction is less expensive, although the complete program has to be reinserted. EAROM (electronically alterable read-only memory) is similar to EPROM except that the program instructions are selectively erasable by electrical methods; this makes correction even more convenient. The latter two features are unlikely to impinge on the business user, however.

Microprocessors

Microprocessors (chips) are limited to relatively few types stemming mainly from three manufacturers — Intel, Motorola and Zilog.

Larger microcomputers tend to have several different processors built into them. The reason for this is mainly to cope with the various operating systems that exist for microcomputing. Another purpose is to make the microcomputer faster by utilizing the additional processors for handling input, output and communications, thus relieving the main processor.

The two significant characteristics of a microprocessor are its word size and its speed of operation. These are complex factors and it is not simple to make comparisons between the various models. In broad terms, the word size is the number of bits dealt with at the same time, i.e. in parallel along the bus. The bigger the word size, the more powerful the processor, other things being equal — which they rarely are. Most microprocesssors now have either 16-bit or 32-bit words.

The speed of a microprocessor, also known as the clock rate or data transfer rate, is the rate at which the data bits are moved around inside it. This rate lies between 5 and 33 million bits per second (megahertz) but a particular microprocessor is not always made to operate at the same rate in different models of microcomputers.

In any case most business applications are dominated by data transfers to and from backing storage and so a high clock rate may not be all that advantageous.

Backing storage

The most common backing storage of microcomputers is the floppy disk (Section 4.2) and usually there are two disk drives per system. Typically one drive takes the software disk whilst the other takes the user's database disk. The main sizes of floppy disk are the $5\frac{1}{4}$ inch and the $3\frac{1}{2}$ inch diameter, although the latter is encased in a rigid container and so it is not really floppy. These disks hold up to 3 megabytes each.

Where a larger amount of storage is needed a Winchester disk (Section 4.2) may be incorporated into the microcomputer system. As used with microcomputers, these have storage capacities of around 50 megabytes. It is also possible to attach several hard disk drives to a number of microcomputers simultaneously so that they can share the operating system, other software and a common database (see local area networks in Section 2.5). It is probable that except for the smallest of businesses a hard disk is needed for most applications.

Visual display units (VDUs)

VDUs in general and microcomputer VDUs in particular are torn between two different types of display. One is to display figures and text, the other is to display graphical representations (graphics) — see Section 3.8.

When considering the capacity of a VDU screen for the purpose of figure and text display, it is the number of lines and the number of characters per line that are of relevance, typically 25 lines of 80 characters each. We are also interested in the definition of the displayed characters and this depends on the number of dots (pixels) composing each character, often this is 9 pixels wide by 14 pixels deep including the borders.

In business applications graphics takes the form of straightforward diagrams and graphs, whereas in technical applications they are far more complex. Nevertheless, even for business graphics the resolution and colours of the display are important. Resolution is dependent on the number of pixels that can be accommodated on the screen, typically 720 pixels wide by 350 pixels deep. Normally there are eight colours available, sometimes sixteen. Much beyond eight and certainly over sixteen, the colours become indistinguishable from each other. And although this does not matter for pictures, it is important that business graphics do not become confusing. For both figures and graphics the size of the screen is relevant, normally this is 12 inches diagonally, but larger and flatter screens are now on the market.

Innovations for microcomputer displays are windows (Section 3.8), icons and variable-shaped cursors. An icon is a symbolic shape displayed to facilitate the user's choice of action, acting as a simple reminder of the possibilities available. A variable-shaped cursor indicates the current state of the microcomputer's processing, e.g. an hour glass indicates that the user has to wait for the results.

Printers

This is normally either a dot (wire) matrix printer or a daisy wheel printer (Section 3.11) with most speeds between 30 and 120 characters per second. Various print bank widths and fonts are available, and also plotting facilities with some models.

Programming

The most common programming language at present in use with microcomputers is BASIC. This is probably owing to its simplicity and widespread use for educational purposes. COBOL, FORTRAN and Pascal and other high-level languages are also available for business and scientific applications.

In business it is unusual for microcomputer users to write their own programs. It is more likely that they purchase ready-made software covering the applications of relevance.

Operating systems

This looks after the compiling and interpreting of the high-level languages used with microcomputers and also the control of programs and files stored on the floppy disks. The most common operating systems for microcomputers are the various editions of CP/M, MS–DOS, PC–DOS and UNIX. (PC–DOS is IBM's version of MS–DOS.) As already mentioned, certain microcomputers can work with several different operating systems, either optionally or as a matter of course. This flexibility gives them greater appeal because prospective users who have existent programs and files are likely to want to transfer them onto new hardware without amendment.

Software

A large amount of microcomputer business software is now on the market. For the most part it splits into six categories. These are as follows:

• Spreadsheets, e.g. Visicalc, Supercalc and Multiplan.

- Database management, e.g. dBASE IV, Paradox and Superbase.
- Word processing, e.g. WordPerfect, Wordstar, DisplayWrite and Multimate.
- Desktop publishing, e.g. Ventura, Pagemaker and Interleaf.
- Integrated software, e.g. Symphony, Lotus 1-2-3 and Framework.
- On-line services, e.g. Delphi and CompuServe.

The above is sometimes called horizontal software as it runs across a wide range of business users and applications. Vertical software is aimed at specific types of companies or users and again there is a massive amount available. The various company software includes antique dealers, hotels, estate agents, solicitors and farmers. The software for user types includes stock control, sales and purchase accounting, payroll, production planning and job costing.

Large microcomputers

The more powerful microcomputers are capable of handling a number of users at the same time and also several concurrent tasks. The multi-user microcomputers are linked to workstations at which the users may be doing either the same or different work from each other. This facility ties in with networking (Section 2.5) such as the use of Ethernet as a local area network system (LAN).

Microcomputers are increasingly acting as terminals linked to a distant or local mainframe. If this arrangement is used in conjunction with multi-tasking (Section 5.3), a flexible and powerful system results. The user could, for instance, download data from the mainframe's database and employ this along with a spreadsheet for financial modelling. This could then be followed by the use of a word processing package in order to create a financial report for management.

Most microcomputers, and espcially the larger ones, have plenty of spare ports and slots, thus allowing for considerable expansion in terms of processing capabilities and attached peripherals. This enables a user to start with a fairly small microcomputer and to expand it as necessary into a multi-tasking, multi-user, network-linked machine.

Portable microcomputers

A portable microcomputer is small, lightweight and battery-powered. This allows it to be carried around and used in cars, trains, airliners, etc. The display is usually a LCD panel providing twenty lines of eighty characters. There is sometimes a built-in thermal printer, a cassette recorder and the necessary software for a particular function. If a modem and communications interface are included, a portable microcomputer becomes a means of data capture and/or message acceptance in conjunction with a distant minicomputer or mainframe.

Portable microcomputers are connectable to various types of printers and to $3\frac{1}{2}$ inch disk drives in a similar way to ordinary microcomputers.

2.5 Data communications

Data transmission

Communications is an extensive subject in its own right, encompassing not only
data transmission but also sound and video transmission via telephone lines, radio
links and satellite links. And in fact with the increasing use of digital transmission
for sound and video, computers have moved into the communications and
entertainment areas. In a book of this size and content it is not practical to include
more than superficial explanations of the various aspects of communications,
nevertheless this section provides the reader with a general understanding of data
communications as far as it impacts on business data processing. Figure 2.2 shows
the main components of a data communications system.

In the context of this book data communications means the transmission and
control of business data as it is moved from one point to another. There follows
descriptions of the main concepts, equipment and techniques employed for these
purposes.

Modems

As explained previously, computers represent data by electrical pulses.
Unfortunately telephone lines are unable to transmit such pulses faithfully owing
to the fact that they were originally designed solely for speech transmission
resulting in distortion of the pulses and consequent errors. Since speech
transmission takes the form of variations in electric current at audio frequencies
along the telephone lines, the computer's pulses must be transmitted in a similar
way.

This is achieved by the use of a 'modem', i.e. a modulator/demodulator. At
the sending end this device converts pulses into variations either in the level
(amplitude) or in the frequency of the electric current transmitted along the wire.
At the received end another modem does exactly the opposite. Thus the sender
and receiver perceive only pulses, whereas the telephone lines carry, in effect,
two levels or frequencies of sound (one for each of the bits 0 and 1). These
processes are known as amplitude modulation and frequency modulation
respectively. Some modems are small enough to be housed inside other equipment
(card modems). Modems will be obsolete when all telephone equipment becomes
digital.

Synchronous/asynchronous transmission

Another aspect of data transmission is the synchronization (or relative timing)
of the pulses when transmitted. Synchronous mode means that in each time

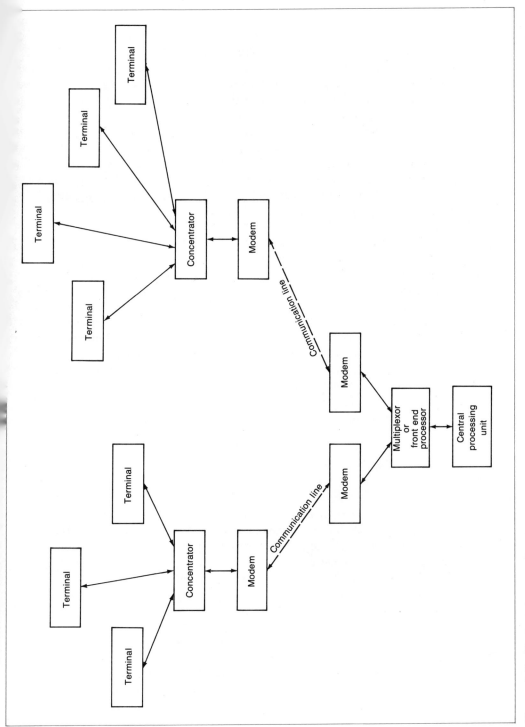

Figure 2.2 Basic structure of a data communications system

interval either a 1 or a 0 pulse must be present during the period of transmission. In other words, the equipment at the receiving end expects a pulse to arrive a predetermined instants, and so there is no need to otherwise indicate their presence. Synchronous mode is best suited to long transmission of data such as with remote job entry. Once transmission has commenced it cannot be interrupted without re-establishing the timing of the pulses.

Where shorter transmissions of data with intervals between them are required, e.g. keyed data, asynchronous mode is more suitable. This mode demands that the receiving end has some method of detecting the start of each character and ensuring that no pulses (bits) are lost. This is achieved by enclosing the bits representing the character by start and stop bits. A complete character actually necessitates 10 bits, i.e. 1 start bit, 7 data bits, 1 parity bit, and 1 stop bit.

Transmission speed (rate)

The rate at which bits are transmitted along a line is measured in bauds. A baud is in effect 1 bit per second, thus a 2,400-baud line transmits a maximum of 2,400 bits in a second. As examples of transmission rates, British Telecom's Datel systems offer lines, either private or public switched telephone network (PSNT), with rates from 200 to 50,000 baud. At the higher rates transmission is in synchronous mode and generally over private lines (circuits).

A means of attaining high speed is parallel transmission. This is where each of the data bits is sent along its own circuit, thus necessitating as many wires as there are bits in parallel. This method is used mainly for short connections such as between a computer and its high-speed peripherals, e.g. disk drives.

Simplex/half duplex/duplex

A simplex circuit means that data can be transmitted in one direction only. Half duplex circuits allow transmission in either direction but not simultaneously, i.e. the equipment at the end of the line takes its turn to transmit with that at the other end. Duplex, or full duplex, means that it is possible to transmit in both directions simultaneously.

Multiplexing

Multiplexing is a means of combining together data from several sources so that it can be transmitted along one communication line.

Thus if several terminals situated in fairly close proximity need to communicate with a distant computer, they are connected to a multiplexor which in turn is connected to a modem. At the computer end this arrangement is in reverse which means that the combined data from the terminals is separated by another multiplexor into individual lots as if they had come along their own lines. In other words the multiplexing is 'transparent' to the user, as are the modems.

There are two main methods of multiplexing — time division and frequency division. Time division multiplexing means that either the bits or the characters being transmitted to or from several terminals are interleaved during transmission. For instance, a bit is taken from each terminal in turn and transmitted in synchronous mode by the multiplexor. At the receiving end the other multiplexor separates the bits and passes them to the computer as complete pieces of data.

Frequency division multiplexing entails several carrier waves each of which carries one lot of data being transmitted. Because each carrier wave has a different frequency, it is possible to separate them at the receiving end and so distinguish between the various lots of data.

A statistical multiplexor (statmux) is an intelligent device that is capable of judging each terminal's instantaneous requirements for line capacity and allocating line time accordingly. In this respect it has close similarities to a concentrator (see below). It also corrects errors caused by line faults and noise, and provides data formatting and network management.

Multiplexors are often integral with modems and concentrators.

Front-end processing

A front-end processor is usually a minicomputer or a microcomputer interposed between the main (host) computer and the multiplexor. Its purpose is to relieve the host computer from the burden of communications housekeeping. That is to say, the front-end processor presents the host computer with complete, error-free data and deals with chores such as message assembly/disassembly from/to packets (see 'packet switching'), parity checking, message labelling (message serial numbering), and removal or insertion of stop-start bits with asynchronous mode.

Concentrators

Even with time division multiplexing it is likely that a high-speed (rate) line is under-utilized. This is owing to the discrepancy between the line speed and the terminal operators' keying rates. For instance, even a 200-baud line has something like five times the capacity of an operator working at top speed. This difference results in many null (blank) spaces in the succession of bits. Thus when it is a terminal's turn to have a bit inserted, none is available.

A concentrator overcomes this deficiency by gathering the bits from each terminal or group of terminals and holding them in its buffer store until there are sufficient to justify forward transmission.

Thus it accepts bits at a low rate and then transmits them in a high-speed burst occupying a period of time division multiplexing. Concentrators are necessary only at the terminal end of a transmission link because, at the receiving end, either the front-end processor or the host computer is capable of sorting out the data.

Multidrop (multipoint) lines

A multidrop line has several terminals or concentrators attached to it. This arrangement reduces line costs but implies that only one terminal/concentrator transmits at a time along the line. Each lot of computer-transmitted data is headed by an identification so that although all the terminals receive it, only the appropriate terminal accepts it. In order properly to control the receipt of data from the terminals, they are 'polled' by the computer or front-end processor. This means that they are asked whether they have data to send and, if so, some or all of it is accepted. Polling entails protocol messages being sent to and from the terminals, and certain terminals may be given priority by being polled more frequently. Various polling arrangements are employed in order to minimize transmission costs, such as 'hub polling'; with this each terminal passes on the protocol messages to the next terminal rather than the computer polling each terminal individually.

Protocols

A protocol is an 'agreement' whereby devices can communicate in a fully understood manner. Owing to the diverse nature of hardware devices, they cannot usually communicate with each other except by means of a protocol unless they happen to come from one manufacturer. The factors entering into data transmission and covered by the protocol include the mode of transmission i.e. synchronous or asynchronous, speed of transmission, full or half duplex, format of the data, and error detection and correction procedures.

A commonly used protocol is 'binary synchronous communications' (BSC) also called 'Bisync'. With this protocol, transmission is synchronous, half duplex and block-formatted using ASCII or EBCDIC coding. Bisync was originally intended for use in a polled environment in which the computer confirms that each block of data from a terminal has been received correctly.

Another protocol is 'high-level data link control' (HDLC) of which there are several variants such as 'synchronous data line control' (SDLC) and X25.

Important features of HDLC protocols are the address field and sequence numbers incorporated into the data. The address allows all devices to be treated equally in that the data travels along with other data until its address is reached. The sequence number enables packets to be put into the correct order if they arrive out of sequence as a result of being transmitted over different routes (see 'packet switching'). HDLC is therefore suitable for statmux techniques in which many different lots of data share a single line.

There are many other protocols devised by manufacturers and communication organizations throughout the world. In an attempt to attain some degree of compatibility the ISO has put forward standards for a framework for all protocols. This is known as the 'open system interconnection' (OSI) model and contains seven layers each with a specific function such as the physical interface, error control, control messages and transparency. OSI can be regarded as a reference ground for protocol and hardware designers so that they are able to introduce new devices and methods with a reasonable level of conformity to existing and other new equipment.

In situations where two devices wish to communicate but employ different protocols it is possible to overcome this problem by using a protocol conversion computer or function.

Data transmission media

Telephone lines

As mentioned earlier in this section, data can be transmitted along a line (also termed a link or channel) at various speeds. The simplest and oldest type of communications channel is a pair of copper wires, i.e. a telephone line. This method is still used extensively and is satisfactory provided the low rates of transmission are acceptable.

Coaxial cables

When higher rates of transmission are necessary, ordinary wires cannot transmit without distorting the electrical pulses representing the data. Coaxial cable, similar to that used for connecting the aerials of domestic televisions, has a much better performance at higher transmission rates. It is employed as the transmission medium both for local and for intercontinental data communications.

Fibre optics

The principle of fibre optics is that data and other information is transmitted in the form of light through very fine glass fibres. The light is actually red or infra-red and is contained within the glass fibre owing to the principle of total internal reflection. In other words, the light is transmitted through the fibre after the style of water in a hosepipe, bends in the fibre making no difference. The glass fibres are contained within a cable that has strengthening and waterproofing properties.

The light is passed into and taken from the fibres by means of transducers, i.e. devices that convert electrical pulses to light and vice versa. Transducing is obviously necessary in order to interface electrically operated equipment such as peripherals and word processors to the optically operated fibres.

The advantages of fibre optics are the following:

- High bandwidth, i.e. a powerful data transmission capability.

- Low cross-talk, i.e. no interference between adjacent fibres.
- Low attenuation, i.e. little loss of signal strength.
- Freedom from interference by external electrical and electromagnetic equipment.
- High reliability.
- Safe because no heat, sparks or electrical voltages are created.
- Economic because glass is less expensive than the copper used in ordinary wires.

The high bandwidth allows data to be transmitted at several hundred megabits per second. The low attenuation permits transmission over distances of up to 5 kilometres without the need for repeaters, i.e. reamplification of the light intensity. The most usual mode of transmission is time division multiplexing and, as each of the large number of high bandwidth fibres in a cable can carry 32 channels, the transmission capability of just one cable is enormous.

Microwave networks

A microwave link is an ultra high frequency (UHF) radio transmission between two line-of-sight points. These points house radio transmitters and receivers (transceivers), known as repeaters. They are sited at strategic positions so as to form a network through which transmissions are routed between any two places. As far as possible the points are on hills so as to give the maximum line-of-sight distance over the horizon. Because of the high frequency of microwaves, and hence their large bandwidth, they are capable of transmitting without distortion.

Communication satellites

A weakness of microwave links is their demand for line-of-sight positioning. Since the horizon intervenes even between high points at distances exceeding a few tens of miles, microwaves cannot be used for transoceanic communications.

To overcome this problem repeaters are installed in satellites launched into geosynchronous orbits several thousand miles above the earth. A geosynchronous orbit means that the satellite maintains a fixed position relative to the earth. The satellite repeater receives radio transmissions from earth and, after amplification, retransmits them to be picked up by receivers within its coverage. Only three satellites are necessary to cover the whole of the earth's surface, and so it is possible to link any two points on earth by means of communication satellites.

In practical terms an intercontinental data communications link uses most of the above media. The first stage would probably be a telephone line or coaxial cable, either private or rented from a common carrier, e.g. British Telecom. This would be linked to a microwave network which takes the data to a radio station from where it is transmitted to a satellite. The satellite retransmits to a distant receiving station, after which the link is the reverse of the early stages. At various stages in the telephone system it is likely that optical fibres are alternatives to wires or coaxial cables.

Distributed processing

A distributed DP system is one with several interconnected points at which processing power, i.e. intelligence, and storage capacity are available. These points may on occasions act autonomously and at other times co-operate in handling a common problem. The locations of the processing points need not necessarily be physically remote from one another or from a central mainframe computer.

The main purpose of distributed processing is to give the end-users of computing facilities the control over and responsibility for their own data. The end-user becomes master of his own destiny to a much greater degree than with batch processing carried out entirely within the DP department. In other words, he has considerable computing power under his control rather than delegating it all to the centralized computer.

Distributed processing presupposes that the user department automatically accepts responsibility for the correctness and completeness of its source data. The department in question is likely to be the only body aware of the source data in use and of the immediate results required from the system. Because the source data as such is not handled by the DP department, the DP staff cannot be held responsible for source data errors or making corrections except when specifically requested by the user department.

A distributed processing system may be composed of several processing points connected together in a wide variety of configurations. The points themselves can be minicomputers, intelligent terminals, microcomputers or mainframe computers.

Broadly, distributed processing systems fall into two approaches – hierarchical and lateral.

Hierarchical (vertical) systems

These have several levels, the most powerful of which consists of one or more mainframe computers forming the central complex of the hierarchy. This complex is capable of handling local batch processing, remote job entry, time-sharing, and the needs of the lower levels in the hierarchy. It is likely that the central complex is large and expensive.

The second level comprises a powerful minicomputer(s) acting as a satellite to the mainframe(s). This must be capable of administering a network protocol so that data and messages can be passed through it between the lower and higher levels. This minicomputer must also be able to handle local batchwork, interactive terminals and, possibly, communication with other minicomputers.

The third level consists of microcomputers or intelligent terminals dedicated to particular tasks such as point-of-sale processing. They are capable of controlling a number of keyboards and VDUs, and of communicating with the second-level minicomputers. At the lowest level of the hierarchy are terminals that have little or no intelligence and so act merely as the means of accepting input and displaying output, i.e. a keyboard and screen.

Lateral (horizontal) systems

These are similar to hierarchical systems except for the omission of the mainframe(s). The minicomputers in a lateral system are autonomous but are capable of communicating with one another. This intercommunication must be flexible in order that various arrangements can be set up. In some situations the minicomputers co-operate in order to create a more powerful processing system, in others the communication is merely the interchange of messages or data.

The co-operation of minicomputers in a lateral system infers that they act as stand-by and back-up computers for each other. These requirements necessitate sophisticated software, and consequently overheads in terms of storage, cost and time must be taken into consideration.

It is also possible to have stand-alone distributed processing in that the minicomputers are substantially autonomous with only occasional connection to other computers. This may occur when it is necessary to transfer fairly large amounts of data to or from the minicomputers. An example of data being sent from several minicomputers to one mainframe or minicomputer is where stock levels are transmitted from branches to head office. An example of the reverse is details of new products sent from head office to all the branches. These procedures are sometimes termed 'bottom-up' and 'top-down' respectively.

Data switching

Data is often transmitted from one point to another along a fixed, permanent communication link, such as between a terminal and a nearby computer. This is satisfactory when the points are in regular communication and no other, occasional, users are involved. When data has to be transmitted between various users and in an unpredictable fashion, a data switching arrangement is necessary. Data can be switched by circuitry (hard wiring) in a similar way to telephone conversations, this method means that a physical circuit is set up and held in existence for the duration of the transmission. Circuit switching is an uneconomic method because the communication path is usually under-utilized during its existence.

Packet switching

A more efficient method of data transmission is message switching, and particularly a variation of this, i.e. packet switching. The main concept of packet switching is that a piece of data, i.e. a message, is fragmented into packets of data of fixed length, e.g. 128 bytes (octets), and transmitted in this form together with its control data. Control data is essentially the identity of the sender and address of the recipient.

Packet switching is achieved through the employment of a packet switching system (PSS), also known as a packet switching exchange (PSE). This system accepts messages and directs them to their destination by examining an 'address header' incorporated into each packet. The address header is derived from that inserted into the original message.

A PSS takes the form of a computer network in which each computer redirects the packets it receives to the next computer along the appropriate route to the packet's destination. Although the original message is fragmented into packets, which may arrive at different times, the PSS ensures that they all arrive at their destination accurately and that they are reassembled correctly. Thus the recipient finishes up with an exact copy of the original message.

The high level of efficiency of packet switching is achieved by interleaving packets, that is to say, packets travel between various points along the same path simultaneously.

The computers employed for packet switching are called 'store-and-forward' computers since they have storage buffers in which the packets awaiting onward transmission are held. They are able to request retransmission of packets found to contain errors on receipt, and retransmit packets at the request of the receiving point. It is also possible for the PSS to replicate packets for transmission to several recipients. Another facility is 'redirection'; this comes into play if the receiving point or a link is out of action. The packets are then redirected to a previously nominated address and the user is informed.

There are two main methods by which data is transmitted through a PSS. The first is a permanent virtual circuit otherwise known as a fixed path protocol, in which all the packets comprising the one call (message) go by the same route. The other method, called a switched virtual circuit or path-independent protocol, transmits the packets of one call via separate routes.

It is also possible to transmit human speech via a PSS because speech is in bursts that can be packeted.

Virtual circuits

This is a facility that allows packets to be transmitted without them all containing the control data. The PSS makes a note of the first packet's control data and of its routeing so that subsequent packets can be treated accordingly. A similar arrangement is a 'permanent datacall'; this is provided by British Telecom for its users who wish to send large amounts of data between fixed points.

Packet switching terminals

The terminals, i.e. points or nodes, connected to a PSS fall into two different types — packet devices and character devices. The former, such as a front-end processor or mainframe, is capable of forming its own packets for injection into the PSS. Character devices, such as keyboard-operated terminals, transmit characters slowly and at random intervals. They therefore need to be interfaced to the PSS by means of a packet assembler/disassembler (PAD), this builds up or breaks down a packet from or into separate characters.

Local area networks

A local area network (LAN) is based on the principle of several users sharing the DP facilities available in one organization by providing them with two-way access via a communications network. For instance, the common use of word processors, printers, microcomputers, databases, storage media, and so on; these are known as 'nodes' in the LAN. A LAN is generally confined to within one building or site but can be extended through the use of repeaters and gateways. The former allows longer communication paths; the latter enables one network to be linked to another.

There are many suppliers of LANs utilizing the various methods described below but typical characteristics are a data transfer speed of 10−20 megabits per second, a network length of up to a few kilometres, and a maximum of 100 nodes or workstations. As well as these characteristics there are three other important aspects of LANs − their access method, transmission mode and network topology.

Access method, sometimes called protocol, is the way in which nodes are permitted to enter data into the network, four of these are described below.

Central control protocol
Central control is the most conceptually straightforward protocol in that all data entering the network is authorized by a single network control microprocessor (controller). Nodes request permission from the controller to gain access to the network or, alternatively, the controller asks each node in turn whether it requires access, i.e. polling.

CSMA-CD
'Carrier sense multiple access with collision detection' (CSMA-CD) means that each node with data to transmit 'listens' to the network. When it 'hears' that the network is clear of other data, it transmits its own. By continuing to listen, the node detects whether its data has 'collided' with another node's data and, if so, it waits a short time before trying again to transmit. If the network is not clear, the node waits and tries again. CSMA-CD is the method used by the well-known LAN, 'Ethernet'.

Empty slot access
This method involves a series of slots passing through the network. Each slot contains its destination address, source address, data and various flags. As each

slot passes a node it is inspected to see whether it contains data addressed to that node. If so, the data is copied by the node and a flag inserted into the slot to acknowledge receipt. The slot returns in due course to the sending node which sees the acknowledgement flag and then removes the data.

When a node needs to transmit, it inserts the data along with its own (source) address and the destination address into the first empty slot it encounters. Empty slot access is used by Cambridge Ring networks.

Token access/token passing
A token is a special signal (flag) that is passed from node to node in the network. Only when a node is in possession of the token can it enter data into the network.

LAN transmission modes
The transmission modes of LANs are of two main types – baseband and broadband.

Baseband transmission is essentially a binary method, each bit being represented by one of two states of an electric pulse passing through the network. It is therefore an inexpensive but 'low bandwidth' method, that is to say, it transmits only a small amount of data at the one time. Baseband is nevertheless suitable for most LANs, and is the mode employed by Ethernet and Cambridge Ring networks.

With broadband transmission, the data is modulated onto a carrier wave. What this means is that a high-frequency electric current (the carrier) is altered in some way to represent the data. The two foremost ways are frequency division multiplexing and time division multiplexing, as explained previously under 'multiplexing'.

Broadband transmission needs a greater bandwidth than baseband, but it can transmit something like ten times as much in a given time. This enables it to handle video and voice transmission in addition to data since these demand a means of transmitting signals at a much higher rate than data. The transmission distance is greater with broadband and there is less interference on the lines.

Network topologies

The topology of a network is its physical layout of computers and other units, all known as nodes of the network. Topologies fall into four main types as described below, but in practice many networks are hybrids of these types.

Tree networks
A tree or hierarchical network, as in Figure 2.3, inevitably means that nodes at the same level do not communicate directly with each other but via the node at the next higher level.

The intention of a tree network is that the large-scale processing is handled by the mainframe, lower-level processing by the minicomputers, and the simplest

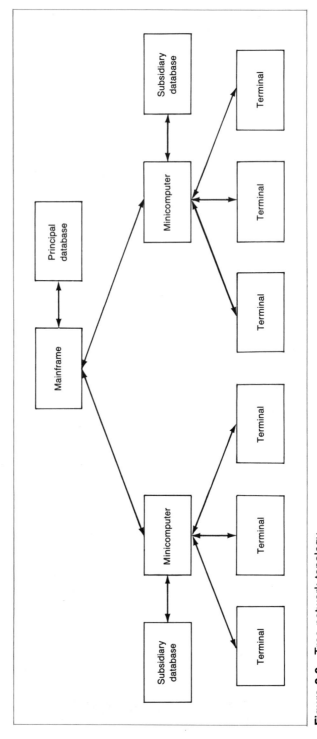

Figure 2.3 Tree network topology

processing by the intelligent terminals or microcomputers. Alternatively the lowest level could be dumb terminals which would merely act as input/output devices.

The minicomputers are physically sited at points intermediate between the mainframe and the terminals so as to reduce transmission costs.

Tree networks tend to be used for large-scale, long-distance networking such as by international airline seat reservation systems.

Star networks

A star network, as depicted in Figure 2.4, has a mainframe or minicomputer as the central node. The lower-level nodes, i.e. microcomputers and/or terminals, are unable to communicate directly with one another but only through the central node.

A star network is most suited to situations with many lower-level nodes wanting access to a central database controlled by the mainframe or minicomputer, such as with on-line banking.

Bus networks

A bus is a main communication channel to which all the nodes are attached. Thus, as shown in Figure 2.5, they are all in direct contact with each other.

This topology especially suits LANs, since nodes can be plugged in or out at will.

Ring networks

As depicted in Figure 2.6, a ring network entails all nodes being linked together on an equal footing. Data is input to the ring by any node and transmitted round it. The appropriate node accepts data intended for it and other data is passed on through the ring to its destination.

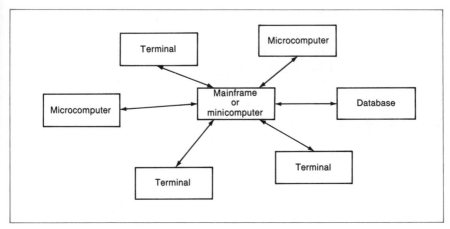

Figure 2.4 Star network topology

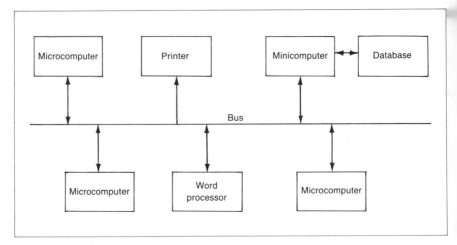

Figure 2.5 Bus network topology

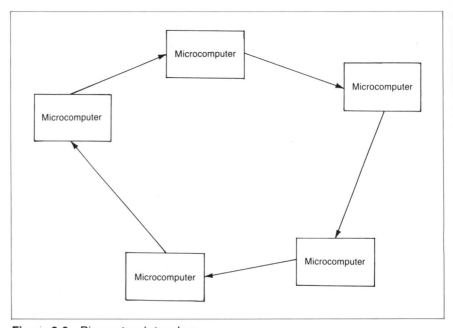

Figure 2.6 Ring network topology

Value added network services

Value added network services (VANS) are a means of simplifying the electronic exchange of data between users of the service. The concept behind VANS is that a user merely plugs into an interface provided by the VANS operating company and the network does all that is necessary thereafter. This service copes with different types of user computers by reconciling their protocols.

A particular VANS is aimed at a certain industry and is tailored to meet its individual needs, e.g. insurance, retailing or local authorities. A VANS may be utilized entirely within the one organization or between different organizations having the requirement for data exchange.

An example of the latter are estate agents and solicitors involved in property conveyancing having access to computer databases in local authorities via microcomputers in their own offices. A similar scheme is in operation for accountants and insurance brokers to have access to databases in insurance companies.

It is intended that VANS will be extended eventually to incorporate a worldwide network of companies and organizations.

Real-time and on-line systems

Real-time DP implies that the input messages and responses pass quickly enough between the environment and the computer to enable the latter to have some degree of control over the former. In the broad sense, real-time systems include plant and machinery control, and defence and space systems, but here we are concerned solely with the usage of real-time systems for business applications.

In a real-time business DP system, source data, i.e. input messages, is transmitted from terminals, often in widespread locations. After the input messages have been processed by the computer, the resultant reply messages are transmitted back to the terminals sufficiently quickly for on-the-spot actions or decisions to be taken.

On-line systems are sometimes regarded as synonymous with real-time, but this is not truly the case; on-line means merely that the data is transmitted directly to or from the computer. The confusion arises because real-time systems are also inevitably on-line; this must be so to attain the necessary short response time.

Response time

An important aspect of a real-time system is its response time. This is the interval of time between the end of the input message and the receipt of the beginning of the reply message. It includes several contributory times such as the transmission times, message queuing and processing, and file accesses. These times have to be kept as short as is economic if a low response time is to be achieved.

The response times acceptable for a real-time system call for careful study because of the many factors implicated, these are technical, economic and psychological. In broad terms, response times for business applications lie between 2 and 10 seconds.

Another factor entering into response time is the 'traffic pattern' of the real-time system. The greater the number of messages handled by the computer in a period of time, the longer the response time tends to be. That is to say, a real-time system is designed to accept an average number of messages per minute, and if the actual volume of messages is above this, the response time increases.

Airline reservation systems

All the world's major airlines now operate real-time seat reservation systems for their flights. These systems are sophisticated, expensive and heavily employed, and it is a matter of fact that the airlines could not function without them.

The main intention behind an airline reservation system is to obtain the extra seat bookings on each flight needed to make it profitable. There is a narrow margin between profit and loss in terms of seats occupied. Since prospective passengers are apt to turn to another airline if they do not get an immediate reservation, a rapid response is imperative.

The seat reservation system of a large airline typically has several thousand terminals situated in the airline's worldwide offices. These are linked to a central database holding up-to-the-minute records of the bookings for the next few months.

By this means and by using sophisticated dialogues (Section 7.5) passengers' enquiries and bookings are handled immediately. In other words, a passenger can reserve a seat on any flight in the foreseeable future from any point in the world.

Real-time banking/building societies

The concept behind real-time banking is that every clerk (teller) has immediate access to all the customers' accounts. This means that a customer is able to withdraw cash and enquire about his account at any of the branches. Also the bank or building society is able to keep a close check on the customer's current balance; thus the system has advantages for both parties.

In most real-time banking systems the terminal comprises a keyboard, a passbook printer and a display screen. The passbook printer is used in order to update the customer's passbook after every transaction. The display screen provides the means for the computer to communicate with the clerk, and the keyboard enables him to transmit transactions and enquiries to the computer.

System security is achieved in a real-time banking system by having more than one computer, by multiple data transmission paths, and by having storage equipment as part of the terminal. This latter facility allows transactions to continue on a local basis during periods of system failure. If this occurs the transactions are copied to the storage medium for subsequent transmission when the system becomes operational.

2.6 Office automation

Also referred to as 'electronic offices', office automation is a conglomerate of various technologies intended to improve the efficiency of office work and also to reduce the huge numbers of office staff presently employed. Office workers have gradually increased their use of semi-automatic machines such as electric typewriters, calculators, photocopiers, tape recorders, etc., over a long period, but office automation is expected to bring about much more extensive changes to their work style.

The principal areas of office automation are: word processing, microcomputers, mainframe terminals, COM and microforms, electronic mail (including facsimile), videotex, electronic funds transfer and desktop publishing.

Word processing (WP)

The increasing need for typed documents combined with the higher cost of manual labour and the reduced cost of microprocessors has resulted in the development of WP on a large and expanding scale in recent years. Initially, the need was primarily to reduce office overheads, such as typing, and in some cases to alleviate a shortage of typists. Subsequent developments in microprocessor technology and its decreasing cost have made it economic to incorporate a wide range of facilities into word processors. This has happened to the extent that a powerful word processor is nowadays available for the equivalent price of yesteryear's electric typewriter.

In its simplest form WP is an enhanced method of typing, i.e. it converts text into the form of typewritten documents but also stores it in magnetic form. The initial stages do not demand a high financial outlay nor necessarily the involvement of departments other than the one concerned. In its more sophisticated form WP can include the composition, recording, transcription, editing and communication of text.

The prospect of a comprehensive WP system in an organization calls for a careful study of the precise requirements. Without this there is the risk of fragmented and incompatible word processors leading to low efficiency of use, and worse, the use of sophisticated equipment for work that could be done on ordinary typewriters. As may be envisaged from the characteristics described below, the adoption of WP can result in a considerable increase in the throughput of typing and allied work.

Applications of word processing

The documents used in offices can be categorized into the following groups:

- One-off texts, such as individualized letters and memoranda.

- Replicated texts, such as standard letters and certain legal documents, perhaps with some degree of individuality.
- Updatable texts, such as reports and manufacturers' manuals that may need amending at regular and frequent intervals.

Of these, the first category is the least likely to attract advantage from WP, apart from increased accuracy and speed in its preparation. The second two categories lend themselves to cost savings and quality improvements, and both gain advantage from the fact that text is stored in magnetic form and can thus be easily retrieved and modified. The magnetic media employed includes floppy disks, hard disks, cards, cassettes and cartridges.

It is apparent from the descriptions of WP facilities that follow as to why these three categories of documents gain advantage to differing extents.

Types of word processors

The hardware of word processors falls into four groups: these are stand-alone, shared logic, mainframe time-sharing, and communicating word processors.

Stand-alone word processors

A stand-alone word processor comprises a keyboard, a VDU, a printer, a magnetic storage device and a microprocessor. The keyboard is similar to that of a conventional typewriter plus a few control keys. The VDU displays twenty to thirty lines of eighty characters, and the printer is of letter quality such as a daisy wheel printer (Section 3.11).

The magnetic storage serves two purposes; one is to hold the texts that are to be processed, the other is to hold the programs of microprocessor instructions. Typically the storage is a floppy disk holding the equivalent of around 120 pages of text. Both the program and the text are transferred into the microprocessor before being accessed.

Shared-logic word processors

Where the amount of work is extensive it is generally more cost-effective to use a shared-logic system rather than several stand-alone word processors. A shared-logic word processor consists of a number of work stations connected to a microprocessor and sharing one or more printers. Thus although a more powerful microprocessor is necessary, it is kept in more constant use and therefore gives better value for money. This is also true of the printer(s) because they operate at a considerably faster rate than keying; two printers, for example, will generally balance the input from eight work stations.

The work stations of a shared-logic word processor can be located at distances of up to several thousand feet from the microprocessor. This is a useful facility as it means that the typists are able to work in separate departments rather than in a centralized office.

Certain shared-logic word processors are equipped with computer peripherals such as line printers, magnetic disks and magnetic tapes. The latter pair of peripherals enables large volumes of text or numeric data to be transferred to a computer for further processing. A line printer allows for the high-speed printing of a large number of documents, most probably containing data read from magnetic media.

Mainframe word processors
The word processor in this case is effectively similar to a computer terminal in that it time shares the computer's processor along with other terminals. The word processor's texts are stored as records in the mainframe's storage media and retrieved and transmitted as and when required. The printed output is either spooled for printing on the mainframe's line printers or transmitted to the word processor's own serial printer.

The employment of a mainframe facilitates transfer of data from a database for incorporation into documents printed by the word processor, e.g. accounts figures; this is known as library selection.

Communicating word processors (CWP)
This type of WP system consists of several multistation word processors each equipped with a communications controller. It is thus possible for each CWP to communicate with a central mainframe and with other CWPs. This means that a CWP is, in effect, a simple electronic mail system because letters typed at one CWP are capable of being delivered quickly and automatically to another CWP some distance away. It is obviously possible to develop sophisticated procedures in order to enhance the communication facilities of offices.

Mode of operation of word processors

The word processor operator, i.e. the typist, keys in the text in a similar manner to conventional typing and then it appears simultaneously on the VDU screen. Also displayed is the status or control information available for guiding the operator with regard to parameter settings; these include margin widths, tabulating (tabbing) distances and print pitch. If during the course of keying a conscious error is made, the operator is able to make an immediate correction to the text on the screen.

The displayed text is also stored magnetically so that, when instructed, the word processor automatically prints the text at high speed. The storage can also hold text created previously and awaiting further editing, processing or printing. This could, for instance, be standard texts for insertion into various replicated documents such as sales literature, product manuals and conveyancing documents.

When a replicated document needs to be customized, i.e. contain individualized text, it is prepared with 'stop codes' inserted at the appropriate points. In operation the text is displayed and the cursor moves automatically from one stop code to the next, thus allowing the operator to make the necessary insertions. An example of this is a standard letter to a company's overdue debtors into which the recipient's name and address, the date and the amount have to be inserted.

Word processor facilities

The precise facilities available with a word processor depend upon the particular model but the list below gives a good indication of what can be expected.

Line wrap-around Automatic 'carriage return', thus allowing the operator to key at a steady rate without bothering about the end of a line.

Centring The text and its headings and titles are automatically positioned between prescribed margins.

Decimal alignment Columns of figures are aligned about the decimal point for ease of comparison and summation.

Page length control The number of lines per page is fixed according to the user's requirements.

Subscripting and superscripting Characters can be printed below or above the normal line such as for scientific applications.

Margin control The text is indented at the left and truncated at the right so as to give even margins.

Title and page number generation This saves the repeated keying of a title common to several pages, and the insertion of the page numbers manually.

Text editing Mainly the manual insertion and deletion of words, sentences, paragraphs or whole pages in existing text with automatic repositioning of the resultant text.

Hyphenation The insertion and removal of end-of-line hyphens according to the repositioning of a word.

Page movement Text is automatically moved to new pages as a consequence of insertions or deletions to previous pages.

Global search and replace Also known as 'exchanging' or 'string search', this means that prescribed groups of words are replaced by other words throughout the text, e.g. the new name of a company replaces its former name throughout a report.

Text (mail) merging Blocks of text from various sources, i.e. keyed and stored, are put together in order to build up a complete text, this can include the copying of text from one document to another. For instance, various blocks of text, including names and addresses, can be selected from storage and inserted automatically into letters according to their type of recipient.

Line spacing Varied spacings to suit type of document.

Spelling checking Each word is looked-up in a stored dictionary holding all the common words plus a few hundred subject-orientated words. The latter can be added as and when they occur. Absence of a word from the dictionary implies a misspelling, and the closest words are then displayed as possible alternatives. A misspelling may result in another word witch [*sic*] is actually in the dictionary and so an error goes undetected.

Glossary   Frequently used words, phrases, sentences and paragraphs are stored and called into use by keying a simple code number, thus saving much keying effort.

Landscaping   This means that a tabulated report can be laid out by positioning the columns of figures and interchanging them as necessary.

Library selection   Certain data unique to a single document are retrieved from storage and inserted automatically, e.g. an individual name and address.

Form outline   The outline, headings and annotations of a blank document appear on the screen, and the document is filled in as the data is keyed. This is similar to form-filling (Section 7.5).

Arithmetic capability   A limited amount of cross casting and column totalling is available for numeric data on documents.

Data processing   The capability of processing data along with words. This means that the word processor acts as a simple computer when necessary, e.g. when preparing straightforward invoices.

Desktop publishing (DTP)

DTP is the employment of a computer in order to create pages of mixed text and illustrations — as in most technical books. The software associated with DTP together with the high-quality printers now available enable this to be achieved straightforwardly and to a high standard. The types of document likely to be prepared in this way include newletters, notices, advertisements and catalogues.

By use of a mouse and VDU, frames are represented on the screen into which text is inserted via the keyboard or from disk storage. In the latter case the text may well have been generated and stored by means of word processing software.

The text can be in several fonts and sizes on the one document. The illustrations are created on the screen by drawing with a mouse-controlled pointer. After a final check the document is copied exactly by the printer as many times as required or, alternatively, printed the once and then photocopied.

DTP facilities include the following:

- A wide range of fonts (typefaces) and print sizes for merging with useful symbols such as arrows and stars.
- Columns of various widths into which the text is fitted automatically using sensible hyphenation. Reorganization of the columns is also automatic.
- Automatic spacing of characters and lines in order to fit the text into the available space.
- Scaling and cropping of illustrations so as fit the available space.
- Page numbers inserted alternately left and right (as in books) in multi-page documents.

DTP has spawned its own terminology, some of which comes from the printing industry; the following are some examples:

Banner   The main headline across the top of the page.
Bullet   Solid blobs printed before pieces of text in order to add emphasis.
Cast-off   A calculation as to how much space text will use on a page.
Crosshead   A small heading used to break up text into easily readable sections.
Footer   A line of text at the bottom of each page giving the publication's title, author's name, etc.
Masthead   Details of person's involved in producing the publication.
WYSIWYG (what you see is what you get)   The representation on the screen is exactly, or very nearly, the same as will emanate from the printer.
Jigging   Moving text around by means of desktop publishing software.

Electronic mail (EM)

Just as electronic funds transfer (EFT) has a natural connection with point-of-sale systems (Section 3.7), electronic mail (EM) ties in naturally with word processing and videotex (see below).

As was suggested in the paragraph on communicating word processors, EM means that letters and documents typed or scanned in one office are delivered very quickly to another office irrespective of its distance. This concept inevitably implies that a computer network using packet switching (Section 2.5) must be employed.

The sender of a letter or document via EM attaches to it the address code of the recipient(s). This accompanies the letter so that it can be directed along the correct routes. It also contains the sender's code and an indication as to the recipient's right to make amendments. This control is necessary because on some occasions a document is sent through a number of offices each of which is permitted or otherwise to add to it. For instance, a final report required by head office might be created from a series of subreports contributed by a series of branch offices. These contributions may need to be in a certain sequence because one office's subreport depends upon the contents of a previous contributing office's subreport.

Similarly it is sometimes desirable to have a notification of delivery, this is achieved by the EM system automatically returning a message to this effect to the sender after delivering his communication. In the case of confidential information sight by the authorized person only is effected by the inclusion of a pass code. This must be matched by the recipient's pass code before the local computer will deliver the contents of the communication.

Other possible features of EM include:

- Automatic redirection of messages if the recipient has moved.
- Authentication of sender for security purposes.

- Notification to sender if a message cannot be delivered.
- Multiple addressing, i.e. the same message being sent to several recipients.
- Recording times of despatch and delivery of messages.
- Message filing and retrieval.
- Automatic accounting and the billing of users.

Facsimile (fax)

Another requirement of EM is for facsimile transmission, i.e. identical copies of documents, diagrams, handwriting, etc. It is obviously advantageous to be able to send such things rapidly between companies, and is sometimes important for these to be exact copies of the originals, e.g. signatures. This latter requirement applies most particularly to legal documents.

Facsimile transmission is achieved by optically analysing the document's appearance at the sending end and thus converting it into a digital representation. The reverse process is carried out at the receiving end so that an exact copy can be produced. This is, in effect, the same as long-distance photocopying.

The main drawback of facsimile is its slowness of conversion, transmission and reconversion: an A4 sheet takes from 40 seconds to several minutes. This problem is caused by the huge amount of data involved: one A4 sheet is equivalent to about $\frac{3}{4}$ million bits, and this is thirty times as much as when it is represented by conventional coding.

Voice mail

A similar arrangement to EM is voice mail, this is the storing and forwarding of digitized speech. There is no need for the sender to be connected to the recipient but merely to speak his message knowing that it will eventually reach the person(s) for whom it is intended, including multiple recipients.

Each participant has his own 'mailbox' from which messages are retrieved by calling on the phone, this may be up to a month after the origination of the message. He then replies in the same way as described above.

IBM's Speechfile is an example of voice mail, this handles not only speech but facsimile and encoded text.

Videotex

Videotex (videotext) is a generic term applicable to a number of information systems. These systems fall into one of two groups — Teletext and Viewdata.

The common characteristic of all videotex systems is that they can make information available to a very large number of people based upon one or more databases.

Teletext

Dealing firstly with the Teletext group, these are essentially an extension of domestic television services. That is to say, pages of information in addition to the usual programmes are transmitted by the television station and received by all the television sets tuned to the channel. In order to make use of this information a keypad and adaptor (decoder) are required, the purpose of which is to select and store the required page.

Teletext is a read-only system in that there is no data transmitted by the user to the computer, and therefore no way of changing the information. The required page of information is seen by keying a digit selected from a succession of displayed lists, i.e. menu selection (Section 7.5).

Only a few hundred pages of information are available with Telextext systems owing to limitations of the television channel capacities. Each page is transmitted and stored between programme frames and as this takes a quarter of a second, it may be necessary to wait several seconds for the required page to appear.

The main purpose of Teletext is to provide information of a general nature such as sports results, weather forecasts, entertainment guides, etc. This is enhanced by a few extra facilities such as recall of up to four preceding pages, combining textual information and subtitles with the pictures in order to assist the hard of hearing, translation into various languages, and news flashes concurrent with the programme.

The most well-known Teletext services in the UK are CEEFAX (BBC) and ORACLE (IBA).

Viewdata

Viewdata uses telephone lines as the communication medium between the computer and the user. The computer's output is displayed on either an adapted television set or a VDU, both equipped with a communications adaptor (decoder) and a numeric keypad or full keyboard.

The user obtains his requirements interactively and not merely by selecting listed items or entering a page number, this results in a lower response time than with Teletext. With publicly available Viewdata systems such as PRESTEL each page received is charged for (although some are free). The user has also to pay for the telephone line usage during the transmission from and to the computer.

PRESTEL accommodates 'closed user groups' (CUG), these are organizations wanting their data to be private to the members of the CUG. Only the members know the pass codes needed for these pages. A CUG system is effectively the same as a private computer with a large number of terminals and could be used, for instance, by a company's salesmen to obtain confidential information in their homes regarding sales volumes, product prices, etc.

Viewdata systems have much larger databases than Teletext, measured in hundreds of thousands of pages. They are thus capable of providing a huge amount of information, both public and private. This information is stored in a network of computers each of which serves its own local users but is also capable of passing the user's request on to other computers when necessary.

Another facility is a 'gateway', this means the interfacing of conventional computer databases with a Viewdata system. Thus a gateway, in effect, creates a computer network with an unlimited number of terminals, computers and databases.

Viewdata electronic mail

The above facilities promote electronic mail via Viewdata (VEM), the principle of which is that a sender can dispatch messages or data to a selected recipient. The sender keys the recipient's address number, the local computer then looks up and displays the recipient's name for validation. Assuming this is correct, the message is keyed-in whereupon the words 'message dispatched' together with the time and date appears. If the recipient's terminal/television is switched on, a message is displayed at the foot of his screen to tell him to switch to the Viewdata channel. Alternatively the message is automatically recorded locally for subsequent display.

A security arrangement can be incorporated whereby the dispatching computer demands a password known only by the authentic recipient before delivering the message. This, of course, prevents the message from being automatically recorded locally.

VEM also caters for multiple addressing in order to dispatch the same message to several (or many) recipients. This could be beneficial for advertisers but may possibly lead to abuse. Other facilities include message playback to check its accuracy, acknowledgement of receipt of a message and certification of receipt by a named person.

An important aspect of VEM could be the use of 'response frames', i.e. pages into which a user can insert data. This means, for example, that a selling company could display its sales lines and the user indicate his requirements and credit card number on the response frame, so initiating the order, i.e. electronic mail order.

Electronic funds transfer (EFT)

The need to pay for goods and services received has engendered a variety of methods of payment throughout history. In recent years these methods have included, in addition to cash, bank cheques, Giro transfers, credit cards, direct debit/credit and standing orders. The UK clearing banks now deal with several million financial transactions per working day, most of which entail the preparation and handling of handwritten or typed documents, such as cheques. Similar situations apply in many other countries. This huge amount of work and immense cost has led the banks and other companies to move towards considering document-free methods of transferring money between bank accounts.

The concepts of EFT are that (a) details of financial transactions are represented by electronic or magnetic means instead of on documents, and (b) accounts are updated concurrently in computer storage by the corresponding debits and credits. The general idea is that the customer has a magnetized credit card which is inserted into the point-of-sale (POS) terminal (Section 3.7), and a code number is then entered. If the card and code correspond, the amount of the bill is entered either via a keyboard or directly from the POS. This allows the customer's balance to be checked and, if sufficient, his and the retailer's accounts are updated automatically.

EFT has now been extended, by means of viewdata, into people's homes, enabling them to inspect their bank accounts, make transfers, settle bills and pay for goods purchased by using their domestic television. This is sometimes called 'home banking'.

A further aspect of EFT is the chip card. This is a card on which a predetermined amount of credit is magnetically recorded and the balance is reduced automatically each time it is used for a purchase. Usually the card is thrown away when the balance reaches zero but some types of card can be reloaded. An extension of this arrangement is a card capable of holding the full details of a bank account; this could be used as above but also linked to a central computer for updating by other transactions such as direct credits and standing orders.

SWIFT and CHAPS

Another application of EFT is its employment by the clearing banks themselves in order to effect transfers of funds between their own accounts with other banks. Such a system, acronymed SWIFT (Society for Worldwide Interbank Financial Telecommunications) caters for interbank transactions at international level such as bank A instructing bank B to transfer funds to bank C's account with bank D. A development of SWIFT is CHAPS (Clearing Houses Automated Payments System), this is a bank clearing sytem operated through British Telecom's packet switching system and intended for the rapid transference of high value transactions.

2.7 Exercises

Exercise 2.1 Office automation

An article in the February 1986 edition of *Management Accounting* stated: 'Within ten years or less, around 50% of business transactions may be conducted electronically.'

You are required to answer *four* of the following, with reference to specific applications wherever possible.

(a) Explain what is meant by the term 'Electronic Office'.
(b) Describe the principal features of an electronic mail system either with a multi-access computer within an organization or using a national network.
(c) Explain what is meant by EFT.
(d) Describe what facilities would be expected within a terminal emulation package.
(e) A number of integrated software packages can be purchased, each of which combines terminal emulation, word processing, spreadsheets and a database. Explain how this integration may prove beneficial to an organisation.

(CIMA stage 2, Inf. Tech. Man., May 1988)

Exercise 2.2   Data communications

The following is a brief description of a centralized computer system providing on-line links with three subsidiaries.

- The central facility is a large mainframe with disk drives, two line printers for document production and a magnetic tape unit for security.
- Each subsidiary has several terminals which are linked via a high speed data transmission line to the central facility.

Required:

(a) Draw the hardware configuration for the above system. Label your diagram carefully to show the following if appropriate: terminal, compiler, front end processor, update, disk drive, tape unit, DBMS, line printer, multiplexor, modem, data communication lines, line concentrator, central processing unit.
(b) With reference to the diagram indicate the stages through which an enquiry (or enquiry transaction) would pass from entry at a user's terminal to the point at which the answer is received by the user.

(CACA level 2, Sys. an. & des., June 1987)

Exercise 2.3   Distributed processing

'Distributed processing is an important option in corporate planning. In such an arrangement mini and/or microcomputers working interactively may well replace much of the processing undertaken on mainframes. Distributed processing may well be based on local area networks (LANs) and be implemented using either "packaged" software or full "turnkey" operations.'

(a) What are the essential elements of the three main types of computer identified in the above statement?
(b) What is meant by

    (i) Distributed processing?
    (ii) Local area networks?
    (iii) 'Turnkey' implementation?
(c) With reference to the above statement, briefly explain how the growth in distributed systems might change the role of the user manager.

                             (CACA level 2, Sys. an. & des., Dec. 1987)

Exercise 2.4 Terminology

Explain the meaning of the following terms:

(a) ROM and RAM;
(b) batch and on-line processing;
(c) mini and main-frame systems.

                             (ICSA part 2, Inf. sys., June 1988)

Exercise 2.5 Data communications

In the case of data transmission and communications briefly describe what the following terms relate to:

(a) modem;
(b) multiplexor;
(c) baud rate;
(d) local area network.

                             (ICSA part 2, Inf. sys., Dec. 1988)

Exercise 2.6 Mainframe configuration

(a) Describe the characteristics and functions of the various elements of a mainframe computer configuration.
(b) State how the operations of the computer and its peripheral equipment are controlled.

                        (ICAEW PE1, Aud., Sys. & DP, May 1988)

Exercise 2.7 Local area networks

(a) What is a local area network? What advantages can be gained from its use?
(b) Describe the following:
    (i) a bus network
    (ii) a ring network
    (iii) a star network.

                        (BCS part 1, Gen. paper I, April 1987)

Exercise 2.8   Types of computers

Discuss the features of micro, mini and mainframe systems and outline the criteria that organizations should adopt on deciding which system to install.

(ICSA part 2, Inf. sys., Dec. 1986)

2.8   Outline solutions to exercises

Solution 2.1

Refer to Section 2.6.
(a) • Office transactions represented and transmitted electronically.
     • Office records held magnetically.
     • Minimum of paper records and manual transcription.
     • Facilities for word processing, extensive accounting and office control software, electronic mail, electronic funds transfer, facsimile.
     • Personnel microcomputers linked to centralized and/or distributed databases.
(b) Refer to 'Electronic mail' in Section 2.6.
(c) Refer to 'Electronic funds transfer' in Section 2.6.
(d) A terminal emulation package enables a microcomputer to be used as a terminal linked to a mainframe or minicomputer. The package handles problems such as protocols, data coding and transmission line speeds.
(e) An integrated package combines together into the one package various types of applications software such as word processing, spreadsheets and graphics. This reduces the effort for certain work, e.g. preparing a cost variance analysis using a spreadsheet program, incorporating results into reports using word processing, and preparing a demonstration of costs using computer graphics.

Solution 2.2

(a) The hardware configuration diagram is similar to Figure 2.2 but with an additional terminal cluster and with the CPU having the disk drives, line printers and the tape unit shown linked to it.
(b) 1. Enquiry keyed in at a terminal.
     2. Enquiry data held in concentrator buffer until sufficient data for transmission.
     3. Data converted from digital to analogue signal by modem.
     4. Enquiry passed along transmission line to receiving modem.
     5. Converted back into digital form.
     6. Enquiry assembled and checked for completeness, etc., by front-end processor and passed to CPU.
     7. Enquiry processed by program and reply message/information created.
     8. Stages (6) to (2) reversed.
     9. Reply displayed or printed at terminal.

Solution 2.3

(a) Refer to Sections 2.2, 2.3 and 2.4.
(b) (i) and (ii) Refer to Section 2.5. (iii) The design and implementation of the
     complete system by an external organization, such as a firm of consultants, with
     a minimum of involvement by the user company.
(c) • Less dependence on the DP department for the processing of data.
     • More involvement of the user staff with consequent need for training in operations
       and software.
     • Possibility of need to recruit DP specialist(s) into user department.
     • Knowledge of contents and methods of database(s) in order to design new systems
       for the user department.
     • Tighter control over source data entry and queries.

Solution 2.4

(a) Refer to 'Memory' in Section 2.4.
(b) Batch processing entails accumulating a batch of transaction data, often outside
     the computer system, before entering it in its entirety into the computer. The
     batch is sometimes sorted into a convenient order before the transactions are
     processed. Thus the result of a transaction's processing is not apparent or
     effective until the end of the batch.
         On-line processing means that the source transaction is entered into the
     computer directly, probably as soon as it arises. Thus it is feasible to obtain an
     immediate response to a query for instance. See also 'Real-time and on-line
     systems' in Section 2.5.
(c) Refer to Sections 2.2 and 2.3.

Solution 2.5

(a) Refer to 'Modems' in Section 2.5.
(b) Refer to 'Multiplexing' in Section 2.5.
(c) Refer to 'baud' in glossary.
(d) Refer to 'Local area networks' in Section 2.5.

Solution 2.6

Refer to 'Structure of a computer' in Section 2.2.

Solution 2.7

(a) Refer to 'Local area networks' in Section 2.5. The main advantages are:
     • users have access to all hardware linked to the LAN, e.g. printers and
       backing storage;
     • users can communicate with each other, and with more distant points via
       gateways.
     • common use of applications software;
     • common access to database records;

- transmission of data between offices.

(b) Refer to 'Network topologies' in Section 2.5.

Solution 2.8

Refer to Sections 2.2 to 2.4.

2.9   References and further reading

Expert systems and artificial intelligence

2.1   Simons, G.L., *Evolution of the Intelligent Machine: A Popular History of AI* (NEC, 1988).

2.2   Silverman, B.G. (ed.), *Expert Systems for Business* (Addison Wesley, 1987).

2.3   Alty, J. and Coombs, M.S., *Expert Systems: Concepts and Examples* (NEC, 1984).

2.4   Chorafas, D.N., *Applying Expert Systems in Business* (McGraw-Hill, 1990).

2.5   Gallagher, J.P., *Knowledge Systems for Business: Integrating Expert Systems and MIS* (Prentice Hall, 1988).

2.6   Martin, J. and Oxman, S.W., *Building Expert Systems* (Prentice Hall, 1988).

2.7   Barrett, M.L. and Beerel, A.C., *Expert Systems in Business* (John Wiley, 1988).

2.8   Bryant, N., *Managing Expert Systems* (John Wiley, 1988).

2.9   Harmon, P., Maus, R. and Morrissey, W., *Expert Systems Tools and Applications* (John Wiley, 1988).

2.10 Coleman, T., *Expert Systems for the Data Processing Professional* (NCC, 1988).

2.11 Mockler, R., *Knowledge Based Systems for Management Decisions* (Prentice Hall, 1988).

2.12 Rauch-Hindin, W., *Guide to Commercial Artificial Intelligence* (Prentice Hall, 1988).

2.13 Beynon-Davis, P., *Introducing Knowledge Engineering* (NCC, 1989).

Computers and computer architecture

2.14 Stallings, W., *Computer Organization and Architecture* (Collier Macmillan, 1987).

2.15 Langholz, G., Francioni, J. and Kandel, A., *Elements of Computer Organisation* (Prentice Hall, 1988).

2.16 Gorsline, G.W., *Computer Organisation* (Prentice Hall, 1987).

2.17 Lippiat, A.G. and Wright, G.G.L., *The Architecture of Small Computer Systems* (Prentice Hall, 1985).

2.18 Long, L., *Computers in Business* (Prentice Hall, 1987).

2.19 Long, L., *Introduction to Computers and Information Processing* (Prentice Hall, 1988).

2.20 Hunt, R. and Shelley, J., *Computers and Commonsense* (Prentice Hall, 1988).

2.21 Gunton, T., *Infrastructure: Building a Framework for Corporate Information Handling* (Prentice Hall, 1989).

Microcomputers

2.22 Ismail, A.R. and Rooney, V.M., *Microprocessor Hardware and Software Concepts* (Collier Macmillan, 1987).
2.23 Protopapas, D.A., *Microcomputer Hardware Design* (Prentice Hall, 1988).
2.24 Rocci, R.J. and Laskowski, P., *Microprocessors and Microcomputers* (Prentice Hall, 1986).
2.25 Curtin, D.P. and Porter, L.R., *Microcomputers: Software and Applications* (Prentice Hall, 1987).
2.26 Long, L. and Long, N., *Microcomputers* (Prentice Hall, 1988).
2.27 Dologite, D.G. and Mockler, R.J., *Using Microcomputers* (Prentice Hall, 1988).
2.28 Macpherson, S., *Understanding Portable Computers* (NCC, 1987).

Data communications and networks

2.29 Green, D., *Business Guide to Communications Systems* (Pitman, 1987).
2.30 Cole, R., *Computer Communications* (Macmillan, 1986).
2.31 Stallings, W., *Data and Computer Communications* (Collier Macmillan, 1988).
2.32 Richardson, A., *Exploiting Digital Communications* (NCC, 1988).
2.33 Beyda, W.J., *Basic Data Communications: A Comprehensive Overview* (Prentice Hall, 1989).
2.34 Housley, T., *Data Communications and Teleprocessing* (Prentice Hall, 1987).
2.35 Preston, M., *What is EDI?* (NCC, 1988).
2.36 Crichlow, J.M., *An Introduction to Distributed and Parallel Computing* (Prentice Hall, 1988).
2.37 Pye, C., *What is OSI?* (NCC, 1988).
2.38 Freer, J.R., *Computer Communications and Networks* (Pitman, 1988).
2.39 Stallings, W., *Local Networks* (Collier Macmillan, 1987).
2.40 Gandy, M., *Choosing a Local Area Network* (NCC, 1987).
2.41 Black, U., *Computer Networks: Protocols, Standards and Interfaces* (Prentice Hall, 1987).
2.42 Lehrmann, M., *Local Area Networking with Microcomputers* (Prentice Hall, 1986).
2.43 Martin, J. and Chapman, K.K., *SNA: IBM's Networking Solution* (Prentice Hall, 1987).
2.44 Tanenbaum, A.S., *Computer Networks* (Prentice Hall, 1988).
2.45 Tangney, B. and O'Mahoney, D., *Local Area Networks and their Applications* (Prentice Hall, 1987).
2.46 Bertsekas, D.P. and Gallager, R.G., *Data Networks* (Prentice Hall, 1987).

Office automation

2.47 Simons, G.L., *Management Guide to Office Automation* (NCC, 1986).
2.48 Barden, R.A., *How to Start in Office Automation* (NCC, 1988).
2.49 Pritchard, J.A.T., *Integrated Office Systems* (NCC, 1988).
2.50 Wilson, P.A., *Introducing Electronic Filing* (NCC, 1986).
2.51 Flewitt, P., *Word Processing* (Macmillan, 1985).

2.52 Gosling, P., *Mastering Word Processing* (Macmillan, 1985).

2.53 Frasson, M-F., *WordPerfect: The Learning Reference and Example Manual 4.2* (Prentice Hall, 1989).

2.54 Crider, J., *WordPerfect Power (5.0)* (Prentice Hall, 1988).

2.55 Pritchard, J.A.T., *Using an Electronic Mailbox* (NCC, 1987).

2.56 Mayer, I., *The Electronic Mailbox* (John Wiley, 1987).

2.57 Milton, R. (ed), *The Desktop Publishing Yearbook 1988* (Database Publications, 1988).

2.58 Burns, D. and Venit, S., *The Electronic Publisher* (Prentice Hall, 1988).

2.59 Pickering, T., *Introducing Desktop Publishing* (NCC, 1989).

2.60 Gosling, P. and Gosling, J., *Mastering Word Processing* (Macmillan, 1988).

2.61 Newman, W.M., *Designing Integrated Systems for the Office Environment* (McGraw-Hill, 1987).

2.62 Hirschheim, R.A., *Office Automation: Concepts, Technologies and Issues* (Addison Wesley, 1985).

3

Data capture and computer input/output devices

3.1 Data capture

Data capture is a general term for the process whereby source data is collected and transformed into a media or form capable of being 'understood' by a computer. Computer input is the transference of the data from the computer-sensible media into the main store of the computer. In some cases these two functions are one and the same, such as with on-line systems.

The collection and means of inputting data have undergone many developments in order to reduce the tremendous burden of data capture. This is just as well since it is a labour-intensive activity and consequently is expensive. It is beneficial to capture data at its point of origin, thereby eliminating the need for keying, by constraining the originator to create it in a computer-compatible form.

The methods described in this chapter cover a wide range, and it is probable that developments of some of these rather than fundamentally new ideas will be employed in the foreseeable future.

Before moving on to the methods it is useful first to consider a few points about the structure of business data. This nearly always takes the form of a group of related data items, called a record, that pertain to an activity or an entity, i.e. to something done or to something that exists. Thus if the activity took the form of depositing money with a building society, the record pertaining to this financial transaction would consist of data items such as the account number, date, amount and branch number. On the whole, the data items of an activity or entity are captured and input at the same time. This is obviously necessary because, for instance, the amount mentioned above only has meaning if tied to a particular account.

Data capture is therefore geared to the acceptance of a succession of similar records during a particular period and via a particular piece of equipment. This means that a key-operator or a source document user repeats the handling of a certain type of record many times during a certain period.

The principle of 'verification' is sometimes employed with key-to-disk and key-to-diskette systems (Sections 3.2 and 3.3). This entails keying the same source data, usually from documents, into the system twice, whereupon it is automatically checked for absolute similarity. Any discrepancies are thus detected and then corrected before the data goes for processing. As a general rule, the data is keyed by two different persons so as to minimize the chance of the same misreading occurring twice.

Key-operating

Because of the large volume of source data handled by many organizations, it is important to have an efficient arrangement for keying it into the system.

The three main aspects of keying are as follows:

Source documents

Clear documents are important since it is possible that both the original and the verifier operator may misread a badly written figure in the same way, with a consequent error reaching the computer. If the operators disagree in their keying, there is a delay while the discrepancy is reconciled. The design of the source document is also of consequence in maintaining a high speed of keying. And although it is not always possible to arrange a document's layout purely to facilitate keying, this should be borne in mind in designing any document that holds source data.

Operator training

The training of keyboard operators has two main aims. First, emphasis on the need for accuracy in keying the data. Second, achieving the ability to key at high speed while maintaining accuracy.

The former is promoted by showing the operators how their work fits into the overall system and pointing out the consequences of erroneous keying.

High-speed keying comes with proper training followed by the use of well-designed source documents. Operators can reach 18,000 key depressions per hour and, as this is an average of five key strokes per second, the operator obviously needs great dexterity and concentration.

Equipment

The technicalities of the keying methods are explained in the sections that follow, here we are concerned with the operating aspects of the equipment. From the operator's point of view the keyboard and the display are the paramount factors and are likely to be the only 'window' through which he or she sees the whole DP system.

The keyboard needs to be well laid-out, light to the touch and designed as far as possible to suit the type of data being keyed. It is likely that in reality the keyboard's layout is similar to a conventional typewriter since this is deeply engrained into office use. Ideally a keyboard should not have keys that are never used and should have extra keys such as a numeric pad if a large amount of numeric data is involved. A numeric pad is a separate set of the keys 0 to 9 to one side of the main keyboard.

3.2 Key-to-disk systems

The essential constituents of a key-to-disk system are a number of keystations, a supervisor's console, a processor, one or more magnetic disks, and one or more magnetic tape drives, as shown in Figure 3.1.

A keystation consists of keyboard, laid out similarly to that of a typewriter, and also either a visual display unit (VDU) or a panel display (Section 3.8). The average number of keystations per system is around twelve but as many as sixty-four are incorporated in larger systems. Each keystation is linked to the processor, and when the input data is keyed it is immediately transferred to an entry buffer. This is an area of storage in the processor holding a few hundred characters and allocated to the individual keystation.

During the keying each field or character is checked automatically for feasibility, and any invalidity results in a message from the processor to the keystation. This results in either an audible or displayed warning and the locking of the keyboard. The operator either corrects the error there and then or inserts a flag into the record to mark it for subsequent correction. Error correction is facilitated by use of the VDU or panel display. These show the current status of the input data, and a cursor on the VDU or a light on the panel display indicates the erroneous data (cursors are explained in Section 3.8).

The checks applied to the input data can be sophisticated including, for instance, the verification or generation of check digits, the creation of batch totals, the use of look-up tables, and the checking of inter-field relationships. These checks are controlled by a read-only program held in the processor's storage. This program can be tailor-made to meet the user's individual requirements or purchased in package form from the range available.

When a keystation's entry buffer has been filled, the data is transferred as a record to a catalogued area on a fixed head disk (Section 4.2).

When a keystation is in verify mode, the appropriate prime record is retrieved from the disk and inserted into the keystation's entry buffer so that it can be compared with the same record as it is keyed for verification. Discrepancies are

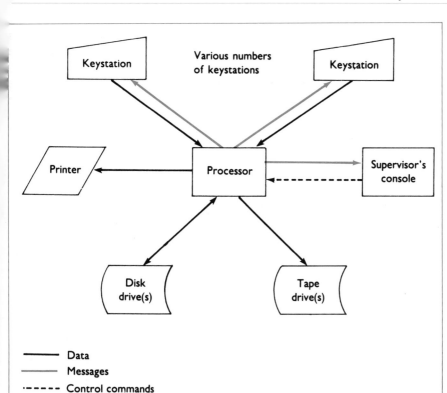

Figure 3.1   Basic structure of a key-to-disk system

displayed on the VDU for correction of either the prime record or the verifying record. Retrieval of the prime record from the disk is achieved by inputting either the record number (assigned previously by the processor), a key field in the record, or the document's reference number, i.e. an arbitrary number assigned by the operator.

Records are subsequently transferred from the disk to magnetic tape on supervisor command from the console. Transfer takes place only after certain conditions have been fulfilled such as verification or correction, and a check that they have not been already transferred. The records are moved into an output buffer on the disk before being written as a block to the magnetic tape.

The supervisor also uses the console to monitor the status of the input batches, to analyse the keystation operators' performances, and to check the usage of the disk storage.

Features of key-to-disk systems

Various key-to-disk systems are now available; below are their principal features.

● The disks hold from a few million to several hundred million characters depending on the model. The amount of storage relates to the number of keystations in the system, and also to the amount of data being throughput.

- The keystations may be sited at distances of up to 1,000 feet from the processor. This is a useful feature if it is desirable to site keystations close to various sources of data, e.g. in factories and dispersed offices.

- Some systems employ communications equipment and are therefore capable of transmitting batches of data from system to system, or to a mainframe computer sited at a considerable distance.

- Line or serial printers are attachable to most systems. This makes the system self-contained for straightforward applications because processing operations may also be programmed into the processor. By combining this feature with communications equipment, a key-to-disk system becomes, in effect, a remote front-end processor.

- File data stored on the disk unit it retrievable via the keystations by utilizing a database management package, this creates a small database system suitable for simple applications.

- Greater control is achieved over keyed input as regards its accuracy, correction, security, operator guidance and progress monitoring. This reduces the need for verification to the extent of elimination from certain applications.

- The main drawback of key-to-disk is its relatively high initial cost if only a few keystations are needed.

- A possible disadvantage is the dependence of the system on the processor. A breakdown results in all the keystation operators being halted in their work unless a standby processor is attached, which obviously entails greater cost.

3.3 Key-to-diskette systems

A key-to-diskette system accepts keyed data and transfers it onto diskettes (floppy disks). These are of lightweight plastic, 20 cm (8 inches) in diameter and coated with a magnetizable material. They hold from 1 to 2 million bytes of data on one or both surfaces. Smaller floppy disks are about 13 cm (5 inches) in diameter and hold between a half and one million bytes.

The source data enters a key-to-diskette system via stand-alone data stations, each of which is equipped with a keyboard and a small VDU. The keyed data is held in a buffer in the data station before being recorded on the diskette. It is also displayed on the VDU in the form of two lines of 40 characters together with a third line to indicate the record's format.

Verification takes place in the usual way by rekeying the data with the data station switched to verify mode. It is sometimes found convenient to split a batch of data by copying from one diskette to another. This facilitates the verification of work by enabling several operators to verify different parts of the same batch.

After being recorded, the data on the diskettes is usually transferred to magnetic tape by means of a data converter. During this process the data converter performs error checking and provides error messages to facilitate correction. It is also possible to input the data into a computer directly from the diskettes, although this is a time-consuming and cumbersome procedure if a lot of diskettes are involved.

Features of key-to-diskette systems

- Check digit verification, field totalling during or after recording, and diskette searching to subsequently retrieve a particular record.
- Data station operator guidance through each source document by means of displayed messages. Ten different record formats at a time can be handled in this way.
- A communication adaptor housed in the data converter, enabling data to be transferred to or from a mainframe computer or another data converter.
- A serial printer attachable to the data station so that hard copy of the diskettes' contents can be prepared.
- The data stations are self-contained and hence there is little possibility of a complete system breakdown.
- The data stations can be sited at dispersed locations in order that the data can be captured close to its source.
- The diskettes are robust enough to be handled and sent through the mail, this encourages dispersed recording and centralized conversion.

3.4 Magnetic ink character recognition (MICR)

The concept behind MICR is that human-readable characters are printed on documents in a magnetizable ink. This enables a magnetic ink reader to recognize the characters for input to the computer.

Magnetic ink characters fall into two categories, known as the E13B font and the CMC7 font; shown respectively in Figures 3.2 and 3.3. The E13B character set comprises the ten numeric digits and four special symbols. The font is of one size only (about 3 mm high), and is very stylized in appearance. The CMC7 character set consists of 10 digits, the twenty-six upper-case alphabetic characters, and five special symbols. This font comes in four different sizes but these are not intermixable on the same document. People have become accustomed to both of these fonts and read the characters with little difficulty.

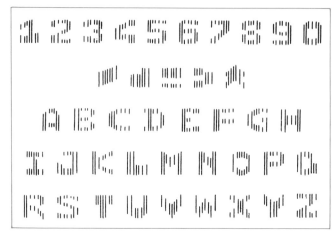

Figure 3.2 E13B magnetic ink font

Figure 3.3 CMC7 magnetic ink font

Usage of MICR

MICR is not suitable as a general method for capturing data for computer input. This is because the imprinting of the magnetic ink characters calls for precise positioning and a high level of print quality control. Also the amount of printing is limited to one line of characters in a predetermined position, thus restricting its flexibility.

E13B characters are used on British and US bank cheques, the line of print incorporates the cheque serial number, a destination code (bank and branch of drawer), the account number and the amount. The three former fields are preprinted before the cheque is drawn, and the amount is imprinted when the cheque passes through the banking system. This is done manually by a key-operated machine called an 'inscriber'.

CMC7 characters appear on European bank cheques and British postal orders. The data on postal orders can be totally preprinted since the amount is predecided.

Magnetic ink readers

These machines are also named 'magnetic character sorter-readers', 'magnetic ink character readers', or 'document processors'. They are capable of reading magnetic ink characters on MICR documents, and either passing the data directly to a computer or storing it off-line.

The MICR document is directed to one of up to thirty-six pockets (stackers) according to a predecided sorting pattern under program control. This capability enables documents bearing a given account number to be selected and is useful in the processing of bank cheques. Magnetic ink readers are also capable of accumulating and printing batch totals, editing documents to ensure that they contain a given number, and checking for correct sequence.

Most models of magnetic ink readers accept intermixed documents of various sizes such as are encountered with bank cheques. Their speed of operation is up to 2,400 documents per minute, which represents a million or more bank cheques per day. This capability is needed in order to handle the large volume of banking transactions carried out (see EFT in Section 2.6).

3.5 Optical mark recognition (OMR)

OMR has been in widespread use since the early 1960s for a wide variety of applications. It entails making small black marks on documents and is a flexible system because the value or meaning of a mark is unique to the particular type of document. Each mark is interpreted by a computer program written especially for that type of document. Putting this another way, an OMR document is designed to hold a number of boxes into which the marks are entered, as shown in Figure 3.4. Each box is annotated, usually in red printing, so that the user readily understands the value or meaning of an entered mark. An optical reader transcribes the marks/no marks into 'ones' or 'zeros' which are then passed to the computer for interpretation into a meaning.

Examples of the possible meanings of a mark are a single digit, a number, an alphabetic character, a binary bit, a plus or minus sign (credit or debit), a day of the week, document identification, or a specific meaning selected from several alternatives. It is also quite common to have several marks representing one digit or number, e.g. a mark in a box annotated '3' and a mark in a box '2' to represent 5.

Thus it is apparent that the only absolute constraint on OMR is the number of marks that can be accommodated on the document. Documents vary in size from about 8 × 8 cm to 25 × 40 cm, the larger sizes being able to hold over 2,000 marking positions. The marks themselves also vary in length from one system to another over the range 3−8 mm, they are normally entered in horizontal rows spaced down the document.

Marking is done with a fibre tip or ballpoint pen, soft lead pencil, typewriter, embossed plate, computer printer, or is printed during the document's

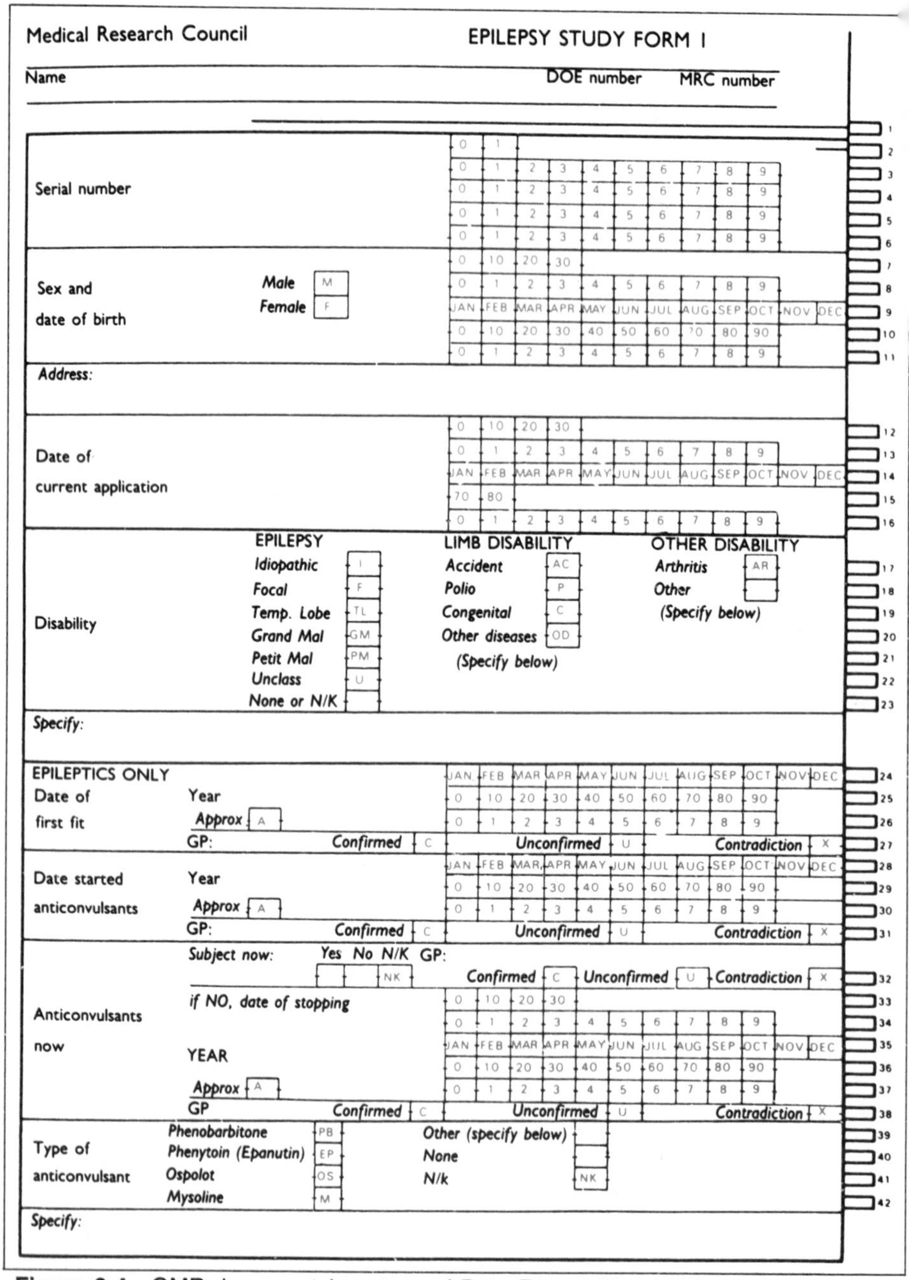

Figure 3.4 OMR document (courtesy of Data Recognition Ltd.)

manufacture. A human error in marking can be corrected by extending the erroneous mark downwards and then making another mark in the correct box. The extended mark is ignored by the optical reader. Some of the smaller models do not have this facility.

It was suggested earlier that a mark can represent a binary bit, and thus several such marks a binary number. This technique is applicable to marking by embossed plates, computer printers and during the original manufacture of the documents, and saves considerable space on the document. It is not a method to be adopted for manually marked documents, as people are confused by binary coding. It is convenient for turn around documents, i.e. documents printed by a computer for subsequent reinput to the system with a minimum of human intervention.

Applications of OMR

There is a wide range of OMR applications in business and also, to a lesser degree, in education and government. OMR documents are particularly suitable as turnaround documents since they are easily prepared and reasonably straightfoward to use.

A few representative applications are described briefly below.

Order forms   An OMR order form contains a printed list of items available and the order quantity is marked alongside each item required. The heading of the form often holds premarked data regarding the customer, salesman, date, etc.

Time sheets   Usually there is one sheet per employee per week on which there is space for marking all the variable data applicable to the payroll.

Surveys   The respondent's answers must be selected from the alternatives on the form by entering marks in the appropriate positions. Certain types of examinations employ this method, i.e. multiple-choice answers.

Diagrams   These are usually exploded diagrams of machines with a marking box near each constituent part. This facilitates ordering the required part because it is easily recognized on the diagram and then selected without writing or code numbers being involved.

Other uses of OMR documents include rent collection, gas and electricity reading, aptitude testing, vehicle inspection, stocktaking, and insurance premium payments.

Features of OMR

- The preprinted headings and annotations must be absolutely clear, and the boxes arranged so as to facilitate speedy marking, perhaps by people with little understanding of the whole system.
- The headings and annotations are printed in red as this makes them photoelectrically invisible.
- Wherever feasible, a control total should be incorporated into the document's marking, e.g. total quantity on an order form.
- A vertical spacing of six marking rows per inch conforms to most line printer

spacings, thus facilitating the preparation of turnaround documents. The documents must then, of course, be manufactured in the form of continuous stationery, and separated after the marks have been printed by the computer.

- Turnaround documents generally require printing in ordinary characters as well as with marks because the recipients are not good at understanding premarking.
- No special equipment is necessarily required for marking.
- The data is captured at source with no intervening keying before reaching the computer, thus minimizing the amount of manual work.
- Unsuitable for alphabetic data unless this is very limited, i.e. the boxes can be annotated with certain alphabetic characters only. This is simply because of the large amount of space needed for full alphabetic data.

3.6 Optical character recognition (OCR)

OCR was at one time regarded as the answer to all computer input problems — what could be better than computers being able to read hand-printed and machine-printed characters in the same way as people? In the light of harsh practicalities and high costs much of the original fervour has evaporated, and the use of OCR is not as extensive as was once predicted. Nevertheless it is incorporated into certain word processing applications through the automatic reading of typed documents.

OCR fonts

Nowadays two main OCR fonts are available, known as OCR-A and OCR-B, and shown in Figures 3.5 and 3.6 respectively. Other fonts also exist but now have much less usage than OCR-A and OCR-B.

OCR-A is an American standard and accommodates the numeric digits, upper-case alphabet and a range of symbols; four different font sizes are available. OCR-B is a European standard covering the numeric digits, upper-case and lower-case alphabets, certain non-English letters and a range of symbols; it has three different sizes.

Certain optical readers will accept other fonts including those printed by typewriters and used in books, thus forming a natural interface with word processing systems. Some optical readers are capable of reading *optically* the magnetic ink font E13B.

The four other main methods of printing OCR characters are preprinting, electric typewriting, computer printing and hand printing. Preprinting is of a high quality, and therefore no misreading of characters should occur. Electric typewriters that are specifically designed for this work can also print precisely, and by changing the printing element a wide range of fonts can be typed.

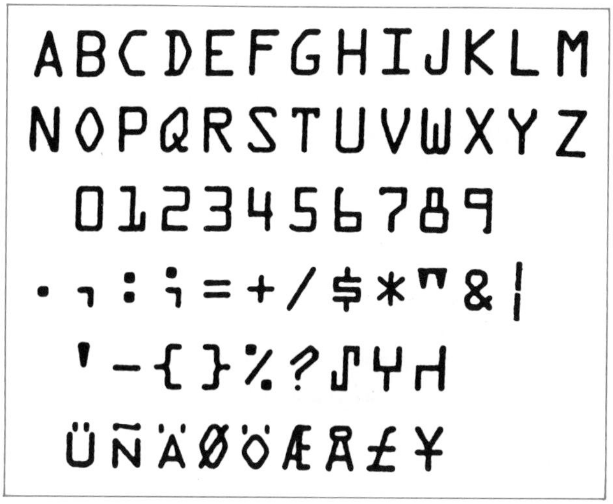

Figure 3.5 OCR-A font

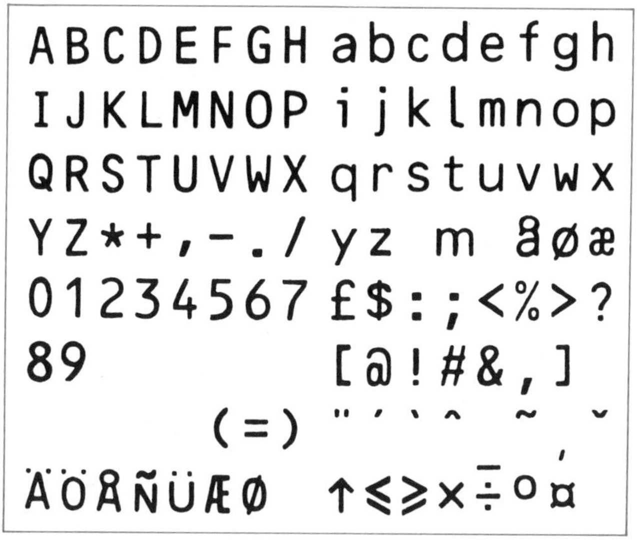

Figure 3.6 OCR-B font

Computer-printed OCR characters are of more dubious efficacy since the standard of alignment of computer printing varies enormously from one model to another, and in any case many computer printers do not have a machine-recognizable font.

Hand printing

As the name suggests, hand printing means the manual printing of characters on documents for subsequent reading by an optical reader. This method is restricted to the digits 0—9 and to a few optional alphabetical characters and symbols. The optical reader's logic allows for some tolerance in the shape of the characters but nevertheless all hand printing must be done carefully.

The limited set of characters is due mainly to the intrinsic similarity in the shapes of certain digits and letters, e.g. zero and 'oh', one and i, etc.

Optical readers

Many models of optical readers have flexibility of use in that they accept a variety of OCR fonts, hand printing and marks. A high level of recognition accuracy is achieved provided the documents conform to the recommendations made by the optical reader manufacturer as regards quality of printing.

Documents of various sizes and thicknesses can be read including cards, labels and continuous stationery. Labels are usually read by means of a hand-held wand reader that is stroked across the labelled goods.

The operational speeds of optical readers vary from around 2,000 documents per minute, when only one or two lines are read, down to 150 per minute when a full page of printing is read. Doubtful characters are either displayed for immediate individual correction or spooled for subsequent corrections as a batch. Output is almost always on-line to a mainframe but alternatively off-line to magnetic tape or diskettes. Some models have a sorting capability under program control so that the documents can be directed to several output pockets (stackers).

Features of OCR

- It is a natural method from the viewpoint of the non-technical user, the documents being clearly understandable to everyone.
- Hand printing requires no special equipment or expertise other than reasonable care but does not allow for the full alphabet.
- The data is captured at source with no interposed keying prior to reaching the computer.
- Turnaround documents are fully printed in clearly readable characters.
- Optical readers are expensive and so are advantageous only to large organizations that have a high level of throughput of OCR documents.

3.7 Bar coding and point-of-sale systems

Several media are grouped together under 'bar coding', although in some ways they are distinctly different from one another. Bar coding is the representation of code numbers or other data in the form of optical or magnetic bars on a data carrier. The data carrier may be a tag, ticket, label, plastic card or a container holding goods.

Bar codes

The two types of bar codes are based on either the European Article Number (EAN) or the Uniform Product Code (UPC).

These two systems are similar, the UPC having been used in the USA for some considerable time. The EAN has been introduced in various countries in Europe (see Figure 3.7) and comprises thirteen digits each of which is represented by two bars. The thickness and spacing of these bars is the means by which each digit is identified. Beneath the bars is printed a human-readable interpretation of the EAN or UPC in OCR-B font.

The thirteen digits of the EAN are usually made up of two digits to identify the country, five for the manufacturer, five for the product and one as a check digit. The UPC is similar except that only one digit is used for the country identifier, making twelve digits in all. By using five digits for the product, it is generally possible to identify uniquely all the products of a company and their variations such as colour, packaging form, weight, size, etc., bearing in mind that five digits cover 100,000 items.

The bar codes are printed on the containers at the time of manufacture and are read optically by either a hand-held reader (scanner or wand) or a static reader. Thus it is possible to identify entities automatically in a wide range of situations. These include goods in supermarkets, items in factory stores, library books and borrowers, and almost anything else.

Badges

A badge (or data carrier) is a stiff plastic card measuring typically 8.5 × 5.4 cm. The data is carried in a magnetic strip on one side of the card. The other side

Figure 3.7   Example of European Article Number bar code

is printed with details of the issuing company and type of card, and also may be embossed with the holder's name and number, expiry data, etc. In some cases the embossing is an OCR font and is used to print copies by means of a simple carbon copying device. These copies can then be read into a computer for accounting or administrative purposes.

The most extensive employment of badges is as bank credit and service cards. They are also used by libraries, for security purposes, for production logging, and for a wide range of other purposes.

Badges have a great versatility and are used more for devices such as cash dispensers than for computer source data. When the latter is the case, the data may be converted into a computer-compatible form such as magnetic tape. On-line computer input via badge readers is also available and operates in conjunction with manual input from a keyboard, switches, etc. Badge readers are intended for sporadic operation, e.g. by workers clocking in, rather than for high-speed input from batches of badges.

Normally a badge carries data that is unchangeable, i.e. static identification, but a newer development is the 'chip card' described in Section 2.6 under EFT.

Tags

A tag is a small card printed or punched in coded form so as to represent an entity. They are commonly attached to goods in shops and removed at the time of sale. The data is then converted into magnetic form before being input to a computer for stock control and sales analysis purposes.

A wide range of tags have been used in the past, notably the small punched cards known as Kimball tags. Currently most tags are printed with EAN bar codes which are read by a hand-held reader (wand).

Point-of-sale systems (POS/EPOS)

Point-of-sale (electronic point-of-sale) systems are used in supermarkets and other large shops in order to cope with a large throughput of customers. Typically such a POS incorporates a scanner, i.e. a bar code reader, and a printer and a keyboard built into each service point, of which there are generally between six and twenty-four.

The sales assistant passes each item purchased across a window in the counter so that the scanner can see the bar code and thereby identify the item. Another method is for the sales assistant to have a hand-held scanner which does the same thing. This latter arrangement is more suitable for large or awkwardly shaped items that could not be passed easily over a static scanner.

When the scanner has read and recognized the bar code, it emits a short sound. If this is not heard the sales assistant repeats the scanning procedure.

The price per unit item and the description are then looked-up automatically by the linked central minicomputer, the cost of each item is displayed and printed at the counter. The customer is thus provided with a printed receipt list showing the description, quantity, price and amount of all purchases.

The keyboard is for entering the prices of items not bar-coded, e.g. fresh vegetables. This operates in conjunction with electronic scales so that the price is computed automatically.

A further facility is for the terminal's printer to print all the entries onto the customer's blank cheque, leaving only the signature to be added. The slight drawback of this is that the printer, being a tally-roll printer, has a narrow print width (about 7 cm). This causes the entities on the cheque to be somewhat misplaced, nevertheless the cheques are accepted by the clearing banks.

The change (if a cash transaction) is also computed and printed at the bottom of the receipt along with the date, time and reference data.

From the point of view of the supermarket's management, the POS enables stock levels to be updated immediately by each sale. This facilitates the prompt restocking of shelves, and also provides an analysis of sales so that sudden surges in demand are detected at an early stage.

Some problems with POS have arisen as a result of discrepancies between the prices marked on the shelves and those stored in the computer, bearing in mind that the goods themselves are not price-marked. Discrepancies tend to occur when prices have changed and have not yet been remarked on the shelves. A possible way round this problem is to have electronically displayed prices, i.e. LCD displays, on the shelves linked directly to the minicomputer so that all price changes are registered simultaneously.

Another significant advantage of POS is that items labelling is almost, if not entirely, eliminated. This is a large saving in terms of man-hours and, additionally, reduces errors that sometimes occur in labelling. There is also the advantage of preventing label swopping by dishonest customers.

3.8 Visual display/keyboards

A visual display unit (VDU) is also sometimes termed a CRT display or a video display. Although strictly speaking a VDU is an output device, it is often employed in conjunction with a keyboard as a means of input. That is to say, the keyboard is used to enter data which appears simultaneously on the VDU's screen, perhaps along with other data deriving from the computer. In any case the characteristics of a VDU apply equally well to its use for both input and output.

A VDU is basically the same as a domestic television set in that it contains a cathode ray tube (CRT) scanned by a beam of electrons. This creates a set of horizontal lines (the raster) along which bright dots are made to appear so as to give the outline of characters and shapes. Typically, characters are five dots wide by seven dots high and appear in lines across the screen. The most common display size is twenty-four lines of eighty characters each but big variations occur between the different models of VDU. Another characteristic of a VDU is its character set (repertoire), i.e. the number of different digits, letters, symbols and shapes that can be represented on the screen. Often the repertoire consists of either 96 or 128 characters of the ASCII set.

The keyboard of a VDU reflects the repertoire to a large extent and, as already stated, has a similar layout to a typewriter but with additional control keys. Control keys do not necessarily cause characters to appear on the screen but send special signals to the computer for purposes such as text editing and cursor movement. A cursor is a symbol such as a line, square or arrow displayed on the screen to indicate relevant data or the next position to be used, it can be moved around the screen by means of the control keys or by program.

Most keyboard are detachable from the screen and so can be interchanged and positioned to suit the operator's convenience.

Operational features of VDUs

The features described below are attained through a combination of hardware and software, and the extent to which the VDU itself, as opposed to the processor to which it is linked, is capable of achieving them depends upon its level of intelligence, i.e. the amount of built-in processing power in the VDU.

Paging and scrolling   Paging is the displaying of a complete screen or page of information at a time and its immediate replacement by another page on request. This is analogous to turning the pages of a book, and so is suitable for inspecting sets of figures or pieces of text that fall into groups.

Scrolling is the movement of information up or down the screen a line at a time so that as one line appears at the bottom another disappears from the top and vice versa. This occurs rapidly and so there is no significant delay in inspecting quite long lists such as stock levels and account balances. Scrolling is only really suitable for lists that are in a known clear sequence, otherwise it is difficult to know which way to scroll to find a particular item.

Sideways scrolling is the movement of the display to the right or left across the screen. This is commonly utilized in spreadsheet programs but is otherwise not really suitable for lists or text.

Form filling   This is a changeable electronic or optical display of a document outline (entry form) together with the relevant headings and annotations. The keyed input data computed entries are displayed within the outline as though they are being entered manually. This method enables the operator always to have a clear picture of the point reached in the work.

An example of the practical use of an entry form is in the preparation of sales invoices from customer order data. The operator enters the account number, the commodity codes (or equivalent) and the quantities sold. At the appropriate points the computer inserts the name and address, descriptions, prices, amounts and other calculated information. See also Figure 7.11.

Double brightness   The various data items on the screen can be displayed at two alternative levels of brightness, these are sometimes called foreground and background data. The essential purpose of double brightness is to differentiate between data so that, for instance, data entered manually is clearly distinguishable from that emanating from the computer. It is also useful for drawing attention to certain data by making it brighter than the rest.

'Highlighting' is where certain data is given a solid bright background, i.e. the dots composing the character(s) are fully bright and the remaining dots in the character space are at half brightness.

'Inverse video' or 'reverse video' is where the characters are created by 'black' dots on a bright background, i.e. the reverse of normal. This is used mainly for headings in larger fonts.

Blinking or flashing   A data item or the cursor is made to flash on and off or from normal to inverse video. This is obviously useful for drawing attention to certain data.

Variable character size   Certain lines are composed of larger characters than normal, e.g. double height and double width. This is mainly for headings perhaps in conjunction with double brightness.

Mouse   A mouse is a hand-held device which when run along the table causes a cursor to move correspondingly on the screen. When the cursor reaches a position of significance, the user presses a button on the mouse and the computer registers that this is of some interest. Thus a mouse is a convenient way of selecting parts of the display without having to use the keyboard. A mouse may either be attached to the VDU by a lead (its tail) or be unattached (tail-less) and operate by ultrasonics.

Touch screens   The concept of a touch screen is that the user is able to indicate items of interest by touching them on the screen. This is achieved mainly by a matrix of fine infra-red beams criss-crossing the screen and being broken by the finger or touching object. Other methods are also available or proposed such as conductive membranes, sound wave reflection, capacitative screens and piezo-electric crystal deformation.

Whatever method is employed, there can be only a limited number of touch points on the screen otherwise their close proximity would cause confusion. A practical approach is to display a menu (Section 7.5) with a touch point alongside each item.

An extension of touch screens is hand-drawing whereby the user by moving his finger across the screen causes lines to appear. This is of more interest in education than business.

Windows   One of the problems with VDUs in business is the need to move frequently from one display to another in order to make cross-references. For example, a customer's recent invoice, his ledger account and his payments history. This problem is largely overcome by having windows, i.e. separate small displays, on the screen simultaneously. Each window is capable of being scrolled, paged or edited individually as though it was on a separate VDU.

A process termed 'zooming' is a means of obtaining a finer degree of detail in the data shown via a window. Windows are frequently used on microcomputers in conjunction with a mouse and icons, sometimes called WIMP.

Graphics   Graphic displays are of two types — raster and vector. Business VDUs are the raster type, as explained earlier in this section, but the closeness of the dots on a high-resolution screen enables them to appear as lines and coloured areas. This implies that a wide range of things can be represented, e.g. graphs, bar charts, pie charts, histograms, 'three-dimensional' representations, logos, icons and very large characters.

Vector graphics involve a different type of VDU that draws solid lines instead of dots.

Colour   Some VDU manufacturers claim that their models are capable of reproducing hundreds and even thousands of colours. In so far as the three primary colours (red, green and blue) can be mixed at various brightnesses this is technically true. In practice the business user is unlikely to need more than a few colours, e.g. eight, for representations such as those above. Judicious use of colours can make a display clearer and more interesting but overlavish employment is likely to be counter-productive by making the display too dazzling for business information.

Audible output   An audible note, sometimes called a bell, is sounded by the VDU whenever circumstances warrant this. This is a convenient way of drawing attention to trouble or a special condition without altering the display. It must be backed up by facilities for detecting the problem and putting things right.

Panel display

This is a panel composed of a set of small tubes which are arranged to change their appearance so as to represent characters. A common use of small panel displays is in pocket calculators and in certain data capture devices.

The tubes are either light-emitting diodes (LEDs) or, more likely, liquid crystal diodes (LCDs). The latter require so little electrical power that it is practical to incorporate a large number into battery-powered portable computers in order to create a twenty-four line by eighty-character display.

3.9   Voice data entry (VDE)

VDE, also termed 'voice input', 'speech recognition' and other names, differs from almost all other methods of data capture in that there is no digital input representing data. The input data is derived from a human voice and because of the wide range of voice sounds, it is very difficult for a computer to interpret that data with complete accuracy.

There are three aspects of VDE: isolated word recognition; connected speech recognition; and speech understanding systems. It is with the first aspect that we are concerned here, but a few words regarding the other two are worthwhile.

Connected speech recognition means that the computer must be capable of interpreting and making use of short strings of words, i.e. structured sentences. This implies the recognition and understanding of certain keywords in a string. Although the computer might not recognize all the words, there is sufficient understanding for certain actions to be initiated.

Speech understanding systems are of a higher level and necessitate the computer 'understanding' the grammatical and intellectual meanings of text and of continuous speech in real time. These aims imply a high level of artificial intelligence, which in turn means the employment of very powerful computers. Inherent factors are speaker independence and differentiation between speech and background sounds. The fifth-generation projects such as ICOT (Japanese), Alvey (US) and Esprit (European) include the above aims as part of their long-term objectives. From the business point of view, speech understanding is unlikely to make any impact for a long time.

Returning to isolated word recognition, this is much less ambitious in that it interprets only a limited set of words, e.g. up to 2,000 in the case of the IBM Tangora speech recognition system, and then only from known persons' voices. That is to say, the computer accepts input data only from persons whose voices it has been trained to interpret. It is trained by the person speaking each word a few times and concurrently inputting the word via a keyboard. This is known as 'training mode' and the computer is thus able to create and store a feature matrix of each word based on its pitch, tone and phoneme characteristics. The feature matrix is, in effect, an average reference pattern for each particular word as spoken by a certain individual. If a person's pronunciation changes for one reason or another, it may well be necessary to retrain the computer.

The input of voice data for actual use is termed 'recognition mode'. If voice data is displayed immediately after being input, it is possible to amalgamate training and recognition modes. This occurs because corrections can be made to misinterpreted input and so the computer can modify the relevant feature matrix. During recognition mode the words are spoken into a small noise-cancelling microphone generally attached to a headband. There must be a short time interval (at least 0.1 seconds) between words in order to separate successive words; this is no problem in practice.

Applications of VDE

In the foreseeable future VDE is unlikely to be employed for the input of a large amount of data as this can be handled by faster and more cost effective methods. VDE is more suited to specialized data involving separate words or short strings of words spoken at intervals. This situation arises especially when the user is totally occupied with his hands or cannot divert his eyes from his task. Similarly VDE is useful for activating a computer or other machine to perform certain tasks.

Examples of VDE applications include the control of luggage and goods sorting/directing mechanisms, such as occur in airports, factories and postal centres. Another application is in slaughterhouses where the weights and qualities of carcases are recorded by VDE.

Voice recognition is also used in security systems, but in this application it is the person rather than the information that is of interest.

A final point worth mentioning is the challenge of language translation in real time, for instance translating Japanese into English down the phone while preserving the essential characteristics of the speakers' voices. This is hardly likely to be achieved in the writer's lifetime but it could within the reader's!

3.10 Computer output

The three principal methods of outputting information from a computer are printing, visual display and computer output to microfilm (COM). And, of these, printing is still by far the most common. Visual display, although in the true sense an output method, is mainly utilized in connection with data input, as explained in Section 3.8. COM has increased in use for certain applications but is unlikely to replace printed documents owing to its inherent need for special viewing equipment.

Voice response (audio output) has also gained limited use but, here again, is unlikely to be adopted extensively for business purposes. This is mainly owing to the human inability to retain in mind more than a few numbers or words at a time.

A significant development was the insertion of microprocessors into peripherals and terminals, thereby giving them a degree of 'intelligence'. This enabled the peripheral to be more autonomous in controlling its own operations, and so alleviate the processing load of the CPU. This built-in processing power also reduces the amount of data needing to be transmitted over communication lines between a central computer and a distant terminal. This is because certain data and procedures are repetitive and of a routine nature and so can often be created by or stored in the terminal itself. An example of this is the outline and headings of a document to be printed or displayed. The printer or VDU could hold these in its own storage after being down-loaded from the computer only once per job instead of for every document.

3.11 Printing

The printer is the workhorse of the computer. During the operation of the computer, it is involved in a massive amount of mechanical effort — far more than the other types of peripherals. It is therefore imperative that the most suitable type of printer is employed for the computer jobs in hand. Computer printers also come in a much wider range of capabilities than other peripherals, and this is reflected in their wide range of costs.

The descriptions that follow are intended to give the reader a broad and comprehensive understanding of printer technology without, hopefully, blinding him with a plethora of figures and technicalities. Some quantitative facts must, however, be taken into consideration otherwise we have no measurable bases of comparison between the different methods and models.

Computer printers fall into three main groups — line printers, serial printers and page printers. These groups can be further categorized as shown in Figure 3.8. The principal reason for categorizing in this way is that it emphasizes their differing capabilities and methodologies.

Line printers

A line printer is characterized by its ability to, in effect, print a complete line at a time. The complete line is printed in a fraction of a second, and a line printer does not normally print less than a complete line at a time. This does not, of course, mean that the line of print has necessarily to be full; gaps may be present in any positions in order to separate the data items printed.

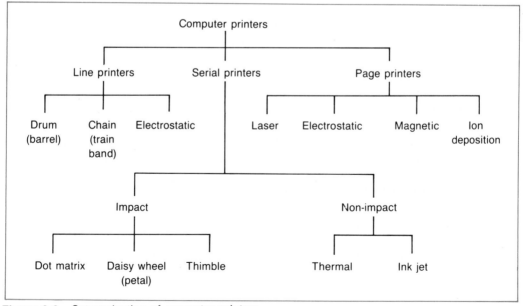

Figure 3.8 Categorization of computer printers

Another factor to remember is that the speed of line printing is independent of the actual amount of print in a line. The reason for this is that line printing is a cyclic mechanical process in which the actual impression of the characters onto the paper is only a part.

The paper (stationery) is sprocket-fed in order to maintain its accurate movement, and consequently needs a column of sprocket holes down each edge. It is also fan-folded with perforations between the sheets so as to facilitate their separation after printing. After a batch of documents have been printed, it is usual to guillotine the edges to remove the sprocket holes.

Copies are made by means of either interleaved carbons or the use of chemically coated paper. The latter has a special coating that is sensitive to pressure and so causes an impression to appear on the copies. Because this entails less overall thickness of paper, the bottom copies are clearer than with carbon copying. It is also possible to use stationery with carbonized backing as the means of attaining selective copying.

There is nowadays a less clear distinction between line printers and high-performance serial printers since their printing capabilities and speeds are similar.

Line printers are of three main types: (a) drum printers, (b) chain, train or band printers and (c) electrostatic printers.

Drum printers

A drum printer comprises a drum (barrel) rotating continuously at high speed, around the circumference of which are embossed the printable characters. One complete set of print characters is embossed on the drum for each and every print position. Thus a print drum with a 64-character print set and a width of 160 print positions holds 10,240 embossed characters on its surface.

The mode of operation of a drum printer is for a set of print hammers (one per print position) to strike the paper against the embossed characters. A carbon ribbon interposed between the paper and the drum causes the appropriate character to appear on the paper. This method is called 'fly' printing because the embossed characters continue moving during the hammers' strikes.

In order for fly printing to be effective, the hammers need to strike very quickly and accurately timewise. Drum printing can usually be recognized by the wavy nature of the printed lines and the slight blurring of the printed characters. The former fault is caused by mistimings of the hammers, and is almost unavoidable in practice.

The principle of drum printing engenders relatively high cost owing to the manufacturing difficulties of the embossed drum, and the need for a means of accurate hammer timing. Printer drums cannot be interchanged by the user and so there is no possibility of changing the character set or font (typeface).

It is for these reasons that drum printers have been largely displaced by chain and band printers.

Chain printers

A chain printer consists of a set of type slugs mounted on a chain which rotates continuously in a horizontal plane. There may be up to eight repetitions of the character set around the chain if the set is reduced in size. This increases the speed of printing since there is less waiting time for a given character to appear.

As with a drum printer, there is a hammer for each print position. This strikes at the exact instant that the appropriate character slug is opposite the print position. Timing is again critical otherwise the print quality is degraded, but the problem of wavy lines is eliminated since the chain moves horizontally and not at right angles to the print line.

An advantage of chain printers is that the chain of type slugs can be changed by the user, and so various character sets and fonts are readily available.

A train printer is essentially the same as a chain printer, and a band printer differs in that it has a flexible metal belt with the characters embossed on it instead of a chain.

Electrostatic printers

A row of closely spaced styli are located across the print bank of an electrostatic printer in such a way that any character can be formed. This is achieved by electrically charging the appropriate styli and then applying them to the surface of special paper. This dielectric surface is capable of holding the charge so that when the paper is passed through a chemical solution, toner (ink) adheres to the charged areas.

Characteristics of line printers

Speeds   From 300 to 3,000 lines per minute, but mostly between 600 and 1,000, spaced six or eight lines per inch vertically. The theoretical maximum speed of a printer is rarely achieved in practice owing to the time taken by vertical spacing and skipping (multiple spacing). Skipping means the high-speed movement of the stationery across blank and preprinted areas.

Print bank widths (print positions or columns)   From 96 to 160 print positions spaced ten or twelve per inch across the line of print.

Character sets   Normally forty-eight, sixty-four or ninety-six characters per set (repertoire) in fonts such as OCR-B and ECMA 11.

Copies   One top document plus five, or six copies if special stationery is used.

Serial printers

Also known as character printers, serial printers print one character at a time across the line of print. This method of printing necessitates only one, or sometimes two, print head(s) being in operation at one instant in a similar way to a typewriter.

In contrast to a conventional typewriter, however, the print head of a serial printer moves across the paper while the paper remains stationary.

As is seen from Figure 3.8, serial printers fall into two categories – impact and non-impact. With the former the print head comes into contact with the print ribbon, generally with sufficient force to enable several copies to be made simultaneously. Non-impact printers inevitably mean only one copy at a time, this is a disadvantage because several copies are usually needed in a business. The extra copies have to be prepared either by repeated printing or by photocopying off-line.

Impact printers are used far more than non-impact, especially in conjunction with microcomputers.

Dot matrix printers

Dot matrix printers, also known as 'wire matrix' and 'needle' printers, form printed characters that consist of small dots. These are created by a column of wires (needles) in the print head, selected ones of which are rapidly protruded to come into contact with the print ribbon. This is repeated several times for each character as the print head moves across the document. The quality of dot matrix printing is determined largely by the number of wires in the column and the number of columns composing each character, i.e. the dots in the matrix, typically 7×5. Quality is enhanced by multiple passing of the print head in order to get interlaced or staggered dots. This is achieved either by having two print heads or by a slight shift of the one head between successive passes. A similar technique provides for oversize characters and special printing such as logos and diagrammatic representations.

Daisy wheel (petal) printers

The printing element of a daisy wheel printer is a rotatable wheel consisting of a number of flexible spokes made of metal or plastic. At the outer end of each spoke is a moulded character, and the wheel is rotated until the appropriate character comes into line with the print hammer. This strikes it against the ribbon so making its impression on the paper.

The wheels are removable and inexpensive and so the user can print in various fonts (typefaces) by having a collection of wheels. Similarly, wheels are easily replaced when they show signs of wear.

Daisy wheel printers are fairly slow and noisy but produce a high quality of print, i.e. letter quality, suitable for use in word processing. Quality is further enhanced by using a software-controlled hammer, this strikes with a force relating to the size of the character being printed.

Thimble printers

A thimble printer is a variant of the daisy wheel printer. It has moulded characters at the end of spokes that are arranged cylindrically in the shape of a thimble.

Ink jet printers

Considerable technological development has gone into ink jet printers but as yet they are a long way behind dot matrix and daisy wheel printers in the numbers sold. The problems of clogging that the early machines encountered have been largely eliminated by subsequent modifications and the use of self-cleaning print heads and ink that dries only on contact with the paper.

A good feature of ink jet printers is their quietness of operation. They are at the top end of serial printer speeds and have great flexibility in their print style. Their capabilities include any font, simulated handwriting, variable size, diagrams, logos, and so on.

Another advantage of certain models is the ability to produce multicoloured printing, up to eight colours are available but it is unlikely that more than two or three are needed for business documents.

The major disadvantage of an ink jet printer is its inability to print more than one copy at a time.

Thermal printers

The print head of a thermal (electrothermal) printer contains an array of heating elements that have electric currents switched through them so as to form the shape of the required character. When the print head comes into contact with the special paper, it burns away an aluminium coating to reveal a black core. Other models employ similar processes including the fusing together of colouring agents held in a surface coating on the paper.

The main drawbacks of thermal printing are the need for special paper and only one copy at a time. They are quiet in operation, however.

Characteristics of serial printers

Speeds
From 40 to 400 characters per second. The effective printing speed is increased by bi-directional printing and by 'look-ahead'. The latter means that the printer has sufficient intelligence to decide whether to print the subsequent line forwards or backwards in order to minimize the print head movement.

Print bank widths
From 80 to about 300 print positions, averaging 132. Dual-stationery drives are

available on some models for printing two documents concurrently. Vertical spacing is either six, eight or ten lines per inch.

Character sets
The usual set is the ninety-six ASCII characters but a much greater number is possible with matrix and ink jet printers. The latter can produce cursive, i.e. imitation handwritten, fonts under software control. In effect, there is an almost unlimited number of fonts and characters available from certain models of serial printers. Others produce the more popular fonts such as OCR-A, OCR-B, and various upper- and lower-case sets.

Page printers

Page printers create a full page of print at a time using one of the techniques described below. They vary in size from relatively inexpensive table-top devices up to expensive but very powerful printing systems (see characteristics). There are four types of page printer — laser, ion-deposition, magnetic and electrostatic.

Laser printers

A laser printer functions by creating an image of a page of print in the form of microscopic dots on the photoconductive surface of a rotating drum by means of a controllable low-power laser beam. A special ink (toner) is then attracted to the laser-exposed areas of the drum. When the paper comes into contact with the drum, the image is transferred and then fused permanently onto it. The drum is then automatically erased before receiving the next page's image. This method uses ordinary blank computer stationery, either fan-folded or a continuous reel. The document's outlines and headings are created by flashing a photographic negative of the document onto the photoconductive drum while printing is in progress.

Ion-deposition printers

In contrast to the laser printer, this method is electrical rather than optical. Ions (charged electrical particles) are created in a cavity, and directed electrically through an orifice onto the dielectric surface of a rotating cylinder. By using an array of orifices and by switching the ions off and on, the required characters are formed as an electric charge image on the cylinder's surface. Toner is then applied to the charged image and transferred to the paper on which it is transfixed by pressure, this is known as cold fusion.

This method enables logos, signatures, etc., to be printed as well as characters in a range of fonts. Ion-deposition printers are smaller and cheaper but lower speed than laser printers, typically forty pages per minute.

Electrostatic printers

An electrostatic page printer functions as described under electrostatic line printers and, strictly speaking that is what they are; their high speed, however, permits them to be regarded as page printers. The characters are created by dots at 200 per inch horizontally and vertically, thus giving a high quality that is not obviously matrix printing. The document outlines are software coded and then stored for printing concurrently with the data. Letterheads and logos are created electrostatically from a changeable metal cylinder. Preprinted stationery can also be used.

Magnetic printers (magnetoelectric)

The basic principle of a magnetic printer is in some ways similar to a magnetic drum. A drum in the printer has a surface that can be coated with rows of tiny spots of magnetism by means of thousands of minute recording heads. As the drum rotates it becomes covered with these magnetic spots so as to form a latent image of the page to be printed. Following this, dry ink particles are brought into contact with the drum's surface and these adhere to the magnetized spots. The ink is then pressurized onto the surface and subsequently transferred onto paper. This method is claimed to be simpler and less troublesome than other methods, largely due to the use of a dry ink.

Characteristics of page printers

Speeds
Quoted at between 8 and 600 pages per minute, this is equivalent to a maximum of about 36,000 lines per minute. The effective speed depends upon various factors such as the number of lines per document and options required, such as double-sided printing.

Character sets
Typically 128 but up to 256 characters per set with a range of fonts and sizes; the character fonts are stored in the printer's storage. The print pitch tends to be more compressed than other printers, e.g. fifteen characters per inch.

Copies
Produced by reprinting the document immediately as many times as necessary. This gives good quality on all copies, and permits differing data between them.

Blanked-out areas and different names and addresses on standard letters are examples.

Intelligence
Built-in microprocessors and storage permit software control, e.g. a job control language for automatically selecting the print requirements for each type of document.

Output
The high rate of throughput of documents necessitate stationery handling facilities (Section 7.3) to be built into page printers. This means that it is possible to feed rolls of blank paper into one end of the system and for printed documents in their final form to come out the other end.

3.12 Speech output

Speech output is also known as audio response, audio output, voice response, voice output and voice answer-back. It is a comparatively little-used method of outputting information or instructions from a computer. None the less it has been adopted for certain specialized applications, and in the long term may find a wider variety of uses including those associated with fifth-generation projects.

The concept of speech output is that computers are capable of producing speech based on a stored digital representation of either words or sounds. In the former case words spoken by a person are recorded, then digitized and stored for subsequent reproduction. Typically, the vocabulary would be a few hundred words. In order to save storage, certain commonly used words are stored separately from the sentence they are in and replaced by a code number after the style of an attribute value table (Section 4.3). They are inserted into the sentence just prior to its output.

Digitized speech is expensive of storage because it is necessary to store the binary value of the sound's amplitude taken at frequent intervals of time. This is called pulse code modulation and demands something like 24,000 bits per stored word. The amount of storage can, however, be reduced significantly by storing the differences between the successive amplitudes rather than their absolute values.

It is also possible to store digitized sounds rather than complete words and therefore create the required words by combining their constituent sounds in the correct order.

Considerations regarding speech output

Before adopting speech output, there are several factors to be taken into consideration.

- Speech cannot be scanned, i.e. if it is not heard or understood, it is necessary to have it repeated.
- The amount of information, e.g. the number of words, that can be stored in human short-term memory is quite low. This is particularly true for numeric data (around seven digits is the maximum that is safely remembered).
- Speech output must have a short response time and be continuous within a grammatical phrase or sentence. Pauses are acceptable but only at semantically appropriate places.
- The stored vocabulary must be capable of being amended so as to meet the changing requirements of the business.
- The quality of the speech must be acceptable to the listener, bearing in mind the environment and nature of his work.

Applications of speech output

Speech output is not a replacement for other methods when it comes to large volumes of output but in certain circumstances it has clear advantages. One of these is when the user is working in a situation demanding intensive effort or concentration of eyes or hands, e.g. highly concentrated work, disabled persons, blind persons, or in darkness or poor light.

A popular business application of speech output is salespersons phoning in their customers' orders. The salesperson attaches a small keypad to a public telephone by means of an acoustic coupler, and then dials the computer. The computer is programmed to instruct him step-by-step in regard to the data to be keyed in, and these instructions are heard through the telephone. After each data item input, the computer responds by repeating verbally the data keyed-in so as to verify its accuracy.

This is a convenient, rapid and economic means of capturing sales orders, mainly because no humans are involved at the receiving end. A large amount of order data is automatically recorded from numerous distant sources and processed to initiate the dispatch of and accounting for customers' orders.

Possible future uses of speech output include the prompts and messages from electronic telephone systems, e.g. advice regarding changed telephone numbers, and credit card checking by means of a telephone link between a retailer and the bank's computer.

3.13 Computer output microforms (COM)

COM is the direct recording of computer output onto microfilm or microfiche (collectively termed microforms). It is a natural successor to the off-line microfilming of printed computer ouput.

Microforms

The two types of microforms are microfilm and microfiche. The former is 16- or 35-mm rolls of film contained on spools or in catridges. Each roll holds from 2,000 to 5,000 pages; a page is a frame containing information from one document.

Generally the pages are positioned single along the roll; this is known as simplex format. By reducing their size it is possible to accommodate two rows of pages along the roll side-by-side; this is duplex format. Duo format is where the pages run along the roll in two rows but have reversed sequence in one row, i.e. it is intended that they are viewed forward along one row and back along the other.

Microfiche is 105-mm film cut up into sheets about 6 inches × 4 inches each holding several hundred pages. The actual number of pages depends upon the reduction ratio, the most common reduction ratios are 42:1 giving 208 pages per fiche, 48:1 giving 270, and 72:1 giving 690.

Microfiche is more compact than microfilm and simpler to view and update. It is generally more convenient to handle a single sheet than a roll, and this is especially true when just one page requires to be changed. With microfiche only the fiche containing the page in question needs replacing whereas with microfilm the whole roll needs to be replaced in most cases. For these reasons microfiche has largely superseded microfilm.

COM recording

COM recorders operate either on-line or via magnetic tape in order to convert the computer's digital representation of data into microforms. The most common method of doing this is for the recorder to photograph the display of a cathode ray tube enclosed within itself. A succession of such displays are photographed so as to fill a microfice or microfilm. At the same time the microform is provided with headings and indexing by means of in-built optical equipment and software. As with many pieces of equipment COM recorders are microprocessor controlled, enabling various formats and reduction ratios to be available.

Another method of recording is by writing directly onto the microform with an electron beam or a laser beam. It is also possible to record using fibre optics. Both these methods also employ optics and software.

After data has been recorded on the microform, it has to be developed. This is done by a processsor which is an enclosed unit operating with dry chemicals. By the employment of laser techniques, recording and processing can be integrated into one process. A high proportion of COM users employ the services of a bureau to prepare their microforms.

Microfilm indexing

Remembering that a roll of microfilm holds several thousand pages, it is obviously a problem to be able to find the required page quickly. This is overcome by a number of indexing methods, most of which involve lines or bars recorded on the microfilm to enable the viewing mechanism to find the required page automatically.

Microfiche indexing

Each fiche has a header in large (eyeball) letters describing its contents. And in one corner of the fiche is an index page holding the coordinates of the other pages on the fiche together with some indication of their contents.

The user selects the appropriate fiche by examining the headers by eye and then views the index page using the reader. The reader is then set manually to display the appropriate page.

Features of COM

Media space
The saving with COM in this respect depends upon the reduction ratio used. Assuming this is 48:1, the effective ratio of paper volume to microform volume is about 60:1 with cartridged microfilm, and 500:1 with microfiche.

Output speed
This is a complex factor owing to the variety of COM arrangements and the need for processing the film. COM recorders operate at 100 to 1,000 pages per minute, and line printers at 300 to 3,000 lines per minute.

In general, a middle-range COM recorder is around 10–20 times as fast as a middle-range printer.

Durability
Microforms have good ageing qualities and, if properly housed, deteriorate less than paper and print. This is especially true in relation to chemical-based printing, which fades rapidly if exposed to strong light.

Costs
The microform medium itself costs less per page than paper. Distribution costs are reduced, especially if mailing is involved, and so are the output handling activities (separating, guillotining, etc.).

Nevertheless the practical cost must take into account the likely need for additional COM equipment and the probability that a printer is available anyway.

Multiple copying
A printer produces five or six copies at a time, whereas a recorder produces only one. If a large number of microform copies is required, replicating equipment is available including units that are capable of making variable numbers of copies as controlled by marks on the originals.

Record retrieval

It is faster with a large amount of output to find a required page of microforms than a page of printed sheets since one of the above indexing methods can be employed in order to facilitate the search.

Reading

The outstanding problem with COM is the need for a reader at each location where the microforms are likely to be viewed. This could be costly if many viewing points exist.

Updating

COM records suffer if they are active as it is not practical to make frequent updates. This also tends to apply to printed records unless the updating is minimal. Updating is possible by preparing a secondary file of microform pages of updates and amendments for inspection along with the primary file. At intervals the two are merged into a new microform file although this is not as automatic as with magnetic media. A similar point is that microforms cannot be annotated by hand as can paper-printed documents.

3.14 Exercises

Exercise 3.1 Printers

What are the essential characteristics of the following computer printers:

(i)   daisywheel
(ii) dot matrix
(iii) laser
(iv) ink jet.

Comment on the range of applications which suit each of them.

(BCS part II, Option A, April 1987)

Exercise 3.2 Peripheral devices

Describe the facilities provided by, the operational characteristics of, and a typical application of three of the following peripheral devices:

(i)   dot matrix or daisywheel printer
(ii) colour graphics terminal
(iii) mouse or trackerball
(iv) modem.

(BCS part I, Gen. paper I, April 1986)

Exercise 3.3 Peripheral devices

Note: Section (a) applies to Chapter 4.

(a) Compare and contrast the following pairs of peripherals:
  (i) magnetic tape and replaceable disks as backing store
  (ii) OCR and MICR as input devices
  (iii) VDU and line printer as output devices.
(b) For each of the peripherals above give an example of usage.

(BCS part I, Gen. paper I, April 1987)

Exercise 3.4 OMR document

Design an order form for use in an OMR system. The form's size is 7 inches wide by 8 inches deep, and the spacings of the marking positions are three per inch vertically and four per inch horizontally. The clear printing is spaced three lines per inch vertically and ten characters per inch horizontally.

The data shown in Table 3.1 is to be contained in each order form.

Table 3.1

Attribute	Picture	Presentation
Customer account no.	9999	Binary marks by computer
Customer name	A(30)	Clear printing by computer
Week number (53 max.)	99	Decimal marks by hand
Salesman number	99	Decimal marks by hand
Commodity descriptions (9)	A(40)	Clear preprinting
Commodity order quantities (9)	99	Decimal marks by hand

Exercise 3.5 Key-to-disk system

It has been decided to install a key-to-disk system for which it is assumed that the average rate of keying is 10,000 keystrokes per operator per hour. The volumes of data to be keyed in an effective working week of thirty hours are:

(a) 6,000 stores issues of twenty characters;
(b) 15,000 job tickets of thirty characters;
(c) 1,200 customer orders of sixty characters;
(d) 1,500 goods received notes of forty characters;
(e) 8,000 daywork tickets of sixty characters.

Decide how many keystations are required if a 25 per cent safety allowance is adopted, i.e. 25 per cent more capacity is to be introduced than is actually required.

Exercise 3.6 Costing of data capture

A company needs to capture data pertaining to monetary transactions. There are 5 million transactions per annum each involving the recording of fifteen digits. Alternative methods under consideration are:

(a) key-to-disk keyed from existing source documents;
(b) OCR handprinting by the clerks who fill in the existing source documents, with ten transactions per OCR document.

Compute the annual costs of each of the two methods, taking into account the costs of the key-to-disk operators, the data media, the off-line equipment and the on-line computer peripherals. The costs shown in Table 3.2 can be assumed (do not take these as accurate for other purposes), overheads are included in these costs.

Table 3.2

Key-to-disk systems with 6 keystations	£600 per month
Key-to-disk systems with 8 keystations	£700 per month
Key-to-disk systems with 10 keystations	£800 per month
Key-to-disk operators	£300 per month
Optical reader	£1,500 per month
Magnetic tape drive	£100 per month
OCR documents	£8 per thousand

Key-to-disk operators work at 10,000 keystrokes per hour for an effective 1,500 hours per annum. One additional magnetic tape unit is required with a key-to-disk system. Existing source document costs are £1,500 p.a. All other costs can be ignored.

Exercise 3.7 Printer timing

Three models of printers A, B and C, are under consideration for producing the output detailed below. Calculate the times taken by each of the three models on the assumption that no other times interfere, i.e. the computer is printer-bound.

Printer A is a serial printer operating at 200 characters per second with one-directional printing. The carriage return (once per print line) takes 200 ms and the average skip rate is 30 ms per line.

Printer B is a line printer operating at 300 lines per minute. The average skip rate is 10 ms per line.

Printer C is a serial printer operating at 250 characters per second with bi-directional printing, i.e. no carriage return time. The average skip rate is 60 ms per line.

Output 1,000 documents each comprising the following:

  (i) three header lines averaging sixty characters each;
 (ii) three line gap;
(iii) eight detail lines averaging 100 characters each;
 (iv) average gap of twenty lines;
  (v) one total line of twenty-five characters;
 (vi) ten-line gap to next document.

Exercise 3.8 Storage space and weight

One million documents 15 inches wide × 10 inches deep × 0.004 inches thick, weighing 8 lb per 1,000, are stored in archival files.

It is under consideration to convert these into other microfiche or roll microfilm.

The microfiches hold 270 pages each, and are 6 inches × 4 inches × 0.01 inches (in jacket), weighing 6 lb per 1,000 in jackets.

The roll microfilm holds 2,000 pages per roll and is contained in a magazine 5 inches × 5 inches × 1 inch weighing 4 ounces each.

Calculate the volumes and weights of the existing documents and of the two alternatives.

3.15 Outline solutions to exercises

Solution 3.1

For technical characteristics of the printers see Section 3.11. Most suitable business applications are:
  (i) Daisywheel
- Reports demanding high-quality print but in only the one font and size.
- Correspondence needing a few simultaneous copies, e.g. word processing or desktop publishing involving one-font text but no graphics.
- Preparation of OCR documents.

 (ii) Dot matrix
- Routine reports needing several fonts but only low-quality print.
- Internal memoranda incorporating variable data extracted from the database, i.e. one copy only of each memo.

(iii) Laser
- Desktop publishing involving graphics and multi-font text.
- Variable data correspondence including logos and headings.
- Reports containing graphics.

 (iv) Ink jet
- Reports demanding coloured graphics.
- Correspondence in imitation handwriting.
- Reports needing a range of fonts and symbols.

Solution 3.2

(i) See Solution 3.1.

(ii) A wide range of graphics software with which it is practical to create an unlimited number of diagrams, charts and pictures. These are modified as required by using 'brushes' and a 'palette' of colours, i.e. mock painting. The technical characteristics are as described in Section 3.8.

(iii) Mouses [*sic*] are explained in Section 3.8. Their main purpose in business is for selecting items on a screen that are of interest or require alteraton, i.e. WIMPs. This is a fairly rapid method that eliminates the need for a keyboard (for selection purposes) but the mouse requires a clear space on what is often a crowded desk.

A trackerball does a similar job to a mouse but is operated by rotating a static housed ball with the fingers. It is, in effect, an upside-down mouse.

(iv) Refer to 'Modems' in Section 2.5.

Solution 3.3

(a) (i) Refer to 'Magnetic disks' and 'Magnetic tape' in Section 4.2.

(ii) Refer to Sections 3.4 and 3.6.

(iii) Refer to Sections 3.8 and 3.11.

(b) (i) Magnetic tape − dumping file records during a long updating run of, say, stock records.

Magnetic disks − holding commodity master records for use in an invoicing run.

(ii) OCR − credit transfer forms preprinted with customer details and the amount due.

MICR − bank cheques.

(iii) VDU − input of customer orders in a mail order company.

Line printer − large-scale printing of routine documents such as invoices and payslips.

Solution 3.4

See Figure 3.9 (this form is not full size).

Notes on solution:

(a) This is obviously a simplistic form in that it holds too few commodities.

(b) The customer account no. is preprinted by computer in binary form.

Table 3.3 Keying requirements

(a)	6,000 × 20 =	120,000 characters
(b)	15,000 × 30 =	450,000 characters
(c)	1,200 × 60 =	72,000 characters
(d)	1,500 × 40 =	60,000 characters
(e)	8,000 × 60 =	480,000 characters
	Total	1,182,000
	plus 25% is	1,477,500 characters

Order Form	Fine Food Company Ltd.									
Customer Name	Salesman number	10	20	30	40	50	60	70	80	90
Gourmet Food Shops		1	2	3	4	5	6	7	8	9
Account number	Week no.	10	20	30	40	50				
____ __ _____ __ ___		1	2	3	4	5	6	7	8	9
Raspberry jam, 1 kg jar		10	20	30	40	50	60	70	80	90
		1	2	3	4	5	6	7	8	9
Blackcurrant jam, 1 kg jar		10	20	30	40	50	60	70	80	90
		1	2	3	4	5	6	7	8	9
Baked beans, $\frac{1}{2}$ kg can		10	20	30	40	50	60	70	80	90
		1	2	3	4	5	6	7	8	9
Vinegar, 1 litre bottle		10	20	30	40	50	60	70	80	90
		1	2	3	4	5	6	7	8	9
Corn flakes, large packet		10	20	30	40	50	60	70	80	90
		1	2	3	4	5	6	7	8	9
Escargots, 100 g jar		10	20	30	40	50	60	70	80	90
		1	2	3	4	5	6	7	8	9
Pickled walnuts, small jar		10	20	30	40	50	60	70	80	90
		1	2	3	4	5	6	7	8	9
Peanut butter, smooth $\frac{1}{4}$ kg jar		10	20	30	40	50	60	70	80	90
		1	2	3	4	5	6	7	8	9

Figure 3.9 OMR order form for Exercise 3.4 (timing marks not shown)

Solution 3.5

Keying requirements are shown in Table 3.3.

Keying capacity is $10,000 \times 30 = 300,000$ key strokes per operator per week.

Thus, number of keystations required is $1,477,500 \div 300,000 \times 2$ (to allow for verifying) $= 9.85$, say 10.

Solution 3.6

Table 3.4 shows the solution.

Table 3.4

Key-to-disk — annual costs
5,000,000 transactions × 15 digits at 10,000 keystrokes
  per hour = 7,500 operator hours
7,500 × 2 (for verifying) ÷ 1,500 hours p.a. = 10 operators

10 operators at £300 per month	£36,000
Key-to-disk with 10 keystations	£ 8,400
Additional magnetic tape unit	£ 1,200
	Total £45,600

OCR hand printing — annual costs
5,000,000 transactions at 10 per document = 500,000 documents

500,000 documents at £8 per thousand	£ 4,000
Optical reader at £1,500 per month	£18,000
	£22,000
Less cost of existing stationery	£ 1,500
	Total £20,500

Solution 3.7

Table 3.5 shows the solution.

Table 3.5

		Printer A		Printer B		Printer C	
		(sec)		(sec)		(sec)	
(i)	3 lines	0.900	3 lines	0.600	3 lines	0.720	
	3 carriage returns	0.600					
(ii)	3-line gap	0.090	3-line gap	0.030	3-line gap	0.180	
(iii)	8 lines	4.000	8 lines	1.600	8 lines	3.200	
	8 carriage returns	1.600					
(iv)	20-line gap	0.600	20-line gap	0.200	20-line gap	1.200	
(v)	1 line	0.125	1 line	0.200	1 line	0.100	
	1 carriage return	0.200					
(vi)	10-line gap	0.300	10-line gap	0.100	10-line gap	0.600	
	Totals per documents	8.415	5.130	2.730		6.000	
	Times per 1,000 docs	140 min		46 min		100 min	

Solution 3.8

Table 3.6 shows the solution.

Table 3.6

Existing documents		
Volume	= 1,000,000 × 15 in. × 10 in. × 0.004 in.	= 347 cu. ft.
Weight	= 1,000,000 × 8 lb ÷ 1,000	= 8,000 lb
Microfiche		
Volume	= 1,000,000 × 6 in. × 4 in. × 0.01 in. ÷ 270	= 0.51 cu. ft.
Weight	= 1,000,000 × 6 lb ÷ 1,000 ÷ 270	= 22 lb
Roll microfilm		
Volume	= 1,000,000 × 5 in. × 5 in. × 1 in. ÷ 2,000	= 7.2 cu. ft.
Weight	= 1,000,000 × $\frac{1}{4}$ lb ÷ 2,000	= 125 lb

3.16 References and further reading

3.1 Marshall, G., *Computer Graphics Applications* (Prentice Hall, 1987).

3.2 Watherworth, J.A., *Speech and Language-based Interaction with Machines* (John Wiley, 1987).

3.3 Yannakoudakis, E.J. and Hutton, P.J., *Speech Synthesis and Recognition Systems* (John Wiley, 1987).

3.4 Fallside, F. and Woods, W., *Computer Speech Processing* (Prentice Hall, 1985).

3.5 Poulton, A.S., *Microcomputer Speech Synthesis and Recognition* (John Wiley, 1983).

3.6 Witten, I., *Making Computers Talk: An Introduction to Speech Synthesis* (Prentice Hall, 1986).

3.7 Wilkinson, B. and Horrocks, D., *Computer Peripherals* (Hodder and Stoughton, 1980).

4 *Computer files and databases*

4.1 Business files

Business procedures, no matter how simple, call for the provision of up-to-date information in relation to the organization's suppliers, employees, products, customers, and so on. These are the 'entity sets' of the business, and each set has certain attributes associated with each and every entity in the set, e.g. a product has its selling price, labour cost, stock-in-hand, past sales quantities, etc. There is a host of terms associated with data structures, including many synonyms; Figure 4.1 shows the more common terms and the ways they interrelate.

In a non-computerized situation, each department in the organization has certain entity sets for which it is responsible. These are usually in documentary form and, as such, do not have the clear-cut structure associated with computer files. Nevertheless the same information about the entities is present, and is extracted and used in manual systems.

Logical records and files

As stated previously, in business there is a natural tendency for entities to fall into sets and for each entity to have several different data items associated with it. This group of data items can be regarded as a logical record. That is to say, as far as the user is concerned the data items are always closely associated with the entity in question and can be identified by using the key of the logical record. The contrast between logical records and physical data, i.e. the way a database holds the data, is discussed in Section 4.4. For the moment we will stick to the logical aspect.

A logical record can consist of any number of different data items associated with the entity's attributes. It may also contain several repetitions of the one data item but with differing meanings, e.g. the amounts spent by a customer in each of the past six months.

Reality	Information	System storage concept	Examples
The things with which the organization is concerned	Facts and figures about the things with which the organization is concerned	The way in which the facts and figures are held for use by the organization	A firm's customers, suppliers, employees, products, etc.
A range of entity sets	A range of entity record sets	Database or schema	All the data appertaining to the above
Entity set	Entity record set	File, logical file, record set or data store	A personnel file
Entity	Entity record	Logical record or record	An individual employee
Several closely associated properties of the entity	Group of attributes	Data item group, data structure or data aggregate	Employee's work history
Property of the entity	Attribute	Data item, field or data element	Employee's grade
Value of property	Attribute value	Data item value	Engineer, grade 3

Figure 4.1 Data structure concepts

Logical records appertaining to the entities within one set can be regarded as forming a logical file. The two principal types of logical record structures are described below. This section should be read in conjunction with the explanation of normalization and relational databases in Section 4.4.

File-record structures

Fixed length records

The simplest structured file is one which contains a separate record for each entity within a set, such as shown in Table 4.1. This applies to an office furniture manufacturer's stock file and has a record for each and every commodity held in stock. Each record in the entity set is of the same length because it contains the same data items for each entity, and corresponding data items are allocated the same space within each record. This is known as a fixed length record and, by definition, if the structure or length of any one record has to be changed, then all the other records must be restructured in a similar way.

Table 4.1 Example A

Entity set	All commodities stocked, e.g. office furniture
Entity	A particular commodity, e.g. desk, 'Executive' style
Attributes of entity (data items)	Catalogue no., e.g. B263 Selling price, e.g. £250.00 Stock-in-hand, e.g. 12

In this example the actual data item values are shown and the record is arranged to hold the maximum value of each of these for any entity in the set. The space allowed in computer storage for the data item is sometimes termed a 'field', but from now on we shall refer only to data items.

Variable length records

The need for variable length records arises for two reasons: (1) where there are differing numbers of data items associated with entities, and (2) where the data items are allowed to occupy different amounts of space (variable length data items). These are shown in Tables 4.2 and 4.3 respectively.

In Table 4.2 products do not all have the same number of consistuent materials, and therefore the records vary in length accordingly.

In Table 4.3, the names and addresses vary in length from one supplier to the next and, in order to avoid wasting space by allowing for the longest, the data items are allowed to occupy only the space they actually need.

A further but less likely reason for variable length records is where data items are nested within other data items. Table 4.4 makes the point, in that each product consists of several materials and each material comes from several suppliers.

Table 4.2 Example B

Entity set	All products manufactured, e.g. gas cookers
Entity	A particular product, e.g. 4-burner cooker in white
Attributes of entity (data items)	⎧ Product no., e.g. 9CW 418 ⎨ Material no., e.g. 38051 ⎱ repeated for each raw material ⎩ Material quantity, e.g. 15 ⎰ in the product

Table 4.3 Example C

Entity set	Suppliers, e.g. timber merchants
Entity	A particular supplier, e.g. Deal & Company
Attributes of entity (data items)	⎧ Supplier account no., e.g. 95026 ⎨ Supplier's registered name, e.g. A.G. Deal & Co., ⎪ Supplier address, e.g. Fir Tree Ave., Woods End, ⎩ Oakhampton

Table 4.4 Example D

Entity set	All products manufactured
Entity	A particular product
Attributes (data items)	⎧ Product no. ⎪ Material no. ⎱ repeated for ⎨ Material quantity ⎱ each raw ⎪ Material supplier no. ⎱ repeated for each ⎱ material in ⎩ Material supplier no. ⎰ supplier of the material ⎰ the product

If a systems analyst finds himself with logical records of this degree of complexity, it is worth making strenuous efforts to simplify them. In any event if the database is to be controlled by a database management system (DBMS), the logical files will be normalized (Section 4.4) as a matter of course.

Anticipating Section 4.4, normalizing means that, in effect, variable-length records are converted into fixed-length records by moving the repeated items into records of their own.

Data items

A data item, also known as a 'data element', is a piece of meaningful data pertaining to an entity, i.e. it quantifies or specifies one of the entity's attributes. In this context an entity is an artefact, person, company or other thing that is represented within the DP system. A data item cannot be sensibly split into smaller pieces, and it is important to give careful thought to their structures as they form the 'bricks' of a database and might need to be accurately specified for use in a data dictionary (Section 4.4).

As is seen from subsequent sections, data items are manipulated, structured, processed and stored in many different ways. And it is only through the processing of data items — from whatever source, that useful information can be output from a computer.

It is useful to categorize data items into three main types, as follows.

Static data items

These are non-changeable in their value and also largely in their layout (picture). Examples are account numbers, commodity codes and dates of birth. It would be only under exceptional circumstances that a static data item changed its value, most likely owing to an error having been discovered, e.g. a person's incorrect date of birth.

The layout of a static data item might be changed very occasionally, perhaps to bring it into line with other similar data items. An instance of this could be changing the layout of dates from the British format of DDMMYY to the American format of MMDDYY (DD = day, MM = month, YY = year).

Code numbers are generally static data items and also tend to be used as the keys of records (see 'Key data items' below).

Dynamic data items

These can expect to be updated at regular intervals as a consequence of activities taking place. A high proportion of data items are of this type and can be regarded as the lifeblood of business records. Examples include stock levels, earnings year-to-year, accounts balances and cumulative costs. In general, dynamic data items have a high level of activity although it is not impossible for a particular data item to remain the same for a long time, e.g. the stock level of a slow-moving stock item.

Changeable data items

A changeable data item generally remains the same for some time, i.e. it is not changed at regular intervals. Nevertheless it may be changed when circumstances enforce this, e.g. a taxpayer's code when his or her allowances are changed. Other examples of changeable data items are VAT (sales tax) rates, sales prices and women's surnames on marriage.

Key data items (keys)

A key is an identifier of a group of data items, i.e. a logical record is identified by its key. Strictly speaking any data item can act as a key at a certain point in time. It is, however, generally code numbers, such as account numbers, commodity codes and so on, that form keys.

A key may be formed from two or more concatenated data items if this is necessary for unique identification. Thus a stock record could need both the store number and the part number to give full identification. If only one of these two data items were present, only partial identification of the stock would be possible, i.e. either where it is or what it is.

A key might not necessarily need to provide absolute identification but only to the extent of the record being one of several or many similar ones. This would be true in the above example if we were interested solely in what stock we have regardless of its whereabouts, the part number would then suffice.

It is also possible for only a portion of a data item to form the whole or part of a key. For instance, the last letter − or more recently the first letter − of a UK vehicle's registration mark denotes its year of registration.

Designatory data items (designations)

A designation, otherwise known as a symbol or flag, serves to indicate the status or a characteristic of the entity, the record or the data item. Normally the designation needs only a small amount of space, e.g. one digit, and it is interpreted by the computer program so that the record or data item is processed in the appropriate way.

Example of an entity designation
Commodities might either be manufactured by the company, purchased from a home-based supplier, or imported. These categories could be recognized by means of an entity designation in each record, with a value of 1, 2 or 3 respectively.

Example of a record designation
A record designation applies to the record itself and not to the entity. If we wish to know whether a record has been referred to during a processing run, the value of a record designation is changed when this happens, e.g. from 0 to 1, so that a subsequent check can be made. An example of this could be in order to detect which commodities have had their prices looked up during invoice printing.

Example of a data item designation
The quantity of a material might be measured in different units from one material to another. Consequently a 'unit of measure' designation is useful, e.g. 1 = units, 2 = metres, 3 = kg, and so on.

Example of a data item status designation (field designation)
Analogously to the record designation, the data item status designation applies to the field and not to the data item itself. Such a designation could for instance indicate whether the stock level of a commodity was changed during a stock updating process.

Characteristics of data items

An important aspect of a data item is its layout or 'picture'. The layout is its structure in terms of the constituent digits, letters or symbols. It is convenient to represent this in a similar way to that used in COBOL. Thus a digit is represented by a '9', a letter (alphabetic character) by an 'A', and either of these or a symbol, e.g. an asterisk, by an 'X'. So a recent UK vehicle registration mark has the picture A999AAA. To save space in writing, a long picture is abbreviated by the use of a bracketed number, e.g. A(30) means a name of up to 30 letters in length.

Another characteristic of a data item is the range of values within which it lies, and of course during processing it is the actual value of a data item that contributes to the result. In this context value means any quantifiable or logical measure of its characteristic. Range means the span from the minimum possible to the maximum possible. For instance, a data item could be the commodity selling price, the values of which range from £10 to £50. Further explanation of data item characteristics is given under data dictionaries in Section 4.4.

For more realistic examples of file records refer to the case study in Chapter 9.

Categories of DP files

There are several ways in which DP files can be categorized but we are here concerned with the usage aspect rather than the technological aspect. The four file usage categories are transaction (movement) files, transition files, spool files and master files.

Transaction files

A transaction file is a logical file of records that relate to events or activities, e.g. orders received, jobs completed, goods dispatched, such files are created at regular intervals geared to the organization's cycles of activities, e.g. payments received each day.

Data such as this is known as source data because it derives from the source of the activity.

Quite often a transaction file is the output of a key-to-disk or other data capture system, and although by this stage it may have undergone a minimum of processing, it is still essentially the original source data.

One of the main purposes of a transaction file is to update or amend a master file, e.g. customers' payments update a sales (debtors') file. Another use for a transaction file is in order to analyse source data either entirely on its own or in conjunction with data read from another file, perhaps a master file. An example of the latter is a cost of sales analysis in which the sales quantities are in the transaction file and the unit costs are taken from a master file in order to compute the cost of each sales analysis total.

It is quite usual during the course of business activities for transaction data to stem from different sources or arrive at various times. This generally introduces a need for some sorting and/or merging of several transaction files before the true processing commences. An example could be stock transactions arising from several stores needing to be combined before updating a common stock master file.

After being used in these ways, a transaction file has served its purpose and is no longer needed except for data security purposes.

Transition files

Transition files derive from transactions files as a consequence of making changes to the latter. These changes may take the form of insertions, deletions and accumulations, including data derived from other files. A transition file is essentially a DP convenience rather than a true necessity and as such can take any form, sequence or layout that is useful in the DP routine.

The advent of more powerful computers equipped with direct access storage has tended to reduce the need for transition files. They are more common to magnetic tape systems, and so are gradually disappearing from the DP scene. Where they are still in use, they are of a temporary nature.

An example of a transition file could be the sales data mentioned under 'Transaction files' after its unit costs have been inserted.

Spool (output) files

Spooling is the process of writing data to a magnetic medium so as to form a temporary file prior to printing or, alternatively, creating a copy of source data before processing it. These processes are necessary when the relevant units, e.g. printer or processor, are not in a position to accept the data. Spooling also means that a copy of the output or input data is available for future reference. Spool files are normally disposed of after a short time, and in fact input spool files are virtually the same as transaction files.

Master files

A master file is a set of records relating to things that exist, i.e. entities, and consequently is of a permanent nature. Its constituent records must be maintained in an up-to-date state so that they can be used to provide accurate data for processing.

It should be pointed out that a master file is a logical concept, and that within a database its physical structure may be entirely different from the way the user regards it. This is of no great consequence to the systems designer, who, at this stage, should think of a master file as existing in a logical form.

There are three main processes that are applicable to master files, i.e. referencing (interrogating), updating and amending.

Referencing a master file

This process implies merely that the computer refers to certain records and makes a note of all or some of their contents without making any changes. This is a very usual procedure and referencing is the *raison d'être* of master file records. A given record may be referenced thousands of times during a single processing run, e.g., looking up the selling price of a popular item during invoicing.

It is an obvious corollary that a master file needs to be brought strictly up to date before being referenced.

Updating a master file

This means that each master record, as and when necessary, is brought into an up-to-date condition. In a payroll routine, for instance, each employee's record is updated as regards his 'earnings to date', 'tax paid to date', and so on, prior to being used for preparing his payslip.

With fixed-length records, updating entails altering the values of the data items in a record without changing its length. Updating variable length records tends to change their lengths because new data items are inserted and others are removed. This would be so for example if an additional material were introduced into a product. This change to the length of a logical record is more apparent than real if a DBMS is in use. The DBMS caters for the change but without necessarily needing actually to rearrange the record itself.

Activity ratios

Several ratios are available as measures of the amount of activity of a file. These ratios can be used to estimate the times taken to process the file. They are not defined absolutely, however, and various names have been applied to them. The reader should not be too disturbed if he or she finds different names in other books.

The ratios defined below are normally in relation to one processing run. They would, however, be just as usefully applied over a period of time provided comparisons are made between periods of the same length.

A record is described as 'accessed' every time it is referenced or updated, i.e. transferred from backing store to main store.

The principal ratios, designated (A) to (E), are defined below:

$$(A) \text{ Record hit ratio} = \frac{\text{Number of different records accessed}}{\text{Number of records in file}}$$

This ratio is never greater than one.

$$(B) \text{ Hit records activity ratio} = \frac{\text{Total accesses to the file}}{\text{Number of different records accessed}}$$

This ratio is never less than one (provided there has been some activity).

(C) Record activity ratio $= \dfrac{\text{Total accesses to the file}}{\text{Number of records in the file}}$

This ratio can be any value above zero (assuming some activity).

Ratio (A) gives a measure of the proportion of live records in the file. A low ratio indicates that many dead or dormant records exist.

Ratio (B) provides a measure of the level of activity of the live records.

Ratio (C) measures the average activity of the records. A high ratio means the file as a whole is busy but gives no indication regarding the pattern of this activity within the records.

Ratio (A) × ratio (B) = ratio (C).

Example using the ratios above
A commodity file comprises 5,000 records. During an invoicing routine 4,000 of the commodities have their prices referenced and this occurs a total of 8,000 times.

(A) Record hit ratio = 4,000 ÷ 5,000 = 0.8
(B) Hit records activity ratio = 8,000 ÷ 4,000 = 2.0
(C) Record activity ratio = 8,000 ÷ 5,000 = 1.6

Thus it is apparent that a fair proportion of the commodities are being sold but that the sales are thinly spread over the commodities within one invoicing routine, i.e. an average of only 1.6 sales per commodity.

Amending a master file
This means the insertion of new records, the removal of obsolete records, and changes to essentially static records. Amendment of a file is also referred to as file maintenance or housekeeping, but these terms also include the general tidying up of the file. The extent to which amendments are made depends largely upon the nature of the entities represented in the file.

Master files tend to fall into one of two categories — semi-static and volatile. Semi-static files are those that are really intended to remain in the same state for some considerable period of time. Volatile files are those that have a high volume of insertions and deletions. A typical semi-static master file is a commodity price file appertaining to a stable range of goods. A good example of a volatile file is a jobs-in-progress file: the jobs therein are perpetually starting and being completed.

It is useful in some situations to have ratios for amendments similar to those for access given above. We might also use a volatility ratio to give a measure of the amount by which a file is changing:

(D) Volatility ratio $= \dfrac{\text{Number of insertions} + \text{number of deletions}}{\text{Initial number of records in the file}}$

This ratio can have any value from zero upwards.

$$\text{(E) Expansion ratio} = \frac{\text{Number of insertions} - \text{number of deletions}}{\text{Initial number of records}}$$

The expansion ratio is a measure of growth of the file and may be any positive or negative value or zero.

Example using the ratios above

During a certain time period the commodity file in the previous example has another 750 commodities inserted into it and 250 obsolete commodities removed.

$$\text{(D) Volatility ratio} = \frac{750 + 250}{5,000} = 0.2$$

$$\text{(E) Expansion ratio} = \frac{750 - 250}{5,000} = 0.1$$

Thus the commodity range is quite volatile and tending to increase in size.

File processes

The principal processes carried out with files are described below; these apply not only to master files but also to transaction and transition files.

Sorting

During sorting, the records in a logical file are brought into the sequence determined by a key in the records. A computer is capable of sorting records into a 'nested' sequence, e.g. to employee number within department number within factory number. This entails multi-key sorting, i.e. the computer looks for several keys in each record and, in effect, treats them as a concatenated key.

In practice, sorting is often by a 'sort generator'. This is part of the computer's software and comprises several sophisticated sorting techniques that are called into use according to the parameters of the file and the sorting requirements.

The need for sorting has diminished with the demise of magnetic tape as backing storage. This is beneficial because sorting is time consuming and therefore expensive in terms of computer usage. Nevertheless there is always likely to be residual need for sorting owing to the wide variety of sequences demanded by business information. More is said about sorting in Section 5.3.

Merging

Merging implies that two or more files in the same sequence are combined into one file. There are two main aspects of merging.

File merging
Two or more separate files of similar records and in the same sequence are merged together so as to form one file. The records in the 'input' files need not necessarily be an exact match, and the 'output' file holds the sum total of the input records. An example of file merging is the bringing together of sales records from the various branches of a firm, there being initially one file per branch and finally one file for the firm as a whole.

Record merging
The corresponding records from two or more 'input' files, usually in the same sequence, are combined into one record in the 'output' file. It is usually the case that the input records all match according to some key, and non-matching records are rejected.

The input files need not necessarily contain similar records. An example is the combination of stock records with cost records on a one-for-one basis prior to preparing a stock valuation report.

An instance of non-matching files is stocks of parts in several stores: one part may be in all the stores, another in only one store.

Matching

Two of more input files, generally in the same sequence, are compared record against record in order to ensure that there is a complete set of records for each key. Mismatched records are highlighted for subsequent action.

An example is a file of purchase orders matched against goods received notes, presorted into order number sequence.

Summarizing

Records with the same key in one file are accumulated together to form one record in the 'output' file. Summarizing usually applies to a file presorted into a certain sequence and the resultant file is in the same sequence. It is, however, possible to summarize a non-sequential, e.g. random, file if it is stored on a direct access device. Records to be summarized are generally of a similar type. An example is the labour costs of a work-in-progress file in which all the costs of each job are summarized together.

Searching

This entails looking for records with certain keys or holding certain data and in some way making a note of these. There may not, in fact, be extraction of data from the records but merely a count made of their characteristics. Several different counts or extractions may be made during the one search. An instance is a search for and count of all ledger records with a debt balance of above a certain amount and the totalling of these balances.

4.2 Data storage media

Before studying the various devices and media used for the storage of data, it is useful to consider the requirements of any large-scale storage system.

Data storage characteristics

- *Low access time.* The average time needed for gaining access to the stored records must be low enough to enable the processing of the data to be accomplished within an acceptable time.
- *Storage capacity.* This must be sufficient to hold all the data needed concurrently during a process.
- *Interchangeability.* The storage device must be capable of being reloaded with the data required for a particular process.
- *Security.* The storage media must hold the data without fear of loss, damage or deterioration over long periods whether it is in use or not.
- *Transfer rate.* The data has to be transferred to and from the storage media at a high enough rate to meet the time restrictions on the work.
- *Cost.* The cost per unit of stored data must be low enough to make the system economical.

The above requirements have resulted in a variety of storage devices and media being utilized over the past 30 years or so. As with most things, it is a matter of balancing one requirement against another while keeping within the acceptable cost.

Magnetic disks

The main backing storage device at present in use for business purposes is the hard magnetic disk. This comprises a drive unit onto which one or perhaps two magnetic disk cartridges are loaded. The drive consists of a control unit and a spindle housing that rotates continuously when switched on. The cartridges are loaded by the operator so as to provide the data currently needed for the job in hand.

A cartridge comprises several flat disks (platters) mounted on a central spindle as shown in Figure 4.2. When mounted it rotates at high speed, e.g. 3,600 r.p.m., enabling data to be read from or written to it. The data is recorded magnetically

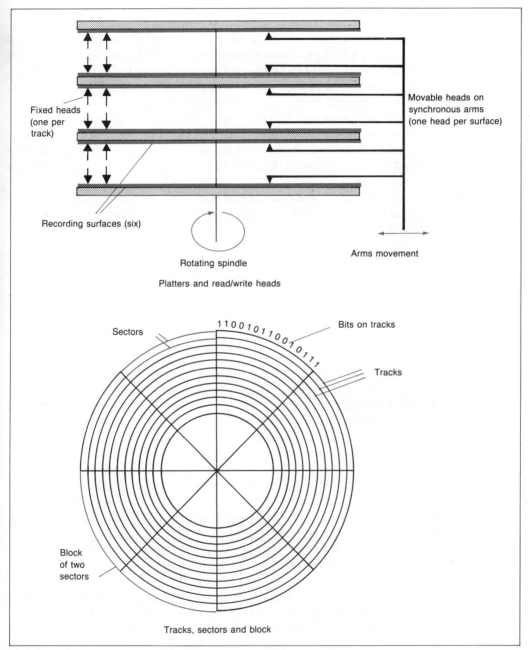

Figure 4.2 Magnetic disk cartridge

on both surfaces of each disk in the form of concentric tracks. A track has a
succession of bits recorded along it to represent characters in either EBCDIC
or ASCII code. Each track is divided up into sectors, often four or eight, and
these are read or written one or more at a time as blocks by means of a read/write

head. To do this it is first necessary to position the head over the relevant track, and as there is usually one head for each surface, all the heads are moved synchronously across the tracks. Once in position all the data on the equiradial tracks can be read or written (transferred) without further movement of the heads. This gives rise to the concept of a 'cylinder', i.e. a set of equiradial tracks, one per surface. More is written about cylinders subsequently.

Certain models of disk units also have a number of fixed read/write heads in addition to the movable heads. The fixed heads are positioned permanently over certain of the outer tracks, there being one head per track, so eliminating the need for head movement. It is therefore sensible to hold the most active data on the outer tracks.

A point of interst about conventional read/write heads is their close proximity to the disk surface. The head is supported aerodynamically by a cushion of air carried by the rotating disk. The principle, known as a flying head, allows the gap between the head and the disk surface to be only a thousandth of a millimetre. This distance is smaller than a smoke particle and only a sixtieth of the diameter of a human hair. It is mainly for this reason that conventional, as opposed to sealed, disk units have to be kept in a very clean atmosphere at all times.

Winchester disks

A particular type of magnetic disk, called a 'Winchester', comprises a number of platters (disks) permanently sealed into an airtight enclosure. This means that all dust is excluded thus permitting the read/write heads to be positioned even closer to the surfaces and so enabling greater recording densities to be employed. The higher recording density means that the disks have greater storage capacity and a higher rate of data transfer. Typical capacities of Winchesters are between 4 and 160 megabytes, and transfer rates from $\frac{1}{2}$ to $1\frac{1}{2}$ megabytes per second.

Another technical feature of a Winchester is the lubricated surfaces allowing the heads to 'land' when the platters cease to rotate. This virtually eliminates head crashes, i.e. the head coming into contact with the surface, so enhancing the reliability of Winchesters.

Winchester platters are either 14, 8, $5\frac{1}{4}$ or $3\frac{1}{2}$ inches in diameter with the smaller sizes coming increasingly into use for small business systems, in some cases in direct competition with floppy disks.

Because they are non-removable, Winchesters require backup arrangements, these are often magnetic tape cartridges or streamer tape (see below). In the case of $3\frac{1}{2}$ inch Winchesters, although it is not possible to remove the actual disks, they are small enough to allow the complete disk drive to be removed thus affording the equivalent facility to removable disks.

Where more on-line storage is needed than can be accommodated on one drive, several drives are connected to the CPU via one disk control unit (channel). An advantageous feature of a system comprising several disk drives is where the disk control unit can be freed from a drive during its rotational delay time. This means that it can transfer data to or from other drives during this period. This is known as 'rotational position sensing' and, in effect, means that several drives can be used concurrently.

Fixed disks

These are essentially all the same as interchangeable disks, described above, except that they are permanently installed in the unit. This gives them the advantages of being hermetically sealed and of being large in size. They are therefore of high storage capacity and are intended to hold both software and the database constantly. This arrangement suits companies that have one major ongoing application such as an airline seat reservation system. It is of course possible when necessary to load and unload the disks using streamer tape.

Floppy disks

Diskettes, generally called floppy disks, are single disks made of flexible plastic and permanently housed in an envelope or a rigid container.

The data on floppy disks is in concentric tracks (about forty) on the outer part of the surfaces and access to it is via a slot in the envelope. The most common sizes are $3\frac{1}{2}$, $5\frac{1}{4}$ and 8 inch diameter disks; the $3\frac{1}{2}$ inch disks have the advantage of a shutter that automatically covers the slot when the disk is not in use, thus preventing accidental damage to the disk's surface. Floppy disks are usually double-sided and, of course, the drive needs to be correspondingly equipped.

Both the drives and the floppy disks themselves are inexpensive, with the result that they are used extensively in personal computers in business and at home. The lower cost means of course that they do not have the capacities and speeds of hard disks; the range of capacities is from $\frac{1}{4}$ to 2 megabytes and transfer rates around 125 to 250 kilobytes per second. As with most technological developments, there is little compatibility between the various models even for disks of the same diameter. This is mainly due to their differing formatting, i.e. the way in which the data is stored and retrieved from the disk.

Logical data layout of disks

Cylinder

The fastest way of reading or writing records on disks is by minimizing the movement of the read/write arms. This is achieved by positioning records needed consecutively on equiradial tracks on the disk surfaces. A set of such tracks is termed a 'cylinder' (seek area), and this has the characteristic that its records can be transferred without further arm movement after the initial positioning (see Figure 4.3).

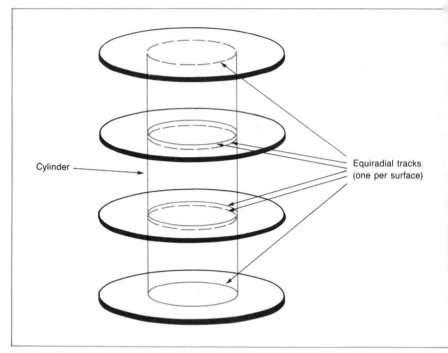

Cylinder

Equiradial tracks
(one per surface)

Figure 4.3 Cylinder concept

In general, records of the same file are located in the same cylinder(s). As seen from Figure 4.3, there are as many cylinders in a cartridge as there are tracks on a disk surface.

Block

A block is made up of one or more sectors and is the slab of data that is transferred to or from the disk surface in one continuous process. A block may be a complete track or a portion of a track depending on the disk model and/or the software in use.

The size of a block (bytes per block) is largely determined by the amount of main storage that can be set aside to hold blocks of data being transferred to and from the disk. A block must comprise an integral number of the disk's sectors.

Disk access times

The total time to move data from the disk to main store comprises:

1. The time to position the read/write heads over the appropriate track (head

of arm positioning time). This depends upon the number of tracks that the heads have to move across and, of course, is zero for fixed heads.

2. The time taken for the disk to rotate until the required block of data arrives at the head (rotational delay time), on average this is half a revolution.
3. The time to transfer (read or write) the data after the head has been positioned over the track and the data block has reached the head.

The head positioning time plus the rotational delay time is known as the access time. The rotational delay time is also termed 'latency' but there is some confusion here as some disk suppliers refer to the access time as the latency and others to half the rotational delay as latency.

The rotational delay time of a disk unit is determined by the rotational speed of the disks, and this also controls the data transfer rate to or from the disk.

Optical disks

Optical disks are a comparatively new development for data storage but their technology is fundamentally similar to the video disks used for entertainment. Mostly they consist of a single removable glass, plastic or metal disk coated on one side with tellerium or platinum protected by a layer of transparent plastic. The disk diameters are mostly between $3\frac{1}{2}$ and 12 inches and they rotate on a spindle in a similar fashion to magnetic disks.

The data is recorded in the form of minute pits burned into the tellerium coating by a finely focused laser beam. These pits are about one micron (a millionth of a metre) across and are in spiral tracks on the disk's surface. The minute size of the pits allows a high recording density, something like 40,000 tracks per surface. Optical disks hold between 0.2 and 5 gigabytes, this is about twenty times greater than magnetic disk cartidges.

The data is read by a low-power laser beam which moves across the surface and is reflected into a photo-cell. The presence of pits causes the laser beam to be amplitude modulated, i.e. varied in intensity, this is interpretable as a binary code. The laser unit is 1–2 mm away from the disk surface, so avoiding the problems inherent to the extremely close proximity of magnetic disk heads.

Optical disks rotate mostly at 1,500 r.p.m. which, allowing for the movement of the laser unit, gives access times of between 60 and 500 ms and data transfer rates of 0.6–3 megabytes per second. They are inherently more robust than magnetic disks owing to the protective layer, burned-in pits and large head gap. This robustness eliminates the need for air filtration and decreases the risk of damage caused by mishandling.

The drawback of optical disks is that the data cannot be erased, so making them non-rewritable. This means that when used for file updating the new file has to be written to another disk or a different area of the same disk. It remains to be seen whether this disadvantage will allow optical disks to become a serious competitor for magnetic disks or, alternatively to be used merely for archival and backup purposes. In the long term there are probably many uses for optical disks, especially in education, technology and document imaging.

A developing aspect of optical disks is the preparation and sale of general information for business use. Examples are government statistics, lists of publications, educational information, legal documents and medical information.

Mass storage media

The leading system is the IBM 3850 Mass Storage System. This loads a high-capacity disk system as and when necessary by transferring data from a number of 'data cartridges' housed in cells. Each cartridge consists of a 3 inch wide magnetic medium inside a protective cover. This is known as a 'mass storage volume' and is capable of holding 50 million bytes of data.

In order to load the disk system, the data cartridges are moved automatically from the cells in which they are housed. These may, if desired, be contained in a fireproof vault so as to provide a high level of physical security.

A typical system consists of 9,440 cartridges giving a storage capacity of 472,000 million bytes. This is just about sufficient to hold the basic data appertaining to every person on earth! Mass storage systems are used only by very large organizations, notably the US government.

Magnetic drums

A magnetic drum consists of a cylinder upon the surface of which data is stored in magnetic form in tracks (channels) running around its circumference, each track having its own read/write head. The drum rotates at high speed (about 3,000 r.p.m.) and as each record passes the track's read/write head, it can be transferred from or to the drum. The drum is mounted so as to rotate about either a vertical or horizontal axis, depending on the model.

A typical magnetic drum has 800 tracks each capable of holding 5,000 bytes, thus giving the whole drum a capacity of 4 million bytes. If the drum rotates at 3,000 r.p.m., the average time (half a revolution) to access a record is 10 ms (a hundredth of a second). This time is known as the latency of the drum. The rate at which data is transferred depends upon the rotational speed and the number of bytes per track. In this case it is 5,000 bytes in 20 ms (one revolution), i.e. 250,000 bytes per second.

The two main drawbacks of magnetic drums are their limited storage capacities (only a few million bytes at the most), and their non-interchangeability. They are also relatively costly per unit of data stored. The main advantages of drums are their low access times and high transfer rates. Nowadays they have almost vanished from business computers in favour of magnetic disks but are still used for applications demanding short response times.

Magnetic tape

The principal use of magnetic tape is now more as a backup medium rather than a primary method of backing storage. It is often used as a depository for disks dumped from fixed data storage, and the increased capacity of disks has resulted in the introduction of cartridge tape and streamer tape to replace the conventional type.

Conventional magnetic tape is in reels of up to 3,600 feet and is made of Mylar plastic tape, $\frac{1}{2}$ inch wide and coated with a magnetic material on one side. During reading or writing, the tape is moved from one spool to another in the same way as with an ordinary tape recorder.

The philosophy of using magnetic tape is that data is read from one reel and written to another. It is impractical to read from and immediately write to the same reel. A reel of tape is loaded on a magnetic tape drive (unit), and so as many drives are needed as reels during a processing run. Thus for simply reading or writing, only one drive is needed, but for updating a tape file, two drives are necessary.

The same principle applies to cartridge tape; this is housed completely within a small box, i.e. cartridge, which makes it more convenient to use than spooled tape. The cartridge has merely to be inserted through a slot in the drive, whereas spooled tape necessitates the loading and perhaps threading of two spools.

Conventional tape is densely packed with magnetic spots in frames across its width. A frame represents one byte and each bit within a frame is read/written by the read/write head for that bit position. The frames thus form tracks along the length of the tape, and normally there are nine tracks across the tape, i.e. eight data tracks and one parity bit track (see Figure 4.4).

Streamer tape

In contrast to conventional magnetic tape, so-called 'streamer' tape does not allow for stopping and starting between data blocks. Streamer tape is either $\frac{1}{4}$ or $\frac{1}{2}$ inch wide, and although having inter-block gaps, passes over these without stopping. The $\frac{1}{2}$ inch streamer tape has long data blocks, up to 16 kilobytes, and has gaps between these merely for technical, i.e. non-utilitarian, reasons. The principle of streaming is that the processor and the tape are matched in speed so as to attain a high rate of data transfer.

Method of use of magnetic tape

Since data is transferred serially to or from magnetic tape, the records thereon usually have to be in sequence. If the records on a tape compose a master file

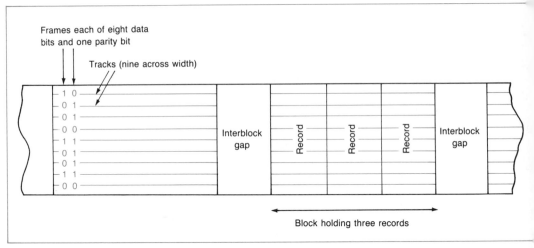

Figure 4.4   Magnetic tape structure

that is frequently updated by transaction records (held in the same sequence on another tape) the transaction records are sorted into the same sequence as the master file prior to the updating run. The updating process consists of reading the brought-forward master records from one tape, updating them, and writing them to the carried-forward tape.

A means of obtaining security is to retain the brought-forward tape of one run until after the completion of the next run. Thus, at any time, three tapes are in existence, i.e.:

- *Grandfather tape* – previous run's brought-forward tape, held for security.
- *Father tape* – this run's brought-forward tape (previous run's carried-forward tape) being read.
- *Son tape* – this run's carried-forward tape being written.

Dumping

Magnetic tape is often employed as a dump for the contents of the main store during lengthy processing runs. If trouble occurs, such as a hardware failure or an operating error, the run can be restarted from the dump point by reloading the main store from magnetic tape and reinputting the transactions that followed after the dump point. The computer's operating system takes care of this procedure.

4.3 Direct access file organization and structures

Storage and access modes

There are three principal modes for storing and accessing records on a disk or in memory — serial, sequential and random.

Serial mode

The records are stored contiguously regardless of their keys (if any). The sole way of accessing serial records is to search through the complete file starting with the first record.

A serial file is normally of a temporary nature awaiting sorting into a useful sequence and as such is likely to be also a transaction file. A serial file may be keyless but there are few instances of this is business. An example is the results of a survey of public opinion in which the respondents are anonymous and the results are merely analysed as an entirety.

Sequential mode

As with magnetic tape, direct access sequential mode normally involves accessing sequentially a file that is stored sequentially. The search for a given record continues onwards from the previous record accessed, examining each record in turn. This method is usually efficient for high-activity files but not for low-activity files. This is because the transaction records need to be sorted, which is time consuming, and little advantage is gained from continuing the search onwards if there are large gaps between the records accessed.

Sequential mode is often associated with a master file held in a certain sequence and updated by a transaction file sorted into the same sequence. A typical example being the updating of stock records held in part number sequence by stock issues and receipts.

Indexed-sequential mode

Indexed-sequential is a mode of storage whereby records are held sequentially and accessed selectively, i.e. selective-sequential access. Groups of unrequired records are skipped past, and this procedure is facilitated by the use of one or more indexes that are consulted prior to searching for a particular record (see 'Indexed-sequential searching').

If the accesses are known to be in the same sequence as the file sequence, the search for a record can continue onwards from the previous record accessed, as with sequential mode.

Indexed sequential files may also be accessed haphazardly, i.e. not in any sequence, without great loss of efficiency provided the index(es) are fairly extensive.

Random modes

This mode means that each record is stored in a location determined from the record's key by means of an address generation algorithm (AGA). There is no obvious relationship between the keys of adjacent records, and the only efficient way to find a record is to use the algorithm.

Random mode is applicable to master files and is unlikely to be of any relevance to transaction files. Thus a master file stored randomly could be updated by transactions in no particular order. Random mode is useful with low-activity files because it is possible to go fairly directly to a wanted record.

The main advantages of random mode are as follows:

- No index is required, thus saving storage space.
- It is a fast access method because little or no searching is involved.
- Transactions do not need sorting, thus saving time.
- New records are easily inserted into the random file provided they are not excessive in number.

The main problem with random mode is in achieving a uniform spread of records over the storage area allocated to the file. This problem is exacerbated if the file is volatile because the AGA tends to become less efficient when it has to deal with new patterns of keys (see 'Randomizing').

Processing modes

When amending or updating files held in a direct-access device, there are two fundamentally different ways in which this can be done; these are known as reconstruction mode and overlay mode.

Reconstruction mode

Reconstruction mode means that the complete original file after amendment or updating is written back to an entirely different storage area. The original records are thus preserved in their original locations and so at the end of the processing run two complete sets of records exist.

Reconstruction mode is only really practical with sequential or indexed sequential files so that all the updates or amendments are done in one go. The new record is then written to the reconstruction area after it has been fully updated. If a master record is updated randomly, the next update must be applied to the record in the reconstruction area. This introduces the problem of finding it unless the reconstructed file is an exact facsimile of the original, this is not always possible if the records expand or increase in number.

At the end of the updating or amending run it is necessary to copy across the unaltered records so that finally a full set is in the reconstruction area. An alternative approach with sequential files is to copy the unaltered records during the updating run. This means that wherever a gap occurs between two consecutive transaction records, all the corresponding master records are copied as they stand.

Reconstruction mode has a security advantage in that, in the event of trouble, the processing run is easily repeated because the original file is still intact. Another advantage in the case of sequential and indexed sequential files is that if records expand during updating, either in number or size, they can be accommodated in the reconstruction area without difficulty, whereas this is not possible if the records have to be written back into their original storage area.

Overlay mode

This mode is usually applicable to a file of fixed-length records that are being updated. The updated records are each written back to their original locations, and it is therefore quite possible that a record is overwritten many times during the course of an updating run.

This method has an inbuilt security hazard owing to the possibility of losing or damaging the original records. It also proves difficult if there is any expansion of records since they cannot then be accommodated in their original space, and so overflow methods are then needed. The security problem is eliminated by making a complete copy of the master file before updating commences or dumping copies at intervals during the updating run.

Reconstruction mode and overlay mode can, of course, be amalgamated within the one process by whatever arrangement gives both operational efficiency and data security of acceptable standards.

Direct access addressing

The key of a record not only identifies it but is also used to decide its storage location, i.e. address, either in memory or on disk. In some cases it is possible to form a unique address for each record. In other cases this is not practicable and so the key gives either a shared address or an approximate address for the record. Address (or location) in this context means a group of bits or bytes in backing storage that are transferable as a whole between the backing storage and the main store.

Self-addressing

Self-addressing is a straightforward method because a record's address is equal to its key's value, e.g. the record with key 458 is stored in address 458. Thus the file is inevitably stored in key sequence. The advantages of self-addressing are as follows:

- it leads directly to the wanted record;
- no indexing or searching is required;
- the key itself need not necessarily be held within the stored record — although it generally is.

The reason for the latter point is that the key is easily computed from the address, and so once a record has been found, its key is easily deduced. This need might arise when a file of records without stored keys is being printed out from storage along with the key of each record.

The drawbacks to self-addressed storage are as follows:

- The records must all be of the same (fixed) length or, if they are of variable length, the storage space per record has to be sufficiently large to accommodate the longest record. Alternatively, variable length records can be split into subrecords chained together (Section 4.3).
- Where records are missing from a set, i.e. those keys are not in use, the corresponding storage locations must be left empty in order to preserve the relationship between the key values and the records' locations.

Self-addressing with key conversion

This method is basically similar to self-addressing except that the key requires a little processing to turn it into the record's address. This leads to either a precise address, i.e. the record's position within a block, or an approximate address, i.e. the block only. Normally the former is possible as follows:

$$b \quad = \text{required block no.}$$
$$p \quad = \text{record's position within the block}$$
$$k \quad = \text{record's key value}$$
$$k_0 \quad = \text{lowest key value in the entity set}$$
$$r \quad = \text{number of records in each block}$$
$$b_0 \quad = \text{number of first block in storage area in use.}$$

Then $b = \left[\dfrac{k - k_0}{r} \right] + b_0$ where $\left[\ \right]$ means the integer value of the quotient,

and $p = $ the remainder from $\left[\dfrac{k - k_0}{r} \right]$ plus 1.

EXAMPLE

Suppose we have 4,000 records with keys 12,000–15,999 held 10 to a block from block no. 1,500 onwards. The problem is to find the location of the record with key 13,874.

Then $b = \left\lceil \dfrac{13,784 - 12,000}{10} \right\rceil + 1,500 = 1,687$, with remainder 4,

thus $b = 4 + 1 = 5$

The required record is therefore the fifth in block no. 1,687.

Ordinal numbers

If gaps occur in a range of keys, as is quite usual owing to entities having become obsolete, the records may still be stored continuously in order to save space. Each key must first be converted into an ordinal number, and this is then employed to determine the record's address by using self-addressing.

EXAMPLE

An entity set has keys 1,001–1,200, 1,351–1,600 and 1,870–1,950. Thus there are two gaps equivalent to 150 and 269 keys respectively, and an initial 'gap' of 1,000 keys.

To calculate the ordinal number of a key:

subtract 1,000 from keys 1,001–1,200 inclusive,
subtract 1,150, i.e. 1,000 + 150, from keys 1,351–1,600 inclusive,
subtract 1,419, i.e. 1,000 + 150 + 269, from keys 1,870–1,950 inclusive.

Thus key 1,915 becomes ordinal number 496, and its record's address is then found by using either self-addressing or self-addressing with key (ordinal number) conversion.

Matrix addressing

In some circumstances it is necessary to find the address of a record held within a multidimensional matrix of records, e.g. a table of sales records covering 400 products sold in twenty sales areas during each of twelve months. The above table therefore holds $400 \times 20 \times 12 = 96,000$ sales records. To find the address of a record, say, of product no. 1,328, in area no. 13 for the seventh month, we must convert each of these to ordinal numbers, as described above.

If the product's ordinal number is P, the area's ordinal number is A, and the month's ordinal number is M, the record's position within the matrix (table) is determined from the formula:

$$(P - 1) \times 20 \times 12 + (A - 1) \times 12 + M$$

This formula assumes that the records are organized in months within areas within products. A different but basically similar formula is used if the table is organized in another way, e.g. areas within products within months.

EXAMPLE

Suppose product no. 1,328 turned out to be the 151st, i.e. its ordinal number $P = 151$, and $A = 13$, and $M = 7$. Then the required record is in position $(151 - 1) \times 20 \times 12 + (13 - 1) \times 12 + 7 = 36,151$ within the table.

This type of problem is quite common in business applications and may, in fact, extend to more than three dimensions.

Randomizing (hashing)

Randomizing applies to randomly stored files, as mentioned previously. The whole aim and object of randomizing is to obtain an even spread of records between the available blocks. This is attempted by using an algorithm (AGA) i.e. randomizing technique, to operate on the keys in order to convert them into pseudo-random numbers. The pseudo-random number is then used to form the address of the record by one of the above methods. With randomizing it is inevitable that an address is shared because the algorithm is bound to produce synonyms, i.e. identical pseudo-random numbers, for different keys. An address is normally that of a block and so several records are assigned to the same block.

A variety of randomizing techniques have been devised, just two of which are explained below. Alphabetic keys are catered for simply by converting the alphabetic character into numeric digits before applying the algorithm. Since the whole object of randomizing is to obtain as even a spread of records as possible, two or more techniques may have to be amalgamated in order to achieve this. It is up to the designer to test the various possibilities on the set of keys taking into account the number of available blocks and existent records.

If the spread of records is uneven then there is the possibility of a block becoming too full and 'overflowing'. This is catered for by one of the overflow techniques explained later in this section.

Prime number division
The key is divided by the largest prime number below the number of available blocks. The remainder from this division is the relative block number, i.e. the number of blocks, after the first. If the key values in a set have no bias in their end digits, non-prime numbers can be used as divisors, but the keys need careful

checking first. Prime number division is a good method for use with sets of keys that have biased values but it is safer to analyse the remainders before adoption nevertheless.

EXAMPLE

If 2,000 blocks are available, the prime number is 1,999. Key 27,859, for instance, when divided by 1,999 gives a remainder of 1,872, and so this is the relative block number for the record with this key.

Extraction
The digits of the key that have the most random values are extracted from it and, after adjustment, form the record's block number. The most random digits can be found by performing an analysis of the digit's values prior to setting up the digit extraction algorithm. If digits are taken from the end of the key, it is termed 'truncation'.

EXAMPLE

The most random-valued digits in a set of keys are found to be the second, third, fifth and seventh; 3,000 blocks are available.
   Key 5,927,016 would therefore become 9,206; this is then multiplied by 0.3 in order to bring it within the number of blocks, i.e. $9,206 \times 0.3 =$ block no. 2,762.

Direct access searching

Whereas addressing determines the location of a record by using algorithmic methods, searching finds the record by scanning groups of records, an index, or both. The simplest method is to examine every record in a file until the required one is found (serial searching). This is prohibitively expensive of time for most files and so a short cut is generally desirable.

Indexed-sequential searching

This method was mentioned previously and a more detailed explanation follows. Assume we have a disk split up into cylinders and blocks as explained in Section 4.2. A cylinder index is created (Figure 4.5) to hold the highest key in each cylinder — of which there are four in this example. Associated with each cylinder is a block index holding the highest key in each block within that cylinder — there are five blocks in each cylinder.

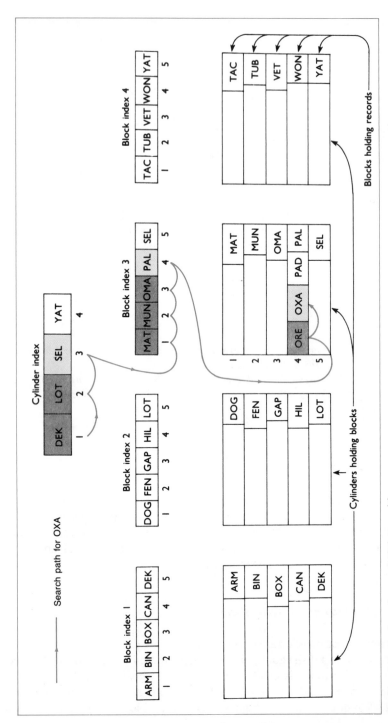

Figure 4.5 Indexed-sequential searching

When searching for a record's key in the index:

1. The cylinder index is examined key-by-key until one is found that is larger than or equal to the wanted key; this directs the search to the appropriate block index.
2. The block index is similarly examined, and the search directed to the appropriate block.
3. The block is searched record by record until the wanted record is found.

The records can be of variable length and need not necessarily be in sequence within a block since all records therein are examined in turn. In practice they tend to be in sequence and so other searching techniques, such as binary searching (see below), may be adopted for searching the block if it contains a large number of records.

The example in Figure 4.5 shows the search path for the record with key OXA.

Binary searching (binary chopping)

This technique may not always be suitable for searching through actual records since they are generally too widely spread in backing storage. It is, however, eminently suited to searching an index held in the main store. The indexes used for indexed-sequential are amenable to binary searching since in reality such indexes are much longer than in the example of Figure 4.5.

The keys in the index to be binary searched must be in sequence and form a complete set. As shown in Figure 4.6, the search starts at the midpoint of the index and then moves half-way to the left or right (down or up) depending upon whether the wanted key is less than or greater than the midpoint key. The key at this half-way point is examined and each move from then on is to the half-way point of the remaining keys. The search ends either when the wanted key is found or when no more keys remain to be sensibly examined.

Figure 4.6 shows the search path for key 81 from among fifteen keys in the

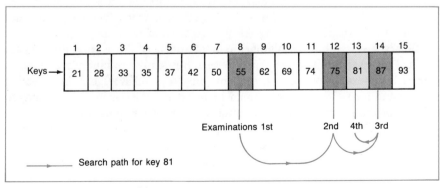

Figure 4.6 Binary searching

index. This example entails the maximum number of examinations of keys, i.e. four, and it can be seen that each move is half the length of the previous one.

In practice, the index is unlikely to be as convenient as this example because it is not always possible exactly to halve each successive move. Complete exact halving is possible only when the total number of keys in the index is $2^n - 1$, where n is any integer (4 in the example). The way round this problem is either to insert dummy entries to make the requisite number, or to simulate dummy entries in the computer program controlling the binary search.

The average number of examinations (comparisons) is $(\log_2 k) - 1$, where k is the number of keys in the index. This is immensely less than with a straight serial search of an index. For instance, if $k = 1,000$ the average number of binary comparisons is about nine as compared with 500 for serial searching.

Block searching

In this context a block is a subdivision of an index (not necessarily associated with a disk). A block is devised to contain roughly the square root of the number of keys in the whole index, e.g. an index of 900 keys would be sectionalized into thirty blocks of thirty keys each. It can be demonstrated mathematically that square-root blocks minimize the total number of index examinations needed to find a key.

The search is first through the block index to find the appropriate block and then through this to find the wanted key. The average number of examinations is $\sqrt{k}$, where k is the total number of keys, i.e. $\sqrt{k}/2$ for the block index and the same for the block itself.

Balanced binary tree searching

A binary tree is a relationship of keys such that the examination of any key leads to one of two other keys. This process is illustrated in Figures 4.7 and 4.8 for a balanced tree, i.e. one with a balanced spread of its branches. The binary tree is actually in the form of an index containing all the keys together with a directory showing the branches stemming left and right from each key.

Binary tree searching is suitable for an unsequenced file because the keys are chained together by the directory. The search is similar to binary searching in that each key examination halves the remaining keys, on average. When creating the file and index, the records should be inserted haphazardly as this tends to create a balanced tree and hence minimize the average number of examinations per search. That this is so is apparent if one constructs a tree for a string of keys in sequence.

Figures 4.7 and 4.8 show the search path for key LIP, i.e. via nodes, 1, 2, 6 and 7. Having found the node containing the wanted key, the node number is easily converted into the record's address.

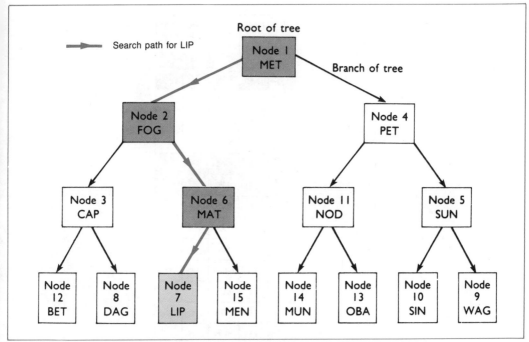

Figure 4.7 Balanced binary tree searching (see Figure 4.8)

An advantage of a tree index is that new keys do not necessitate the rearrangement of existing keys. Similarly, deletions can be made without leaving too many redundant nodes since these are eventually refilled with new keys. A new key is eligible for inserting into a node provided it is greater than all keys to its left and less than all keys to its right. Thus if the key MAT were deleted, it could be replaced by any key between LIQ and MEM inclusive.

A deleted key cannot be removed from the index without being replaced as this would destroy the continuity of the search. Instead a marker is inserted into the node to indicate its redundancy and invite later replacement by a qualifying new key.

Unbalanced tree searching

An unbalanced tree gives preference to the more commonly used keys by siting them in the nodes nearer to the tree's root. They are thus found more quickly during a search but the tree is inevitably unbalanced as a consequence. The simplest method of achieving this priority is simply to load the records into the file, and consequently the keys into the tree index, in descending order of frequency of usage.

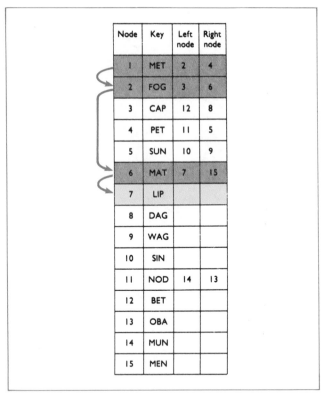

Node	Key	Left node	Right node
1	MET	2	4
2	FOG	3	6
3	CAP	12	8
4	PET	11	5
5	SUN	10	9
6	MAT	7	15
7	LIP		
8	DAG		
9	WAG		
10	SIN		
11	NOD	14	13
12	BET		
13	OBA		
14	MUN		
15	MEN		

Figure 4.8   Binary tree index (corresponding to Figure 4.7)

Parsing

When keys are inserted into an index, it often turns out that portions of the keys are identical between adjacent keys. There is then scope for saving index space by holding each group of common digits or letters once only; this is called parsing and is a method of data compression. As shown in Figure 4.8, the index is split into several levels and the search moves through the levels a digit or group of digits at a time.

Figures 4.9(b), (c) and (d) show three alternative search arrangements for key 5,278,391 through the keys listed in Figure 4.9(a); several others are also possible. In practice, the need for markers to separate the segments of keys slightly reduces the storage saved through parsing. The theoretical number of digits in each index is shown in Figure 4.9.

Key position estimating

Where a set of keys is fairly static, it is worthwhile analysing its content in order to be able to estimate the position of a wanted key. The search then starts at

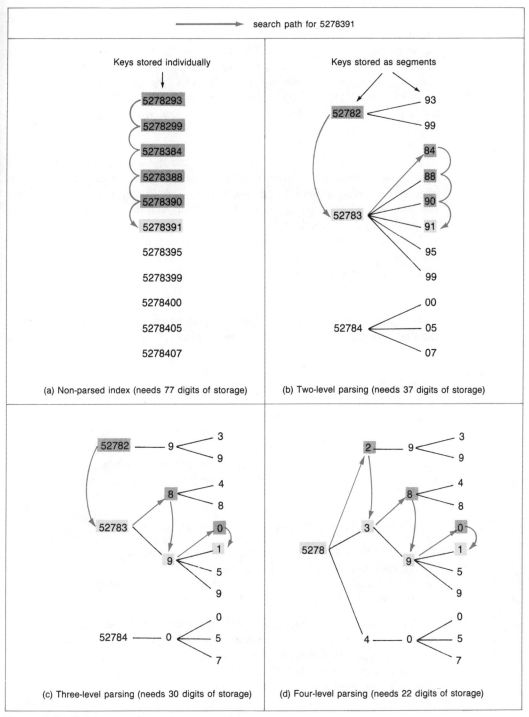

Figure 4.9 Parsing — alternative arrangements

this position and moves up or down the index a key at a time until the wanted key is found.

An example is in Figure 4.10. This table gives the fractions of the whole where the first letters of a set of surnames start. Thus if we have 80,000 surnames in a sequential index and wish to find CLIFTON, the search commences at the 12,720th, i.e. $0.159 \times 80,000$. If this turns out to be CLEGG the search moves forward a surname at a time; if CLOUGH, backwards. The point here is that in course of time the file will change and so the C surnames might not start exactly at the 12,720th.

A closer estimate of the key position is made if a double table is employed containing a separate set of fractions for the second letter of the surname. This is necessary because these do not concur with the first letter fractions. Strictly the table should hold 676 fractions, i.e. one for each pair of initial letters, but this is perhaps not worthwhile except for very long indexes.

If we use the table in Figure 4.10 (as it stands) in order to obtain a closer estimate for CLIFTON by using the first two letters, the calculation is based on the fraction at which L starts among the Cs, i.e.

$$80,000 \times [0.159 + 0.522 \times (0.238 - 0.159)] = 16,019.$$

This assumes that the second letters are spread statistically in the same way as the first letters, this is not really so but is near enough for practical purposes.

Overflow methodology

The methods of addressing and searching for records explained in the previous sections have merely mentioned 'blocks', the assumption being that a record is found in its 'home block'. The home block of a record is the one in which it is normally housed. If, however, it cannot be accommodated therein, it is directed to an 'overflow block' by one of a number of overflow handling methods.

Causes of overflow

With a sequential file the reasons for overflow are as follows:

- a variable length record expands during updating so that it can no longer be accommodated in its home block;
- a new (fixed or variable) record needs to be inserted into its home block but this has insufficient space left for it.

With a random file, overflow occurs for another, fundamental, reason. When records are distributed by a randomizing technique, it is a fact of statistical probability that, even though the algorithm is perfect, there is a maldistribution of records between blocks. This is analogous to a roulette wheel in that for a given number of spins some compartments receive more balls than others. A disk's blocks are equivalent to the roulette wheel's compartments, and the records to the balls.

In view of this unavoidable maldistribution, a practical way of minimizing

1st letter	Fraction at start	1st letter	Fraction at start	1st letter	Fraction at start
A	0	J	0.472	S	0.766
B	0.029	K	0.503	T	0.864
C	0.159	L	0.522	U	0.907
D	0.238	M	0.565	V	0.909
E	0.281	N	0.635	W	0.916
F	0.306	O	0.655	X	0.998
G	0.336	P	0.667	Y	0.998
H	0.379	Q	0.719	Z	0.999
I	0.467	R	0.721		

Figure 4.10 Table for key position estimating

the overflow of a random file is to load the more active records first so that they are the least likely to be directed to overflow areas.

Handling overflow
Since overflow is unavoidable, we must be prepared to deal with it. The simplest method, if the overflow is minimal, is to accommodate an overflow record in the block following its home block. The search then starts at the home block and continues through successive blocks until the record is found. This method soon falls down when the amount of overflow increases because the blocks become jammed with each other's records, so aggravating their own overflow.

Overflow chaining
Specific storage areas are assigned to overflow blocks either within the same cylinder as the corresponding home blocks (cylinder overflow area) or as one area for all overflow (independent overflow area). The former method has the advantage of time saving because no arm movement is involved in going to the overflow area. The latter method gains by saving storage space because cylinder overflow areas tend to be left partially empty.

Whichever method is adopted, the computer must be directed to the overflow block. This is achieved by incorporating the number of the overflow block within each home block.

Data structures

There is a considerable range of data structures with many variations on the main themes. They tend to be used more in system software and database management systems than in user-designed systems. Nevertheless the DP student should be aware of the meanings and advantages of the main data structures.

Chains

A chain is a string of records each of which is connected to another record by means of a pointer. The pointer is held within the record and provides the address of the next record in the chain. From the application programmer's point of view the chained records are contiguous because the system software finds the group of logical records related to the first one demanded.

Chains are useful when logical records vary considerably in length because they can then be made up of various numbers of chained fixed-length physical records (as mentioned for self-addressing). Chains are also advantageous for linking logical records with similar characteristics, e.g. the 'hinges' in Figure 4.11.

The extent to which the chaining of logical records is viable depends largely upon the volatility of the file. Deletion of records poses problems owing to the need to change pointers, and this is particularly awkward when chains intersect, i.e. contain a record common to more than one chain. File amendment problems are eased if a chain is two-way so that both the preceding and succeeding records have a pointer.

Rings

A ring is a string of records linked by pointers in a similar way to a chain but with the final record pointing back to the head of the ring. Rings may be either one-way or two-way, and may intersect with other rings.

The two-way ring in Figure 4.12 could apply to a ledger account, the head of the ring being the account identification and the linked records being transactions pertaining to that account. Although not shown, this ring could intersect with another ring applying to some other attribute of the transactions.

As compared with chains, two-way pointers are more secure since a break in the ring caused by a damaged pointer is overcome by going around the ring the other way. The records in a ring may also all be connected by pointers to the head of the ring. This is not shown in Figure 4.12 for the sake of clarity.

Trees

A tree consists of a hierarchy of nodes, the highest of which is the tree's root (the tree can be regarded as upside down). A node (element) may be a single record, a group of records or any other storage concept. Figure 4.7 is a simple tree structure. The main characteristic of a tree is that no 'child' (node at one level) has more than one 'parent' (linked node at the level immediately higher).

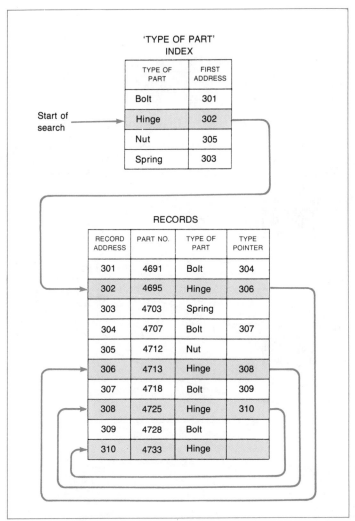

Figure 4.11 Chained logical records showing linking of 'hinge' records

A parent can, however, have any number of children — not just two as in the binary tree.

The node at the end of a branch is sometimes called a 'leaf' and the children linked to one parent a 'family'. A child is also known as a 'member' and a parent as an 'owner'.

Networks (plex structures)

A plex structure has its elements (nodes) linked to other elements at any level. A child can have more than one parent and be linked to its grandparent or higher

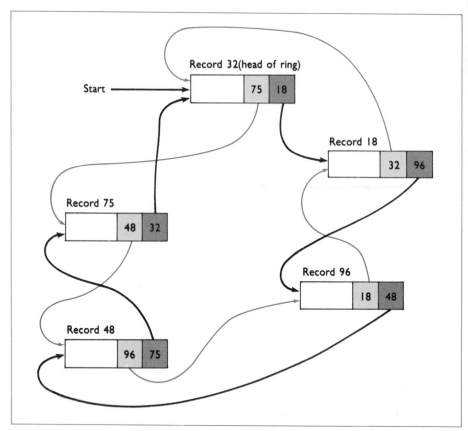

Figure 4.12 Two-way ring

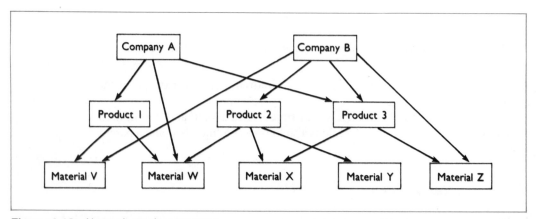

Figure 4.13 Network or plex structure

level. The hierarchical aspect ceases to have meaning in the more complicated plex structures as it becomes unclear as to which level is which.

Figure 4.13 illustrates a situation where two companies supply products composed of materials, and also the materials themselves. The main advantage of a plex structure is that it is possible to link together all the characteristics of any entity without these being held in the entity's record. Thus, in the example in Figure 4.13, it is immediately apparent from company A's record that company A supplies products 1 and 3, and material W.

A network may also contain elements that are mutually linked, with the result that all elements are of equal status. For example, companies trading with each other could be linked and so two such companies would have links in both directions if they sell to each other.

Inverted lists and files

Whereas a conventional record contains an entity identifier (key) together with the attribute values of the entity, an inverted list shows the attribute value followed by a list of the identifiers. A group of inverted lists comprise an inverted file, and this may be completely or partially inverted depending whether all attributes are included as lists.

Figure 4.14 is a completely inverted file for students, each of whom has three attributes — his course, year and sponsor. An inverted file is useful for rapidly finding the entities in a given attribute value. If more than one attribute value is applicable, the computer selects the entities from one inverted list and matches them against those from the other lists. If looking for the names of unsponsored BA Business Studies students, for instance, BAKER, GREEN and LLOYD are extracted from the left-hand list and matched against COOK, FOX and GREEN from the right-hand list. This leaves GREEN as the only qualifier. Inverted lists are incorporated into certain types of databases.

Attribute value tables

It is apparent from even the brief file in Figure 4.14 that attribute values appear repeatedly in both the normal and the inverted file. To save storage space in either case, an attribute value table is employed. As is seen from Figure 4.15 the record does not hold the actual attribute value but a pointer instead. The pointer indicates where the value is to be found in the attribute value table.

Thus, many records may point to one entry in the table, and this need not necessarily be in any particular order; also it can hold values of different types of attributes, as in Figure 4.15 in which courses and sponsors are intermixed.

Short-length attribute values, such as 'IBM' and 'Nil', may not be worth putting in the table and so are contained in the record itself in the usual way. This is also true for infrequently occurring values.

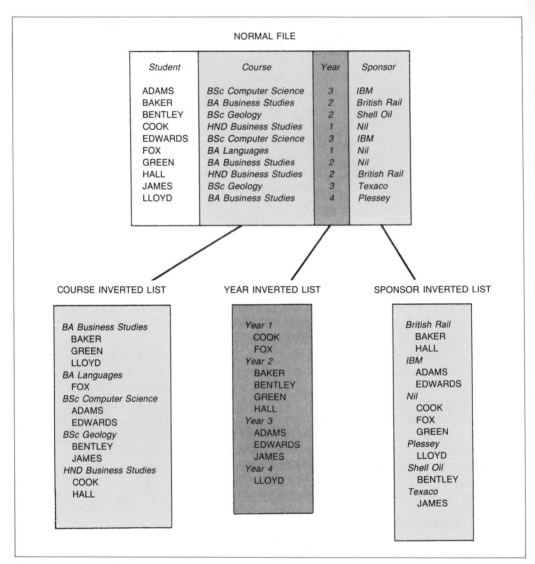

Figure 4.14 Completely inverted file

4.4 Database methods

Background to DP files

In the early years (1960s) of business DP, the majority of computers were equipped with magnetic tape, and later disks, to hold files. More often than not the files

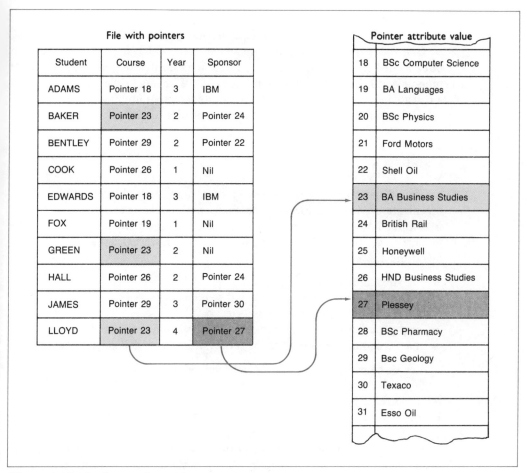

Figure 4.15 Attribute value table
Note: The red lines indicate Lloyd's course and sponsor.

were held sequentially and each one was complete in itself for the purposes and applications it served. Commonly, there were master files appertaining to payroll, sales, purchases, and so on. By and large, these files contained little or no redundant data, i.e. minimal duplication of entity values.

As more applications were added to the DP system in later years, the likelihood of redundant data increased. This could well be true, for instance, of master files covering stock control, production control and production costing. Data items such as material costs, operation times, component descriptions and batch quantities appeared in two or all three of these files.

Another aspect of the development of business DP is the introduction of management information systems. Management information requirements may, on the one hand, be straightforward, being based on data derived from only one or two files. On the other hand, managers may demand information of a sophisticated nature calling for the complex integration of data from several files.

Generally when new routines are added to the DP system, the files have to be expanded or modified. This reorganization means that the existing application programs using these files have to be amended. With large-scale DP, this involves a considerable amount of systems design and reprogramming effort.

As a result of these problems the concept of a 'database' came into being.

Databases

Briefly, a database is a collection of data supporting the operations of the organization. More specifically, a database entails creating and maintaining data in computer storage in such a way that it is usable for many purposes. In order to have an efficient database there are certain characteristics that must be met, i.e. it must:

- be substantially non-redundant;
- be program independent (data independence);
- be usable by all the programs;
- include all the necessary structural interrelations of data;
- have a common approach to the retrieval, insertion and amendment of data.

Let us consider these requirements individually.

Non-redundancy
Bearing in mind that redundancy is the duplication of identical data in the computer's storage, it may well attract certain problems. The three main dangers with redundant data are: (1) the probability of contradiction between the values of the data items in different files; (2) the waste of storage space; and (3) the problems of updating identical data items so that the master files are all equally valid.

Occasionally a minimal amount of redundancy is accpetable, such as when the need for data security or rapid access is paramount. If this is the case, it should be a definite decision so that the system can be planned to cope with duplicate updating and thereby eliminate the possibility of contradictory data values.

Data independence
This means that the data and the programs are mutually independent. That is to say, the data can be moved or restructured without the need to make alterations to the programs. Similarly an enforced program change does not call for rearrangement of the data layout.

These points are of great importance because if data independence is not achieved the programmers inevitably find themselves in a tail-chasing situation. Some DP staff have found themselves totally occupied in amending existing programs and file structures with the result that it has not been possible to introduce new applications.

Program usage
A database needs to be usable by not only all the existing applications but also by all foreseeable applications. These are ambitious aims,. but none the less a database must be open-ended so as to accept new sets of data items and changes to existing data item sets.

In practice this means that all possibilities as regards data usage must be considered from the outset. The compilation of data for the database needs to be far wider than that envisaged for merely the initial routines. In many cases it is impractical actually to store all the possible data initially, but it is nevertheless advantageous if its existence is known from the start.

Data interrelationships
These are necessary owing to the fact that the various applications use data in different ways. One application may demand a link between an employee's name and his pension contribution, another between his tax payment and his previous employer. Requirements such as these impose stringent demands upon the database's accuracy, security and flexibility, necessitating extensive use of the methods described in Section 4.3.

Common approach
This is in the interests of understanding and simplicity. Although application programmers are not concerned with the database's structure and techniques, a common approach simplifies the database control programs and facilitates the database administrator's work.

A helpful feature towards a common approach is the adoption of a data dictionary (see later in this section).

Logical and physical data

Logical data is the way data is seen by the systems analyst and the applications programmer. In the course of their work these people put together entity attributes and so form the logical records and files. The particular way in which this is done depends largely upon the future usages of the files and the need to maintain them in a completely up-to-date state.

Physical data is the actual structuring of data on the storage media. This is likely to be entirely different from the logical aspect of the data. Physical data independence implies that the physical storage techniques and the storage hardware can be changed without affecting the application programs.

The practical considerations of limited storage space and processing time tend to impose restrictions on the extent of data interrelationships that are possible. Even sophisticated databases have limitations and it is therefore important for the systems designer to get some measure of priorities in this respect. If necessary, several independent databases are maintained as a means of simplifying the interrelationships.

In order to achieve this latter aim it is necessary to have a software interface between logical data and physical data. This go-between is called a database management system (DBMS).

Database management systems (DBMSs)

A DBMS could be defined as a system that organizes the storage of data in such a way as to facilitate its retrieval for many different applications.

The characteristics of logical data are decided by the user's need for flexibility in processing data. In many business situations there is an unlimited range of demands upon the data; new problems and consequent new arrangements of data occur frequently. The characteristics of physical data are decided by the need for high performance of the computer. These two requirements tend to come into conflict and it falls to the lot of the DBMS to reconcile them as far as is possible.

It is apparent that DBMSs involve a high level of complexity in their design. The techniques described in the preceding section are employed within all DBMSs to some extent, and in many cases extended to a higher level of sophistication.

Features of DBMSs

Bearing in mind that a DBMS on a mainframe or minicomputer may be required to handle a number of different systems concurrently, e.g. batch processing, on-line enquiries and transaction processing, it is obviously a complex and expensive item of software. It needs to interface tightly with the operating system and in fact the demarcation between these two pieces of systems software is very blurred in some cases.

Another complexity that imposes demands on a DBMS is a distributed database. The DBMS must then be capable of enabling a user at one location to access a database on a distant computer by using his own language and system procedures. That is to say, the distance and differences between the two systems must be transparent to the user.

The newer DBMSs, including those intended for use with microcomputers, have a wider range of functions and capabilities. As indicated above, some of these facilities are closely tied to the functioning of the operating system.

Examples of these facilities are the following:

- Screen formatting for ease of data entry (see entry forms in Section 8.5).
- Record and file locking to make multi-user systems secure.
- Sorting records into any sequence.
- Creation of an audit trail.
- Logging of transactions.
- Control of user passwords.
- Acceptance of user-written programs for enhancing the DBMS.

- Acceptance of high-level languages as a means of making changes to the contents of the database.
- Validation of data.
- Parameter-controlled report generating.
- Dynamic creation and maintenance of a data dictionary.

Databases and DBMSs consist of three main structural types — hierarchical, network and relational, and in some cases these are amalgamated within one DBMS.

Hierarchical databases

A hierarchically structured database is a top-down or branching tree arrangement. Each data item falls within a higher-level data item and so on to the top of the tree. Thus if the hierarchical database contained data pertaining to company employees, it could be organized into factories, departments and employees. This method facilitates the rapid retrieval of data provided it involves coming downwards through the hierarchy, e.g. if the employee's factory and department are known. If, on the other hand, higher-level details are not known, then the nature of a hierarchical database necessitates a long search, perhaps examining every record.

Figure 4.16 shows this simple hierarchical structure, and Figure 4.17 is the way in which the corresponding records appear.

An instance of a hierarchical database is IBM's IMS (Information Management System).

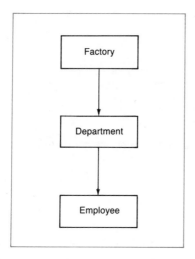

Figure 4.16 Hierarchical data structure

```
┌─────────────────────────────────────────┐
│  Factory–Department                       │
├─────────────────────────────────────────┤
│  Factory 1   Bristol                      │
│     Dept. 3A        Metals stores         │
│     Dept. 3B        Liquids stores        │
│     Dept. 11        Purchasing            │
├─────────────────────────────────────────┤
│  Factory 3   London                       │
│     Dept. 2         Security              │
│     Dept. 10        Costing               │
├─────────────────────────────────────────┤
│  Factory 5   Derby                        │
│     Dept. 1         Machine shop          │
│     Dept. 8         Sales                 │
└─────────────────────────────────────────┘
```

```
┌─────────────────────────────────────────┐
│  Department–Employee                      │
├─────────────────────────────────────────┤
│  Dept. 1    Machine shop                  │
│     2573       Watkins       £156.00      │
│     2593       Bates         £123.75      │
├─────────────────────────────────────────┤
│  Dept. 2    Security                      │
│     2588       Brown         £122.50      │
│     2655       Williams      £155.00      │
├─────────────────────────────────────────┤
│  Dept. 3A   Metals stores                 │
│     2591       Porter        £150.00      │
│     2672       Cox           £171.00      │
├─────────────────────────────────────────┤
│  Dept. 3B   Liquids stores                │
│     2633       Moore         £168.75      │
│     2679       Forbes        £190.00      │
├─────────────────────────────────────────┤
│  Dept. 8    Sales                         │
│     2569       Jones         £125.00      │
│     2580       Smith         £170.00      │
│     2618       Palmer        £178.30      │
├─────────────────────────────────────────┤
│  Dept. 10   Costing                       │
│     2625       Ambler        £205.00      │
├─────────────────────────────────────────┤
│  Dept. 11   Purchasing                    │
│     2548       Moss          £110.00      │
│     2703       Parker        £215.00      │
└─────────────────────────────────────────┘
```

Figure 4.17   Hierarchical database

Network databases

The above example is shown as a network structure in Figure 4.18; this is the same style as the structure in Figure 4.13.

There is a more direct connection between data items at the various levels

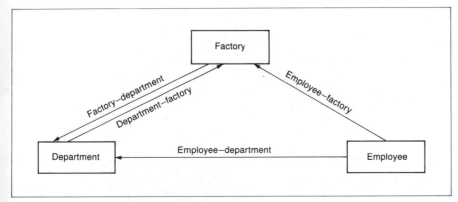

Figure 4.18 Network data structure

than with hierarchical databases. This is brought about through the use of pointers linking data at different levels.

In Figures 4.18 and 4.19 the directions of the arrows indicate the paths through which data is found. Thus in the way that this network database is constructed, it is possible easily to find an employee's factory and department from his employee number. It is also straightforward to find the departments in each factory and the factory that any department is in.

If it was required to ascertain which employees are in a particular department or factory, more points would be necessary.

A network database involves a more complicated DBMS and occupies more storage space than a hierarchical database.

Examples of network databases are IDMS and Total.

Relational databases

A relational database can be regarded as consisting of a number of two-dimensional arrays of data items, i.e. otherwise known as flat files.

The mathematical theory of sets upon which the concepts of relational databases is founded introduces some new terminology that we have not so far mentioned. Whereas up to now we have referred to a record, this is known in this context as a 'tuple' and the data items are called 'domains'. The connection between domains within a tuple is called a 'relation'. The point about using these new terms is that they refer to the database structure and not to the logical structure as seen by the user. For the sake of simplicity it is the intention to stick to the terms data item and record in this section.

Figure 4.20 illustrates the flat files of the relational database of the example. Although this diagram shows the department—factory relationship in department

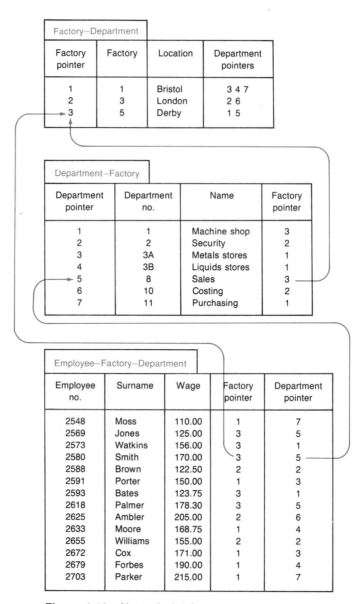

Figure 4.19 Network database

sequence, the DBMS could, if advantageous, also hold it in factory sequence. Much depends on the numbers of factories and departments and the consequent amount of searching and indexing involved, such as in Section 4.3.

Examples of relational database systems are DB2, Oracle and Ingres.

Factory no.	Location
1	Bristol
3	London
5	Derby

Department no.	Factory no.	Name
1	5	Machine shop
2	3	Security
3A	1	Metals stores
3B	1	Liquids stores
8	5	Sales
10	3	Costing
11	1	Purchasing

Employee no.	Surname	Department no.	Wage
2548	Moss	11	110.00
2569	Jones	8	125.00
2573	Watkins	1	156.00
2580	Smith	8	170.00
2588	Brown	2	122.50
2591	Porter	3A	150.00
2593	Bates	1	123.75
2618	Palmer	8	178.30
2625	Ambler	10	205.00
2633	Moore	3B	168.75
2655	Williams	2	155.00
2672	Cox	3A	171.00
2679	Forbes	3B	190.00
2703	Parker	11	215.00

Figure 4.20   Relational database

Normalization

In order to allow for the flexible use of data held in a database and to minimize the effect of application changes on the database structure, a process termed 'normalization' has been developed. It has been established that there are three main types of normalization, i.e. normalized relations. These are known as first normal form (1NF), second normal form (2NF) and third normal form (3NF). There follows a brief explanation of the meanings of these three main forms and of two lesser-used forms (4NF and 5NF).

Suppose we have several branches, each of which deals with a number of customers. Each customer has an account number and transacts purchases (debits) and payments (credits) from time to time. Each customer also has a name and

Branch no.	Account no.	Name and address	Postcode	Tel. no.	Balance	Transaction			
						No.	Date	Type	Amount
15	36895	Jones, 4 High St., Warwick	WK5 3MS	251—6734	215.93	228651	6.5.90	DR	65.82
						228704	9.5.90	DR	38.50
						228841	11.5.90	CR	15.00
15	36899	Todd, 18 Martin Rd., Stoke	ST2 7GM	158—3541	1265.83	227091	14.4.90	CR	90.00
						228604	28.4.90	DR	78.90
						228935	18.5.90	DR	57.83
17	35206	Cater, 2 Byron Ave., Ryde	IW7 2AH	393—0206	489.21	228711	9.5.90	DR	95.75

Figure 4.21 Unnormalized record

address, a post code and a telephone number, and the account has a current balance.

In completely unnormalized form this data might be in the form of the records shown in Figure 4.21.

1NF

To convert a record into 1NF the repeating groups must be put into records of their own, and so Figure 4.21 becomes as Figure 4.22. It should be noted that each transaction takes with it the account number to which it applies. The process of converting to 1NF in effect turns each variable-length record into several fixed-length records.

Accounts Details

Branch no.	Account no.	Name and address	Postcode	Tel. no.	Balance
15	36895	Jones, 4 High St., Warwick	WK5 3MS	251—6734	215.93
15	36899	Todd, 18 Martin Rd., Stoke	ST2 7GM	158—3541	1265.83
17	35206	Carter, 2 Byron Ave., Ryde	IW7 2AH	393—0206	489.21

Transactions Details

Transaction no.	Account no.	Date	Type	Amount
227091	36899	14.4.90	CR	90.00
228604	36899	28.4.90	DR	78.90
228651	36895	6.5.90	DR	65.82
228704	36895	9.5.90	DR	38.50
228711	35206	9.5.90	DR	95.75
228841	36895	11.5.90	CR	15.00
228935	36899	18.5.90	DR	57.83

Figure 4.22 1NF records

2NF

A record is in 2NF provided it satisfies the conditions for 1NF and also all non-key data items are fully functionally dependent on the primary key. In our example the name and address is dependent only on the account no. not the branch, i.e. the name and address can be found it we know the account no. only. Similarly, the transaction details relate only to the transaction and not to the account, i.e. the amount, etc., is known if we know the transaction no. only.

The 2NF is obtained by creating new records for the accounts and transactions as Figure 4.23.

3NF

A record is in 3NF provided it satisfies the conditions for 2NF and also no non-key data item is functionally dependent on any other non-key data item. In the

Branch–account relationships	
Branch no.	Account no.
15	36895
15	36899
17	35206

Account–transaction relationships	
Account no.	Transaction no.
35206	228711
36895	228651
36895	228704
36895	228841
36899	227091
36899	228604
36899	228935

Accounts details				
Account no.	Name and address	Postcode	Tel. no.	Balance
35206	Carter, 2 Byron Ave., Ryde	IW7 2AH	393—0206	489.21
36895	Jones, 4 High St., Warwick	WK5 3MS	251—6734	215.93
36899	Todd, 18 Martin Rd., Stoke	ST2 7GM	158—3541	1265.83

Transactions details			
Transaction no.	Date	Type	Amount
227091	14.4.90	CR	90.00
228604	28.4.90	DR	78.90
228651	6.5.90	DR	65.82
228704	9.5.90	DR	38.50
228711	9.5.90	DR	95.75
228841	11.5.90	CR	15.00
228935	18.5.90	DR	57.83

Figure 4.23 2NF records

example the post code and telephone no. are dependent on the name and address, i.e. if we know the address, the post code is known, and if we know the name and address, the telephone number is known.

To convert into 3NF these data items are put into another record as Figure 4.24.

It is apparent from the normalization procedures described above that relational databases, although straightforward in principle, can be cumbersome to store and organize. They involve the creation of virtual files, i.e. replicated data of a temporary nature that is transparent to the user. This replication causes them to occupy a large amount of storage.

Branch–account relationships

Branch no.	Account no.
15	36895
15	36899
17	35206

Account–transactions relationships

Account no.	Transaction no.
35206	228711
36895	228651
36895	228704
36895	228841
36899	227091
36899	228604
36899	228935

Accounts details

Account no.	Name and address	Balance
35206	Carter, 2 Byron Ave., Ryde	489.21
36895	Jones, 4 High St., Warwick	215.93
36899	Todd, 18 Martin Rd., Stoke	1265.83

Names and Address Details

Name and address	Postcode	Tel. no.
Carter, 2 Byron Ave., Ryde	IW7 2AH	393—0206
Jones, 4 High St., Warwick	WK5 3MS	251—6734
Todd, 18 Martin Rd., Stoke	ST2 7GM	158—3541

Transactions Details

Transaction no.	Date	Type	Amount
227091	14.4.90	CR	90.00
228604	28.4.90	DR	78.90
228651	6.5.90	DR	65.82
228704	9.5.90	DR	38.50
228711	9.5.90	DR	95.75
228841	11.5.90	CR	15.00
228935	18.5.90	DR	57.83

Figure 4.24 3NF records

4NF and 5NF

It is possible in some cases to continue the process of normalization to 4NF and 5NF. 4NF is relevant to a situation where the key data item has multi-valued dependencies, i.e. several things of the same type are related to it. For instance, a name and address may have more than one telephone number. In order to be in 4NF, the name and address details in Figure 4.24 have to be split into a record for each telephone number.

In doing this the post code is replicated in these records. 5NF avoids this by puting the post codes and the telephone numbers into separate records each linked to the name and address.

Data dictionaries

A data dictionary (DD) is a store of information that describes and specifies the characteristics of each piece of data used in a system. In other words it is an electronic glossary defining each of the data items incorporated in the whole system. A DD may also include definitive descriptions of processes within the system.

The main point about having a DD is that experience has shown time and time again that data easily becomes ambiguous. People are inclined to give different names to the same thing, and the same name to two or more different things. For instance, one person may refer to the 'stock number' and another person calls it the 'commodity code'. Similarly programmers are apt to employ different names for the same data item in their programs, e.g. STKNO and COMCDE.

A DD attempts to obviate these problems by pinning data down according to clear definitions. Each piece of data has the following characteristics ascribed to it:

Name meaningful, standardized and preferably constructed in a program-defined form such as in COBOL, e.g. STOCK-NO.
Description a brief explanation of the meaning of the data item.
Aliases a list of alternative names that have been used for the data item, e.g. STKNO as an alias of STOCK-NO mentioned above.
Related data it may be useful to draw attention to data that is closely connected with or has a similar name to the data item although it is not an alias, e.g. VAT status and VAT rate.
Range of values a data item may have a continuous range of values, in which case only its maximum and minimum values are included. Alternatively, the values may be discrete, e.g. discount rates of 0, 10 and 20 per cent only, or one fixed value, e.g. a fixed price. The other possibility is a coded value, e.g. 10 = Bristol, 11 = Southampton, and so on.
Layout this is the 'picture' of the data item as it exists outside the computer

and so is conveniently specified and held in the form explained under 'picture' in Section 7.4.

Encoding   an indication of the form in which the data is encoded, e.g. 1 = binary, 2 = ASCII, 3 = EBDIC and so on.

Editing   a specification of any editing or special checks that the data item must undergo, especially on input, these are discussed under data validation in Section 8.4.

Other characteristics of a data item that may be included in a DD are as follows:

Ownership   the department that initiates the data item.
Users   the departments that refer to it.
Systems and programs   that reference or update it.
Security and privacy   restraints imposed upon its use.

These latter features take the DD towards becoming a data encyclopaedia (see below).

Data dictionaries come in a variety of types: some are stand-alone, others relate to a certain DBMS. Small DDs of up to a few hundred items can be maintained manually using a card index system. Larger dictionaries are automated, generally through the employment of a DD package (Section 5.4). An automated dictionary has the advantage of being able to provide a variety of useful listings and reports. Examples are a full alphabetic list of all items, a selected list based on the first few letters of the name, a search facility for letter groups, i.e. to find items whose names are not completely known. Most DBMSs have an automated DD incorporated into them.

The work of creating and maintaining the DD falls upon the data administrator – if such a post exists, and in any case it is important that all DD entries are channelled through one person.

It is also possible that the DD is kept up-to-date by the software using it, this is called an active DD.

Reference 4.16 gives further information on DDs.

EXAMPLE OF DATA DICTIONARY

This example covers one data item taken from the case study in Chapter 9, i.e. 'article number'. In practice the information below would be entered on special forms that are part of the system design but are merely listed here for the sake of brevity.

Name   Article number, program form ART-NO.
Description   A number unique to each and every individual article. Even though two or more articles are identical, they still have their own article numbers.
Aliases   Article no., AN.

Related data
1. Article description/description — a brief non-definitive descriptive name for general information only.
2. Category — each article falls into one of nine categories (see layout).
3. Manufacturer — each article in category 2 (watches) is from one of ten manufacturers including an 'others' group, i.e. from a smaller manufacturer not specifically nominated (see layout).

Range of values Minimum value 10000, maximum value 99999.

Layout Five numeric digits only, i.e. picture is 99999.

The first digit denotes the broad category (numbered 1–9) into which the article falls.

The second digit of category 2 (watches) denotes the manufacturer.

Encoding ASCII.

Editing Limits (range) check in every input program. The limits are reassigned from time to time according to current usage.

Ownership Owned and allocated by the Goods Receiving Section.

Users All departments.

Systems and programs Used in every process and program in the stock control and sales analysis processes.

Security and privacy Creation and allocation of article numbers is restricted to the Goods Receiving Section only.

Data encyclopaedias

An evolvement of the DD is the data encyclopaedia (DE). This is a wider concept that includes additional information to that described above. This information is aimed at specifying the data item's usage, and so it includes details of the processes, data flows and data stores (files) associated with it.

A DE is a combination of the following:

- Document specification form (Figure 6.3, Section 6.4)
- Data usage chart (Figure 6.4, Section 6.4)
- Output analysis chart (Figure 7.5, Section 7.3)
- Logical file record specification (Figure 7.7, Section 7.4)
- Data item utilization chart (Figure 7.8, Section 7.4)

4.5 Exercises

Exercise 4.1 File organization

Describe three different methods of file organization, outlining the advantages and disadvantages of each method. Also, for each method, give a typical application where a particular method of file organization may be used in preference to the other methods.

(ICSA part 2, Inf. sys., June 1987)

Exercise 4.2 Database/indexed-sequential files

(a) Describe the information processing requirements that led to the development of database systems.
(b) Explain the basic principles of indexed-sequential files and their implementation.
(c) Describe briefly an application where indexed-sequential files would be more suitable than a database system.

(BCS part 1, Gen. paper II, April 1986)

Exercise 4.3 Searching techniques

Distinguish carefully between the following searching techniques

 (i) linear
 (ii) binary chop
(iii) hashing
(iv) binary tree

by informally describing the algorithms and by deriving relative time and space complexities in each case.

(BCS part II, Option D1, April 1986)

Exercise 4.4 Binary tree searching

(a) Create a binary tree index for the keys as under, entering them in the order shown.
    58, 77, 94, 40, 49, 45, 63, 18,·72, 75, 25, 76.
(b) Delete keys 63 and 40, insert further keys 70, 46, 33 and 91, reconstruct the index.
(c) In what order should the 12 keys in (a) be entered to make the tree more balanced?

Exercise 4.5 Normalizing

A company manufactures products by assembling components together. The components are either bought-out, i.e. fully completed, or made-in from raw materials. The latter take various forms such as sheets, liquids, bars, etc. Each form has a unit-of-measure (UOM) code, i.e. 1 = metres, 2 = square metres, 3 = kilograms, 4 = litres. Components have a designation to indicate whether bought-out (= 1) or made-in (= 2).

The company's production planning file holds the data items shown below. Transcribe these into 3NF and list the figures as per Figure 4.24. They are deliberately unordered.

Product no., description, assembly time

Component no., description, quantity per product, supplier no., supplier name, BO/MI designation ⎱ repeated for each component in product

Raw material no., description, quantity per component, supplier no., supplier name, UOM code ⎱ repeated for each made-in raw material in component

Product no. 325 is a Trolley and contains components B1378 (six off), M496 (one off) and B2284 (four off), and takes a time of 0.35 to assemble. B1378 is supplied by AGD Ltd, B2284 by White & Co., M496 is made-in from three raw materials, i.e. 0.6 square metres of sheet steel (no. 43750), 1.5 metres of steel bar (no. 40605) and 1.2 litres of black paint (no. 32809).

All steel materials are supplied by VG Steel Ltd (no. 4381), all paint by Premier Paint Co. (no. 2659).

B2284 is a 6 inch wheel, White & Co.'s no. is 1126, M496 is a chassis, B1378 is a bracket, AGD's no. is 1759.

Exercise 4.6 Database terminology

Within the context of the database explain what is meant by each of the following terms:

(a) data independence;
(b) data integrity;
(c) data redundancy;
(d) data security.

(ICSA part 4, Man. sys., June 1988)

4.6 Outline solutions to exercises

Solution 4.1

The technicalities of the three methods below are described in Section 4.3.

(a) Indexed-sequential
Advantages:
- copes with variable length records,
- fairly fast searching,
- deletion of a record does not affect searching provided its key is left in the index.

Disadvantages:
- indexes occupy considerable memory,
- new records are insertable only if space is left in the blocks,
- records must be stored sequentially and need reorganizing when blocks overflow.

Application: A payroll master file applicable to a fairly static set of workers. The payroll would probably be processed in the same sequence as the file, and minimal alterations to the range of records, i.e. low volatility.

(b) Binary tree

Advantages
- records stored unordered but need sorting for sequential printout,
- rapid search for wanted record,
- new records easily added to index and file.

Disadvantages:
- needs frequent reorganization if file is volatile,
- index occupies a very large amount of main store,
- keys of deleted records must be left in the index, this is more of a problem than with indexed-sequential owing to the much greater number of keys in the index.

Application: A reservations file such as hotel rooms or airline seats. With these the file grows steadily, is interrogated frequently, and is abandoned at the end of the period.

(c) Binary chopping

Advantages:
- rapid search of either the index or the file,
- handles variable length records provided the index holds addresses of records.

Disadvantages:
- index occupies considerable memory,
- keys stored sequentially in index and records must also be in sequence unless index holds record addresses,
- arrangements needed for unsuitable number of keys,
- does not facilitate insertion of records.

Application: A relatively small file to be processed entirely in main store and undergoing changes only at predetermined intervals. This might be a product master file of a firm offering a fixed range of goods during the year.

Solution 4.2

(a) Refer to 'Background to DP files' in Section 4.4.
(b) Refer to 'Indexed-sequential mode' and 'Indexed-sequential searching' in Section 4.3.
(c) There is not a great deal of advantage in having a database system where only the one main file is involved. Thus an accounts payable file appertaining to a fairly static set of suppliers would be catered for adequately by an indexed-sequential file.

Solution 4.3

(i) Linear searching means the same as serial searching, i.e. starting at the beginning and examining each item (key or record) in turn. If the items are wanted sequentially and they are in this sequence, the search can continue from the last item found. An unordered (no sequence) set must always be searched from its beginning.

This method takes a large amount of time but no extra storage, only the records or keys themselves, i.e. no indexes.

(ii)–(iv) Refer to Section 4.3 for algorithms, the space-time characteristics are shown in Figure 4.25.

Method	Time	Space overheads	Comments
Linear	Large	Small	No index
Binary chop-indexed	Small	Fairly large	
Binary chop-unindexed	Fairly large	Small	
Hash	Very small	Fairly large	Space needed for insertions and overflow
Binary tree	Small	Fairly large	Large index

Figure 4.25   Characteristics of methods of searching

Solution 4.4

(a) and (b), see Figure 4.26
(c) There are numerous possible orders for the keys, such as 63, 76, 45, 25, 58, 75, 77, 94, 18, 40, 72, 49.

This order gives four levels as against six in the original order. Construct a tree diagram to prove this.

Solution 4.5

Refer to Figure 4.27.

Solution 4.6

(a) Refer to 'Data independence' in Section 4.4.
(b) Data integrity refers to the necessity of maintaining the contents of the databse or files in an accurate, complete and up-to-date state.
(c) Data redundancy means that certain data items are held in the database more than once, i.e. their values appear in several places. Normalization in relational databases removes redundancy.
(d) Data security is intended to preserve data against accidental or wilful damage or loss. It is a wide subject covered briefly in Section 7.7.

Node no.	Key	Left node no.	Right node no.
1	58	4	2
2	77	7	3
3	94		
4	40	8	5
5	49	6	
6	45		
7	63		9
8	18		11
9	72		10
10	75		12
11	25		
12	76		

(a)

Node no.	Key	Left node no.	Right node no.
1	58	4	2
2	77	7	3
3	94	14	
4	33	8	5
5	49	6	
6	45		13
7	70		9
8	18		11
9	72		10
10	75		12
11	25		
12	76		
13	46		
14	91		

(b)

Figure 4.26 Binary tree indexes of Exercise 4.4

4.7 References and further reading

4.1 Johnson, L.F. and Cooper, R.H., *File Techniques for Data Base Organisation in COBOL* (Prentice Hall, 1986).
4.2 Bamford, C. and Curran, P.F., *Data Structures, Files and Databases* (Macmillan, 1987).
4.3 Tharp, A.L., *File Organization and Processing* (John Wiley, 1988).
4.4 Fernandez, J.N. and Ashley, R., *Tape and Files* (John Wiley, 1985).
4.5 Martin, J. and Chapman, K.K., *DB2: Concepts, Design and Programming* (Prentice Hall, 1989).
4.6 Loomis, M.E.S., *Data Management and File Structures* (Prentice Hall, 1989).

Product details

Product no.	Description	Assy. time
325	Trolley	0.35

Product–component relationships

Product no.	Component no.	Quantity per product
325	B1375	6
325	B2284	4
325	M496	1

Components details

Component no.	Description	Supplier no.	BO/MI des.
B1375	Bracket	1759	1
B2284	6 inch wheel	1126	1
M496	Chassis	—	2

Suppliers details

Supplier no.	Supplier name
1126	White & Co.
1759	AGD Ltd.
2659	VG Steel Ltd.
4381	Premier Paint Co.

Component–raw material relationships

Component no.	Raw material no.	Quantity per component
M496	32809	1.2
M496	40605	1.5
M496	43750	0.6

Raw materials details

Raw material no.	Description	Supplier no.	UOM code
22809	Black paint	2659	4
40605	Steel bar	4381	1
43750	Steel sheet	4381	2

Figure 4.27 · 3NF records of Exercise 4.5

4.7   Gillenson, M.L., *Database: Step-by-Step* (John Wiley, 1985).

4.8   Peterson, W.W. and Lew, A., *File Design and Programming* (John Wiley, 1986).

4.9   Atre, S., *Data Base: Structured Techniques* (John Wiley, 1988).

4.10 Mayne, A., *Data Dictionary Systems − A Technical Review* (NCC, 1984).

4.11 Mayne, A. and Wood, M.B., *Introducing Relational Database* (NCC, 1983).

4.12 Hughes, J.G., *Database Technology* (Prentice Hall, 1988).

4.13 Tanenbaum, A.M. and Augenstein, M.J., *Data Structures Using Pascal* (Prentice Hall, 1986).

4.14 Harbron, T.R., *File Systems* (Prentice Hall, 1988).

4.15 Inmon, W.H. and Bird, T.J., *The Dynamics of Data Base* (Prentice Hall, 1987).

4.16 Kendall, K.E. and Kendall, J.E., *Systems Analysis and Design* (Prentice Hall, 1988).

4.17 Stanczyk, S., *Theory and Practice of Relational Databases* (Pitman, 1989).

4.18 Date, C.J., *An Introduction to Database Systems* (Addison Wesley, 1986).

4.19 Date, C.J., *Relational Databases: Selected Writings* (Addison Wesley, 1985).

4.20 Hanson, O.J., *Essentials of Computer Data Files* (Pitman, 1985).

Programming and software

Whereas 'hardware' means the equipment used for DP, 'software' means the programs used by computers. It can be largely taken as including application programs, utility programs, operating systems, translators (assemblers and compilers), subroutines and application packages. These and related topics are explained briefly in the succeeding pages, largely from the aspect of systems analysis. Readers needing further information about programming languages and techniques are directed to the references at the end of this chapter.

Computers, in spite of their technological sophistication, are useless without a considerable amount of software. In fact no other artefact relies so heavily upon human instructions before it can function. In contrast, no other artefact can accomplish such elaborate tasks in terms of repetitive logical processes and approach so closely to the impression of having intelligence.

5.1   Programming

This section is not intended to teach the reader how to write actual programs. There are many other books dedicated to that aim (see references at the end of this chapter). It does, however, provide an introduction to programming concepts and some details of several programming languages.

As is seen from Section 2.2, a computer functions by obeying a string of instructions (the program) in succession. This tends to be repeated for each piece of data input and for each record accessed from a file. The program instructions are held in the main store and passed one by one, usually from contiguous locations, into the control unit. Here they are 'decoded' so that the control unit can set up the circuits and units appropriate for obeying the instruction. Computers obey instructions at a rate of millions per second, and it is common to indicate a computer's internal speed in mips (millions of instructions per second).

A computer program is created by a programmer using a system analyst's specification of the job in hand (Section 7.6). The programmer also prepares his own 'specification' so as to be absolutely clear in his own mind what he is trying to accomplish and how he intends to set about it. Except for the most trivial programs, it is unwise to start writing instructions without having either a program flowchart or a structured representation of what is to be programmed.

Machine and low-level languages

The instructions as actually stored and decoded by the computer are in the form of sets of bits (ones and zeros). In the very early days of computers, the programmer composed the instructions in this form — an extremely tedious task! These sets of bits are the 'machine language', and nowadays no true machine language application programming is carried out. The nearest is a symbolic language, in which each part of the instruction is written in the form of letters or digits.

For instance, 'A3,287' could mean 'add the contents of the main store address 287 to the contents of register 3 of the CPU'. A stage further is the use of symbolic data addresses instead of actual addresses, in which case the above instruction might be 'A3, BAL'. The first part of such an instruction is the 'operation code', the latter part (3, BAL) is the operand.

The above type of instruction is a 'single-operand' or 'single-address' instruction. Some machine languages have two-address instructions, and although these take more bits, they are more powerful and so the program as a whole tends to be shorter, i.e. needs fewer instructions. A symbolic language is a machine-orientated low-level language because there is a one-to-one relationship between the source program (written) instructions and the object program (machine) instructions.

Branching, looping and address modification

In the above example, the operation code is an arithmetic function, i.e. add. As well as the usual arithmetic functions, machine languages have a variety of other functions of various types. These are needed in order to move data from one address to another, to input and output data, and to obey alternative instructions by branching along different paths in the program.

Branching is an important aspect of program construction because it enables the computer to execute different instructions dependent on the outcome of a test or decision. For instance, a test applied to an accounts balance to determine whether it is debit or credit, followed by the appropriate procedure. It is quite common for several tests to be chained together, e.g. whether the balance is debit or credit and, if debit, has it been so for more than four weeks?

Another important aspect is looping. This is the repetition of certain program instructions by looping back as many times as necessary. For instance, if it is required to print a string of accounts balances held in storage, the program goes round a print loop once for each account.

It is also perfectly usual to nest one or more loops inside another. The program enters the outer loop and proceeds until it encounters the inner loop, it goes round the inner loop as many times as necessary, then continues along the outer loop. On reaching the end of the outer loop it returns to the start.

The point of looping is that it minimizes the volume of program instructions and so saves storage. In some cases it would be practically impossible to achieve a result without looping, e.g. if several thousand procedures had to be repeated.

Looping involves two main aspects apart from the actual processing purpose of the loop. One is a modification to the address of the data item or record being processed. Thus when we print the accounts' balances, the program has to be modified prior to each loop in order to get the next account. The other aspect of looping is to know when to stop, this is achieved either by counting a preknown number of loops or by repeatedly testing a data item until it has reached a value that indicates the end of the looping.

Subroutines

It is often necessary to repeat a group of instructions several times at different points in a program. In order to save writing these instructions over and over again, and as a means of saving storage space, the group of instructions are formed into a closed subroutine.

The program calls the subroutine whenever it is needed, but before doing so it inserts the return address into the operand of a branch instruction at the end of the subroutine. Figure 5.1 shows a closed subroutine.

In contrast, an open subroutine is inserted as part of the main program (see macros). This is done when it is used once only in the program, thereby obviating the need for branching and modifying. An open subroutine is often used in several different programs.

EXAMPLES OF CLOSED SUBROUTINES

Calculating square roots, conversion of date held as number of days, since say 1900, into conventional date format, conversion of monetary amounts in pence into usual format for printing, e.g. 0025782 into £257.82, calculation of number of days between any two dates (for interest calculation).

EXAMPLES OF OPEN SUBROUTINES

PAYE calculation (income tax), VAT calculation (sales tax), note and coin analysis (wage packet make up).

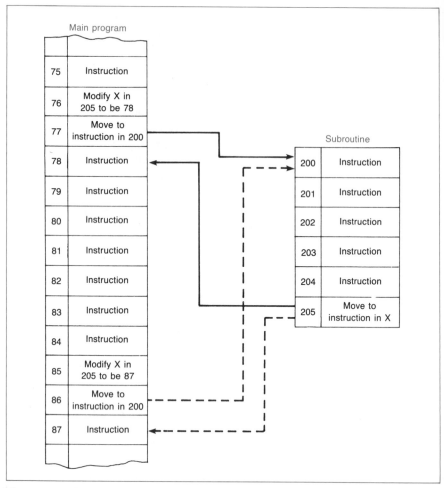

Figure 5.1   Structure of a closed subroutine

Subroutines that are used frequently are often written in machine code in order to avoid repeated compiling/interpreting and to minimize running time.

Assemblers

An assembler is a special program written in machine language used to translate, i.e. convert, symbolic language instructions (the source program) into machine language instructions (the object program). This is done on an instruction-for-instruction basis and, at the same time, various subroutines and macros (see below) are incorporated into the object program. The assembler is also able to detect syntax errors in the source program so that thse can be corrected before the program is tested.

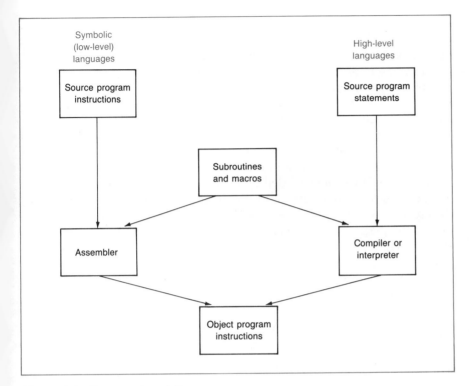

Figure 5.2   Program translation

The student will find Figure 5.2 useful in understanding the terms used in connection with this general topic.

Macro instructions

A macro instruction is written as part of the source program and translated by the assembler into several object program instructions. This saves time and effort when programming since all the commonly used open subroutines can be defined as macros. Macros are not, however, as economical with main storage as are closed subroutines because the instructions are stored repeatedly, i.e. once for each time the macro is required.

Structured programs

It is no doubt already apparent that programs and programming can reach high levels of complexity. This is unavoidable if the application or problem is complicated but nevertheless the program must be understandable. That is to say, it must not reach such a level of intricacy that no one but the original programmer is able to follow through it subsequently. Programs have to be understandable because they often need changes made to them during their lives, probably due to unavoidable external circumstances.

This requirement for clarity engendered the concept of structured programming and the development of certain programming languages, e.g. Pascal and Ada, directed towards this idea.

The concept of structured programming is that all programs should consist of a number of modules, i.e. groups of instructions or statements, and that these should be largely independent of each other, i.e. have minimum coupling.

Each module has to be headed by a title (label) in order clearly to identify it. The same title should also be used on structure charts (Section 7.6) so that the program and chart are cross-related unambiguously. It is also advisable to insert a brief explanatory statement, e.g. a REM statement as in BASIC, at the start of each module as a reminder of its function. Similarly each module needs a clearly defined end point, e.g. a RETURN statement or a special symbol.

Earlier in this section subroutines were explained, and the question arises as to the relationship between modules and subroutines. The answer is that there is no absolute relationship. A module may call a subroutine(s) and a subroutine is often split up into modules in a similar way to a complete program.

Module coupling

Coupling means the interaction between modules. There are a number of ways in which coupling can occur, and these are of differing acceptability in terms of the efficiency of the structured program.

Data coupling
Data coupling means that the modules interact only to the extent of data items being passed from one module to another. This is not only unavoidable but necessary to a significant extent in order to achieve the desired results. An example of data coupling is module A passing a gross amount of money to module B in order to determine the amount of discount allowed. Module B receives the gross amount, and by using the discounting rules, is able to calculate the amount of discount. This in turn is passed to other module(s). Thus the only coupling between modules A and B is the data item 'gross amount': this is weak coupling.

Control coupling
With control coupling one module exerts some degree of control over another module. This comes about by module A passing a flag, signal or switch to module B so as to affect B's processing procedures. For instance, as an extension to the discount process described above, module A could also pass a flag to B to indicate which of a set of discounting rules to apply. In this case the modules are more closely coupled because a change to the discounting rules involves both modules.

Module B needs to have the new procedure inserted; module A needs to have the means of selecting the new flag.

Environment coupling

If two modules use the same area of memory or backing storage for their own data, they are coupled via the environment. This type of coupling would probably not be apparent from the program's structure chart (Section 7.6). With a high-level programming language, using the same variable name in the two modules for different data items is tantamount to environment coupling.

Environment coupling should be avoided as it can cause problems if one module is amended so that the storage area is not entirely vacant when the next module comes to use it.

There are also stronger types of coupling but these are best avoided if at all possible.

Module cohesion

A module should be 'cohesive', i.e. perform one identifiable function only preferably on the one data stream. Cohesiveness, also termed 'binding', enables a clear connection to be seen between a structure chart (Figure 7.19) and the corresponding program because a cohesive module has a single entry point and a single exit point.

There are various forms of cohesion and of differing desirability. Functional cohesion implies that the module has a clear, self-contained function and therefore is not affected by changes to other modules; this is highly desirable. Less desirable types of cohesion are such as coincidental inclusion of functions in a module, similar but otherwise unconnected functions, and time-related functions.

Module structures

The modules of a structured program are of three kinds — sequential (serial), selective (decision) and iterative (loop). A sequential module is a set of serially performed actions with no branching or looping involved. A selective module entails branching within it but the branches join before the exit point. An iterative module contains loops in it but again has only one exit point.

As far as practical it is desirable that a module contains only one of these structures. Thus if a program includes a decision followed by a loop, these are better separated into two different modules.

It is quite straightforward to construct programs composed only of these three kinds of modules. If this is done in conjunction with the principles of minimum coupling, maximum cohesion, single entry and single exit: the result is a structured program.

Overall structure

A structured program is generally controlled by a main (driver) subroutine which calls other subroutines as required. A subroutine consists of one or more modules, each of which can call other subroutines. In every case the subroutine returns the program to the calling subroutine (as in Figures 5.1 and 5.3).

By giving each subroutine and module its own label, the path of the program is easily traceable. These methods are tidier and clearer than merely branching off indiscriminately and not necessarily returning to the same section of the program. If the latter procedure is adopted, a program is likely to become a cat's cradle of branching points and paths.

EXAMPLE OF STRUCTURED PROGRAM

This is the outline of a simple program for creating a sales report based on sales in various areas within several countries. For each country its areas' sales have to be aggregated to form the country's sales total, this is then converted into the equivalent sterling sales. By repeating this procedure for each country, the sales report is created and printed.

The process is shown in Figure 5.3, and is based on a fictitious language which uses the commands GOSUB, DOMOD, RETURN and REPEAT. GOSUB causes the program to go to the subroutine with the specified label, from which it returns to the driver subroutine. DOMOD causes the program to execute the specified module, after which it moves on to the next statement, i.e. another DOMOD or a REPEAT or RETURN to calling subroutine.

It is seen from Figure 5.3 that the driver subroutine calls two other subroutines in turn for each country. The subroutine 'Aggregate' accumulates the sales in the areas to give the country's sales. The subroutine 'Result' consists of three modules, the first of which looks up the exchange rate and the name of the country. The second module calculates the equivalent sterling amount, and the third prints the name of the country and its equivalent sterling sales.

Although this simplistic example is perhaps over-moduled, it illustrates the point of structured programming. It also demonstrates the three types of module described above, i.e. selective (Print), iterative (Collect) and sequential (Calc and Rate-name).

5.2 High-level languages

High-level languages were developed in order further to ease the work of programmers by making the programming language more procedure-orientated. Whereas low-level language instructions tend to be machine-orientated, the

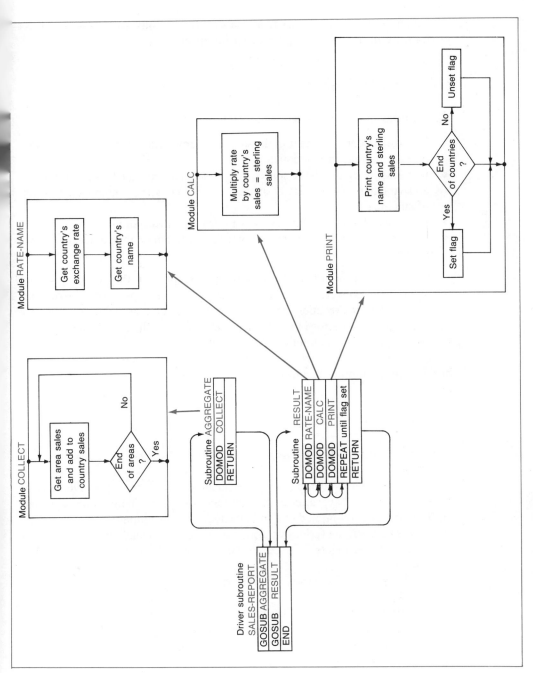

Figure 5.3 Structured program chart

'statements' of a high-level language are closer to natural English or other natural languages.

A high-level source program is translated, i.e. converted, into an object program by means of a compiler or an interpreter.

Compilers and interpreters

The features of a compiler are as follows:

- it translates one statement in the source program into several, perhaps many, object program instructions;
- it checks for errors in the source program statements, such as invalid words and violation of the rules of syntax, i.e. the construction and relationship of statements;
- open and closed subroutines, and macros are incorporated;
- the programmer ends up with a compiled program on magnetic storage and a printed copy, if required.

An interpreter is similar to a compiler except that the source program statements are converted one at a time into object program instructions immediately before execution, and so no object program is available as a complete entity. If there is an error in a statement detectable by the interpreter, an error message is returned on entering the statement.

There follow brief descriptions of a few of the better-known high-level (3GL) business programming languages.

Third-generation languages

COBOL (Common Business-Oriented Language)

COBOL is an extensively used high-level language and since around 1960 several versions (dialects) have appeared. Although the original intention was that COBOL should be compiled and run on any model of computer, there are small differences between the various versions and so the corresponding compilers must also differ. Nevertheless COBOL is now employed for many business DP applications.

A COBOL program consists of four divisions:

1. *Identification division* — this identifies the program.
2. *Environment division* — specifies the computer(s) to be used for compiling and processing.
3. *Data division* — specifies the format and characteristics of the files and data to be processed by the object program and relates these to the names used in the procedure division.

4. *Procedure division* — comprises the statements in the source program; this is the main part of a COBOL program.

The statements (sentences) of the procedure division are made up of 'verbs' and 'names'. The verbs are from a predetermined set of about twenty in all. Examples are ADD, MULTIPLY, MOVE, GO TO, READ and ALTER.

The names are created and assigned to data items by the programmer so as, in effect, to enable the compiler to find the data items in the computer's main store.

Below is a short piece of COBOL programming for computing the amount to be paid to a worker who receives time-and-a-half for hours worked above forty and normal rate up to forty hours.

The names adopted for this module are WORKED-HOURS, OVERTIME-HOURS, PREMIUM-HOURS, PAID-HOURS, RATE and AMOUNT-PAID.

    25 SUBTRACT 40 FROM WORKED-HOURS GIVING OVERTIME-
        HOURS.
    26 IF OVERTIME-HOURS IS NEGATIVE GO TO 30, OTHERWISE
        GO TO 27.
    27 MULTIPLY OVERTIME-HOURS BY 1.5 GIVING PREMIUM-
        HOURS.
    28 ADD PREMIUM-HOURS TO 40 GIVING PAID-HOURS.
    29 GO TO 31.
    30 MOVE WORKED-HOURS TO PAID-HOURS.
    31 MULTIPLY PAID-HOURS BY RATE GIVING AMOUNT-PAID.

For further information about COBOL, see References 5.9–5.17.

BASIC (Beginners All-purpose Symbolic Instruction Code)

BASIC is a straightforward high-level language intended for use in a time-sharing environment, in this respect it is particularly beneficial in educational institutions. It is also employed extensively with microcomputers in education, the home and business.

One of the difficulties with BASIC is the welter of dialects currently in use. A dialect is a version of BASIC, usually stemming from one of the microcomputer manufacturers. Dialects have been developed largely in an attempt to be competitive, and usually involve additional features, particularly in relation to graphics. Examples of BASIC dialects are Microsoft BASIC, Apple BASIC and BASIC 2, and many others.

Essentially BASIC consists of statements made up of verbs and variables. The verbs are similar to those in COBOL but there are a larger number. Variables are data items with names assigned to them that in effect become the addresses of their locations in the main store. A variable name must be unique and generally consists of one or a few alphabetic characters, perhaps followed by a digit. The interpreter or compiler stores and accesses the data items by utilizing their variable names.

Shown below is the module as described above but written in one of the dialects of BASIC. In this, wh means worked-hours, ph paid-hours, rh rate per normal hour, and ap amount-paid.

```
25   IF wh > 40 THEN ph = 40 + 1.5 * (wh − 40) ELSE ph = wh
26   ap = ph * rh
```

For more on BASIC see References 5.18−5.23.

Pascal

Pascal is a high-level language named after the famous seventeenth-century French mathematician. It was expressly designed as a language to make programming more systematic and•disciplined, and in these respects lends itself to structured programming. It is, however, more difficult to learn than are COBOL and BASIC, and so is unlikely to be accepted as a language for microcomputer users.

Pascal's syntax is in a formal arrangement known as Extended Backus−Naus Form (EBNF). For example:

```
program = title statements "."
```

means that a program is defined as a title followed by statements followed by a period; title and statements are further defined using the same form.

Pascal uses a range of special symbols in its vocabulary such as brackets and punctuation marks. It is efficient at handling sets, stacks, queues, lists and arrays, so making it powerful for programs that involve arranging and processing groups of data items.

In the following example the variables are the same as in the BASIC program.

```
IF wh > 40
THEN ph: = 40 + 1.5 * (wh − 40)
ELSE ph: = wh
ap = ph * rh
```

See References 5.24−5.33 for further details of Pascal.

FORTH

FORTH is an intermediary between high-level languages and assembly languages, but is easier to learn than most of the latter.

It is compiled into a set of subroutines yet has the easy debugging of an interpreted language. Like most other languages, FORTH comes in several versions, with the attendant confusion.

It is a stack-based language, this means that the data items being processed are held in a stack (like an in-tray). They are taken in turn from the top of the stack and results returned thereto in a last-in first-out (LIFO) mode.

In order to make efficient use of the stack principle, instructions are written in a form known as reverse Polish notation. With this the data items are followed by the operator and this is applied to the data items when they reach the top of the stack. The expression to calculate the paid hours in the previous examples would be written:

wh 40 − 1.5 * 40 +

wh would be positioned at the top of the stack.

FORTH has an extensive set of operators (around 180) which can be combined into powerful statements.

See References 5.34−5.41 for further details of FORTH.

PL/1 (Programming Language 1)

PL/1 was created by IBM in the early 1960s as a general-purpose, high-level programming language for both business and scientific applications. It is designed so that simple programs can be constructed without a knowledge of the full language. The concept is for the programmer to utilize a subset of PL/1 with which he is familiar. This is referred to as 'modularity' although it has no direct connection with structured programming.

A PL/1 program is composed of blocks of statements called 'procedures', these may form part of larger blocks after the style of subroutines. Each procedure is compiled separately starting with the lowest, and they can thus be used in several different programs.

Below is the short piece of program used previously, the meanings of the words are the same as in the BASIC example.

```
IF WH > 40
THEN
    PH = 40 + 1.5 * (WH−40);
ELSE
    PH = WH;
AP = PH * RH;
```

For more information about PL/1 see References 5.42−5.46.

C

The C programming language was introduced as early as 1972 but did not become well known until the 1980s. The rise in its popularity is due largely to the increased use of the UNIX operating system whose software is written mostly in the C language.

C is claimed to be a flexible language, thus giving the programmer freedom, power and ease of use. In order to obtain the full power of C it is necessary to have UNIX as the associated operating system.

An error-checking program called 'lint' is applied to a C program before compilation, which is just as well because C is a difficult language for non-specialists.

See References 5.47–5.56 for further details of C.

RPG (Report Program Generator)

RPG was introduced by IBM in 1964 as a language for constructing programs to tabulate and summarize data in sequential files. RPG II and RPG III, improved versions, were introduced later and since then have been implemented by several other computer manufacturers.

RPG has narrow applicability and is really suitable only for DP applications that either update master files (sequential or random with RPG II), or print reports based on files. It is sometimes combined with another language in order to achieve the full requirements of all DP applications.

RPG is a declarative language in that the programmer specifies what a report consists of rather than how to produce it. This is achieved through the employment of specification forms to define input, calculations, output and file characteristics. Thus, although RPG is efficient and straightforward for the programming of many business applications, it is too inflexible for general DP purposes.

See References 5.57–5.60 for more details of RPG.

Fourth-generation languages

A fourth-generation language (4GL) is a higher-level language than third-generation languages such as COBOL and C. In other words it demands fewer lines of manual coding to achieve a given task and is less verbose in its written form. It is difficult to be definitive about 4GLs because this is largely a matter of opinion.

Nevertheless it is generally accepted that a 4GL must be easy to learn, have a programming productivity of at least 10:1 over COBOL and incorporate facilities for prototyping (Section 6.9). It is also accepted that 4GLs are slow in executing the job in hand, and that they need powerful processors.

In the early 1980s it was thought that 4GLs would bring programming capability to end-users but since then it has been recognized that this is not feasible. As a matter of interest the same was suggested for third-generation languages in the early 1960s. It is now accepted that 4GLs are more of a professional programmer's tool than an end-user's, but none the less certain types of 4GL lend themselves to end-user application.

One of the main characteristics of 4GLs is that they are non-procedural, i.e. the programmer states what needs to be done rather than how it is done. This implies that the 4GL software decides the procedure, whereas the programmer merely declares the requirements.

4GLs are usually programmed interactively; this means that programming errors are detected at an early stage. This is reinforced by the fact that 4GLs are generally interpretive. Interactive programming reduces, or even eliminates, the need to remember a set of mnemonic statements as these are replaced by selection from menus and by use of semi-natural language. Similarly, screen graphics in which the programmer fills in the blanks and extensive use of WIMPs contribute to ease of programming.

4GLs in the broad sense consist of the following types:

- Spreadsheet-based, e.g. Lotus 1-2-3 and Multiplan. These include concise syntax and powerful commands, making them of a higher level than earlier spreadsheet software. There is, however, a limit to what can be achieved through the spreadsheet approach.
- Database-based, e.g. dBASE IV and Oracle. These are based on the management and interrogation of databases.
- Application (code) generators, e.g. Ideal, Telon and Natural. This type utilizes form-filling on screens related to systems design. They are then compiled to generate COBOL coding.
- Information centre-based, e.g. Focus, Ramis II and Nomad II. These are capable of producing complex reports, handling sophisticated queries and generating intricate graphics.

An extensive range of 4GLs is now available which with time will no doubt shrink considerably. This large range is in some ways detrimental as it reduces portability and dilutes programming expertise.

5.3 Systems software

Utility software

Certain DP requirements are common to a high proportion of computer users and so generalized utility software is available to meet this need. Utility software is intended to be sufficiently flexible to meet most user's requirements and is tailored to meet their precise needs by means of parameters entered prior to use.

Some or all of the utility programs described below may be incorporated into the operating system that is used with a particular computer.

File conversion
This covers the transference of data from any medium to any other, e.g. magnetic tape to magnetic disk. This may be done either as an exact copy or with simultaneous editing and validation.

File copying

An exact copy of the file is made and written to the same storage medium, e.g. a replica of data records on disk is made on another disk area.

File reorganization

As explained in Section 4.3, direct access files overflow and consequently the overflow records are stored in designated blocks. This is acceptable up to a point but from time to time it is necessary to reorganize the file so as to remove the overflow. This entails reorganizing the cylinder and block indexes, and transferring overflow records back into their home blocks.

Sorting

Quite often it is necessary to arrange records into a certain sequence based on the values of their keys, as described in Section 4.1. A number of factors enter into the choice of the sorting method that is the most suitable. These are the following:

- the length and positions of the key field(s) within the records;
- the number and average size of the records to be sorted;
- the desired sequence (ascending or descending);
- the degree of sequentiality already present in the set of records;
- the hardware units available, e.g. the number of magnetic tape decks.

The above parameters are used by a sort-generator to set up the most suitable type of sorting program.

Dumping routines

These transfer the program and its working data to the backing storage at regular intervals. A dump routine is used in conjunction with a restart program, which reloads the main store with the program and working data.

Housekeeping operations

These are programs or parts of programs not directly concerned with the solution of the problem in hand. Examples are clearing areas of storage now redundant, writing magnetic tape labels, updating common data in records, e.g. the current date, and so on.

Trace routines

These entail the dumping, display or printing of the program or other contents of the main store during program testing to facilitate error detection.

Multiprogramming

The earliest computers were capable of merely carrying out the operations of input, processing and output in succession for each lot of data. Modern computers process several jobs at the same time. This concept is known as 'multiprogramming', and necessitates holding several application programs in the computer's main store simultaneously.

To accomplish multiprogramming, an 'executive' or 'supervisor' program is employed to control the application programs. The executive program has the power to interrupt a running program and pass control to another program. This happens when, for instance, a line printer signals that it is ready for another line of print. The executive program interrupts the current program, loads the print buffer with data waiting to be printed and then returns control to the original program. The printer then prints from the buffer autonomously while processing of current data continues.

When two running programs both require the same printer, the supervisor allows them both to proceed concurrently. One program is allowed to output to the printer as it runs. The other's output is loaded to disk, i.e. spooled, for subsequent output when the printer becomes free.

It is necessary to hold the executive program permanently in main store, i.e. it is main store resident. The application programs, on the other hand, are moved in and out of partitions of the main store so as to suit the jobs being currently carried out.

Virtual storage

The concept of virtual storage is to enable a program to address more storage than is currently in the main store. Without virtual storage a program needing, say, 3 megabytes of main storage cannot be run on a computer with only 2 megabytes.

Virtual storage operates on the principle of holding programs on disk and transferring segments (pages) of the programs into main store for execution. This is a complicated process, known as 'paging' or 'segmentation', and is controlled by a special program in the operating system (see below). The pages of main store assigned to each program are adjusted dynamically in order to maximize the efficiency of the multiprogramming.

Operating systems

As mainframes and minicomputers became more powerful, their ability to run jobs in multiprogramming mode outran the abilities of their human operators. The set-up times of the jobs being run became proportionally greater with the result that the computer remained idle during these times. An operating system precludes this by allowing the operator to stack jobs for subsequent continuous processing.

It should be remembered that in some DP departments the computer carries out a wide range of activities, e.g. in educational institutions. These include the translation of source programs into object programs, especially compiling, and the running of a wide range of jobs. Often the jobs can be segregated into two main types — background and foreground. Background jobs are regular and of known duration and operational requirements. Foreground jobs are occasional and of less well known characteristics. Operating systems endeavour to maintain a balance between the requirements of these various jobs.

An operating system consists of a suite of programs, one of which, the master, kernel or executive program, remains resident in the main store. This program controls the other operating system programs in the suite and between them they control the application programs.

The requirements of an operating system for microcomputers are not entirely the same as for larger computers. Nevertheless they have many similarities and play an important role in the use of microcomputers. For several years the dominant microcomputer operating system was CP/M (control program/monitor).

In recent years several other operating systems have moved into competition with CP/M and these have brought with them new capabilities such as multi-user and multi-tasking. A multi-user operating system is capable of being shared by several processors at the same time thus only one copy need exist. A multi-tasking computer handles several independent tasks simultaneously.

Microcomputer operating systems are sometimes integrated with business applications software, i.e. the operating system includes various application packages among its suite of programs. This applies particularly to office automation applications. Thus in some cases a range of applications software is controlled by the operating system and supplied automatically with the microcomputer. Examples of such software include word processing, electronic mail, networking, spreadsheets, graphics and file handling.

When considering a microcomputer and its operating system, a number of factors should be taken into account.

- The amount of memory occupied by the operating system.
- Does it permit fast running of the application programs?
- How many processors and VDUs can it control simultaneously?
- What choice of programming languages does it allow?

Well-known microcomputer operating systems are:

- CP/M-86, CP/M-68 and other versions: these are 16-bit multi-tasking versions of the original CP/M.
- MS—DOS and PC—DOS: 16-bit single-user systems.
- DOSplus. An enhanced version of MS—DOS covering CP/M programs.
- UNIX: a 32-bit multi-user system with file handling capabilities, based on the structured language C.
- XENIX: an offshoot of UNIX.

Functions of an operating system

- *Priority assignment* — jobs awaiting execution are scheduled according to either a predetermined or a dynamic assignment plan.

- *Control of multiprogramming* − as described above.
- *Spooling* − the control of input/output peripherals in order to achieve their best utilization.
- *Communication* − control of data transmission between terminals and the computer, and computer-to-computer.
- *Dynamic allocation* − of main and backing storage, including virtual storage.
- *Database* − control of the database management system.
- *Software control* − of assemblers, compilers, utility software and subroutines so that these are immediately available when required.
- *Operator communication* − via the console printer or VDU.
- *Operations log* − maintenance of details of all jobs carried out by the computer.
- *Debugging and editing new programs*, in conjunction with the compiler, and passing error messages to the user.
- *Application package control* − especially with microcomputers, as described above.

Job control languages

Each job coming under the control of a mainframe or minicomputer's operating system is specified by its 'job description'. The operating system is told how to carry out a job by a job control language. This comprises a number of control commands that may be retrieved from disk storage along with the job data.

Below is a selection of typical job control commands.

EXECUTE − carry out the current program.
SORT − sort a disk file.
ABORT − abandon the current job.
DELETE − removes a program or file from storage.

5.4 Application software

Application software comprises the programs that are written specifically to achieve results appertaining to the company's activities. In other words, application software is user-orientated as opposed to systems software which is computer-orientated.

Application software comes from two sources, i.e. the company's own DP staff or from external agencies. It is necessary to compare the cost and staffing problems of maintaining the company's DP staff against the cost and risk of relying upon software suppliers.

In the early years of DP, purchased software was often found to be too restrictive and badly documented so that apart from payroll, which is largely legislation-bound, it was not readily accepted. More recently there has been an increased use of purchased software, especially as applied to microcomputers. Firms using microcomputers do not generally have DP staff and, since other staff are fully engaged with their normal work, it is necessary to purchase application programs.

Application packages

A business application package is a complete suite of programs together with the associated documentation. It covers a business routine, and is usually supplied by a computer manufacturer or software house, on lease or purchase.

A package is normally intended to meet the needs of a number of different user companies. In order to achieve this aim, most packages are of modular design and so can be constructed on a building-brick principle to cater for the needs of the individual user. A package often also contains a number of options, these are selected by the user by the insertion of parameters before use.

Of the many different applications covered by packages, those prominent are financial accounting, auditing, payroll and stock control, and in most cases it is important that these applications are integrated with each other. Thus the sales accounting, purchase accounting, nominal accounting and stock control should be integrated so that the final accounts, i.e. balance sheet, profit and loss statement, etc., can be produced automatically.

In addition to these general packages are those that are directed to specific types of user companies. Examples of these are for stockbrokers, insurance brokers, estate agents and travel agents.

Advantages of application packages

The following benefits should accrue from the adoption of an application package.

- *Implementation* — of an application is quicker and possibly cheaper.
- *System design, programming and system testing* — are minimized.
- *System documentation* — is provided with the package.
- *Portability* — from the existing computer system to any new computer adopted by the user.
- *Efficiency* — in terms of speed, storage requirements and accuracy.

Considerations regarding application packages

Definition of requirements
The user company cannot abandon the study of company objectives, systems investigation and consequent definition of DP requirements. In these respects the approach is the same as when designing a DP system for in-house programming.

Study of range

A range of packages should be examined in depth before a choice is made, and existing users of the packages should be consulted for their practical experiences and opinions. It should be remembered that the more commonly used packages result in presure on the suppliers to keep them up-to-date.

Interfacing

How easily does a package interface with the user's own routines, both existing and future? This applies particularly to the database and data dictionary.

Amendments

At least one member of the user company staff must be completely conversant with the detailed operations and capabilities of the package adopted. This facilitates in-house tuning and making subsequent amendments. Moreover, it is important that a package's output is fully meaningful to the end-users.

The package supplier must be in a position to supply all the necessary on-going amendments, especially those required through legislation such as for taxation.

Performance

How efficient is the package in terms of its average and maximum run times on the computer? What resources does it demand such as peripherals and amounts of main and backing storage?

Contract terms

The terms of the contract should embrace factors such as the terms of payment, supplier's assistance with implementation, extent of documentation and future maintenance.

As mentioned above, microcomputers have engendered the development of a large amount of software. This has tended to fall into the main types explained below. Versions of these types of packages are available for mainframes and minicomputers also.

Spreadsheet software

A spreadsheet, also known as a worksheet, is a multi-purpose method that is usable for a variety of planning, modelling and forecasting purposes, e.g. budgeting, sales analysis and break-even analysis.

The principle of a spreadsheet is that is simulates a large matrix of cells within each of which a data item or formula can be held. Once in a cell, the data item or formula can be replicated, moved, sorted, filed, printed and so on, at will. These facilities provide the means of easily and rapidly processing the data without the user needing to write a program as such. The spreadsheet is controlled by a set of user commands in conjunction with a small menu that appears at the bottom of the screen.

A display of cells, i.e. a window, is scrolled up or down and right or left so that any cell may be inspected at will. The display shows around 160 cells at a time out of many thousands that exist on one spreadsheet. Some versions allow different areas of the spreadsheet to be displayed and scrolled simultaneously but independently, i.e. several windows. It is also possible to transfer data from one spreadsheet to another so as to build up the final file or document.

To take a simple example of using a spreadsheet, suppose we wish to create a table of mortgage repayment accounts for various amounts loaned and various repayment periods. The usual procedure would be to enter manually the appropriate formula into one cell and then replicate it in modified form in certain other cells. There would be one cell per amount/period combination and the modified formula in each cell would represent an actual amount/period combination. Having done this, all the formulae are automatically evaluated so giving the repayment amounts. These are then printed along with headings and annotations to form the required table.

It must be emphasized that this simple example is by no means the limit of spreadsheet capabilities. An almost limitless range of work can be performed to give a wide variety of results. Among the better-known spreadsheet programs are Multiplan, Supercalc and Visicalc.

Word processing software

The concept and features of word processing (WP) are explained in Section 2.6. These are so commonly required as to permit the development and utilization of standard packages. A feature of WP software is its ability to interface with other text that automatically incorporates the relevant names, descriptions and numeric data.

The well-known WP software packages include Wordstar, WordPerfect and Easywriter.

Database management software

Databases and DBMSs are described in Section 4.4. DBMS software for mainframes and minicomputers are closely related to the computer itself and supplied mostly via the computer manufacturer. These packages are largely geared for use by professional DP staff and are completely isolated from the end-user.

At the microcomputer level progress has been quite different. A considerable number of DBMS packages are available, some of which do not really justify the name. The salient features of microcomputer DBMSs are their user-friendliness and breadth of capabilities.

Data dictionary software

Data dictionaries (DDs) are explained in Section 4.4. A DD package may be either stand-alone or related to a particular DBMS. In any event it is obviously imperative that the DD interfaces with any existent database or DBMS. Names of some established DD packages are Datamanager, Lexicon and Data Catalogue.

Accounting and other software

A wide selection of software is available for business applications such as payroll, sales, purchase and nominal ledgers, stock control, financial modelling, survey and statistical analyses, operational research and graphics.

5.5 Exercises

Exercise 5.1 Structured programming

From the following narrative of a labour costing procedure in a construction firm, draw up a structured program chart as per Figure 5.3.

The purpose of the procedure is to create and print a weekly report showing the labour cost to date of each contract and each job within the contract, together with numbers and name. Each contract has a number and a name, each job has a number. Jobs extend over several weeks and their ongoing labour costs are updated weekly from data on worktickets (WTs) already stored serially.

A WT is issued for each period of time that an employee spends on a job. It holds the job no., employee no. and the number of hours spent. Each employee has a standard hourly cost rate.

Exercise 5.2 Software packages

Describe the features that you would expect to find in each of the following application software packages:

 (i) spreadsheet;
 (ii) database;
 (iii) word processor.

Briefly explain how each of these packages could be of benefit to a company, and for each describe two tasks that could be undertaken by that package.

(ICSA part 2, Inf. sys., June 1988)

Exercise 5.3 Fourth-generation languages

Explain what is meant by a 'fourth-generation language'.

Describe the salient characteristics of one such language and discuss its usefulness.

(BCS part II, Option C, April 1986)

Exercise 5.4 Software terminology

Explain the meaning of the following terms:

(a) operating systems;
(b) interpreters;
(c) utilities;
(d) flowcharts.

(ICSA part 2, Inf. sys., Dec. 1988)

Exercise 5.5 Modular programming

(a) Explain the advantages of using a systematic method for designing computer software. illustrate your answer by reference to a particular method.
(b) Discuss the features that make a programming language suitable for modular programming. What are the attributes of a good module.

(BCS part I, Gen. paper II, April 1986)

Exercise 5.6 Programming

You are required to:

(a) State, with reasons, which *high-level* programming language you would expect to be used in *each* of the following situations:
　　(i) the implementation of a stock control system for a large company manufacturing a wide range of stationery products;
　　(ii) the analysis of experimental data in the research department of a company designing electronic products;
　　(iii) the teaching of structured programming in the computing department in a college;
　　(iv) the maintenance of the business records for a small trader writing his own programs on a microcomputer.
(b) Give an explanation of *each* of the following terms, in relation to programming, with an example illustrating the use of each:
　　(i) machine language;
　　(ii) compiler;
　　(iii) source program;
　　(iv) interpreter;
　　(v) editor.
(c) Explain what is meant by structured programming.

(CIMA stage 2, Inf. Tech. Man., Nov. 1987)

5.6 Outline solutions to exercises

Solution 5.1

See Figure 5.4.

Solution 5.2

(i) Refer to 'Spreadsheet software' in Section 5.4. Spreadsheets are of benefit in that they allow users with a minimum of computer knowledge to achieve results quickly. No programming ability is required and the software guides the user towards his or her objectives.

    A spreadsheet task is explained in Section 5.4. Another suitable application is in determining parts requirements for a production schedule. The spreadsheet cells are loaded with the parts quantities per product, the product quantities are entered and the program rapidly calculates the total requirement of each part. This is repeated for every schedule.

(ii) Refer to 'Database management software' in Section 5.4 and to Section 4.4 for features of databases.

    A database management package enables its user to create, amend, interrogate and process files without the need for programming on his part.

    A simple but useful employment of a database package could be the creation of a file of names and addresses of prospective customers for the benefit of the sales force. Thereafter the prospects could be sorted into useful lists, e.g. prospects in a certain sales area over a given size.

    A second example entails the searching of multiple files e.g. extracting an employee's address from the personnel file, his tax paid from the payroll file and his superannuation contributions from the pensions file in order to provide information for the Inland Revenue.

(iii) Refer to Section 2.6 for the capabilities of WP. The most well-known task performed by WP packages is the preparation of standardized but variable-content correspondence, i.e. sales letters containing person's names and individualized figures.

    Another use is the preparation of reports by merging together blocks of text from other literature, e.g. an overall sales performance report.

Solution 5.3

Refer to 'Fourth-generation languages' in Section 5.2.
FOCUS
- mainframe and microcomputer versions;
- own relational database;
- modular form of purchase, i.e. input, dialogues, displays, report generation, graphs, financial modelling, statistics;
- huge gain in programming productivity over 3GLs;
- sophisticated database interrogation including non-FOCUS files;
- interactive involvement during processing.

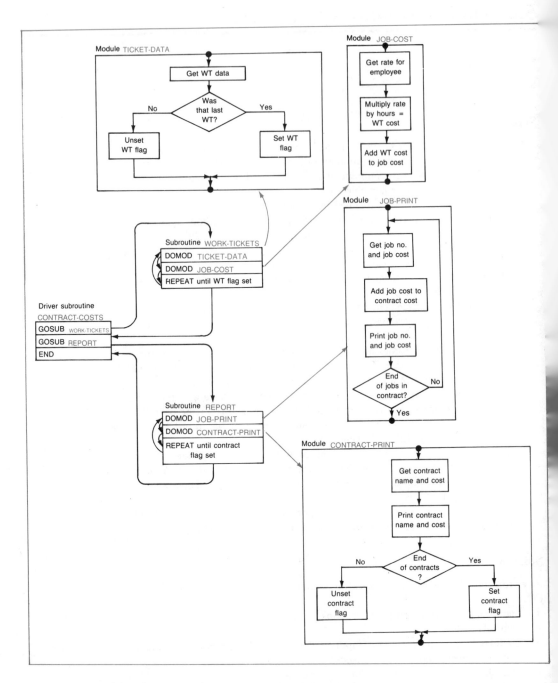

Figure 5.4 Structured program chart for Exercise 5.1

Solution 5.4

(a) Refer to 'Operating systems' in Section 5.3.
(b) An interpreter is a program for translating high-level language statements (the source program) into machine language instructions (the object program). Each source program statement is translated and executed individually before the interpreter moves on to the next statement.
(c) Refer to 'Utility software' in Section 5.3.
(d) A flowchart is a diagram composed of symbols and flow lines depicting the order in which a procedure or a program operates. Flowcharts have been largely superseded by similar but clearer methods such as data flow diagrams. Refer to 'Flowcharting' in Section 7.6.

Solution 5.5

(a) Refer to 'Structured programming' in Section 5.1.
(b) • Easy and clear identification of modules.
     • Simple means of entering and exiting modules.
     • Commands (verbs) to provide good control over looping.
Refer to 'Structured Programming' in Section 5.1 for attributes of modules.

Solution 5.6

(a) (i) COBOL
     (ii) FORTRAN or ALGOL
     (iii) Pascal
     (iv) BASIC
(b) (i) Refer to 'Machine and low-level languages' in Section 5.1.
     (ii) Refer to 'Computers' in Section 5.2.
     (iii) Refer to 'High-level languages' in Section 5.2.
     (iv) Refer to Solution 5.4(b).
     (v) A piece of program or a subroutine for checking the layout and completeness of input data.
(c) Refer to 'Structured programming' in Section 5.1.

5.7 References and further reading

General programming

5.1 Bornat, R., *Programming from First Principles* (Prentice Hall, 1986).
5.2 Johnston, H., *Learning to Program* (Prentice Hall, 1985).
5.3 Cluley, J.C., *Introduction to Low Level Programming for Microprocessors* (Macmillan, 1988).

5.4   Hehner, E.C., *The Logic of Programming* (Prentice Hall, 1984).
5.5   Ghezzi, C. and Jayayeri, M., *Programming Language Concepts* (Prentice Hall, 1988).
5.6   Backhouse, R.C., *Program Construction and Verification* (Prentice Hall, 1986).
5.7   Meyer, B., *Introduction to the Theory of Programming Languages* (Prentice Hall, 1988).
5.8   Goldschlager, L. and Lister, G., *Computer Science: A Modern Introduction* (Prentice Hall, 1988).

COBOL

5.9   Brown, P. and Gwillim, V., *User Guide to COBOL 85* (NCC, 1985).
5.10   Longhurst, J., Rainey, W. and Longhurst, A., *COBOL* (Prentice Hall, 1988).
5.11   Cassel, D., *Introduction to Structured COBOL and Program Design* (Prentice Hall, 1988).
5.12   Spence, J.W., *COBOL* (West Ed. Pub., 1988).
5.13   Abel, P., *Cobol Programming: A Structured Approach* (Prentice Hall, 1989).
5.14   McCracken, D.D. and Golden, D.G., *A Simplified Guide to Structured Cobol* (John Wiley, 1988).
5.15   Grauer, R.T., *Structured COBOL Programming* (Prentice Hall, 1987).
5.16   Boillot, M., *Understanding Structured COBOL* (West Ed. Pub., 1986).
5.17   Myers, S.E., *Structured Cobol with Business Applications* (Prentice Hall, 1988).

BASIC

5.18   Horn, L.W. and Boillot, M., *BASIC* (West Ed. Pub., 1986).
5.19   Gosling, P., *Practical BASIC Programming* (Macmillan, 1982).
5.20   Boillot, M., *BASIC: Concepts and Structured Problem-solving* (West Ed. Pub., 1988).
5.21   Brinkman, R., *Programming in Structured BASIC* (Macmillan, 1984).
5.22   Diehr, G., Barron, T. and Munro, T., *BASIC Programming for the IBM Personal Computer* (John Wiley, 1987).
5.23   Castek, J., *Structured BASIC Programming on IBM Personal Computers* (John Wiley, 1988).

Pascal

5.24   Moseley, L.G., Sharp, J.A. and Salenieks, P., *Pascal in Practice: Using the Language* (John Wiley, 1987).
5.25   Lamphrey, R.H., MacDonald, R.M. and Roberts, M.W., *Programming Principles Using Pascal* (John Wiley, 1985).
5.26   Chivers, I.D., *A Practical Introduction to Standard Pascal* (John Wiley, 1986).
5.27   Findlay, W. and Watt, D.A., *Pascal: An Introduction to Methodical Programming* (Pitman, 1985).
5.28   Graham, N., *Introduction to Pascal* (West Ed. Pub., 1988).
5.29   Watt, D.A., *The Professional Programmer's Guide to Pascal* (Pitman, 1988).
5.30   D'Alarco, H.T. and Sutherland, R., *Problem Solving with Pascal* (Collier Macmillan 1988).
5.31   Lamie, E.L., *Pascal Programming* (John Wiley, 1987).

5.32 Welsh, J. and Elder, J., *Introduction to Pascal* (Prentice Hall, 1988).
5.33 Crawley, W. and McArthur, W., *Structured Programming Using Pascal* (Prentice Hall, 1988).

FORTH

5.34 Brodie, L., *Starting Forth* (Prentice Hall, 1987).
5.35 Winfield, A.F.T., *The Complete FORTH* (John Wiley, 1983).
5.36 Tracy, M. and Anderson, J.J., *Mastering Forth* (Prentice Hall, 1989).
5.37 Salman, W.P., Tisserand, O. and Toulout, B., *FORTH* (Macmillan, 1984).
5.38 Brodie, L., *Thinking Forth* (Prentice Hall, 1984).
5.39 Oakey, S., *FORTH for Micros* (Newnes, 1984).
5.40 Feierbach, G. and Thomas, P., *Forth Tools and Applications* (Prentice Hall, 1985).
5.41 Kelly, M. and Spies, N., *Forth: A Text and Reference* (Prentice Hall, 1986).

PL/1

5.42 Abel, P., *Structured Programming in PL/2 and PL/C* (Prentice Hall, 1985).
5.43 Hughes, J.K., *PL/1 Structured Programming* (John Wiley, 1987).
5.44 Reddy, R. and Ziegler, C., *PL/1: Structured Programming and Problem Solving* (West Ed. Pub., 1988).
5.45 Kennedy, M. and Solomon, M.B., *Structured PL/Zero Plus PL/One* (Prentice Hall, 1988).
5.46 Pollack, S.V. and Sterling, T.D., *A Guide to PL/1 and Structured Programming* (Holt, Rinehart & Winston, 1980).

C

5.47 Plum, T., *Learning to Program in C* (Prentice Hall, 1983).
5.48 Mullish, H., *The Spirit of C: An Introduction to Modern Programming* (West Ed. Pub., 1987).
5.49 Kerninghan, B.W. and Ritchie, D.M., *The C Programming Language* (Prentice Hall, 1988).
5.50 Bronson, G., *A First Book of C* (West Ed. Pub., 1988).
5.51 Barclay, K.A., *C: Problem Solving and Programming* (Prentice Hall, 1989).
5.52 Ammeraal, L., *Introduction to C for Programmers* (John Wiley, 1986).
5.53 Miller, L.H. and Quilici, A.E., *Programming in C* (John Wiley, 1986).
5.54 Berry, R.E., Meekings, B.A.E. and Soren, M.D., *A Book on C* (Macmillan, 1988).
5.55 McKay, P., *The Professional Programmers Guide to C* (Pitman, 1988).
5.56 Swartz, R., *Doing Business with C* (Prentice Hall, 1989).

RPG

5.57 Myers, S.E., *RPG II and RPG III with Business Applications* (Prentice Hall, 1982).
5.58 Stern, N., Sager, A. and Stern, R.A., *RPG II and RPG III Programming* (John Wiley, 1986).

5.59 Bux, W. and Cunningham, E., *RPG and RPG II Programming: Applied Fundamentals, a Job Approach to Learning* (Prentice Hall, 1980).

5.60 Myers, S.E., *RPG II with Business Applications* (Prentice Hall, 1979).

Other third-generation languages

5.61 Smith, A., *APL: A Design Handbook for Commercial Systems* (John Wiley, 1987).

5.62 Mason, J.A., *Learning APL: An Array Processing Language* (John Wiley, 1985).

5.63 Brown, J.A., Pakin, S. and Polivka, R., *APL2 at a Glance* (Prentice Hall, 1988).

5.64 Welsh, J. and Elder, J., *Introduction to Modula-2* (Prentice Hall, 1988).

5.65 Ural, S., *Introduction to Programming with Modula-2* (John Wiley, 1986).

5.66 Feldman, M.B., *Data Structures with Modula-2* (Prentice Hall, 1988).

5.67 Sutherland, R., *The Professional Programmer's Guide to Modula-2* (Pitman, 1988).

5.68 Wiener, R. and Sincovec, R., *Programming in Ada* (John Wiley, 1985).

5.69 Watt, D.A., Wichmann, B.A. and Findlay, W., *Ada: Language and Methodology* (Prentice Hall, 1987).

5.70 Gehani, N., *Ada: An Advanced Introduction* (Prentice Hall, 1989).

5.71 Dawes, J., *The Professional Programmer's Guide to Ada* (Pitman, 1988).

5.72 Pyle, I.C., *The Ada Programming Language* (Prentice Hall, 1985).

5.73 Schnupp, P. and Bernhard, L., *Productive Prolog Programming* (Prentice Hall, 1987).

5.74 Crookes, D., *Introduction to Programming in PROLOG* (Prentice Hall 1988).

5.75 Jones, G., *Programming in Occam* (Prentice Hall, 1987).

5.76 Jones, G. and Goldsmith, M., *Programming in Occam-2* (Prentice Hall, 1988).

Fourth-generation languages

5.77 Martin, J., *Fourth Generation Languages – vol. I: Principles* (Prentice Hall, 1985).

5.78 Martin, J. and Leben, J., *Fourth Generation Languages – vol. II: Representative 4GLs* (Prentice Hall, 1986).

5.79 Martin, J. and Leben, J., *Fourth Generation Languages – vol. III: Fourth Generation Languages from IBM* (Prentice Hall, 1986).

5.80 Watts, R., *Application Generators Using Fourth Generation Languages* (NCC, 1987).

5.81 Bernknopf, J., *A Practical Guide to 4th Generation Programming Languages* (McGraw-Hill, 1989).

UNIX

5.82 Barden, R.A., *UNIX in the Office* (NCC, 1989).

5.83 *Unix Products for the Office* (NCC, 1988).

5.84 Christian, K., *The UNIX Operating System* (John Wiley, 1988).

5.85 Nishinuma, Y. and Espesser, R., *UNIX – First Contact* (Macmillan, 1987).

5.86 Bach, M.J., *The Design of the UNIX Operating System* (Prentice Hall, 1986).

5.87 Bird, R., *The Professional Programmer's Guide to Unix* (Pitman, 1988).

Other operating systems

5.88   Keller, L., *Operating Systems* (Prentice Hall, 1988).
5.89   Finkel, R.A., *An Operating Systems Vade Mecum* (Prentice Hall, 1988).
5.90   Lister, A.M. and Eager, R.D., *Fundamentals of Operating Systems* (Macmillan, 1988).
5.91   Tanenbaum, A.S., *Operating Systems: Design and Implementation* (Prentice Hall, 1987).
5.92   Bic, L. and Shaw, A.C., *Logical Design of Operating Systems* (Prenctice Hall, 1987).
5.93   Allen, M., *Working with DOS* (Prentice Hall, 1988).

Spreadsheets

5.94   Anderson, J.J., *Business Computing with Lotus 1-2-3* (Prentice Hall, 1986).
5.95   Osgood, W.R. and Curtin, D.P., *Preparing Your Business Plan with Lotus 1-2-3* (Prentice Hall, 1985).
5.96   Moore, S., *Using Lotus 1-2-3, Release 3.0* (Prentice Hall, 1989).
5.97   Gilligan, J., *Easily into Lotus 1-2-3* (Macmillan, 1988).
5.98   Remenyi, D. and Nugus, S., *Lotus 1-2-3 for Financial Managers and Accountants* (McGraw-Hill, 1988).
5.99   Thomas, T.E., *Financial Decision Making with Visicalc and Supercalc* (Prentice Hall, 1985).
5.100 Gosling, P., *Easily into Supercalc 4* (Macmillan, 1989).
5.101 Greenfield, W.M. and Curtin, D.P., *Accounting with Symphony* (Prentice Hall, 1986).
5.102 Graff, L. and Cohen, N., *Financial Analysis with Symphony* (Prentice Hall, 1986).
5.103 Osgood, W.R. and Curtin, D.P., *Preparing Your Business Plan with Symphony* (Prentice Hall, 1985).

Word processing

5.104 Crondahl, J., *Wordprocessing with IBM's DisplayWrite Series* (Prentice Hall, 1986).
5.105 Cassel, D., *Wordstar Simplified for the IBM Personal Computer* (Prentice Hall, 1984).
5.106 Simons, C., *Easily into Wordstar* (Macmillan, 1988).
5.107 McClure, R., *Fast Access WordPerfect* (Prentice Hall, 1987).
5.108 Scanlon, L., *Multimate on the IBM PC* (Prentice Hall, 1986).
5.109 Gosling, J., *Easily into Multimate Advantage II* (Macmillan, 1989).
5.110 Milan, M., *Using the Amstrad Word Processor* (NCC, 1986).

Desktop publishing

5.111 Pickering, T., *What is Desktop Publishing?* (NCC, 1988).
5.112 Pickering, T., *Introducing Desktop Publishing* (NCC, 1989).
5.113 Lewis, J., *Interleaf* (Prentice Hall, 1987).
5.114 Lewis, J., *Pagemaker for the IBM* (Prentice Hall, 1987).
5.115 Lewis, J., *Using IBM PC Storyboard* (Prentice Hall, 1988).
5.116 Milan, M., *Desktop Publishing with the Amstrad PCW* (NCC, 1987).

6 Systems investigation

6.1 General aspects

Systems investigation, often loosely referred to as systems analysis, is not a precise science. It is more of an art augmented by a logical approach to the definition and recording of facts. We cannot always predefine the precise objective of the exercise, in other words the aims of a systems investigation are often rather broad at its commencement. Although the objectives have been defined by management in quite clear terms, it does not always follow that these are immediately translatable into investigation procedures. In fact, the systems investigation inevitably starts as a reconnaissance, perhaps prolonged, in its early stages. As the picture unfolds, it becomes more apparent where to look next, and eventually what to do and how to do it.

It is better if the systems analyst, as an investigator, avoids starting out with preconceived intentions in mind. Because a certain method applied on previous occasions solved most of the problems it does not follow that this will again be the case. Often it is more beneficial to look for differences in the present situation than to reach back for a previous solution.

Each circumstance and problem should be seen as part of a bigger situation. Consequently the investigator is well advised to keep 'why' as much in mind as 'what, when, who, where and how'. There is obviously no one answer to all the differing situations but there is usually plenty of scope for innovations and lateral thinking in system development. As a general rule, try not to meet a problem head-on, don't reach for the sledgehammer until the nutcrackers have been considered.

It is also interesting to remember that the person closest to a problem is often the least able to find a solution. Although it is realized that things are not as efficient as they could be, he or she cannot always see past a psychological barrier to the essential ideas beyond. And thus, in course of time, he or she comes to accept the situation as being inevitable and unalterable, methods as inviolate, and documents as sacred. The systems analyst must guard against being led into this trap during the course of the systems investigation work.

The advent of fourth-generation techniques (4GTs) including fourth-generation languages (4GLs) has introduced the likelihood of new approaches to systems investigation and design, such as prototyping. More is written about prototyping in Section 6.9, but for now prototyping can be regarded as a number of methods used to enable systems analysts and end-users to be certain that they are 'talking the same language'. That is to say, the end-user is drawn more closely into specifying what is required by being enabled to see the outcome of a system at a much earlier stage. This facilitates making decisions, and alterations, thereby moving more rapidly towards the final specification.

Figure 6.1 shows diagramatically a number of stages in systems investigation

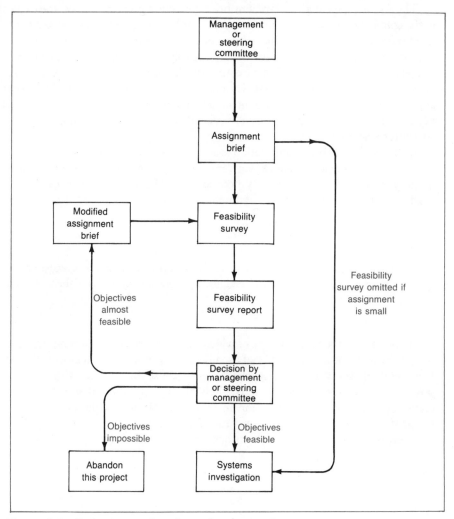

Figure 6.1 Early stages of systems development

work from the initial objectives through to the detailed fact finding. These stages are explained in full in the ensuing sections of this chapter.

Assignment briefs

As shown in Figure 6.1, an assignment brief is a directive from management or the steering committee to the systems department. Where a steering committee (Section 1.5) exists, the assignment is drawn up by its members. If there is no steering committee, an assignment brief is prepared by the senior manager responsible for management services or, alternatively, by the manager of the department most affected by the assignment.

The significance of an assignment brief depends a great deal upon the extent of the company's present information system. Where a computer system is already in operation, it is likely that the assignment will lead to an extension of its use. It must not, however, be assumed that expanding a computer's utilization is necessarily a trivial exercise. If the existing applications and database are not both open-ended, there may be a considerable amount of work in integrating a new application. This type of assignment sometimes arises as a result of a manager's need for further information, usually related to that already coming from the computer system.

If the need for further information is accepted by the steering committee after taking into account the systems work involved, it is generally possible to draw up an assignment brief in entirely precise terms. Because the manager knows what he wants, the aims of the assignment are clear and can be specified exactly.

EXAMPLE

'Design a system to provide a stockholding report of bought-out parts based on the updated month-end stock positions. The contents and layout of the report are to be shown on the attached specimen.'

In the case of a company whose previous computer use has been either minimal or non-existent, the assignment brief usually covers a much larger area of activities. It is inevitably couched in less specific terms because the aims are wider and the possibilities greater. Although it is likely in this situation that the steering committee has computer utilization in mind for solution of the problem, it is better if this idea is not put forward too strongly. The systems analyst will do a better job if he starts out with an open mind.

Main aspects of an assignment brief

Aims of the assignment
These are in broad terms in the case of a general feasibility survey or more specific for a detailed systems investigation. Certain of the aims are liable to be amended

as a result of the findings from the feasibility survey. A revised assignment brief is then prepared before commencement of the systems investigation. This is shown as the iteration in Figure 6.1, which may be repeated several times.

This process of moving towards the precise requirements is abetted by utilizing prototyped results (Section 6.9) if the manager or steering committee is unsure of the possible outputs of the new systems.

Authorization

The assignment brief acts as an authorization as well as a directive, and should be regarded as a request from top management for all staff to co-operate in the proposed survey or investigation.

In this respect the staff should be made aware of the existence and broad purpose of the assignment so that they do not come to regard it as an undercover operation by the systems/computer people.

Scope and limitations

The scope of the proposed systems work is indicated in the assignment brief, including any limitations or dictates imposed upon it. These may be absolute and unalterable such as a definite starting date for the new system or a top limit to the expenditure incurred by it. As far as possible constraints should be avoided as they tend to restrict the true potential of a new system.

Assistance

Information which may be of use in the investigation or design of system is provided. This includes factors such as proposed changes in the company's policies or structure, reference to previous work of a similar nature, names of persons who can be of immediate assistance, and the company's relationship to outside bodies.

Human aspects of systems

The initiation of a systems investigation often causes disquiet in the minds of the staff in the departments concerned. An investigation, probably to be closely followed by changes within the company, is very disturbing to some people.

The systems analyst, by being aware of the possible consequences for people, is in a position to allay apprehension and encourage interest and participation. It is therefore worth giving some consideration to the main reasons for apprehension and the ways in which it can be alleviated.

Career prospects

Middle-level staff, having reached a position a few rungs up the promotion ladder, are inclined to believe that a new system will damage their career prospects. It cannot be denied that a few careers have been damaged by computerization but, on the other hand, many have been greatly enhanced.

For the most part, middle-level staff are able to play an important role in the development and functioning of computer systems. They must, however, adopt a flexible attitude towards their workrole and position, and be willing to learn and operate new methods.

Job security

The possibility of redundancy tends to apply more to low-grade clerical staff since their jobs are more vulnerable to computerization. This is particularly the case where work is of a mundane nature requiring no great level of intellect. Also it must be admitted that computers are often installed in a company for the express purpose of reducing clerical costs. In many situations, however, it has turned out that there have been no actual redundancies in spite of the original intention to cut costs.

As with middle-level staff, low-grade clerical employees can enhance their career prospects by accepting changes and taking advantage of the resultant opportunities. These include a willingness to be retrained into DP jobs such as computer operators, data preparation clerks, keyboard operators and computer programmers. These possibilities should be borne in mind by the systems analyst when assessing future staff requirements.

Explanations

Where extensive changes are to be introduced in a company, the departmental staff may find themselves feeling totally confused. They cannot see how their work skills and jobs can be accommodated into the new system. This is largely because they do not as yet understand the new system or even the general concepts of computerization.

Starting at the investigation stage, it is useful if the systems analyst endeavours to allay these fears by explaining ideas about the ways in which the staff may fit into the new system. This is no easy task in the early stages because the staff's relevance to the new system has not yet become apparent.

Nevertheless staff are encouraged and reassured by seeing input screens or computer-produced results that they recognize and understand. This is a point at which early employment of prototyping can be advantageous.

Involvement

If the departmental staff can be made to feel that they are in some way contributing towards a new system, they are less likely to be apprehensive and more likely to be enthusiastic towards changes. They then believe that, to some degree, they are in control of their own destinies. One way in which involvement is brought about is by organizing project teams (Section 6.2), another is by encouraging the propagation of suggestions and ideas.

During the early stages of the investigation, the departmental staff should be shown films and given short talks to stimulate their interest in new methods. This approach is especially relevant to computer methodology and the usage of microcomputers, computer terminals and word processing in offices.

Systems analysts

The work of most systems analysts is in establishing and maintaining computer-based systems in the fields of business and administration. Their employers are industrial and commercial companies, national and local government departments, financial institutions, computer manufacturers, hospital boards and consultancy firms.

It is evident from the above that the range of work undertaken by systems analysts as a whole is very broad. The tasks of an individual systems analyst are, of course, much narrower during any one period of time, but nevertheless provide plenty of scope for innovation.

Duties of systems analysts

What are the specific duties of the systems analyst?
1. Investigating the existing information usage, systems and procedures of the company with a view to discovering inefficiencies and problems. Of major interest are areas of work incurring high costs, long throughput times and considerable clerical effort.
2. Analysing the findings of the investigation so that they can be used effectively in designing a new system.
3. Designing a new system that increases efficiency, minimizes problems and achieves the objectives set for it by the steering committee.
4. Testing and implementing the new system, including its appraisal before and after implementation, its documentation and continuing maintenance.

Programmer/analysts

A programmer/analyst is a combination of the jobs of systems analyst and programmer. The factors entering into the desirability of this arrangement are as follows:

The size of the company
If the company is small, there may not be scope for the two distinct occupations. The dual role of programmer/analyst provides more flexibility in assigning work

since on some occasions the work load demands analysts and on others programmers.

Communication between analyst and programmer

Two people working on the same problem do not always communicate with one another all that well. They perhaps fail to appreciate each other's capabilities, function and job problems, and this lack of empathy creates a communication gap.

The communication problem obviously disappears with the dual role, and so a number of larger companies have adopted the programmer/analyst policy for this reason.

Conflict of personal attributes

Systems work calls for a fair amount of extroversion and ability to communicate orally, especially during the investigation stage. The programmer's job, on the other hand, demands great concentration whilst working individually. It is unusual for the one person to have the attributes necessary for these two dissimilar tasks.

The increasing use of 4GLs will alleviate this dichotomy from the systems analyst's aspect. As it becomes simpler and quicker to create computer programs, there are greater prospects of more programmer/analysts.

The attributes of the systems analyst

As is the case for many other occupations, an extensive list of desirable attributes is compilable for systems analysts. And, although it is unlikely that any one person possesses all the qualities described below, they indicate the most suitable type of person. They also help the aspiring systems analyst to know the qualities to cultivate and the training to acquire.

Education and training

Nowadays a high proportion of systems analysts have degrees, diplomas or professional qualifications. The disciplines of most immediate application are business studies, data processing, accounting, information systems, computer science and management studies.

The more desirable areas of knowledge and expertise are:

- An understanding of the aims and purpose of the company from the point of view of its management.
- The procedures, techniques and problems entering into the following:

  Financial and management accounting
  Stock and stores control
  Personnel administration
  Production planning and control

Sales and marketing
Operational research and statistical methods

A systems analyst is clearly not expected to be fully conversant with all these areas but some knowledge of each is desirable.

- The methodologies of systems analysis and computer-based DP. Some knowledge of computer programming strategy is useful but there is no need for great expertise.
- The capabilities and purposes of computers, allied equipment and software. The systems analyst must, however, guard against becoming a computer addict as this tends to produce a machine-orientated instead of a problem-orientated approach.
- The sociological psychological and legislative factors relating to computerization and automation.

Personal qualities

The qualities listed below are to be regarded as ways of behaving and thinking that facilitate the work of the systems analyst.

- *Confidence* − a self-assured manner but not in any way supercilious.
- *Responsibility* − a willingness to accept the consequences of his decisions.
- *Creativity* − the ability to innovate and so avoid automatically applying old solutions to new problems.
- *Patience* − a readiness to listen and to explain, repeatedly if need be.
- *Communicability* − oral and written, so as to transmit information about, and enthusiasm for, new methods.
- *Logicality* − the ability to comprehend both the overall concept and the detail of a problem, and to think it through to a logical solution.
- *Persistence* − to obtain information not easily procured and gain results not easily attained.
- *Empathy* − the ability to self-project into the position of the person with problems.
- *Diplomacy* − in dealing with staff whose jobs are in jeopardy or who are inclined to be unco-operative.

Present situation and system

It is an unwise systems analyst who attempts to introduce a new system without first closely researching the relevant existing systems and situations, and the company's aims and problems. This would be 'shooting in the dark' at an 'undefined target', and so the chance of success would be negligible. It is impossible to imagine a situation where no information whatsoever is needed before a new system is designed. Even when there is no existing system, or for that matter no existing organization, there must still be some aims and purpose for future systems. Without at least some indication of these, a new system cannot even be conceptualized.

This is still the case even when a prototyping approach is adopted. It is sometimes suggested that systems investigation is unnecessary when using prototyping because new versions of a system can be prepared so rapidly that a heuristic approach is viable. This philosophy is risky and is best shunned except for the simplest of applications. It is more pragmatic to employ prototyping to augment the conventional systems development life cycle (SDLC) (see Sections 6.9 and 7.1).

It is all very well to say 'define the problems'; this is simple only if the problem definitions are expressed in broad terms. Aims such as increasing the company's profitability, reducing overheads, keeping within the departmental budgets, and satisfying customers' demands are all major problems that spawn a host of minor problems. All aspects of problem definition must therefore be investigated, and this entails discovering as much as possible about the present and future situations.

It is vital to find the facts appertaining to the present situation, and especially when a computer-based system is to be introduced or extended. Computers do not like vagueness and are adept at turning it into chaos. Their programs, input/output and database must be defined precisely if they are to be properly utilized. Inaccuracies, particularly in business programs, may cause the computer to run amok and so make a fool of its programmer and an enemy of its user. A user never quite trusts the computer again after erroneous results have been received from it.

Ideas for improvements

As well as actual facts about the existing situation, there is room for the consideration of people's ideas. Provided these are clearly recognized as subjective judgements and are differentiated from facts, they make a valuable contribution to the design of a new system. The analyst should therefore be on the lookout for well-founded ideas and should encourage the staff to put forward their suggestions during the investigation stage.

At a later stage these ideas can be encapsulated into specimens of input/output layouts in the course of prototyping so that the user is able to confirm that the ideas are understood.

Checklists

It would be convenient to have a comprehensive checklist showing all facts to be collected and questions to be asked during the course of a systems investigation, and merely to fill in the answers. This method is not recommended, however, unless the systems analyst has in-depth knowledge of the applications in queston.

This is because working from a predecided list does not bring to the surface the more subtle information and latent ideas. An individualistic approach does this more satisfactorily. None the less, within a given situation a simple checklist acts as a useful *aide-memoire*, especially for the less experienced systems analyst.

Information required

It has been suggested that a systems investigation should be carried out with no thought for the future usage of the facts gathered. The concept behind this idea is that the investigation is then completely unbiased in its findings and so all possibilities are given equal consideration. Interesting as this approach may be, it is likely to result in the accumulation of more facts than are truly relevant. In practice, most investigations are carried out with certain possible outcomes in mind.

One type of information that could be usefully gathered almost without limit are entity attributes for inclusion in the data dictionary. If there is any possibility of an entity being involved in a system, it is wise to collect information about its attributes.

6.2   Planning the systems investigation

It is unwise to attempt to work to a rigid timetable in planning a systems investigation, for the reasons that (1) the amount of work involved cannot be predicted precisely, and (2) the investigators are dependent upon the availability of the departmental staff whom they wish to interview.

As regards the first point, approximations of the time needed will have been made as a result of the feasibility survey. This means that a rough timetable can be prepared showing the weeks during which each project team or individual will be engaged in each project.

The employment of a Gantt chart is beneficial in that it gives a clear indication of the arrangements, and actual progress can be marked thereon. It is probably not worthwhile using network analysis (Section 8.4) at this stage owing to the imponderables involved.

The following points are to be remembered when planning a systems investigation.

- Investigate the applications or departments in the order of their natural sequence of activities, e.g. customers' orders before accounts receivable. This implies that normally the first applications investigated are those involving the most source data.
- Work from the senior staff downwards, seeking the permission of every

manager or supervisor before investigating his department's activities or interviewing his staff.

- Make arrangements well beforehand for visiting the departments so that the departmental staff can make preparations.
- Arrange for the investigation to be officially announced so that everyone concerned is aware of its imminence and legitimacy.

Project teams

The concept behind project teams is that the future users of a system should be involved in its design and implementation. They also take part in the investigation work because users have a deep knowledge of existing systems.

In a large company several project teams are formed at an early stage of the investigation, each team comprising a mixture of systems analysts and user department staff. Project teams are organized in a variety of ways dependent upon the particular circumstances, and are assigned to the areas under investigation. Each team consists of three or four members who work closely together.

Organizing project teams

- Each application area or department to be investigated is regarded as a project. Projects are planned to occupy a pre-estimated period of time, usually a few weeks. The senior systems analyst administers the project teams and defines the boundaries of each project.
- A team includes at least one member who is familiar with the day-to-day working of the department or area under investigation. This person is assigned to the team on a full-time basis throughout the duration of the project.
- The members of project teams drawn from user departments probably need some training in systems investigation methods. They then work with an experienced systems analyst for a few weeks before undertaking investigations on their own.
- In some circumstances project teams are composed of a mixture of business analysts and technical analysts. The former are responsible for defining the business problems precisely, and the latter for arriving at technical solutions.
- Each project team has a leader who is the most experienced systems analyst in the team. This appointment is temporary in that it lasts for only as long as the arrangement is advantageous. It is important to maintain flexibility and so teams need to be reorganized from time to time.
- Regular meetings, say fortnightly, take place between project team leaders in order to ensure that no gaps or overlaps occur in the areas under investigation. A record is kept of the progress made by the date of each meeting.

Feasibility surveys

A feasibility survey (study) acts as a reconnaissance for the systems investigation coming later. As is seen from the aims stated below, it provides information to facilitate a later in-depth investigation. In situations where the extent of an investigation is strictly limited or where the background information is already well known, the feasibility survey can be omitted.

The main sources of information gathered during a feasibility survey are top and middle (line) management. It is not necessary to unearth a large volume of detailed facts at this stage, and so lower levels of staff are not usually involved.

The major purposes of a feasibility survey are as follows:

Realism of assignment

To decide whether the aims stated in the assignment brief are realistic within the imposed constraints. Most aims are attainable if unlimited time and money are available, but this is never the case! If the assignment's aims are found to be unrealistic, it is necessary either to revise them or to remove the constraints.

Principal work areas

To determine the principal work areas relating to the aims stated in the assignment brief.

This information permits planning of the full investigation, including the optimum deployment of systems analysts and project teams between the departments and applications involved. It is also possible to arrive at estimates of the times needed for the various parts of the investigation, and hence their costs.

Scope for improvements

To discover the applications and departments where scope exists for saving money, time or effort. It is possible that the problem areas identified during the feasibility survey do not coincide with the aims stated in the assignment brief because they were not then recognized as problem areas. Nevertheless wherever there are large amounts of office work, administrative procedures or active information files, their lies potential for savings. Similarly, in work areas involving high levels of stock, sales or production, it is possible that more efficient planning could yield benefits.

Specialist assistance

To determine whether any specialists will be required in the systems investigation.

It may be found that problems exist that are not amenable to solution by conventional methods. Some specialist knowledge is therefore needed and this may not be available within the systems department or the project teams.

Typical of such knowledge are operational research techniques, statistical methods and investment appraisal techniques.

The specialist knowledge may be subsequently provided by persons within the organization or alternatively by external agencies if not available internally.

It is also possible that one or more of the systems analysts could be trained to cope with the problem.

Feasibility survey report

Generally it is best if the results of a feasibility survey are reported to management only briefly. The contents of the report are based on the four purposes described above. Suggestions and reasoned arguments are included so that the steering committee is able to decide whether to sanction further investigation or, alternatively, to reconsider the assignment's aims.

6.3   Users' information requirements

As explained in Chapter 1, information is closely connected with the aims and control of the company. And since, in essence, information is the only product of the new system, it is worth giving some thought to the company's need for it. During the systems investigation and later, in the systems design phase, the systems analyst concerns himself with finding the precise information needed by all levels of staff.

In this context information can be taken to include all useful output from the system. That is to say, all the reports, lists, etc., that stem from, and are needed in order to perform the company's activities. Information varies, for instance, from a financial report for the managing director at a high level to an employee's payslip at a low level.

Since no company is static, it is to be expected that changes in information requirements will be demanded in the course of time. It is part of the systems analyst's job to attempt to predict these changes and make provision for them in the new system. This is obviously a difficult task since even medium-term, let alone long-term, prediction is hazardous. In most cases all that is definite is that changes are likely to occur and that they will be of a certain type. A straightforward example of an almost certain change is to the income tax rates and brackets. When the new system is designed a simple method of accommodating such changes is built into it.

The main aspects of information requirements are as follows:

What information is required and by whom?

Bearing in mind that the information will most probably come from a computer and that this has either to be programmed or software purchased for it, absolute precision in defining the information should be aimed for. Lack of precision means that either changes have to be made later or that the user ultimately receives second-rate information.

There is a clear need for precision in the contents of information, and in this respect it is vital that the systems analyst and the prospective user are talking about exactly the same thing. For instance, the user's understanding of the term 'stock level' could be the quantity of an item in the warehouse unallocated at the end of each day; the systems analyst might see 'stock level' as the current, minute-by-minute, quantity of the item that exists anywhere in the firm. Differences in understanding of this nature may not come to light until it has come into operation. In either event, repetition of work, problems and financial cost may result.

Other important aspects of information are its form of presentation, i.e. screen or printed, and its layout (format).

The layout of information is the relative positions of the informational items together with the headings and annotations on the document or screen. It is not usually too difficult to put together a sample print or display for the user's approval. One of the problems in DP is that layouts which seem straightforward to DP specialists sometimes seem complicated to users, and so the layout of information should not be left entirely at the discretion of the analyst. Prototypes are useful in this respect.

The other main factor entering into the preparation of information is its sequence. This applies particularly to lists and tabulations that are to be used for reference purposes. A user may require a list in several sequences dependent on its purpose. Whatever the need, clear agreement regarding the sequence has to be arrived at. Here again a sample is helpful and especially when nested sequences are involved, e.g. order no. within account no. within week no. sequence.

Turning to the point of who requires the information, we are concerned with who is really going to make use of it. In other words, to whom should the documents be delivered immediately after printing and/or who should have a VDU on his or her desk? A situation to be avoided if at all possible is the passage of information via a hierarchy of managers, many of whom may have little or no interest in it, and a consequent delay in the information reaching the person(s) who have to act upon it.

Every document produced by a computer should have a recipient's name associated with it. Merely addressing a stack of documents to a department often results in no one person actually making use of the information thereon.

When is the information required?

The time of delivery or availability of information has to be agreed so that the user knows for certain when it will be available. This time usually depends on source data being received on time by the DP department. This point needs emphasizing especially if the user is responsible for submitting the source data.

A time of delivery or availability may be:

1. *The time of day*, day of the week, or within a certain time after a variable event, e.g. within 24 hours of a production hold-up.
2. *On demand*, i.e. when requested by the authorized recipient.

On-demand information is often requested by the user entering a query into a terminal, it is therefore important for the systems analyst and user to agree on the types of query information required. There are broadly two main types – immediate-access enquiries and longer-access query information. The former is generally a case of the user inputting a small amount of data and getting a small amount of information in return. For instance, entering a sales area number to get the value of sales in the area for the previous week. Longer-access information tends to be larger in volume, e.g. a query calling for a long list of product sales. This might take several minutes even with a mainframe and so is better sent later in document form rather than via the terminal.

The important point at this stage is that users are made aware of what is reasonable to demand as immediate access information and what they will have to wait a short time for. See 'On-demand reports' in Section 1.3.

3. *On exception*, i.e. when the information is found to contain figures outside a predecided range. As explained under 'Exception reports' in Section 1.3, the computer is programmed to pick out the exceptions and so these must be clearly agreed and defined during the systems investigation.

For what purpose is the information required?

Information is sometimes asked for in order that the recipient can use it to do further work so as to create additional information.

Some users have little understanding of a computer's capabilities and so do not ask for the additional information. This is especially true for situations involving logical decisions. Some people, while accepting that computers can do arithmetic, do not realize that many business decisions are also programmable.

6.4 Usage and flow of data

The usage of data and its flow within the company are the means through which control and planning are achieved. Data moves around the company mainly in documentary form, and consequently all documents have to be carefully scrutinized during the investigation. The data, and the documents themselves, may originate internally or come from external sources. After origination, documents are passed from hand to hand before being dispatched, filed or destroyed. By tracing their movements and noting the entries made at each stage, it is possible to obtain a clear picture of the flow of data and the build-up of information in the company.

From each department the following information needs to be obtained:

- What documents are originated and how many copies are prepared?
- What entries are made on each document and what work does this involve?
- Where are the documents sent after origination or processing?
- What documents are received from other departments or external sources?
- What data is extracted from each document and for what purpose?
- What documents are held in files, for what purpose, and for how long?

The answers to these questions are cross-checked between departments and any discrepancies are reconciled by further investigation.

Document usage

In this context documents can be regarded as any form, card, list or sheet used in the company for holding data. A document may also be part of a conventional file, i.e. a permanent document held with a number of similar documents.

Almost all documents consist of two essential parts — headings and entries. Internal documents start life as preheaded but otherwise blank forms, and entries are made during their use in the company. Externally originated documents arrive with entries already inserted but further ones may be added internally. Pitfalls to be watched out for are out-of-date and incorrectly headed documents. These are avoided by inspecting current live documents and asking their users to validate their contents. Similarly, unusual symbols or coloured entries on documents need investigation as they might have special importance to the user.

Nowadays many documents used in companies stem from the computer. From the systems investigation aspect these are no different from other, non-computer, documents. Their headings and entries are just as suspect and it is therefore wise to investigate them in the same way as for other documents.

Document specification

A convenient and accurate way of noting the meanings of a document's entries is to use a document specification. One such form is filled out for each type of document and a live specimen of the associated document kept with it. Referring to Figures 6.2 and 6.3, the square-outlined reference (T1) is the analyst's document reference and is unique to the particular type of document. The red circled letters on the specimen document, known as entry references, are entered thereon to cross-reference the entries to the document specification form. On some types of document there are several entries of a similar nature, e.g. the jobs on the works order in Figure 6.2. These similar entries are all covered by one reference letter.

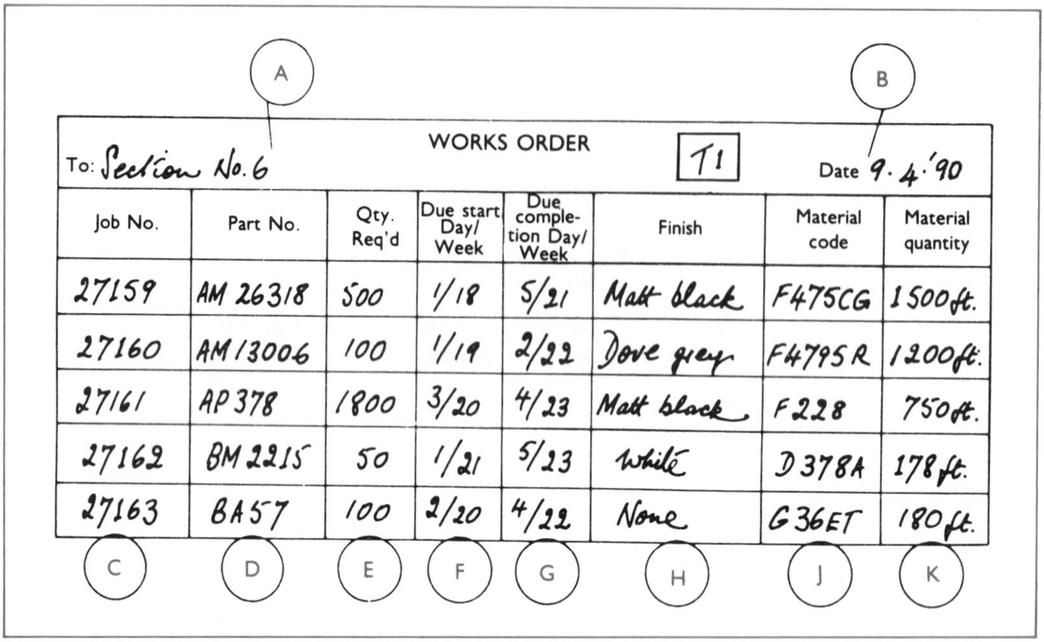

To: Section No. 6 — WORKS ORDER — T1 — Date 9.4.'90

Job No.	Part No.	Qty. Req'd	Due start Day/ Week	Due completion Day/ Week	Finish	Material code	Material quantity
27159	AM 26318	500	1/18	5/21	Matt black	F475CG	1500ft.
27160	AM/13006	100	1/19	2/22	Dove grey	F4795R	1200ft.
27161	AP 378	1800	3/20	4/23	Matt black	F228	750ft.
27162	BM 2215	50	1/21	5/23	White	D378A	178ft.
27163	BA57	100	2/20	4/22	None	G36ET	180ft.

Figure 6.2 Specimen document (works order form T1 in Figure 6.6)

For the most part the document specification (Figure 6.3) is self-explanatory but perhaps 'picture' calls for some elucidation. A '9' in the picture means that the corresponding position may have any value from 0 to 9, 'A' means A to Z. 'X' means either 0 to 9 or A to Z, and 'B' means a blank position. In order to reduce the size of a picture, it is conventional to put a bracketed number after the picture character to show how many times it is repeated, e.g. A(5) is equivalent to AAAAA. The purpose of noting an entry's picture is in order to plan its storage and usage in a computer system, this is especially pertinent to the creation of a data dictionary (Section 4.4).

EXAMPLE OF PROCEDURE

The procedure described below is the basis for the data usage chart in Figure 6.4 and the data flow diagram of Figure 6.6.

Narrative of works order procedure

1. Three copies (yellow, white and blue) of each Works Order (T1) originate in the Production Planning department. The job numbers are extracted from the Jobs Register (F1) and ticked off therein. The material codes and

Document Specification					
Name of document			Originating Department		
works Order Form			*Production Planning*		
Document reference		Date filled out	No. of copies		Systems analyst
T₁		*5. 7. '90*	*1 + 2*		*H.D.C.*
Initial distribution	*1. Supervisor (yellow Copy)* *2. Operator (white Copy) via Supervisor* *3. Production Planning (Blue Copy) to W.I.P. file*				
Remarks	*Section Supervisor ticks off jobs on his copy on completion*				

Entry ref.	Item description (heading)	Max items per doc.	Picture	Entered by	Remarks
A	*Section number*	*1*	*9*	*Planner*	
B	*Date originated*	*1*	*99/99/99*	*Job clerk*	*Day / Month / Year*
C	*Job number*	*5*	*9(5)*	*"*	*Taken from job register*
D	*Part number*	*5*	*AA 99999*	*Planner*	
E	*Quantity required*	*5*	*9999*	*"*	
F	*Due start, day/week*	*5*	*9/99*	*"*	*usually 5 but sometimes 6 working days per week*
G	*Due completion, "*	*5*	*9/99*	*"*	*do*
H	*Finish*	*5*	*A(12)*	*"*	
J	*Material Code*	*5*	*A999AA*	*Asst. Planner*	*Taken from parts spec. file*
K	*Material quantity*	*5*	*9999*	*"*	*Computed from parts spec. file*

Figure 6.3 Document specification form

quantities per part are derived from the Parts Specification file (F2), and the material quantity computed (quantity per part × quantity required).

2. The yellow and white copies of the works order are passed to the section supervisor, who passes on the white copy to the operator and retains the yellow copy. The third, blue, copy is filed in the Work-in-progress file (F3) in job number sequence.

3. On completion of a job, the section supervisor fills out a Job Completed form (T2) with two copies (pink and white). He retains the pink copy (for three months), and passes the white copy to the Production Planning department. Here is is checked for scrapped work and, if present, a Scrap Report (T3) is filled out and filed until the end of the month. All the white copies are then inserted into the Jobs Completed file (F5).

4. At the end of the month, the scrap reports are sorted into finish code within part number within section number sequence, and analyzed to create the scrap analysis (T4).

Data usage charts (grid charts)

Each document entry (also known as a data item) is liable to appear on several different documents, mainly as a consequence of it being transcribed from one document to another. An entry may also originate by being calculated from other entries, or be internally created as a result of the company's activities, or be received from external sources. In order to maintain a check on the multiple usage of data items, and to ensure no unnecessary duplication of data a 'data usage chart' is created, an example of which is shown in Figure 6.4.

Each transaction and file document is given a reference and wherever an entry appears on a document, a code is inserted into the appropriate position in the data usage chart. This code can be conveniently cross-referenced to the flowchart as demonstrated by Figures 6.4 and 6.6.

The meanings of these codes are as follows:

T = transcribed from the transaction document denoted by the reference, e.g. section number on the job completed form is copied from the works order form (T1).

C = calculated from other entries.

E = received from an external source and first recorded on this document.

I = originated internally and first recorded on this document.

F = transcribed from the file document denoted by the reference, e.g. job number on the works order is copied from the job register (F1).

Data flow diagrams

The two main methods of illustrating data flow are data flow diagrams (DFDs) and ISO/BSI flowcharts. The latter has now largely been superseded by DFDs

Document/display		Data items														Remarks
Name	Ref.	Section no.	Job no.	Part no.	Quantity reqd.	Due start date	Due completion date	Finish	Material code	Material qty.	Qty. completed	Qty. scrapped	Actual completion date	% scrapped	Material per part	
Jot reqists	F1	T1	I													Jot not ticked off as used.
Parts spec. file	F2	I	I											1		
Works order	T1	F2	F1	I	C	I	I	I	F2							Quantity required is computed from other data.
Jot completed form	T2	T1	T1	T1			I	I	C	I	I	I				
W.I.P. file	F3	T1	T1	T1	T1	T1	T1	T1	T1	I	I	I				
Scrap report	T3	T2	T2				T1			T2	T2		C			Quantities are summarised totals.
Scrap analysis	T4	T3	T3				T3	T3		C	C		C			
Jot completed file (print copies)	F4															As T2
Jot completed file (white copies)	F5															As T2
Scrap report file	F6															As T3

Figure 6.4 Data usage (grid) chart

as these are clearer and neater. Readers interested in ISO/BSI flowcharting should see Reference 6.11.

A DFD has four types of symbols, as shown in Figure 6.5, and is annotated in a similar way to a flowchart. A DFD concentrates on the flow of data rather than on the movement of documents, although in many cases these are the same thing.

The names annotated in the DFD should, in the final version, be identical to those in the data dictionary. The precise nature and contents of each data flow needs to be ascertained. This is done in a similar way to that explained previously for documents even if the data flow is not in document form, e.g. data keyed into an on-line terminal.

Figure 6.6 is the DFD of the works order procedure explained above.

6.5 Current activities

Cyclical nature of business activities

Nearly all business activities are performed on a regular cycle. For instance, wages are prepared weekly, sales statements monthly, stock evaluation annually. There are usually good reasons for these cycles within the existing system but they should not be assumed to be immutable. With a new system, advantages might be derived from modifying the activity cycles, and so the true reasons for the existing cycles ought to be ascertained.

Prominent among these reasons are the following:

- *Agreement* – e.g. with trade unions to pay workers weekly.
- *Legal* – e.g. financial statements prepared annually.
- *Phasing* – to interface with other activities, e.g. stock evaluation is needed for the annual balance sheet.
- *Control* – to provide regular information for decision-making, e.g. monthly factory loading reports to decide extra resources required.
- *Custom* – it has always been done that way!

The times of the day or the days of the week when tasks are carried out are decided by the activity's cycle. Some activities are scheduled backward from a finish deadline, others forward from a start point. An example of the former is the payroll routine, which hinges upon the agreed time at which the workers receive their pay packets. All the payroll work has to be fitted into the period between the end of the pay period and this deadline. An example of forward scheduling is the preparation of the periodic sales analysis (sales statistics). This activity is triggered by the final sales figures arriving at the end of the sales period, and the analysis is then prepared as quickly as possible.

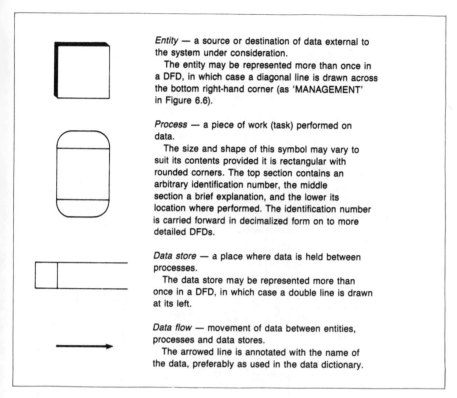

Entity — a source or destination of data external to the system under consideration.

The entity may be represented more than once in a DFD, in which case a diagonal line is drawn across the bottom right-hand corner (as 'MANAGEMENT' in Figure 6.6).

Process — a piece of work (task) performed on data.

The size and shape of this symbol may vary to suit its contents provided it is rectangular with rounded corners. The top section contains an arbitrary identification number, the middle section a brief explanation, and the lower its location where performed. The identification number is carried forward in decimalized form on to more detailed DFDs.

Data store — a place where data is held between processes.

The data store may be represented more than once in a DFD, in which case a double line is drawn at its left.

Data flow — movement of data between entities, processes and data stores.

The arrowed line is annotated with the name of the data, preferably as used in the data dictionary.

Figure 6.5   Data flow diagram symbols

Certain activities proceed without any apparent cycle. Handling customers' orders is sometimes of this nature in that orders arrive continuously and are dealt with in a steady stream day after day. The cycle of these orders varies considerably depending on their rate of arrival and the consequent workload but generally there is some target cycle such as goods being dispatched within 24 hours of receipt of order.

A new system will have greater processing power and consequently achieve results in a shorter time. This leads to an amended timetable of activities. Computers, for instance, are commonly operated for 16–24 hours per day and also at weekends. This enormous increase in processing power enables jobs to be started later or alternatively, completed earlier.

The factors to be considered in relation to activity cycles are as follows:

- When are the deadlines, and are they absolute or relative to other activities?
- When are the start points, and are they decided by internal or external circumstances?
- Could an activity be cycled either more frequently or less frequently with advantage? Dispatching bills daily instead of monthly, for instance, could result in prompter payments and fewer bad debts.

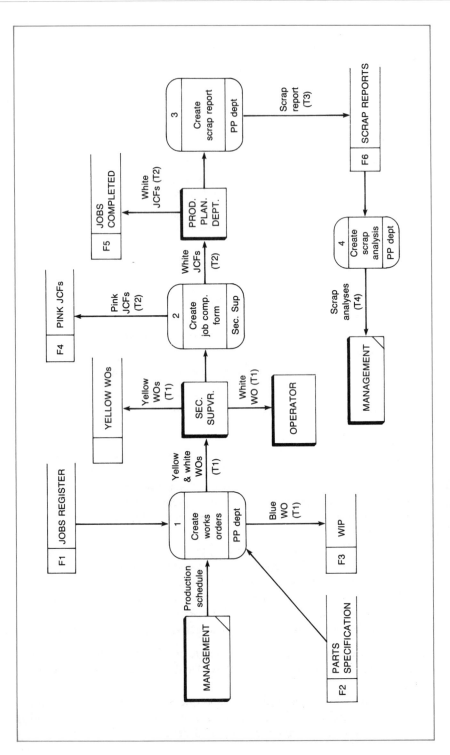

Figure 6.6 Data flow diagram of works order procedure

- What time allowances are made for uncontrollable factors? Delivery times of goods and letters, for example.

Activity cycles are conveniently recorded on a chart such as the weekly payroll in Figure 6.7. Monthly cycles call for a similar but extended version of this chart.

Activity processes

Every business activity consists of several processes (tasks); some are trivial, others are complex, but whichever is the case the analyst must be certain that he understands them and that none has been overlooked.

For each process the following information is needed:

- What numbers of documents, of all types, are handled?
- What enquiries are made; what information is demanded, how soon, and for what purpose?
- Do variations occur in the above; if so, in what way and for what reasons? Seasonal variations are common, and random variations also occur.
- What calculations are made in the course of handling documents and dealing with enquiries?
- What reference is made to file documents (data stores)? This includes the updating of file records and the creation of new ones.
- Are controls imposed on the process? These could be feasibility checks (Section 7.5) applied to the data handled or the creation of control totals and audit figures.
- What decisions are made and what follows as a result of each decision?

Decision trees and tables

It has already been suggested that certain processes involve decisions, a simple example of this is the scrap report decision above. Where a decision is straightforward and with only a few possible outcomes, there is no difficulty in specifying what is involved. In some cases, however, there are a number of related decisions leading to a large number of outcomes.

It is possible to construct a decision tree in which the decision points are shown as diamond-shaped symbols such as those in Figure 6.8. This method soon reaches its limit, however, owing to the sheer size of the tree if there are more than a few related decisions. A more convenient method is to employ a 'decision table'. This takes the form of a table on which are shown 'conditions' (decisions) and related 'actions' (outcomes). The four parts of a decision table are shown in Figure 6.9. Each column of entries is known as a rule and is given an arbitrary rule number.

The aims in preparing a decision table are (1) to ensure that all conditions and their associated actions are included, and (2) that all the rules are both logical

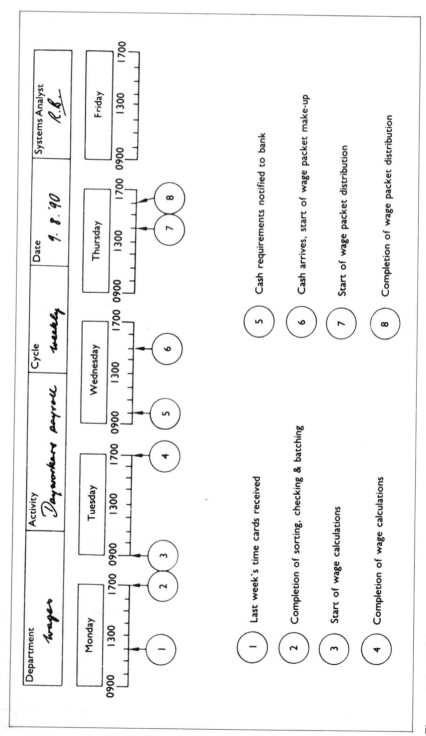

Figure 6.7 Activity cycle chart

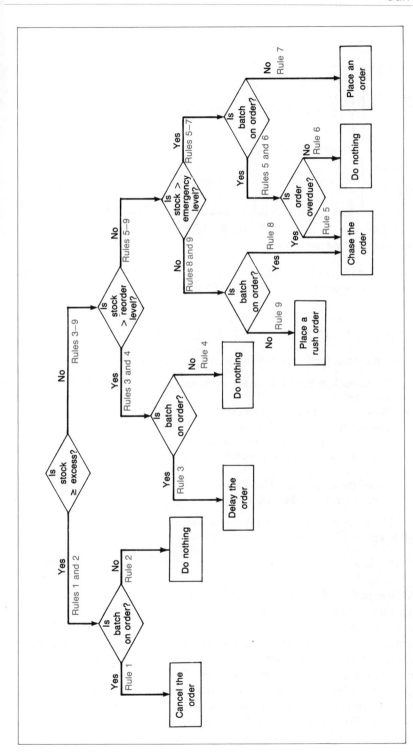

Figure 6.8 Decision tree of stock control procedure

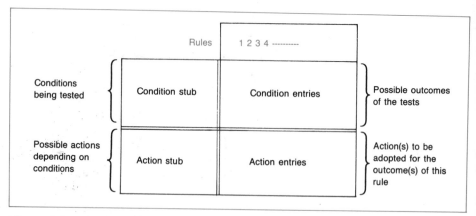

Rules   1 2 3 4 ----------

Conditions being tested

Condition stub

Condition entries

Possible outcomes of the tests

Possible actions depending on conditions

Action stub

Action entries

Action(s) to be adopted for the outcome(s) of this rule

Figure 6.9 Format of decision table

and clearly understandable. There must obviously be no ambiguity whatsoever as this would negate the whole point of this method.

EXAMPLE OF USE OF DECISION TREE AND TABLES

A stock control procedure follows the rules outlined below:

- If the stock-in-hand is at or above the excess level, any batch on order is cancelled.
- If the stock-in-hand is greater than the reorder level but below excess level, any batch on order is delayed.
- If the stock-in-hand has dropped to or below the reorder level, an order is placed unless a batch is already on order, in which case it is chased if overdue.
- When the stock-in-hand has dropped to the emergency level, any batch on order is chased, otherwise a rush order is placed.

The above procedure is shown as a decision tree in Figure 6.8 and as two different decision tables in Figures 6.10 and 6.11.

As is seen from Figures 6.10 and 6.11, the condition entries and the action entries may be in either 'limited' or 'extended' form. A limited condition entry consists of either a 'yes' or a 'no' or is irrelevant (Y, N and − respectively). An extended condition entry is either in descriptive or in quantitied form. Similarly, a limited action entry comprises one or more crosses in each column to indicate the action stub(s) or otherwise a blank.

Limited entries inevitably mean that more details are needed in the stubs than with extended entries. They also tend to result in more rows appearing in the action parts of the decision table. It is also possible to have a decision table with limited conditions and extended actions, or vice versa.

Rules	1	2	3	4	5	6	7	8	9
Is stock ⩾ excess?	Y	Y	N	N	—	—	—	—	—
Is stock > reorder level?	—	—	Y	Y	N	N	N	—	—
Is stock > emergency level?	—	—	—	—	Y	Y	Y	N	N
Is a batch on order?	Y	N	Y	N	Y	Y	N	Y	N
Is order overdue?	—	—	—	—	Y	N	—	—	—
Cancel the order	X								
Delay the order			X						
Do nothing		X		X		X			
Chase the order					X			X	
Place an order							X		
Place a rush order									X

Figure 6.10 Limited condition/limited action decision table of stock control procedure

There are no hard and fast rules as to which arrangement to adopt in a decision table, each situation has to be judged on its own merits. Generally speaking, limited entries are clearer to follow but they can become extensive in number when many decisions are involved.

Exceptions to the norm

It is the ability to cope with the exceptions that makes or breaks a system. During the systems investigation the analyst is perpetually looking out for exceptions, and indeed, exceptions to the exception. The information he acquires about the present system naturally tends to apply to the normal state of affairs rather than the unusual. It is therefore important to appreciate what is meant by exceptions.

Special procedures

These are associated with abnormal situations such as the following:

- the registration of new employees;
- the paying off and deregistration of leavers;
- the recording of a new product's details;

Rules	1	2	3	4	5	6	7	8	9
Stock-in-hand?	≥ Excess	≥ Excess	< Excess and > reorder level	< Excess and > reorder level	≤ Reorder and > emergency level	≤ Reorder and > emergency level	≤ Reorder and > emergency level	≤ Emergency level	≤ Emergency level
State of batch on order?	Placed	Not placed	Placed	Not placed	Overdue	Placed and not overdue	Not placed	Placed	Not placed
Action regarding the order	Cancel order	None	Delay order	None	Chase order	None	Place an order	Chase order	Place a rush order

Figure 6.11 Extended condition/extended action decision table of stock control procedure

- the validation of a new customer's creditworthiness;
- chasing potential bad debts;
- *ad hoc* reports demanded by management;
- sudden and unexpected procedural changes as caused by strikes and other disruptions.

Abnormal workloads

These tend to occur at certain times of the year, mostly owing to seasonal fluctuations in sales demand. They also occur randomly due to unforeseen circumstances and chance factors. An example of an unforeseen circumstance is the liquidation of a competitive company causing an increased demand for the company's products. A chance factor might be an unexpected weather pattern creating a sudden demand.

Peak workloads are of particular relevance in the designing of real-time systems because they have to be handled immediately by the computer and without degradation of service.

Periodic additional work
This occurs at predecided times owing to annual holidays, stocktaking, changeover of the sales range, and financial year-end work.

Error-correction procedures
These are designed to cope with errors in procedures, missing data, mistakes in calculations and misunderstandings in requirements. By understanding the error-correction procedures currently adopted, the systems analyst is better able to design equivalent procedures for the new system.

If the new system's input is on-line, errors are detectable at an earlier stage and are therefore easier to correct. Nevertheless it has to be clearly understood what errors might occur and how best to correct them.

Overtime working
Overtime is caused not only by high workloads but also by bottlenecks preventing work starting until insufficient time remains before a completion deadline. Many businesses have peak workloads intrinsic to their trade at certain times of the year. These demand additional resources not available except through overtime working.

Staff absence and machine breakdowns
Although these contingencies do not usually occur frequently, it is advisable to be aware of the standby arrangements in case they impinge upon the new system.

6.6 Current system costs

This section should be read in conjunction with Section 7.9 as this discusses the costs and savings of a new system.

There are few things that make as much impact upon business managers as the chance of either saving or making money. If management is presented with a clear statement showing potential savings in costs from a new system, it is more readily accepted. Tangible cost savings, such as those brought about by quantifiable reductions in staff, equipment and materials, are straightforward to explain. Intangible cost savings are less easy to quantify, and often no definite monetary value can be placed upon them. Nevertheless, intangible costs are important since they may be greater than realized, and tend to increase. If at all possible some figure should be put on intangible costs so that they can be judged in comparison with other costs.

EXAMPLES OF INTANGIBLE COSTS

- Hold-ups in production caused by the late ordering and/or late delivery of materials.
- Loss of orders due to overpricing of quotations, goods out of stock or overloading of production facilities.
- Overstocking of slow-moving items.
- Obsolete stock clogging the stores or warehouse.

Cash flows

Existing costs can be split into recurring expenditure and capital (fixed asset) costs. Recurring costs are those incurred at regular intervals such as wages, materials, rented equipment and overheads. Capital costs are applicable to the outright purchase of permanent items such as office machines and equipment, computers, furniture and premises. From the financial accounting aspect, capital costs are covered by depreciation incorporated into the financial statements. In other words, the cost of a capital purchase is disposed of on paper by spreading it over a number of years. Nevertheless, in spite of the depreciation concept, the cash for the purchase still has to be found, and the supplier paid either directly, or indirectly via a financing institution.

By combining all the relevant costs, a cashflow pattern covering past time periods can be created and these costs are projected into the future. The extent to which future costs are accurately predictable depends largely upon how far the projection stretches. It is not normally too difficult, however, to cover the new few years with reasonable accuracy.

A scientific approach to evaluating and comparing the costs of projects is to discount future cash flows back to their present values. In other words to calculate the net present value (NPV) of all future costs and savings. The higher the NPV, the more desirable the project as an investment venture. Thus when comparing two or more alternative projects, their respective NPVs are computed and, other things being more or less equal, the project with the higher NPV is chosen.

A simple case of discounting is to suppose we are to receive £10,000 one year from now and the current borrowing rate is 15 per cent, then the NPV of this amount is £10,000 ÷ 1.15, i.e. £8,696 (to the nearest pound).

EXAMPLE OF CALCULATING NPV OF A PROJECT

A company intends to purchase a computer system for £450,000 and expects to make savings during the first few years of its use as shown in Table 6.1. The money for purchase has been borrowed at an interest rate of 20 per cent. It is assumed that the system will last for five years.

Table 6.1

Period	Costs	Savings	Discount factor	Present value
Start	£450,000		1.000	−£450,000
1st year	£100,000		0.833	−£ 83,300
2nd year		£150,000	0.694	+£104,100
3rd year		£300,000	0.579	+£173,700
4th year		£400,000	0.482	+£192,800
5th year		£400,000	0.402	+£160,800
			NPV =	+£ 98,100

Other methods of investment appraisal are payback period, returns/outlay (savings/costs) ratio and internal rate of return. The former two are simple but crude, the latter is sophisticated but difficult to compute. See Reference 6.13 for more on investment appraisal.

Sources of cost information

Primary sources of cost figures in large organizations are the costing department and the budgetary control department. These departments are able to provide actual costs, operating budgets and cost variances analysed under cost heads. Unless the system analyst is a cost accountant, he is wise to ask for help in interpreting these figures.

Another difficulty entering into the costing of the existing system is that it is unlikely to be supplanted completely by the new system. The miscellany of tasks remaining will eventually require costing along with or as part of the new system so that cost comparisons can be made equitably.

Staff costs

If cost information is either not available or is unsuitable, the analyst must compute the costs himself. There is not a lot of advantage to be gained, however, from a very detailed costing exercise. For the moment, the systems analyst is concerned with approximating the costs of the present activities that could be replaced by the new system.

Machine and equipment costs

In addition to labour costs, the systems analyst is also interested in existing machine (including computers) costs, material costs and overhead costs. Machines and equipment are either rented, leased, hire-purchased or purchased outright. If one of the first three methods has been adopted, the cost is easy to determine but long-term contracts may prevent any immediate reductions in these costs with the introduction of a new system. If the machine has been purchased outright, it is necessary to apportion its cost over its estimated life to obtain an annual cost. The company's depreciation policy gives some guidance here but this may not truly represent the actual annual costs.

Office equipment, such as filing cabinets and furniture, has a long life and therefore its annual cost is low. Generally, office equipment of this nature continues in use with a new system and so, in effect, its cost can be ignored. If it is the intention to purchase new equipment, the old equipment is written-off since it will have long since been paid for and its scrap value is negligible.

Office materials comprise mostly stationery, especially that associated with sales procedures, e.g. order forms, bills, invoices, statements. In a strongly sales orientated company it is likely that these costs are fairly high and will tend to remain so, therefore a careful investigation is desirable.

Overhead costs cover items such as indirect labour (e.g. office cleaners), indirect materials (e.g. cleaning materials), heating, security, and so on. The apportioning of overhead costs between departments is a fairly complicated business and becomes impossibly so if attempted between individual activities. In most cases it is not unreasonable to assume that the overheads of the present and future systems will balance out. Failing this, the systems analyst should enlist the assistance of the cost accountant in estimating, allocating and apportioning overheads.

6.7 Entity sets

In this context an 'entity' can be taken to mean any artefact, person, company or activity with which the company is concerned and about which data is kept.

An 'entity set' is a group of the above items that have a common characteristic in terms of usage or physical attributes.

Entity sets include, for instance, amongst many others:

- the products manufactured by a company;
- the customers of a bank;
- the workers employed in a factory;
- the machines installed in a factory;
- the students in a college.

Entities fall into three types — real, activity and conceptual. Real entities are actual things, e.g. products; activity entities are happenings, e.g. financial transactions; conceptual activities are more abstract, such as cost centres.

The main reason why entity sets are of interest is that they form the data framework for the new system. By discovering their characteristics and understanding their usages, they can then be incorporated into the new system more beneficially.

The full understanding of entity sets is of especial importance prior to designing and creating a database and the associated data dictionary (Section 4.4).

The relevant characteristics of each entity set are:

How many different entities are at present in the set and how is the number changing over time?

With some sets the number is almost static, whereas others fluctuate violently even within a short period. We are mainly concerned with how many entities might have to be catered for within the foreseeable future. This is relevant to the amount of backing storage needed to hold the database or the files. It is equally significant for microcomputers holding a few thousand entities on a floppy disk as for a mainframe holding a few million on several volumes of hard disks.

How is the set inherently subdivided?

In almost every case there are several ways in which the entities in a set can be separated into groups. Bank customers, for instance, could be split into personal accounts and business accounts, and the former further segregated into deposit accounts and current accounts.

The present size of each group and, as far as possible, its future size should be ascertained. This information relates to the different ways in which these groups will be processed.

What attributes apply to the entities?

The attributes of an entity set give rise to the data items that need to be held in the database. Attributes are sometimes extensive in number and, at this stage, the systems analyst may be uncertain as to their relevance to the new system. The answer is to become aware of the existence of all attributes, and to gather information about those that are clearly relevant.

The sort of information needed is the same as explained under data dictionaries in Section 4.4.

Examples of attributes and data items are given in the case study in Chapter 9.

What code numbers apply to the entities?

In this context, code numbers are the attribute(s) that in some way identify the entity. Thus, a code number of a bank account is its account number.

By reading 'code number design' (Section 7.2), the reader will become aware of the need for information about code numbers. The main points at this stage are to establish the existence of code numbers pertaining to the entity set and discover what meanings, if any, can be deduced from them. It is also important to establish the precise layouts (pictures) of each set of code numbers.

Bearing in mind that code numbers used in computer-based DP must give unique identification, this is a convenient point at which to determine a code number set's validity. That is to say, is there a one-for-one relationship between the entities and the code numbers. Any suspicion that this is not the case, calls for further investigation and, if necessary, rectification or possibly complete replacement of the set of code numbers.

Entity modelling

Entity models, also known as entity relationships and logical data structures, are a method of analysing information acquired in the process of systems investigation. It is a technique that is used in methodologies such as SSADM (Section 7.11), Information Engineering (IE) (Section 7.11) and Multiview. The precise approach differs slightly between these methodologies and so the explanation that follows covers the main points only.

An entity model shows diagramatically the relationship between sets of entity types or, in fact, between any things of interest to the business. These include concepts, e.g. costs, as well as objects but not unquantifiable things such as 'order processing' since this is a process. The main advantage to be gained from constructing entity models is that the analyst is more certain that all relationships have been noted. They reduce the possibility of a system being designed which has had an important relationship accidentally omitted. Such an omission could seriously delay the implementation of the system while it is corrected. This would be so if, for instance, the fact that 'subjects' in Figure 6.12 were not realized as being composed of 'modules'.

From Figures 6.12 and 6.13 it is seen that entity models may be illustrated in two main ways. One way (Figure 6.12) is to show the entity types as rectangles

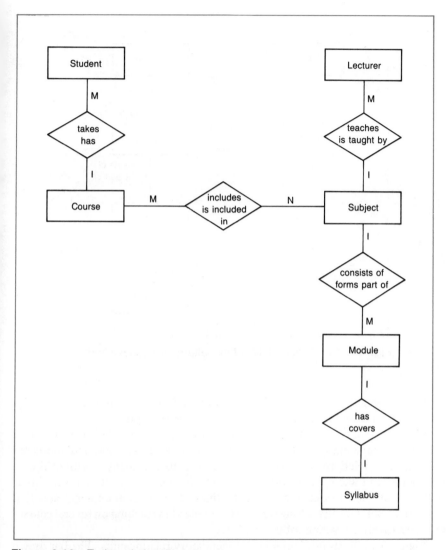

Figure 6.12 Entity relationships

linked by diamonds which indicate their relationships. The designations M, N and 1 signify whether a relationship is one-to-one (1 and 1), many-to-one (M and 1) or many-to-many (M and N). In this context 'many' can be taken to mean two or more.

A one-to-one relationship is such as module and syllabus, i.e. there is only one syllabus for a module and there is only one module that has a particular syllabus.

An example of a many-to-one relationship is students on a course. A course has many (or at least several) students but a student does only one course at a time.

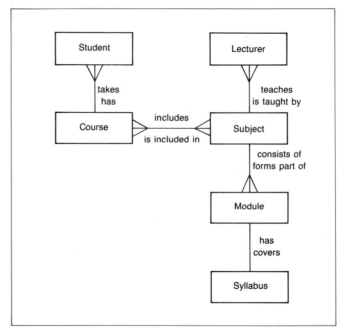

Figure 6.13 Entity relationships (alternative convention)

Many-to-many is exemplified by courses and subjects. A course includes several subjects and a subject is often part of several courses.

Figure 6.13 illustrates the same relationships as Figure 6.12 but is drawn in a different convention, i.e. the IE convention, in which symbols and annotated lines indicate relationships, crow's feet representing a 'many' relationship.

Figure 6.14 shows a relationship in which there is an alternative, this is indicated by the short curves across the lines. The diagram demonstrates that at a certain point in time a lecturer may be involved in teaching on several courses or alternatively be taking sabbatical leave.

Figure 6.15 illustrates optional and mandatory relationships. The bar drawn across the line means that a student must be registered as taking a course (even if temporarily absent). The circle indicates that a course can exist (for a time at least) without any student registered as on it.

A point to be remembered about entity modelling is that the diagrams can be misleading. The analyst must be absolutely clear in his own mind as to precisely what the entities and relationships mean.

Even in the simple example in Figures 6.12 and 6.13, some degree of ambiguity exists. Does a lecturer teach a subject, as shown, or does he really teach a module? In the long term he would generally be regarded as teaching a subject, whereas for a shortish period it is convenient to regard him as teaching a module. A semantic question is whether a lecturer teaches a subject or students.

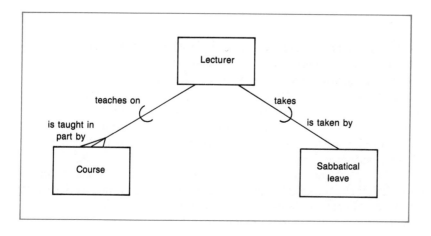

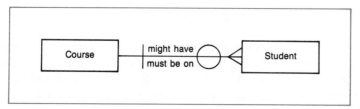

Figure 6.15 Mandatory and optional entity relationships

6.8 Fact-finding methods

Interviewing

In common with many other human activities, the art of interviewing is better learned through practice than from books. Nevertheless some guidelines are useful, especially to the beginner. Interviewing is an indispensable part of fact finding and, if well conducted, provides valuable information about policies, procedures and situations that might not be apparent from documents.

There are several guidelines to help the interviewer, as explained below, but over and above these comes the need for a flexible approach. Interviewees range from company directors to junior clerks, and cover a wide spectrum of ages, social backgrounds and personal attitudes. A systems analyst has to some extent to be 'all things to all men'. This does not imply, however, that he merely adopts a role-playing posture − this would soon be detected by the interviewees with his consequent loss of their regard.

Interviewing top management

Top managers are concerned with strategic decisions and this ought to be reflected in the level of questions put to them. They should be encouraged to explain objectives, major problems, large-scale developments, and the like. Questions about petty details of the company's operations will only serve to irritate them. The discussions at this level cover aspects such as impending mergers, takeovers, new markets, new product ranges, expansion of manufacturing or service facilities and future reorganizations; also the present structure of the line management and their responsibilities.

In particular, the systems analyst discovers from top management the information they need in achieving their aims. At the same time, he is in a position to explain the potentialities of DP systems from their point of view, and particularly if the manager is unfamiliar with computer-based systems.

Interviewing line management

Here the interviews are more concerned with tactical planning and the related information. Most line managers have ideas for improving the present system if facilities were available. They are also able to elucidate on the organization and the staffing of their department, thus enabling the systems analyst to discover who else to interview and what aspects to investigate. This is also a convenient time for seeking permission to interview the manager's staff.

Interviewing operational staff

Operational staff are best not encouraged to put forward policy suggestions even though, in some cases, they are only too keen to do so. Questions are restricted to details of the interviewee's duties and, if necessary, they are asked to demonstrate their work rather than describe it. It is important at this level to allay the feelings of apprehension that arise when changes are on the horizon.

Another worthwhile point to remember is that operational staff are more likely to be politically sensitive towards management and it is therefore advisable for the systems analyst to maintain a strictly neutral attitude in this respect. By friendliness, avoidance of condescension and showing an interest in their work, the co-operation of operational staff is generally secured.

Guidelines to interviewing

- The interviewer should brief himself on the position and general duties of the interviewee; and also, of course, on the subject of the interview. Interviews are either structured or unstructured, if the former approach is chosen, a plan for the interview has to be devised.

- Arrange the time, place and subject of the interview well beforehand so that the interviewee is able to make arrangements regarding his work, and to collect together documents and information related to the subject of the interview. If there is likelihood of continual interruptions or eavesdropping, the interview should be arranged to take place away from the interviewee's normal workplace.

- Put the interviewee at ease by providing a quiet, interruption-free environment. If a tape recorder is used, explain why and reassure the interviewee that it is not for subsequent 'inquests'.

- Listen more than talk, yet say enough to keep the discussion going along the right lines. Avoid leading questions, aim towards short questions and long answers. Take written notes as one's memory is unreliable; if it is felt necessary, prepare beforehand a draft of the questions.

- Interview only one person at a time, thus eliminating arguments between staff and reducing the diffidence of reserved persons. If a manager calls in members of his staff to answer specific questions, encourage them to depart as soon as this has been done. Similarly, discourage a manager from attending an interview involving one of his staff as this tends to inhibit the latter.

- Control the interview by minimizing digressions, separating opinions from facts, and not allowing generalizations to obscure the true situation.

- Do not attempt to cover too much ground in one interview. After one hour, at the most, temporarily conclude the discussion and arrange to resume in the near future. Long interviews suggest that either the interviewee is being allowed to digress or that the discussion is becoming bogged-down.

- Conclude with a brief resumé of the ground covered, asking whether any major points have been omitted, and leave an opening for further discussion. Any dubious information is verified by sending a memorandum later; with operational staff this is best done via the department manager.

Reference 6.9 gives a more detailed exposition on interviewing.

Questionnaires

The adoption of questionnaires as a fact-finding tool is not as straightforward as the inexperienced systems analyst might assume. It is wise to give careful consideration to their employment and design. The main difficulty lies in the avoidance of misunderstandings because the respondent cannot easily ask about vague or confusing questions. Similarly, the systems analyst cannot always pursue answers that might lead to further information. Questionnaires should be used only when no other method of fact finding is practicable: they supplement rather than replace other methods. If time and circumstances permit, a trial run should be carried out using a small number of representative persons prior to the full survey.

Situations suited to questionnaires

- Where the systems analyst is located at a considerable distance from the staff to be questioned, e.g. managers of widespread branches.
- Where there is a large number of respondents such that interviewing is prohibited by the time available, e.g. a large sales force.
- As a means of verifying information found by other methods. The questions in this case must be framed so as to avoid leading the respondent.
- When the questions are simple and call for direct answers, preferably when they are to be selected from a list of answers shown on the questionnaire, i.e. multiple choice.
- When a full set of replies is not necessary in order to determine the facts. People tend to give low priority to filling out questionnaires, and therefore the response is rarely 100 per cent. The sample returned must, however, be large enough to provide a reasonably accurate picture of the situation.

Guidelines to questionnaire design

- Give a brief explanation of its purpose if this is not self-evident from its contents.
- Bear in mind the level of intellect and likely interest of the respondents.
- Keep the questions short, unambiguous and unbiased, and, whenever possible, give multiple choice answers from which one is to be selected. In any case do not pose questions that necessitate a long answer.
- Avoid overmuch branching and skipping in the structure of the questionnaire, e.g. 'if the answer is "yes" to go to Question 8; if "no" omit the next two questions'.
- If the survey is extensive, give consideration to the use of OMR documents in order to reduce the manual work in analysing the answers (Section 3.5).
- Impose a deadline by which the questionnaire has to be returned. A prepaid addressed envelope is beneficial if the respondent is without secretarial help.

Observing

Observing entails watching the departmental staff carrying out their various tasks. It is a time-consuming activity and therefore not to be indulged in without a definite purpose. As a rule people do not take kindly to being observed at their work, so this is one of the systems analyst's more delicate tasks. Any attempt to quantify the staff's activities by timing their actions is likely to result in a distorted measure of their work and so a work-study approach is inappropriate in this context. When aware of being observed, people tend to modify their behaviour, sometimes subconsciously, in order to project a good impression, e.g. working harder.

These remarks must not be taken as implying that observing is always a waste of time and effort. When done discreetly, this method yields information unobtainable through other methods and much depends upon the nature of the work in the department. Observing the operational staff carrying out a routine clerical function yields little new information. On the other hand, watching people at work in a diversified department often brings to light numerous tasks and problems not discovered previously.

It must be borne in mind, however, that even an extensive period of observation may not expose all the problems. At best it is possible to get only snapshots of a continuously changing scene, and these may lead to a distorted impression of the true picture if not supported by other methods of fact finding.

The aspects of a department's work revealed by observing are:

Interruptions to the normal flow of work   These are caused by callers from other departments, telephone calls received and made, and visitors from outside the company.

Informal communication of information   This is between members of the department, callers and visitors, and over the telephone. Since no paperwork is involved, this type of information flow might go undetected if not observed.

The usage of files of documents   Included here is the non-routine reference to file documents in order to handle queries, often received by telephone. In an already computerized system, it is possible to observe how the staff make use of computer printouts and VDU displays.

The balance of the workload   This applies to the different times of the day or week, and between the various members of the department.

Operational inefficiencies   The observable factors here are bad working conditions, machines and equipment in poor condition, absence of authority or leadership, and insufficient understanding of the procedures.

Reading

The problem with reading as a fact-finding tool is in knowing what to read and when to stop. Companies have virtually unlimited amounts of documents and literature, and it is therefore important that the systems analyst is not swamped by them. It is best to be guided by the department staff who appreciate the problem and are willing to select the relevant material.

Literature worth perusing comprises:

Reports of previous surveys and investigations   The more recent of these are likely to contain valid information and conclusions, but even the older reports may contain facts and ideas bearing upon modern systems. The older the information, however, the more stringently must it be verified before being acted upon.

Company instructions (or the equivalent)   These documents provide useful information regarding the company's organization, administrative procedures, policies and future developments. Company instructions are likely to exist only in the larger, highly structured companies and in government departments.

Sales literature and company information booklets   These enable the analyst to acquire an overall and broad view of the company's activities and organization.

Job descriptions   These should confirm the positions, duties and responsibilities of the staff as noted during interviewing.

Existing DP system documentation   This includes the documents as described in Section 7.10.

Management reports   These encompass a wide range of management information and form a good starting point for discussions *re* future requirements.

Procedure manuals   It is not likely that procedure manuals are in great profusion as most companies do not have them. Where they do exist, they should form a helpful background to present procedures.

Forms and documents   The need to investigate these has been explained in Section 6.4.

Measuring

When facts are unobtainable through other methods or when their accuracy is suspect, measuring or estimating is employed. It is not a method recommended for general use since it absorbs considerable time and demands great care. Measured factors include quantities, times, intervals and rates. The tools of measuring are counters (mechanical or electronic), rules, clocks, stopwatches, pocket calculators, scales, and last but not least, the human brain. In most cases measuring yields an approximate figure but nevertheless this is acceptable for its purpose.

EXAMPLES OF MEASUREMENTS AND COUNTS

Quantities (numbers):
of stock record cards held; of staff employed in the wages department.

Times:
to prepare a set of sales statistics; to deal with a query from management.

Intervals:
between the month-end and dispatching the last sales statement; between the issue and return of job tickets.

> **Rates:**
> of arrival of customers' orders per day; of issue of parts from stores per hour.

Each of these factors has certain inherent characteristics, i.e. maximum, minimum, average (mean, mode or median), spread (e.g. standard deviation) and distribution pattern, and so the analyst needs to be clear as to precisely what he is attempting to measure. For instance, merely to find that an average of 200 customers' orders arrive per day is not necessarily of great import. More consequential is the fact that this figure rises on occasions to 500 per day, and that all orders have to be dealt with on the day of receipt.

Sampling

A systems investigation often necessitates determining a figure that can be found only by measuring a sample drawn from the entire group. This is usually because the entire group (known as the 'population') is too large to be measured completely and so a sample is measured in the hope that this is representative of the population.

> ## EXAMPLE OF SAMPLING
>
> The average number of items on sales invoices is found by inspecting a sample of, say, fifty invoices and counting the number of items on each of these. If it is found that the numbers of items are closely grouped, it is safe to use simply the average of the sample. A wide spread of the numbers of items in the sample leaves considerable doubt as to the average being sufficiently accurate to represent the population.

Sampling theory enables us to calculate the size of the sample needed to attain a given probability of being within an acceptable tolerance of the true (population) average. For instance, in counting the invoice items, we might be content if we are 90 per cent certain that the sample average lies within plus or minus one of the population average. Alternatively, sampling theory tells us the probability of our sample's average lying within a predecided acceptable tolerance.

Verifying facts

Verification of the facts acquired from the systems investigation covers two different aspects. One is to verify that the accuracy of a quantifiable fact has been determined to within an acceptable limit. It must be realized that it is almost impossible and not really productive to aim for absolute accuracy in most figures. They are constantly changing and so a completely accurate measure applies only to one moment in time. The main point of verifying this type of fact is in order to eliminate large errors, e.g. a quantity accidentally recorded as ten times too big.

The other aspect of verifying is in order to ensure that activities are performed and situations exist as reported. There are obviously slight discrepancies between one person's account of events and the next person's, nevertheless all accounts should be substantially in agreement and any major differences reconciled before proceeding to make use of the facts.

The answers a systems analyst receives in response to his questions may be erroneous, and mainly for one of the following reasons.

Ignorance of the subject matter

If the respondent does not fully understand the matter under discussion, he may refuse to admit this and so make guesses at the answers. An isolated guess is likely to go undetected but a string of guesses should be detectable and thus expose the respondent's lack of knowledge. There is also the possibility of the occasional erroneous reply even though the respondent knows the subject matter quite well: he simply makes a genuine mistake.

Misunderstanding the question

In many cases, an experienced analyst is able to detect a misunderstood question and so rephrase it. The worst state of affairs is when a discussion diverges from the true subject owing to a succession of erroneous answers and consequent inappropriate questions. This situation should not occur for long with an experienced systems analyst.

Deliberate misrepresentation

Fortunately this is an uncommon reason for incorrect answers. It is possible, however, that the respondent has something either to hide or to gain by distorting the truth. The former reason is usually associated with incompetence, idleness or even fraud, the latter with 'empire building', promotional prospects or job security.

Mistakes are less likely to derive from documented information but even with this the systems analyst should not assume that 'everything in print is correct'. The greatest dangers here are obsolete documents and out-of-date information on documents, and so their dates of origination are significant.

Methods of verifying

The prime method of verification is by comparing the factual information obtained from two or more sources. The snag is that the sources might stem from the same original information and so are not really independent.

Another means of verification is to analyse more deeply the information acquired. This is done by ascertaining that the constituent figures in the information combine together to give the supposed result.

A third means of verification is common sense. This is a combination of business experience and intelligent supposition.

Analysing facts

After collecting together the facts and figures pertaining to the existing situation, the systems analyst studies these in order to formulate ideas for inclusion in the new system. Apart from the qualitative aspects of the facts, he can use two statistical techniques to detect certain characteristics in the figures, these are trend analysis and correlation analysis. A systems analyst needs a general understanding of these, even if only to appreciate what is involved so that he knows to call for specialist assistance if need be. Brief explanations of these techniques follow, fuller details are available from most books on statistics.

Trend analysis

Trend analysis is based upon time series analysis, and comprises a number of techniques helpful to the systems analyst in predicting future figures from past figures. Prediction is important, for instance, where there is a changing or fluctuating situation such that there could be a considerable difference between the present workload and that of a few years hence. It cannot be emphasized too strongly that prediction is no substitute for good intelligence about impending events. It is far more useful to acquire effective information about future events than to make the most sophisticated forecasts.

The main aim is to remove seasonal, cyclical and random variations from the past figures in order that any steady trend is revealed. There are three main methods of revealing a linear trend in a set of figures, i.e. graphing, semi-averages, and least squares. The method to adopt depends largely upon the computing power available and the amount of data to be analysed.

Graphing

This is simply a matter of plotting past figures on a graph, and drawing by eye the best line through them. It is difficult to define what is meant by the 'best' in this context except to say that it is the line which, on the whole, is nearest to all the points on the graph. The more recent points should take preference if the points lie in a markedly curved area. This is tantamount to saying that, if necessary, the best curve should be drawn through the points.

Whatever line is drawn, it can be projected for a few time periods into the future with, hopefully, a reasonable degree of accuracy. In any event, it is likely to be more accurate than merely assuming that the recent figures will continue to hold.

Semi-averaging

This is a crude but simple method of assessing the linear trend in a set of figures. The principle is to split the past figures into two equal or nearly equal groups and to compute the average value of each group. The difference between these averages is then divided by their distance apart, i.e. the number of time periods between them. The result is a rate of change of the figures that can be projected into future time periods.

The least-squares method (regression analysis)
This is the most scientific in that it determines mathematically the straight line running through the set of figures. Put another way, it finds the equation of the straight line that minimizes the average distance between itself and the figures as plotted on a graph. The equation can then be used to compute the figures applicable to future periods.

Other, more sophisticated techniques, include exponential smoothing and the Box–Jenkins method.

Seasonal variations
Superimposed on the linear trend of a set of past figures may be a seasonal trend, occurring to a greater or lesser extent each year. This is often masked by random fluctuations and so not immediately apparent from a visual inspection of the figures or a graph.

By computing the linear trend, as already described, and subtracting the trend figures from the actual figures, we are left with the deviations. In order to detect a seasonal trend the figures must be available for monthly or at least quarterly periods. The average deviation for a given month or quarter taken over a number of years is a measure of seasonal variation. In practice it is desirable to examine the figures for five years or more before coming to any conclusions about the significance of seasonal variations.

Correlation analysis

Correlation is a measure of the strength of the relationship between two variable quantities. That is to say if one quantity changes, does the other quantity also change, either in the same or the opposite way? The strength of this relationship is measured by the correlation coefficient (r). If $r = 1$, there is a perfect positive relationship, i.e. the two variable quantities are linearly related, one increasing at a proportional rate to the other. If $r = -1$, there is a perfect negative relationship, i.e. the rate of decrease of the one is proportional to the rate of increase of the other. If $r = 0$, there is no linear relationship, i.e. the quantities are random relative to each other or have an irrelevant relationship. As a rule of thumb, if r is above 0.7 or below -0.7, there is a relationship worth investigating. This is a rough rule of thumb and, of course, common sense needs to be used before effort is expended in this way.

It cannot be over-emphasized that merely because two variable quantities are found by correlation analysis to be statistically related, it does not follow that they are necessarily related in any other way. That is to say they might not be causally or logically connected in any way whatsoever. A favourite pastime of anti-statisticians is to demonstrate the existence of significant correlation coefficients between obviously unrelated variables.

Within the sphere of systems investigation, however, there is a reasonable chance that two statistically related variables are either causally or logically connected; for instance, the amounts due on bills receivable and the times taken before payments are received. If a statistical relationship is established, then a causal connection is worth looking for and further investigating.

Multiple correlation analysis

This is a more sophisticated technique enabling a measure of correlation to be obtained between several different sets of variable quantities, e.g. vehicles in use, road deaths and the maximum speed limit.

It is unlikely that a systems analyst will find the need to employ multiple correlation analysis but if he does, the assistance of a statistician may well be necessary.

6.9   Prototyping

The conventional approach to systems development is through the systems development life cycle (SDLC), after the style of Figures 6.1 and 7.1. These diagrams show several iterative paths that are of course necessary in order to obtain further information or make changes to previous design features. The need for changes is often caused by misunderstandings of the prospective user's requirements. It is also caused by the user not being clear as to what it is possible for him or her to expect. Although for simple applications the amount of iteration is generally minimal, for a large and complex application it can be everlasting − or so it seems. Thus any method that minimizes replication of effort on the part of both the systems analyst and the user is obviously desirable.

Prototyping is a collection of techniques for reducing misunderstandings and clarifying requirements. It is usable during both the systems investigation and systems design stages − and the earlier in the SDLC it is used, the greater the advantage.

Prototypes are amended and presented several times during the SDLC in a form dependent on the stage reached. By so doing there is the potential for early amendments to weaknesses in the designed system and, in an extreme case, for its abandonment. These possibilities exist because prototyping involves the close participation of prospective users, and consequently their reactions are readily perceived.

Prototyping is particularly beneficial in situations where the application(s) is not clearly defined. On the other hand, for well-understood, fully definable applications, prototyping is probably not worth while. An example of the former situation could be a firm of estate agents setting up a system for holding and interrogating a database appertaining to properties on their books. Although the estate agents have previously done the same thing by means of a card filing system, they find it difficult to imagine a computerized system. They would be greatly reassured by the sight of their data on a screen and by the opportunity of calling it up themselves through a hands-on method. If the prototype makes them believe that the computer is totally under their control, they become more confident and so more inclined to suggest relevant information and suitable screen formats.

An instance of a well-defined application could well be sales invoicing and accounting. The work is well understood as it has been carried out for a long period and there is nothing to be gained from changes. Thus the new system is to be a replica of the previous sytem from the input/output aspects, and so prototyping is unnecessary.

Tools for prototyping

In order for the systems analyst to be able to construct prototypes promptly, a speedy and straightforward method has to be available. In this respect fourth-generation technology (4GT), and, in particular, fourth-generation languages (4GLs) (Section 5.2), forms the cornerstone of prototyping.

There are a host of techniques available even though, strictly speaking, there is no absolute definition of what constitutes 4GT. In broad terms, however, 4GT could be said to include any technique or language that furnishes sophisticated results with a minimum of human effort.

Types of 4GT are given below.

Screen generators (screen painters)

A screen generator is a tool for creating displays on VDU screens quickly and easily. The principle is that the analyst 'draws' or 'paints' the required layout on the screen by means of a mouse, a pointer, a palette and a keyboard. This enables lines, icons and coloured areas to be represented on the screen and then headed and annotated with text and data from the keyboard.

By this means it is feasible to create any document or other layout on the screen, and to modify the layout and its contents according to the wishes of the user.

Facilities are available for inserting items from a data dictionary such as titles, headings and annotations. Also available are preformed skeletons of menus and forms for the subsequent entry of data, and icons for helping with the choice of requirements.

Graphics

In business terms graphics implies the representation of data in the form of graphs, histograms, pie charts, bar charts, pictograms, etc. (see also Section 8.5).

These representations are generated by the 4GT without recourse to programming on the part of the analyst. Thus it is possible, for instance, to show a histogram based on real data so that a manager can confirm that this prototype meets his needs.

Report generators (report writers)

A report generator is software for quickly creating a report from data in the database. The content and format of the report are specified through the use of a non-procedural language, i.e. a 4GL, or alternatively by filling in screen forms. The report generator retrieves, sorts and summarizes the appropriate records and it is also capable of performing rudimentary processing, e.g. calculating percentages. The report's format, headings, annotations and totals are controlled through the 4GL, or alternatively are entered automatically by default. In this way a user is encouraged to set up his own reports during prototyping.

Fourth-generation languages

4GLs are explained in Section 5.2, and from there it is clear that they are invaluable for prototyping owing to their flexibility and ease of use.

Categories of prototypes

There is always the danger in categorizing that the things in question become regarded as completely dissociable. With prototyping this is a significant point because in practice some or all of the categories described below and shown in Figure 6.16 might be incorporated into the prototyping of the one system. The various applications and procedures may be prototyped in different ways or perhaps not at all. The reader should therefore accept the following methods as being approaches rather than clear-cut categories.

Non-working prototypes

With this approach the prototype is a dummy and is usable only for the purpose of demonstrating input procedures and/or output formats. The prototype is incapable of actually processing data but merely reproduces results that have been predetermined and then incorporated into the programs. Accordingly the results are unreal, i.e. false, and so a non-working prototype is unsuitable for realistic user interfacing.

Although this is deceitful, it is nevertheless a valid approach so long as the users are aware of the truth of the matter. Its main purpose is to illustrate the layout of screens, documents and reports irrespective of their contents. As a matter

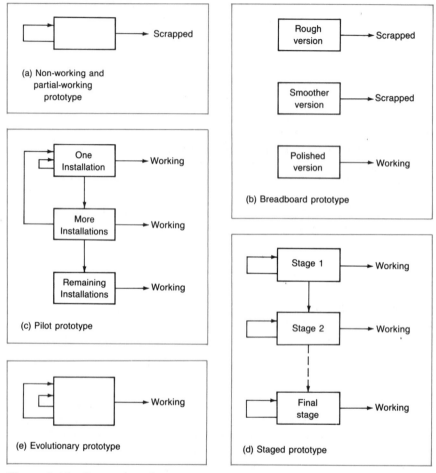

Figure 6.16   Categories of prototypes

of interest this method has been used for thirty years or more in sales environments to show computer printouts. (See Section 6.3).

A non-working prototype is scrapped after the end of its usefulness.

Partially working prototypes

This method could also be termed an 'interfacing' prototype because it is intended to allow users to operate it as a system that gives responses to certain input. Any input to which the prototype cannot give a correct response is rejected so that there is no chance of users being misled.

The prototype is arranged to check input, giving appropriate responses and moving through a succession of dialogue messages. When an input message calls for a substantial piece of output, e.g. a longish report or list, this may have to be simulated because the necessary processing is not yet programmed. This is acceptable so long as it is made clear that the output is not real.

As with a non-working prototype, a partially working prototype is scrapped after fulfilling its purpose.

Breadboard prototypes

The term 'breadboard' is taken from electronic engineering, it implies a rough-and-ready but working arrangement. It was originally a circuit held on a wooden board but in our case is a computer application.

A breadboard prototype is constructed mainly with speed of creation in mind, and consequently is inefficient in terms of speed of operation and usage of storage. This is the result of it being written in a 4GL.

It is possible to have user interfacing because the prototype actually works but it must be emphasized to the user that the final system will be much more efficient. It is also possible for it to make use of an existing database.

The breadboard prototype is scrapped after noting its strengths and weaknesses and replaced by a new version constructed from scratch, probably written in a third-generation language. This in turn is eventually scrapped to be replaced by a final, polished version that becomes the working system.

Pilot prototypes

A pilot or first full-scale prototype is applicable to situations involving a number of installations doing the same work, e.g. a point-of-sale system in a chain of supermarkets. The principle is for the prototype to be introduced into one or a few of the installations so as to enable weaknesses to be detected. These are removed before the prototype is installed in further locations. Generally an application that is suitable for pilot prototyping is fairly straightforward technically; the problems tend to arise from the human aspect.

A pilot prototype is likely to encompass the full range of activities of the application. This means that most of the systems design and programming will need to have been done before initiating the prototype. It is also likely that the complete database is needed, e.g. with a point-of-sale system all the prices, descriptions, etc., must be available from the outset.

Staged prototypes

Staged or incremental prototyping implies that a start is made with only certain features of the full system. Further features are added stage by stage, and the prototype is checked at each stage. A stock control application, for instance, could start simply with the updating of the stocks in hand, then move on with stock evaluation, usage analysis, demand forecasting, automatic reordering, and so on.

At each stage of the prototyping, user interaction is important in order that weaknesses and misunderstandings are not compounded in the next stage.

Once a stage has been shown to be fully correct and complete, using real data, it can be rewritten in a 3GL so as to speed up the whole process of prototyping. The contents of the files may have to be enhanced at each stage but this need not be a problem if allowed for from the start.

With staged prototyping it is preferable that iteration occurs within each individual stage rather than between several stages. The final stage, when fully accepted, becomes the working system.

Evolutionary prototypes

An evolutionary prototype is in some ways similar to a staged approach. But whereas staged prototyping entails adding a succession of separate but closely associated stages, evolutionary prototyping allows the one integral application to evolve through a succession of increasingly refined phases.

It is obviously not always practicable to employ evolutionary prototyping because most applications do not lend themselves to this approach.

As an example, suppose we have an hotel room reservation system for which a file exists holding details of the rooms and their current bookings. The first phase is for the user merely to make enquiries regarding room availability. When this procedure has been agreed, the next phase could be to insert the procedure for making bookings. Thereafter the prototype is refined by the addition of procedures such as cancellations, changes, special requirements, and so on.

6.10 Exercises

Exercise 6.1 Interviewing

You are required to carry out fact-finding interviews with a manager and a number of his staff regarding their current manual office system.

Describe how you would:

(i) Structure and carry out the interviews.
(ii) Validate the data collected.

(BCS part I, Option D, April 1986)

Exercise 6.2 Feasibility survey

A small company has for some years being using a computer bureau for the processing of billing, payment of creditors and payroll systems. The company is considering purchasing a computer on which it will run these applications and others which it will develop in the future. You have been asked to prepare a report on the implications of this proposed course of action.

Required:

(a) Identify and describe six major issues which you would consider in an investigation of the feasibility of the proposal.
(b) Suggest an outline structure for the report.

(CACA level 2, Syns. an. & des., June 1987)

Exercise 6.3 Systems investigation

Describe the methods by which a systems analyst can document the features of an existing system prior to developing a systems definition.

(ICSA part 4, Man. of sys., Dec. 1986)

Exercise 6.4 Systems investigation/prototyping

Luxury Furs Ltd has a chain of twelve retail shops selling ladies' fur coats. It operates a low volume, high price, business and each garment is allocated a separate stock number in the manual stock records system operated at head office. All sales are for cash which is banked intact each day. Each shop renders, by post to head office, a daily sales report which is supported by copy sales dockets and a bank paying-in slip. The following are the head office routines:

1. The daily sales sheets and supporting information are received by the sales/stock audit department who check the sheets, stamp them to show that they have been checked and update their manual stock records. They then pass them in daily batches to the cashier who enters the amount banked into his analysis cash book, the daily total of which is transferred to the appropriate column in the main cash book.
2. Each week the cashier calculates the VAT element of sales cash, transfers it to a separate column in his analysis cash book and prepares a sales report for the business showing the sales for each shop for the week and for the year to date compared with similar information for the previous year. This is submitted to the sales manager.
3. Each week the cashier receives a bank statement which he checks against his cash book and prepares a bank reconciliation.
4. Each week the cashier prepares a cash book summary which is passed to the accounts department to be posted into the nominal ledger. In

addition to updating the nominal Sales and VAT accounts, the accounts department apply the fixed cost of sales percentage to the sales figure to provide a cost of sales figure which is used to update the respective shops' Stock and Cost of Sales accounts.

5. All purchases are delivered to the head office warehouse where they are checked, ticketed and assembled for despatch weekly to the branches under cover of priced despatch notes. Copy despatch notes are passed to sales/stock audit department for use as a stock record and to the accounts department to update the nominal ledger.

6. Suppliers' delivery notes are passed by the warehouse under control of pre-numbered goods received notes to the sales/stock audit department to update the head office stock records before passing the delivery notes to the accounts department to hold pending receipt of the respective invoices.

7. At the end of each four-week period, each shop takes stock and submits stock sheets to the sales/stock audit department who value them at cost, having checked the cut-off and goods in transit. The accounts department sends a copy of the nominal ledger Stock accounts for each shop for the period to the sales/stock audit department who agree the closing balances of these with the closing stock values shown in their manual stock records. When these have been agreed, the totals are compared with evaluated totals of the stock sheets submitted by the shops and any discrepancies between the two are reported, on a standard form, to the sales manager.

Requirements

(a) Prepare an overview manual procedures flow chart showing, in outline, the involvement of the various departments concerned in the above routines, and

(b) design a monthly branch stock discrepancies report in a suitable form for the sales manager.

(ICAEW PE1, Aud., sys. & DP, May 1987)

Exercise 6.5 Decision tables

Prepare (a) a decision tree, (b) a limited condition/extended action decision table and (c) an extended condition/limited action decision table, to specify the circumstances described below.

'A company's customers are either home or foreign, a company customer or an individual person, known or unknown to the company's credit controller, and either able or not able to provide an acceptable reference.

Credit is allowed to some customers depending on the above factors as follows.

Home companies known to the credit controller are allowed credit of up to £1,000, if unknown £400. Foreign companies with an acceptable reference get £700, otherwise £300. Individuals who are home customers and provide an acceptable reference get £100, otherwise no credit. Foreign individuals are allowed £50 on providing an acceptable reference, otherwise nothing.'

Exercise 6.6   Data usage chart

Prepare a data usage chart to incorporate all the documents, files and data items involved in the following situation.

'Orders are received by telephone and an order form (T1) filled out with the details of the order, i.e. commodity code, quantity ordered, order date, also customer's account number looked up in the name and address file (F1). When the goods are subsequently dispatched a dispatch note (T2) is filled out with the same data as on the order form plus dispatch data, quantity dispatched, and customer's name and address (from F1). Later an invoice (T3) is prepared; this is copied from the dispatch note but quantity ordered is omitted. Additionally the commodity price and VAT rate are looked up from a price file (F2) and entered; also the commodity value, VAT amount, and amount payable are all calculated and entered.'

Exercise 6.7   Data flow diagram

Draw a data flow diagram for the following procedure:

- When a goods received note (GRN) is received from the goods inwards section, the corresponding order copy (OC) is extracted from the goods ordered file.
- The data on these two documents are compared, and if not entirely alike, a discrepancy form (DF) is filled out and this together with the GRN and OC are sent to the inquiries section.
  If the data are alike, the OC is stamped 'goods received' and attached to the GRN; they are then filed pending receipt of the corresponding purchase invoice (PI).
- When a PI arrives, it is checked for various errors, and if any are found the PI is photocopied and this is filed for future reference. The erroneous PI is returned to the supplier with a covering letter.
  If the PI is error-free it is stamped 'checked OK' and the corresponding GRN and OC are extracted from the file.
- The data on the PI is checked against that on the GRN and OC. If there is any discrepancy, all three documents are attached together and sent to the inquiries section.
  If the data are alike, the PI is stamped 'passed for payment' and filed for subsequent payment. The GRN and OC are filed together in another file.

Exercise 6.8 Entity relationships

Construct an entity relationship diagram in the IE convention for the following situation:

'A company consists of several departments, each having a number of employees. Each department has a manager who must be on the monthly payroll. Other employees are on either the monthly payroll or the weekly payroll, and are members of the sports club if they so wish.'

Exercise 6.9 Data flow diagram

Create a data flow diagram to illustrate the following procedures:

'Mowell Ltd. is a company manufacturing lawn mowers and allied equipment. These products are assembled from sub-assemblies (made-in) and parts and raw materials (bought-out). Sub-assemblies are made from parts and raw materials.

At quarterly intervals management issues the forward Production Programme (PP), this gives the quantity of each product to be manufactured in the programme.

The PP is first passed to the Production Planning Department (PPD) where it is broken down into its constituent sub-assemblies, parts and raw material gross requirements. The sub-assembly gross requirements are passed to the Stock Control Department (SCD) where they are netted against unallocated stocks.

The sub-assembly net requirements are passed back to the PPD for breaking down to give the parts and raw materials gross requirements.

All the parts and raw materials gross requirements (both from sub-assemblies and from products) are passed to the SCD for netting against unallocated stocks. The net requirements are then passed to the Purchasing Department (PD) for forming into purchase orders to be sent to the appropriate suppliers.'

6.11 Outline solutions to exercises

Solution 6.1

(i) and (ii) Refer to 'Interviewing' in Section 6.8.

Solution 6.2

(a) Major issues

    (i) *Capital and running costs.* The purchase costs of a microcomputer and associated software are likely to be substantially less than the bureau charges taken over a few years. Against this saving are the extra cost of staff for operating the microcomputer system. If, as is probable, the data volumes are small, only one or two operators will be needed. Their salaries will most likely be balanced by other savings.

(ii) *Systems development.* Although the work is currently performed by a bureau, presumably in accordance with requirements, it may well be necessary to investigate and develop new systems. Much depends on the company staff's in-depth understanding of the present applications and the bureau's willingness or obligation to provide information about the quirks of the system.

(iii) *Software.* Following point (ii), it is important for the staff to understand fully what is required of purchased software. Payroll, unless it has unusual features, is unlikely to be a problem. Billing and payment of creditors are more uncertain, and will need close comparison with the capabilities of the purchased software.

(iv) *Hardware.* It is important to confirm the amounts of data so that the size and number of microcomputers, printers and storage can be ascertained. The main problem here is likely to centre on the volumes of manually keyed input. Associated with hardware estimates is the possibility of further developments in regard to applications and networking.

(v) *Security.* Logical security of data and files should be ensured by the correct back-up procedures and adequate stand-by hardware in case of failure. Microcomputer prices are so low that even the smallest company could afford two of everything.

Staff security might be a problem *vis-à-vis* payroll information. Some firms use a bureau for senior staff payroll for this reason. In this case the computer payroll printouts could be on masked payslips and the system operated by only trustworthy staff.

(vi) *Changeover problems.* These include disruption of existing procedures, reallocation of staff duties, training of staff, rearrangement of office accommodation, possible recruitment of a DP specialist, and the setting up of master files, i.e. payroll, purchase ledger, sales ledger and others.

(b) Structure of report

The report must cover the points mentioned above and be structured similarly to below:

- Objectives of proposal.
- Present method's strengths and weaknesses.
- Proposed method's advantages and disadvantages.
- Comparison of estimated costs.
- Outline schedule for implementation.
- Conclusion with recommendatons.

Solution 6.3

Refer to the following:

- 'Document specification forms' in Section 6.4
- 'Data usage charts' in Section 6.4
- 'Flowcharts' in Section 6.4
- 'Data flow diagrams' in Section 6.4

- 'Activity cycle charts' in Section 6.5
- 'Decision trees' in Section 6.5
- 'Decision tables' in Section 6.5
- 'Entity relationship diagrams' in Section 6.7

Solution 6.4

(a) Refer to Figure 6.18.
(b) Refer to Figure 6.17.

Solution 6.5

(a) Refer to Figure 6.19.
(b) Refer to Figure 6.20.
(c) Refer to Figure 6.21.

Solution 6.6

Refer to Figure 6.22.

Solution 6.7

Refer to Figure 6.23.

Abbreviations used:
GRN Goods received note
OC   Order copy
PI   Purchase invoice
DF   Discrepancy form

Branch stock discrepancy report as at 28.10.89 (period 15)				
Branch No. Name	Branch stock value at cost	HO stock value at cost	Discrepancy Dr	Cr
1 Bedford	8050.60	8595.75	545.75	
2 Reading	7948.50	7593.00		355.50
3 Winchester	6853.00	6853.00		
12 Bristol	5262.00	5675.00	413.00	
Totals	95311.75	95586.95	2433.50	458.30
Total net discrepancy			1975.20	

Figure 6.17 Branch stock discrepancy report for Exercise 6.4

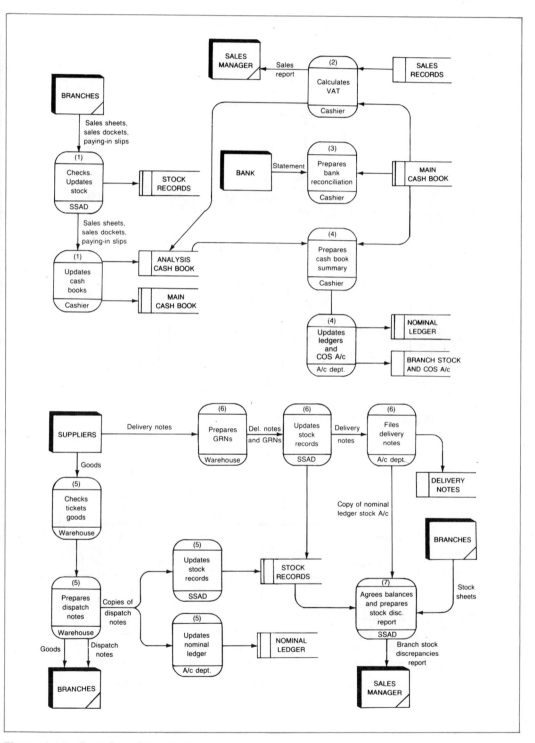

Figure 6.18   Data flow diagram of manual procedures in Exercise 6.4

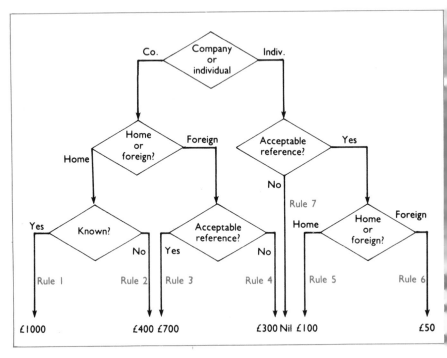

Figure 6.19   Decision tree of Exercise 6.5

Rules	1	2	3	4	5	6	7
Company customer?	Y	Y	Y	Y	N	N	N
Home customer?	Y	Y	N	N	Y	N	—
Known?	Y	N	—	—	—	—	—
Acceptable reference?	—	—	Y	N	Y	Y	N
Credit allowed £	1000	400	700	300	100	50	Nil

Figure 6.20   Limited condition/extended action decision table of Exercise 6.5

Rules	1	2	3	4	5	6	7
Type of customer	Co.	Co.	Co.	Co.	Indiv.	Indiv.	Indiv.
Location	Home	Home	For.	For.	Home	For.	—
Information available	Known	Nil	Ref.	Nil	Ref.	Ref.	Nil
Credit allowed £1000	×						
Credit allowed £400		×					
Credit allowed £700			×				
Credit allowed £300				×			
Credit allowed £100					×		
Credit allowed £50						×	
Credit allowed Nil							×

Figure 6.21 Extended condition/limited action decision table of Exercise 6.5

Name of document	Document ref	Customer account no	Order date	Commodity code	Quantity ordered	Customer name & address	Dispatch date	Quantity dispatched	Commodity price	Commodity VAT rate	Commodity value	VAT amount	Amount payable	Remarks
Order form	T1	I	E	E	E									Orders received by phone
Dispatch note	T2	T1	T1	T1	T1	F1	I	I						
Name and address file	F1	I				E								
Invoice	T3	T2	T2	T2	T2	T2	T2	T2	F2	F2	C	C	C	
Price file	F2			I					I	I				

Figure 6.22 Data usage chart of Exercise 6.6 (Meanings of codes as in text.)

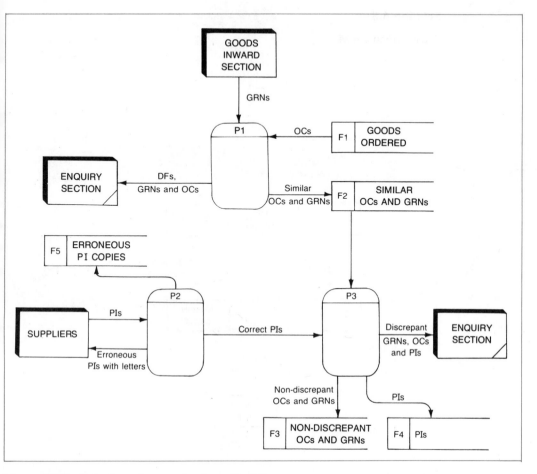

Figure 6.23 Data flow diagram for Exercise 6.7

Processing notes:
P1 OC corresponding to GRN is extracted from file (F1),
    Data compared
    ● if alike, OC stamped, attached to GRN and both filed (F2).
    ● if not alike, DF filled in and sent to inquiries section with OC and GRN.
P2 PI checked
    ● if correct, PI stamped and corresponding GRN and OC, are extracted from
      file (F2).
    ● If erroneous, PI photocopy made and filed (F5), original PI returned to
      supplier with covering letter.
P3 PI checked against corresponding OC and GRN,
    ● if no discrepancies, PI stamped and filed (F4), OCs and GRNs are filed
      together (F3).
    ● if discrepancies, all three documents are attached together and sent to
      inquiries section.

Solution 6.8

Refer to Figure 6.24.

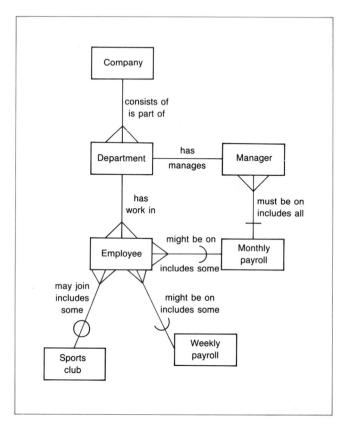

Figure 6.24 Entity relationship diagram for Exercise 6.8

Solution 6.9

Refer to Figure 6.25.

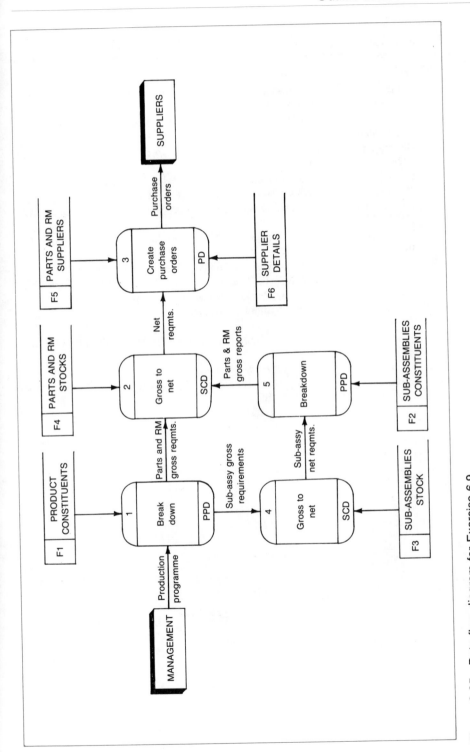

Figure 6.25 Data flow diagram for Exercise 6.9

6.12 References and further reading

6.1 Smith, J.M. and Kokotovich, N.M., *Documenting an Organization's Computer Requirements* (John Wiley, 1985).

6.2 Garland, J.L., *How to Develop Business Information Systems for End Users* (John Wiley, 1986).

6.3 Burch, J. and Grudnitski, G., *Information Systems: Theory and Practice* (John Wiley, 1986).

6.4 Garcia, R.R., *Human Factors in Systems Development* (NCC, 1988).

6.5 Martin, C., *Computers and Senior Managers* (NCC, 1988).

6.6 Law, D. and Longworth, G., *Systems Development: Strategies and Techniques* (NCC, 1987).

6.7 Longworth, G., *Getting the System You Want – A User's Guide to SSADM* (NCC, 1988).

6.8 Martin, J., *User-Centre Requirements Analysis* (Prentice Hall, 1988).

6.9 Kendall, K.E. and Kendall, J.E., *Systems Analysis and Design* (Prentice Hall, 1988).

6.10 Skidmore, S. and Wroe, B., *Introducing Systems Analysis* (NCC, 1988).

6.11 Data processing Flowchart Symbols, Rules and Conventions, BS4058: 1973 (BSI, 1973).

6.12 Recommendations for Decision Tables Used in Data Processing, BS5487: 1977 (BSI, 1977).

6.13 Arnold, J. and Hope, T., *Accounting for Management Decisions* (Prentice Hall, 1990).

6.14 Guide to Design Structure Diagrams for use in Program Design and other Logic Applications, BS6224: 1982 (BSI, 1982).

Systems design

7

7.1 Design philosophy

In Chapter 1 the iterative nature of systems analysis and, in particular, problem definition are discussed against the background of business organization and the need for information. Chapter 6 describes the various aspects of systems investigation; the facts found in this stage form the basis for the design of a new system. As is shown in Figure 7.1, systems design and implementation is also an iterative procedure. Except for the most straightforward of systems, it is not feasible to design a system by working through a series of precise steps. Each decision taken during systems design tends to result in a rethink of the previous steps, and this continues until eventually the whole system takes shape.

This philosophy is epitomized by the procedures involved in prototyping. As explained in Section 6.9, prototyping inevitably causes rethinking and, to some extent, redesigning of the system. As is seen from Figure 7.2, there is a variety of loopbacks connected with the different categories of prototyping. It is quite likely that several of these alternatives are employed in the one systems development life cycle (SDLC).

Figure 7.2 depicts in broad outline the relationships between the conventional SDLC and the five categories of prototyping. Following an examination of the results from a prototype, the SDLC either moves forward to the succeeding activity or returns to a previous activity. The latter is either to correct or complete work done previously or to start the next cycle of the SDLC.

Designing anything, be it physical, artistic or social, is a creative process absorbing something of the designer's personal stamp. With a data system, the design process is logical and yet calls for lateral thought. A logical approach implies systematic moves towards the end-product, each step being the result of decisions based upon the previous steps. At the same time consideration of the capabilities of people and equipment enters into each decision.

Lateral thought means the encompassing of ideas in the broadest sense, perhaps outside the usual DP functions and equipment. The systems designer

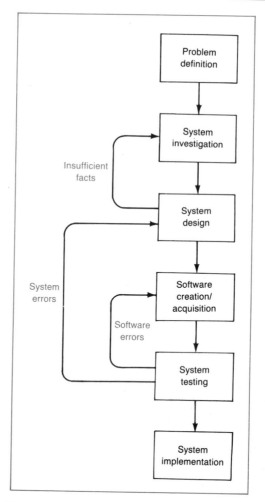

Figure 7.1 Systems development life cycle

should endeavour to free his mind from preconceived notions, and look at each problem on its own merits. A danger with systems design is that the systems analyst overplays his experience by immediately adopting previous solutions for new situations.

Objectives of systems design

Practicality

The system must be capable of being used over a long period by competent but average-intelligence persons. It is no use designing a system that needs geniuses to operate and maintain it.

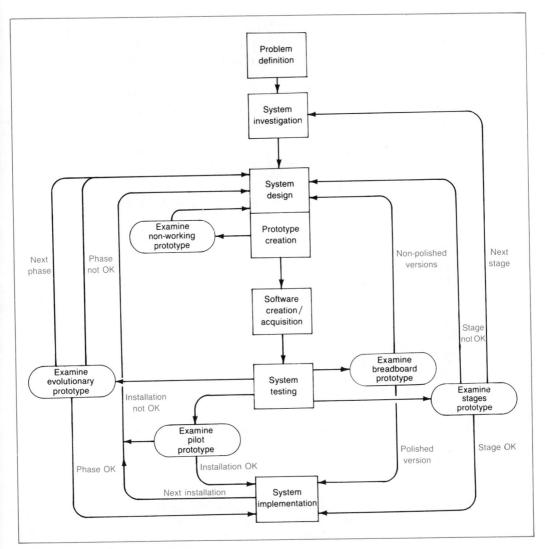

Figure 7.2   SDLC and prototyping

In this respect it has to be borne in mind that the eventual users of the system may have had no involvement in its design and prototyping. To them it is completely new and not a little daunting, so practicality and, if possible, simplicity are of great importance.

Efficiency

The best use should be made of people and equipment. Efficiency involves the accuracy, timeliness and comprehensiveness of the system's output whilst at the same time making good use of the available facilities. In this context, accuracy means the inclusion of all relevant data rather than arithmetical correctness.

Timeliness implies the regular production of information in sufficient time for it to be truly useful to its recipient.

Comprehensiveness means that the information from data processing is of the breadth and depth needed for decisions to be taken. And in more mundane procedures that all the data is taken into account.

Least cost

It is obviously desirable to aim for minimum cost provided the system fulfils its other requirements. We must be certain that when comparing different systems costwise, we are comparing like with like.

It is likely nowadays that the major ingredient in cost is staff since hardware costs have diminished considerably. Thus any factors that reduce staff costs are beneficial provided the work is done at least as well by automated methods.

Flexibility

A system needs to be responsive to the changes inevitably requested by its users. The system also needs to be 'portable' from one computer system to another.

No business is static and so it is inevitable that changes will be necessary. Although it is not practical to cater for every possible change, it is wise to build into the system a means of introducing the more obvious future changes.

Security

Several aspects are included here — hardware reliability and the associated fallback and standby procedures, physical security of data, and the detection and prevention of fraud and abuse (Section 7.7).

Planning and control of systems design

As with systems investigation, it is pragmatic to employ a project team approach to systems design. A project team may be responsible for the design of one or several routines or applications. Within a team it is usual to find several different skills, some members being business orientated, others technically minded. This mixture tends to induce a balanced approach and consequently a practical method evolves.

If the overall system is extensive, several project teams may be involved, in which case it is imperative that they maintain close contact. This eliminates misunderstandings, omissions from the designed system and duplicated effort.

As seen from Figures 7.1 and 7.2, systems development as a whole follows through a life cycle. Associated with the SDLC are the categories of prototyping adopted according to the circumstances. A complex situation may well arise in which the activities in the SDLC and the various aspects of prototyping are closely interconnected.

A DP system can be regarded as consisting of three components i.e. output, logical files and input, surrounded by its environment. The actual processing aspects of business DP, although important, are usually the least difficult to design. Provided the above three components are correctly designed, processing falls into place automatically.

A logical approach is to start with the output since the end requirement defines what is needed in the input and logical files.

This is still true even when a database already exists since by working backwards from the output requirements it will soon become evident if data is missing from the database. It is sometimes argued that to start with the output is not a good idea because future output requirements cannot always be foreseen at the time a system is being designed. This is manifestly true but the alternative approach of analysing all the data that might possibly be needed at some time in the future is far more problematical. In some cases there is a vast amount of irrelevant data which if incorporated into the database would impose a drag on its efficiency and thus on the system as a whole.

As with most things, it is a matter of pragmatism and compromise. Whereas a large organizaton has an army of systems analysts and programmers to build up a comprehensive database, a small firm has neither the time nor the resources to so do.

The methodologies described in Section 7.11 have been designed to make systems development more accurate, logical and complete. This is laudable but it remains to be seen to what extent these methodologies are adopted, especially by smaller organizations.

7.2 Code number systems

In a computer-based business system it is inevitable that code numbers (which can include alphabetic characters) are needed, this is in order to identify uniquely every entity in each entity set. The greater the number of entities within sets, the more significant are the code numbers since there is an increased chance of misidentification. For practical purposes it is impossible to identify, uniquely and unerringly, even as few as a hundred different entities if only their descriptions are available for this purpose.

It is probable that sets of existing code numbers will have been found during the systems investigation, and that these are satisfactory for the present system. Unfortunately they are not always suitable when moving from a manual to a computer-based system. The foremost reason for this is that code numbers employed in non-computer systems do not need to be as precise in their layouts as those for computer use. A computer utilizes a code number as the sole means of both identifying and locating a data record and there are no half measures in this respect.

The existing ranges of code numbers therefore need to be carefully examined before being accepted as suitable for a new system. If they are suspect as regards their uniqueness, completeness or efficacy, new sets need to be devised.

Required characteristics of code numbers

Uniqueness

Each entity type should have one unique code number so as to eliminate the possibility of misidentification. If an entity type needs to have two (or more) different kinds of code numbers as alternative means of identification, e.g. a part number and drawing number, then they must be unique within the kind and the two or more kinds need to be recognizable, i.e. a part number should not be thought to be a drawing number.

Brevity

The layout of a set of code numbers should not be any longer than is necessary subject to being consistent with its purpose and structure. Since seven digits is the most that people can hold in their short-term memory, it is advantageous if the code number is no longer than this.

Consistent pictures

Within a given set all the code numbers should have the same picture (Section 6.4). That is to say, the numeric digits and the alphabetic letters lie in the same relative positions in all the numbers. It is also beneficial if the code numbers are all of exactly the same length, which is really the same thing as having similar pictures. By having this consistency it is simpler to check a code number's accuracy and completeness, both manually and computer-wise.

In this respect leading zeros are best avoided. And it is generally the custom to use only upper-case, i.e. capital, letters.

Distinct pictures

Where various sets of code numbers are used in the one system, it is preferable that each set has its own unique picture. This allows for clear recognition of the set and so prevents misidentification due to two identical numbers being in two different sets, e.g. a product number 2751 and a part number 2751.

Symbols and spaces

Code numbers of over six characters are easier to use manually if broken up by hyphens, obliques or spaces. As these are not of great use to the computer, unless in effect separating different numbers, they are best removed before or during entry to the computer.

Similarly other symbols should not be used.

Visual and audio recognizability

If a set of code numbers is to be used extensively in manual procedures, it is worth considering choosing characters that are as distinct as possible from each other.

Avoidance of letters such as I, O, Q, S and G is helpful because these letters are similar in appearance to other letters and digits, e.g. 1, 0, 8, 6 and others.

Similarly the letters rhyming with 'e' are best avoided if code numbers need to be spoken either by persons or by computers.

Expansibility

The structure and size of a set of code numbers must be chosen so as to allow for additions if there is any chance of expansion in the number of entity types. If it is the intention to re-use the code numbers of obsolete items, great care has to be taken that the items are gone forever.

Assigning code numbers

The designing of code number systems and the assignment of code numbers to entities must be done centrally. The systems department or organization and methods (O&M) department is responsible for these procedures so that there is no chance of confusion arising. If departments are allowed to create their own code number systems, duplicated codes and double usages soon appear. A central record should be kept of all code numbers assigned, these being clearly linked to the corresponding entities.

The means of linking codes to their entities may be through drawings, written specifications, suppliers' or manufacturers' descriptions, photographs or microfilms.

In many instances the biggest problem is to ensure that an ostensibly new entity has not been assigned a code number previously. This applies particularly in the engineering industry where many similar components and materials are used.

Before adopting any code number system and applying it to an entity set, it is advisable to examine the set for any inherent classifications. That is to say, do the entities have any characteristics that are usefully incorporated into their code numbers? Books are a good case in point; these are classified according to the well-known Universal Decimal (Dewey-decimal) Code (UDC) system. This is obviously advantageous in libraries for indexing and locating purposes.

Classifying entities and then assigning classification codes does not necessarily provide unique identification. This is apparent in a library, where many different books are seen to have the same UDC number. Thus, since unique identification is generally called for with business entities, further coding has to be appended to the classification code.

Described below are the better-known classification and coding systems. These can generally be combined in order to obtain the most suitable system.

Classification schemes

Hierarchical classification

The UDC system, mentioned above, is a good example of hierarchical classification. The concept behind this method is that every entity falls into a subgroup of a larger group, which in turn forms part of an even larger group.

In a properly designed hierarchical classification system, each entity has one place only where it fits into the system. It is convenient if each level of classification can be catered for by one digit position in the code, i.e. not more than ten groups in each level (coded 0–9).

The assignment of digits is entirely arbitrary and their meanings are discernible only in relation to the classification at higher level.

EXAMPLE OF HIERARCHICAL CLASSIFICATION

Suppose we wish to classify the various means of passenger transport. Table 7.1. is an example of transport classified into three levels. Thus the classification codes are, for instance, airliners 111, cars 322, sailing yachts 212.

Faceted classification

In this system each position in the classification code has its own independent meaning. In contrast to hierarchical classification, a position does not have to be associated with a higher level in order to ascertain its meaning. This enables faceted classification to be more easily interpretable both by human beings and by computers.

Table 7.1

Higher level (first digit)

       1 = air transport
       2 = sea transport
       3 = land transport

Middle level (second digit)

air   [1 = winged aircraft
         [2 = helicopters

sea   [1 = displacement vessels
         [2 = surface vessels

land   [1 = railway trains
         [2 = road vehicles

Lowest level (third digit)

air, winged   [1 = airliners
                    [2 = light aircraft

air, helicopters   [1 = large
                    [2 = small

sea, displacement   [1 = powered
                    [2 = sailing

sea, surface   [1 = hydrofoils
                    [2 = hovercraft

land, rail   [1 = electric
                      2 = diesel
                    [3 = steam

land, road   [1 = coaches and buses
                      2 = motor cars
                    [3 = motor cycles

EXAMPLE OF FACETED CLASSIFICATION

A range of machine screws is to be classified according to four characteristics – material, diameter, head shape and finish (Table 7.2) Thus 5 mm chromium-plated brass round heads are classified 2312.

Code number schemes

Serial code numbers

Serial code numbers are assigned to entities in an entirely arbitrary way with no information conveyed by the code number itself. This is quite a usual method of appending to classification codes in order to provide full identification of every

Table 7.2

Material (first digit)
1 = stainless steel
2 = brass
3 = steel

Diameter (second digit)
1 = 3 mm
2 = 4 mm
3 = 5 mm

Head shape (third digit)
1 = round head
2 = countersunk
3 = pan head

Finish (fourth digit)
1 = no finish
2 = chromium plated
3 = zinc plated
4 = painted

---

entity. Serial coding has the supreme advantage of simplicity and low redundancy, i.e. a high proportion of the available numbers can be utilized.

> ## EXAMPLE
>
> All cars have code numbers starting with 322, followed by a serial code of three digits to give absolute identification of each particular model, e.g. a Ford Escort might be coded 322001.

Serial numbers, if allocated chronologically, can be usefully employed to determine the relative priorities of transactions such as customers' orders.

Non-transposable code numbers

This is a variation of serial coding and is intended to minimize errors in copying and key codes. The concept is that no pair of adjacent digit positions is assigned values that are interchangeable to form another code number. For example, if code 135 has been assigned, 153 will not be. This method considerably reduces the number of available code numbers but this does not matter as long as there is sufficient capacity within the range of digits available.

Sequential code numbers

The code numbers are assigned to the entities incrementally after the latter have been arranged into some natural sequence. Typically, customer account numbers are assigned in alphabetical order of customers' surnames. This method is not viable if new entities are to be introduced later unless gaps are left between the code numbers.

A partial sequential code number is based on the first part only of a name, say the first two letters. Insertions are facilitated because larger gaps can be left between groups of code numbers, any new entity is assigned the next available code number within the relevant group.

Block code numbers

A block coding system splits up a set of serial or sequential code numbers into blocks as determined by some general characteristic of the entities.

The blocks of code numbers when assigned should allow for further additions to each block.

EXAMPLE

Parts used in a factory might, for instance, be block coded as follows:

General bought-out parts	1000 to 3999
Special bought-out parts	4000 to 4599
Made-in parts	4600 to 9999

Interpretative (significant digit) code numbers

In an interpretative code number all or some of the digits are equal to one or more of the actual quantitative characteristics of the entity.

This method of coding, although obviously useful, calls for careful thought in design. A clear understanding of the characteristics of the entities is needed – both present and future – otherwise new characteristics can appear that are not compatible with the system as devised.

EXAMPLE

Interpretative coding applied to machine screws could indicate their diameter and length. Thus a 6 mm diameter screw 35 mm long would be coded 635. Additional digits would be used to indicate its colour and other characteristics so as to provide uniqueness.

Mnemonic codes

A mnemonic code, as the name suggests, is intended to act as an *aide-mémoire*. Generally all or part of the code number is derived from the entity's description or name, thereby bringing it to the user's mind. There are no particular rules for creating mnemonic codes except that the most obvious parts of the description are used in the code number.

EXAMPLE

Mnemonics for cities might include LDN for London, NYK for New York, TKO for Tokyo, etc. Mnemonic codes are suitable only for small sets of entities otherwise they defeat their own purpose.

Derivable code numbers

Situations arise in which it is advantageous to be able to derive or at lease surmise a code number from a description and vice versa. In this context description also includes names and other data items related to the entity in question. The general principle behind derivable code numbering is to transcribe all or certain characters of the description into numeric digits of the code number.

EXAMPLE

The letters of the alphabet are assigned numbers 10–35 respectively. The first three letters of surnames are then assigned these numbers. Thus, the surname CLIFTON becomes code number 122118.

The obvious problem with this method is duplicated code numbers, e.g. with CLIFFORD and CLIFTON.

7.3 Design of output

All output from a DP system, be it a complex management report or a simple error message, is derived from one or more of three sources — input data, stored data and computation. We are therefore concerned with the combination of sources that provide each item of output. We are also concerned with the timing of the required output in relation to the receipt of source data, the updating of logical files and the demands of the system's environment.

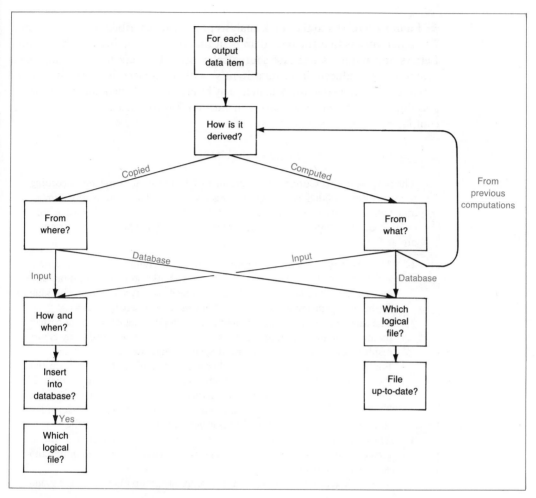

Figure 7.3   Derivation of output data items

Output analysis charts

Figure 7.3 shows the paths followed in deriving the origins of each output data item. By working backwards from the output, the derivation of data items becomes apparent. This procedure is followed for each set of outputs and ensures that no items are overlooked. From this procedure it is possible to create an 'Output analysis chart' as shown in Figure 7.5. This document is filled out for each group of associated inputs, stored data and outputs. The stored data is, of course, also used for other outputs but need to be entered on each output analysis chart.

These charts are a fundamental part of the data dictionary or encyclopaedia, either as they stand or after conversion to a standardized form.

Figure 7.5 relates to the stock analysis procedure described below. On Figure 7.5, a tick means that the data item is in the source at the head of the column. Letters and numbers indicate source references. C refers to something being computed or deduced from data item(s) with references beneath the C, and parentheses indicate that the data item may be erroneous or incomplete. The letters and digits thereon are used again in Section 7.6 to illustrate the design of a computer-based stock analysis system.

EXAMPLE – STOCK ANALYSIS

The purpose of this routine is to create an analysis of the stock in hand according to its cost value subdivided into groups. Each stock item has a commodity number and falls into one of several groups. A grand total of the stock cost is also computed. The resultant report is as shown in Figure 7.4. The steps in the routine are as follows:

1. The quantity of each item in the warehouse is counted and entered on a serially numbered stock form (S1) along with its commodity number and rack number. The latter is noted merely to facilitate any subsequent checking as the one item might possibly be held in several separate racks.
2. The data on each stock form is input to the computer and checked for correct pictures (layouts) and that the stock quantity has been entered. Any errors result in error message P1 being displayed, and the data is rejected.
3. For each item the commodity number is used to look up the cost price and the group number from the commodity master file (D1), held on disk. If the master record is absent from the master file, error message P3 is printed. This omission may be due to either an invalid commodity number on the stock form or a new commodity not yet added to the master file.
4. The stock item value (cost price × stock quantity) is calculated; if this is greater than £9,999.99, error message P2 is printed, and the commodity is omitted from the analysis.
5. The stock item value is added to the appropriate group total and to the grand total.
6. At the end of the analysis, the group totals along with their group numbers and the grand totals are printed to form the stock analysis report (P4), as shown in Figure 7.4.

Phasing of output

Each output document or report needs to be scheduled in relation to the times of:

- the receipt of the associated inputs,
- the updating/amendment of the master files,
- the completion of preceding computer runs.

The receipt of source data is usually connected with activities taking place in the system's environment, e.g. jobs completed in a factory, goods received into the stores.

```
           STOCK ANALYSIS

     Group no.     Stock value

        1           4963.82

        2           5013.09

        3            687.52

        4           1739.76
        |              |
        |              |
        |              |


     Grand total   63580.64
```

Figure 7.4 Stock analysis report

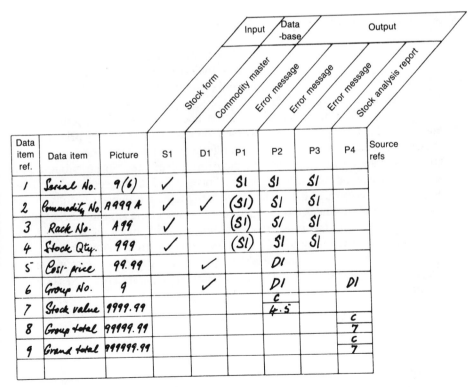

Data item ref.	Data item	Picture	S1	D1	P1	P2	P3	P4	Source refs
1	Serial No.	9(6)	✓		SI	SI	SI		
2	Commodity No	A999A	✓	✓	(SI)	SI	SI		
3	Rack No.	A99	✓		(SI)	SI	SI		
4	Stock Qty.	999	✓		(SI)	SI	SI		
5	Cost-price	99.99		✓		DI			
6	Group No.	9		✓		DI		DI	
7	Stock value	9999.99				c/4.5		c/7	
8	Group total	99999.99						c/7	
9	Grand total	999999.99						c/7	

Figure 7.5 Output analysis chart

The master files are updated/amended by source data at some stage, and so this must also be phased-in with the preparation of output. In the above example, the master file needs to be updated with cost price changes prior to the stock analysis routine.

Similarly, a computer run may rely on using data derived from another run, and so cannot proceed until this has been completed. Job costing, for instance, often depends upon the apportionment of factory overheads derived from a preceding set of computations.

Sequence of output

The sequence of the items of information in an output report, or of the documents in a set, may be a deciding factor in designing the DP system. In general it is faster and more straightforward to hold file records in the same sequence as the predominant output. This, in turn, tends to imply that the input is also in this sequence. These simplistic rules of thumb fail when the output is required in several different sequences.

The sequence(s) of an output report should be shown on the report itself as this may not be apparent from its contents.

Design of documents and displays

It is important that computer-printed documents and VDU displays (screens) are well designed because, in many cases, they are the only contact between end-users and the DP system. The layout and contents must be absolutely clear, and the presentation of a good standard.

To facilitate the designing of an output document, a 'print layout sheet' is employed. This is simply a form on which there is a space for every print position shown full-scale. When designing an output document, the headings, annotations and figures are entered by hand on the print layout sheet so providing a full-scale facsimile of the computer's printing. This applies both to preprinted headings and to computer-printed data. The former need to be positioned carefully so that the computer's printing can be aligned precisely under the appropriate headings.

A specimen print layout is depicted in Figure 7.6. This is the layout for one of the reports in the case study (Chapter 9), and is shown as a computer printout in Figure 9.28. In this example all the printing is computer output, i.e. no preprinting. That in black is the same on every report, that in red varies between reports.

Design features of printed documents

- All information must be unambiguous, thus necessitating clear headings and annotations. These are either preprinted as with payslips and invoices; or

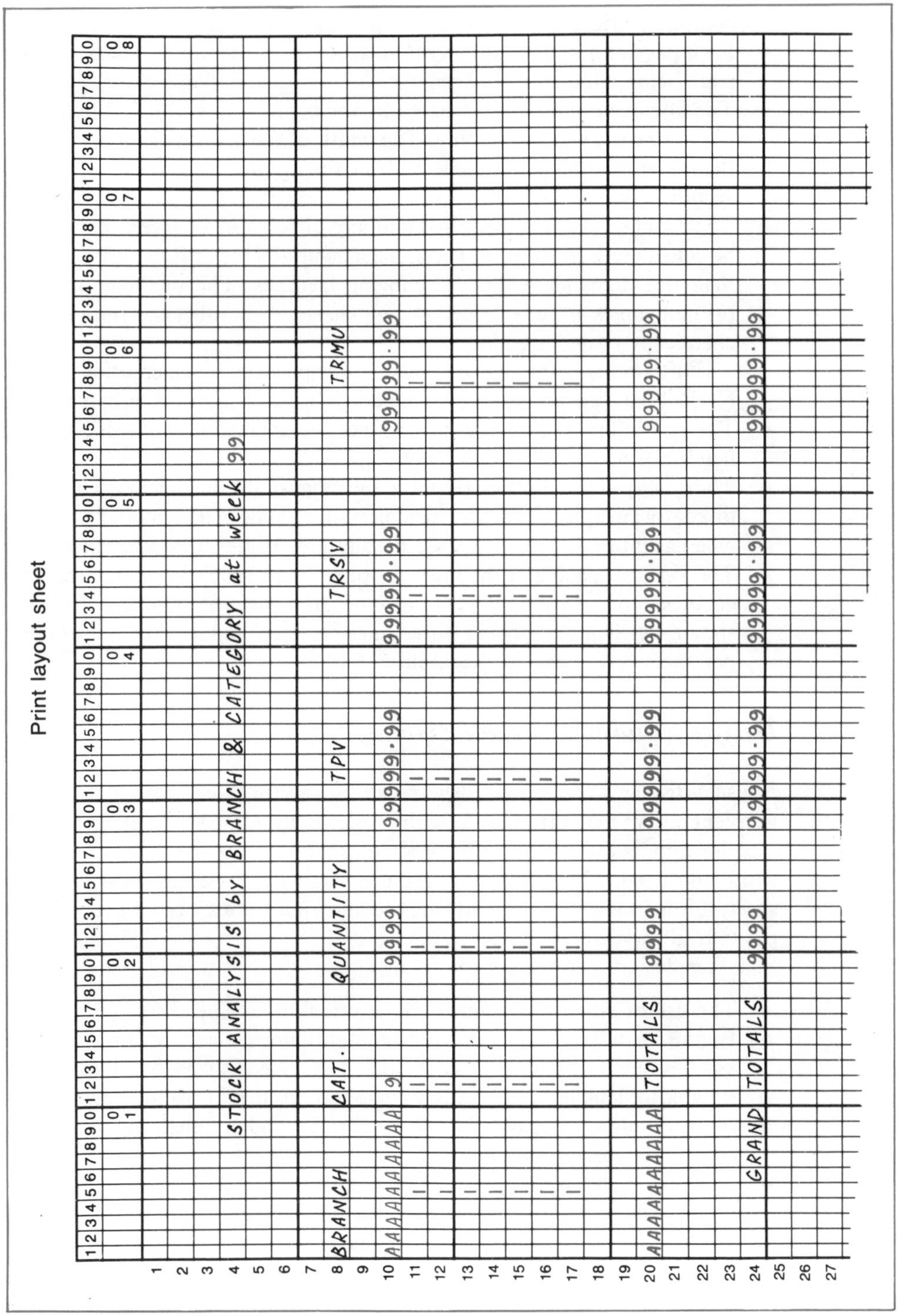

Print layout sheet

Figure 7.6 Specimen print layout

computer-printed, as with most reports and analyses.

- Each page of output is numbered so as to detect the loss of a page, the final page being annotated 'last page'.
- The document's width is dictated by the print bank width and by external requirements, e.g. enveloping. The width of the printing cannot be greater than that of the print bank and so the information must be laid out accordingly.
- The number of copies required and any differences between them need to be considered. Most printers can manage up to four or five copies but more than this demands additional copying facilities. The methods of making printed copies are interleaved carbon sheets, carbon-backed stationery and chemically coated stationery.

    Differences between the contents of copies can be catered for by either blacked-out areas on the copy stationery or blank areas in the carbon backings.
- The possibility of utilizing turnaround documents by employing OMR or handprinting.
- The quality of the printing relates to the usage of the documents. Those going to external recipients, such as customers, need to be of a high-quality printing, whereas internal documents are usually acceptable in dot-matrix printing.
- The vertical spacing of the lines of print. Single spacing (six lines per inch) enables about sixty lines to be printed on a sheet of standard continuous stationery. Double spacing (three lines per inch) reduces the lines to thirty per sheet but enhances readability.

Design features of visual display

A visual display's content and layout call for careful thought since it is a more transient output than printing. As with printed output, the layout of visual display is entirely under the control of the program, subject to keeping within the screen's width and height. Designing the layout is facilitated by using a display layout sheet, this is similar to a print layout sheet in that it has a space for every possible position in the display.

Other design features are the following:

- The use of larger characters and various fonts for headings and titles.
- Paging versus scrolling. Paging suits output information that falls into natural batches such as can be accommodated on one display. Scrolling is more suitable for long lists, especially if the user needs to scan up and down the lists.
- Inverse video, flashing, double brightness and highlighting in order to emphasize certain data items.
- The use of colour and graphics as a means of presenting information in a more easily recognized form; and icons to facilitate selecting requirements. Various graphical presentations are available such as those described in Section 8.5 under the heading 'Diagrammatic techniques'.
- The use of windows in order to display different lots of information simultaneously.

Handling printed stationery

The output subsystem also includes the handling and distribution of the continuous stationery coming from the printer. Various processes are entailed such as those described below, and machines are used if justified by the amount of output.

Decollating This is the removal of the interleaved one-time carbons from multipart sets, and the separation of the continuous sets.

Bursting The pulling apart and stacking of the perforated sheets.

Recollating Recombining the copies after removal of the one-time carbons.

Guillotining Cutting instead of bursting the continuous stationery gives a better finish as the rough edges left by the perforations are removed.

Trimming The stationery is cut vertically to remove the sprocket holes; it may also be cut into several widths or reduced in width.

Folding The separate forms are folded, usually to fit a standard envelope.

Enveloping Insertion of forms into envelopes and sealing the envelopes.

Mailing The automatic franking of envelopes, recording the cost, and handover to the delivery firm.

Copying The reproduction of multiple copies of output documents off-line, usually by photocopying.

Distribution Arrangements are made for expeditious delivery of the output documents to the recipients. This is facilitated by a distribution list printed by the computer at the head of each document or batch of documents.

7.4 Design of logical files

The techniques and hardware of files and databases are discussed in Chapter 4; at this point we are concerned mainly with the contents and layouts of logical files. A logical file is the way in which the user sees a set of records as regards their contents, sequence and identification. It is likely that the database management system actually handles the data in an entirely different way but this need not concern the systems designer. The decisions regarding contents are associated with the outputs required, and so Figures 7.3 and 7.5 can be used. The systems analyst should also look to the future, as far as this is foreseeable, in regard to the data contained in logical files.

Environmental aspects of logical files

Registration

This is the work involved in maintaining a register of code numbers and linking them to the items they represent. It is obviously important to ensure that no code number is allocated to two separate items and that no item has more than one code number. Registration is a tedious activity in companies that have extensive sets of items requiring code numbers. And although computers are helpful in this respect, it is usually still necessary to have a manual procedure for identifying the items themselves.

Amendment and updating

Requests for amendments to file records are best made on a standard form, dated and authorized, so that no contradictions or duplications can occur. Only authorized persons in the user departments should be allowed to request amendments to master file records. User departments should be informed when a file has been updated or amended so that the staff know the precise state of the records, especially if on-line interrogation occurs.

Control

The control counts and totals used in a DP system usually originate from source documents. They are carried forward through the system, and at each state of the amendment or updating need to be reconciled with the user department's control figures. The user staff may be able to suggest the most suitable data items for use as controls.

Inspection

At regular intervals and during periods of low activity, the logical files can be systematically scanned by the computer for actual and incipient errors. The extent to which this process is worthwhile depends largely on the complexity of file contents. Contact between the users, and the systems analyst enables suitable inspection routines to be designed.

Logical file record specification

Figure 7.7 is an example of a specification of a logical file record. The entries on this document derive from the output analysis chart, and are intended to provide sufficient details for creating and maintaining the logical file. Further details for the file include the file labels, data item positions within the record, and block lengths. The database management system also determines many of the technicalities of the records, and the data item names should conform to those in the data dictionary (Section 4.4). And, of course, the logical file record specification is a contributory set of information for creating the data dictionary and the data encyclopaedia.

The main purposes of this specification are:

- to ensure that no data items are omitted from the records;
- to estimate the storage space needed for the file;
- to gain a picture of the sizes of the records, especially if they are of variable

Logical file record name		Ref.	No. of records						
Part Master		*F5*	*6,500*						

Data items		Picture	Avge. length	Value		No. per rec			Remarks
Ref.	Name			Min.	Max.	Min.	Av.	Max	
1	*Part No.*	*AA 999*	*As picture*	*—*	*—*	*1*	*1*	*1*	
2	*Drawing No.*	*9(5)*	*"*	*15000*	*80000*	*1*	*1*	*1*	
3	*Part description*	*A (30)*	*20 chars*	*—*	*—*	*1*	*1*	*1*	
4	*Std. material cost*	*99.99*	*3 digits*	*50p.*	*£70*	*1*	*1*	*1*	
5	*Std. labour cost*	*99.99*	*"*	*£4*	*£95*	*1*	*1*	*1*	
6	*Mfg. cycle time*	*99*	*2 digits*	*1 week*	*35 week*	*1*	*1*	*1*	
7	*Machine No.*	*99*	*"*	*—*	*—*	*1*	*6*	*20*	
8	*Operation time*	*99.9*	*"*	*1 min.*	*25 min.*	*1*	*6*	*20*	

Figure 7.7 Logical file record specification

length, in order to decide upon block sizes, and searching and addressing techniques to be adopted.

Data item utilization

A data item utilization chart (Figure 7.8) shows the data item used by each processing run. The intention of this is to tie together the data items needed in a run and the logical file(s) holding those data items.

File storage modes

If a database is in use, the actual methods of storage are as determined by the DBMS, and so need not concern the systems analyst. Where a database is not used, the following modes of storage need to be considered. These are discussed in Section 4.3 and so only brief reminders are given below.

Serial mode   Only suited to records devoid of keys.
Sequential mode   Suitable for high-activity files but the transactions require sorting into the same sequence as the master file.
Indexed-sequential mode   Suitable for fairly high-activity files especially if the transactions tend naturally to have the same sequence as the file.
Random mode   Beneficial where the transactions cannot be sorted, e.g. with on-line and real-time systems.

Logical file record name		Ref.							
Part Master		*F5*							
Process ref.	Job name	Data items used (refs.)							
		1	2	3	4	5	6	7	8
M5	*Part Master Creation*	C	C	C	C	C	C	C	C
M6	*Part Master Amend*	R	A	A			A	A	A
P3	*Job costing*	R			R	R			
P8	*Machine loading*	R					R	R	R
B2	*Material buying*	R		R	R				
P6	*Std. cost changes*	R			U	U			

Figure 7.8 Data item utilization chart
Key: C = created: U = updated; A = amended; R = referenced.

The decision between the above modes should be based on a calculated assessment of their relative advantages for a particular application, and not on a rule of thumb. The factors entering into the assessment are:

- the activity of the file (Section 4.1);
- the access time of the disk;
- the time taken to sort the transactions;
- the efficiency with which random mode can be used, i.e. the efficiency of algorithms in relation to the volatility of the file;
- the effect of volatility on indexes and addressing methods.

Storage estimation

An important aspect of systems design is the estimation of disk storage space required to hold the logical files needed on-line at the one time.

Disk storage has to hold the following:

- application programs;
- system software;
- all the records used by the run, plus space for new records created and the expansion of records, including overflow areas (Section 4.3).

The logical file record specifications are the starting point for storage estimation. These give the average record length for each file, but over and above this an allowance has to be made for wasted space in each record and each block.

These estimations do not take overflow into account. As was seen in Chapter 4, overflow occurs with volatile and high-activity files, especially if variable-length records are entailed. A variety of statistical methods are used for estimating overflow but it still remains problematical owing to the vagaries of business files.

Distributed database

In some DP systems it is inevitable that the files are held centrally at one point. This is necessary if a number of terminal users require access to the same records in order to update them.

In other cases there is no absolute need to hold all the records centrally and it becomes a matter of debate as to which records should be held where. In a building society, for instance, it is likely that the majority of customers transact only or mainly at their local branch office. It is therefore uneconomical to transmit their transactions over long distances to a head office computer.

There are no easy rules for deciding upon the location of files but the guidelines are as follows:

- Would local files reduce the volume of communications traffic (messages, transactions, etc.)?
- Is there a real requirement for all terminal users to update the same records?
- If terminal users need to reference records, how often do these records require to be amended or updated? For instance, prices of commodities being sold may change from time to time.
- Can local files be utilized for checking source (input) data? This may be advantageous if it avoids the transmission of erroneous data.
- Do the records in a file fall into natural groups that can be held in dispersed locations?
- To what extent is it necessary to merge or compare records of a similar type? Stock records, for instance, may need to be amalgamated only once a year for stock evaluation purposes.
- Where does the responsibility lie for amending file records? If this is at head office, it is necessary to inform all holders of distributed files when amendments have been made?
- Is the security of files held locally satisfactory? In the event of loss or corruption of file records, can they be recreated locally?
- Failure of a centralized mainframe would isolate the database from all users, whereas failure of a local database would affect only the local users.

Systems design aspects of distributed processing

From the systems design aspect the following criteria need to be taken into consideration in deciding the suitability of distributed processing.

- Do the user departments need the capability of the straightforward processing of large amounts of source data with a rapid turnround?

- Is it preferable that the source documents remain continuously in the possession of the user departments? This may be advantageous, for instance, where there is a large number of enquiries and amendments pertaining to customers' orders.
- Can the necessary processing be accomplished by access to locally held files, rather than central files? This could be the case if the file records applied only to the department but not if they required to be updated and/or interrogated by the whole organization.
- Is the output of the central computer mainly documents or information required locally rather than centrally?
- Is it advantageous for source data errors and omissions to be detected immediately on input, and is this feasible without access to central files?
- Is there a security risk in transmitting data over transmission lines? If so, local processing may be preferable to the adoption of encryption techniques before transmission. Alternatively, does a security risk arise through the local staff having access to processing power and file records?
- Are the user departments so remote that data transmission costs and error rates would be high? Alternatively, would the physical transmission of source documents and/or output documents be too risky or time consuming?
- Would there be a requirement to move data, file records, programs or software from computer to computer if distributed processing was installed? If this is a requirement, a communications network protocol system will be needed in order to control these movements. Similarly, the DBMS will be more complete owing to the likelihood of one computer needing access to records controlled by other computers.
- Can the user department operate largely autonomously but with occasional transfers of data to or from other computers? For instance, a local minicomputer may be employed for sales invoicing with daily transference of sales ledger data to the central mainframe.

7.5 Design of input

The design of the input subsystem starts with the origination of the source data. This may be internally such as in the offices, on the factory floor or possibly by management. Alternatively, source data may originate externally from customers, suppliers, the general public or government departments.

Data acquisition

Acquisition of source data may be via the mail, telephone, telex, orally, automatically (source data automation) or from terminals. Whichever is the case, the systems designer must ensure that the source document or on-line input is well structured and fully understood by the users. This is particularly important when the source document is filled out by hand for subsequent keying and, in some cases, the document needs redesigning for this purpose.

The problem of illegible entries on a document may be alleviated by better form design, typing instead of handwriting, OMR, or OCR handprinting. The entries on externally originated documents are more difficult to control but may be improved by originating these documents internally before dispatching to the external agency, i.e. turnaround documents. This allows the documents to be preprinted with most of the pertinent data. A customer order form, for instance, contains a complete list of items alongside which the customer merely enters the order quantities. Also preprinted are the customer's account number, name, address, etc.

Batching

Source documents are made up into batches of a suitable size by the originating department. For each batch a set of control counts and totals is created. Care should be taken that this does not become too onerous, with the result that more errors occur in creating control totals than are eliminated by their utilization. Typical controls are:

- the number of batches;

and for each batch:

- the number of documents;
- the batch serial number and date of origination;
- the total number of items on the documents;
- totals of certain data item values;
- totals of suitable code numbers (hash totals).

Batches sometimes occur naturally, such as the orders arriving in one mail delivery. In other cases a batch is created either at certain points of time or whenever sufficient documents have been accumulated.

Code number entering

Wherever possible the originators of source data should be spared the onus of entering code numbers. This is achieved by having the code numbers pre-entered, as with turnaround documents, or avoiding code numbers entirely by positioning the data on the source document to indicate the item, as with OMR documents (see Figure 3.4).

In many cases these solutions are not practicable, and so the originator must be assisted in getting the code number correct. The points to remember are:

- keep the code numbers as simple as possible (Section 7.2);
- provide boxes on the document to encourage neatness;
- ensure that the user has a clear and up-to-date list from which to transcribe the code numbers;
- consider the use of check digits (later this section);
- build feasibility checks into the data acceptance run (see below);
- incorporate a proper procedure for dealing with erroneous or missing code numbers;
- with on-line data, provide a displayed list from which to select the relevant code number or, alternatively, the item by its description without the code number being involved, e.g. using a touchscreen (Section 3.8).

Data validation

Ideally all data presented to a system is fully correct and complete. Unfortunately, in practical situations, this aim cannot always be achieved, so we must do what we can to detect errors at an early stage. Data received from external sources, such as customers' orders, is generally less controllable than internally originated data, and so this demands even greater checking. Computer-based systems lend themselves to extensive checking procedures, and this is particularly so with interactive systems, e.g. dialogues (later this section).

The main types of error that might occur are source recording, data preparation (although data verification eliminates most of these), incorrect batches of input data, missing data, duplicated data and incorrect file records (e.g. out-of-date records). The three main types of data checks are input validation, feasibility checking and check digits.

Input validation

This is more of an absolute proof than is feasibility checking because the computer-based system checks the input data against known values. Generally this entails the computer looking up a record from its files in order to ensure that the input relates to an existent entity. Before processing a customer's order, for instance, the computer makes an initial check to ensure that the customer number and the catalogue numbers thereon do actually exist. By discarding orders containing non-existent customer numbers and catalogue numbers at an early stage, difficulties are minimized later. Similarly there may be only one date that is acceptable to a particular processing run and any others are rejected as out-of-date.

Validity checks are well worthwhile since they eradicate confusion and backtracking, especially in complex and sophisticated systems.

EXAMPLE OF INPUT VALIDATION

Certain on-line input systems, such as those employed by mail-order companies, impose immediate checks on the orders for accuracy and validity.

The actual procedure is that orders are received from sales agents, keyed into VDU terminals and vetted by the computer for acceptable agent number, correct item (by comparison of keyed and stored price of the item) and valid unit of quantity. Where applicable, a list of options is then displayed so that the order clerk can select the requirement, e.g. the colour of an item of clothing. This method reduces errors by imposing a limit on the option selection and allowing the order clerk to use common sense when the order is unclear.

Flashback (echo) checks

With this method of input validation the computer responds to an input by returning data that in some way confirms or at least strongly implies the accuracy of the input. For instance, the input of an account number could result in the account holder's name being flashed back. In most cases this would provide confirmation of the correctness of the input as the operator already knows the account name.

Feasibility checking

Feasibility checks look for the likelihood of error as well as for definite errors. From the explanations below of the various types of checks, the student will understand their purposes and practicability.

Picture checks (layout checks)

The data item's picture (Section 6.4) is checked against the acceptable picture(s) and any difference results in rejection of the data item. Ideally there would be only one picture for the data item but in some cases several are applicable, e.g. UK vehicle registration marks.

Picture checking is mostly applied to code numbers as these often have an intricate layout. It is also possible that a particular position within a data item can be checked as having one or a limited number of values.

Limits checks (range checks)

Every data item has a minimum and a maximum value whether it be input, output or at an intermediate stage of processing. These limits may be as wide as the data item field allows, e.g. 0000−9999 in a four-digit field but often this is not the case and so a check against the acceptable limits is advantageous.

EXAMPLE OF INPUT LIMITS

The heights of army recruits are measured and subsequently this data item checked as being within the limits $5-6\frac{1}{2}$ feet. Although it is possible that heights outside this range are encountered, this is unlikely and, in any case they can be validated before being accepted into the system.

> ## EXAMPLE OF OUTPUT LIMITS
>
> The amounts of domestic electricity bills are checked as being within the range
> £1–300 before being dispatched to consumers. Those of less than £1 are then
> annotated with a message telling the consumer to withhold payment until the
> next bill. Those of over £300 are scrutinized for errors and possibly withheld
> pending rereading of the meter.

Fragmented limits checks (subrange checks)

These are basically similar to limit checks except that there are several smaller
ranges within which the data item should lie. A block coding system lends itself
to this type of check if there are definite gaps between the blocks of code numbers
(Section 7.2).

One part of a code number may indicate the range within which another part
must lie, e.g. if the code number starts with any of the letters D, M or W, the
four digits that follow must lie within the range 2,500–6,999.

Restricted values checks

In this case, the data item can legitimately have only certain predetermined values,
any others being invalid.

> ## EXAMPLE
>
> A commodity is sold in round dozens only, an order quantity is therefore restricted
> to 12, 24, 36 up to and including say, 1,200.

Combination checks

In this context, 'combination' means the joining together of two or more data
items, such as by adding or multiplying their values. After combination, the result
is checked by one of the above methods, usually a limit check. The point of
combination check is that the data items may pass their own limit checks but
become infeasible when combined together.

> ## EXAMPLE
>
> In costing stores issues, the quantity is checked with limits 1–50, the cost price
> with limits £1–80. The cost value (quantity × cost price) has a combination
> check imposed with limits £1–100. Thus, an issue of twenty units whose cost
> price is £10 each, although passing both limit checks would fail the combination
> check.

Compatibility checks

The concept here is that two, or possibly more, data items are checked for mutual consistency. The parameters of the check imposed on one data item are determined by the value of the other data item.

> ### EXAMPLE
>
> A customer's order for goods worth £50, although normally acceptable, is checked for compatibility with the customer's existing debt. This is found to be £300 and of long standing. Since these amounts are incompatible within the company's trading terms, the sale of the goods is stopped.

Compatibility checking often necessitates the setting up of a table to be stored within the computer. This contains sets of compatible figures and is referred to when carrying out a compatibility check.

> ### EXAMPLE
>
> Data resulting from medical inspections of children includes their ages, heights and weights. By compatibility checking this data against a stored table, ridiculous errors are detected, e.g. a four-year-old weighing 150 lb.

Probability checks (reasonableness checks)

These can be any of the above checks, the outcomes of which are judged against a table of probability of the data being erroneous. The purpose of probability checking is to minimize the investigatory and corrective work following the detection of a possible error. Data only just outside its limits would merely be reported and allowed to proceed. A greater variance would result in the data being held in a suspense file pending investigation, and a large variance in rejection of the data.

Dependency checks

This check means that if one data item is present then so must be another. It could be extended to cover groups of data items dependent on other groups.

> ### EXAMPLE
>
> A series of discount prices each of which must have the appropriate quantity accompanying it.

Check digits (self-checking numbers)

A check digit is appended to a code number, or sometimes to other numbers, in order to detect errors arising when the number is transcribed manually. Although check digits are not infallible, a very high proportion of errors (over 99.9 per cent) are detected.

The desirability of employing a check digit system depends largely upon the length of the code number. The longer the code number the greater the possibility of error, and therefore the more desirable the check digit. Shorter codes (up to five digits) have a lower error rate and so check digits are less advantageous. It could be argued that by appending a check digit to a short code number, not only is the amount of work in copying it increased but also the chance of making a transcription error. A rule of thumb is that it is generally beneficial to append a check digit to code numbers of six digits or more if they are transcribed frequently.

Types of errors
Errors made in copying numbers are as follows:

- *Transcription error* − these are simply a mistake in copying one or more of the digits, e.g. 65302 becomes 65802.
- *Transposition errors* − two adjacent digits are interchanged, e.g. 24981 becomes 24891.
- *Other errors* − include errors such as single and multiple shifts, double transpositions, and the insertion and omission of digits.

Modulus-11 check digit system
This system is the most commonly used and is available as a facility in a wide range of equipment. Modulus-11 provides a high level of security and the method of computing the check digit is as follows:

1. Multiply each digit in the code number by its weight. The weight for the least significant digit is 2, the next least significant digit's weight is 3, and so on.
2. Add together the above products.
3. Divide this sum by 11.
4. If the remainder is 0, the check digit is also 0.

If the remainder is not 0, subtract it from 11 to give the check digit. A check digit of 10 is usually written as 'X'.

Checking a code number with Modulus-11 check digit

1. The check digit is given a weight of 1.
2. Steps 1−3 above are repeated, and if the remainder is 0, the code number is correct.

EXAMPLES OF CREATING MODULUS-11 CHECK DIGITS

Code	2 7 9 3 5	3 4 6 3	9 3 7 0
Weights	6 5 4 3 2	5 4 3 2	5 4 3 2
Products	12 35 36 9 10	15 16 18 6	45 12 21 0
Sum	102	55	78
Sum ÷ 11	9, remainder 3	5, remainder 0	7, remainder 1
Check digit	11 − 3 = 8	0	11 − 1 = 10 = X
New code	279358	34630	9370X

Other check digit systems

Many other check digit systems have been devised but comparatively few put to practical use. The main point to remember is that the larger the divisor and hence also the remainder, the greater tends to be the system's degree of security. With more check digits, there is less probability of an erroneous code number happening by chance to have the same check digit as the correct one.

A convenient divisor for some situations is 23 (largest prime number below 26). This gives remainder of 0–22, which can be expressed as letters of the alphabet, thereby minimizing the overall length of the code numbers.

Creation and verification of check digits

Many types of equipment used for data preparation and capture are capable of automatically creating and/or verifying check digits. This applies particularly to the modulus-11 system. Once a check digit system has been established the user need hardly be aware of its existence. The check digits are created and/or checked automatically by, for example, a key-to-disk system, or are manually copied or keyed from existing documents. Thereafter the check digit is automatically verified whenever the code number is input to a computer. This is done by the computer's program; the necessary subroutines are readily available.

Correction of errors in source data

Errors and omissions, having been detected, need a smooth procedure for dealing with them. The ways of treating errors are as follows:

- Either the data item or the complete record is rejected completely and a message is sent to the originator. The erroneous transactions may be logged in order to ensure that the correct data is resubmitted later.
- The data item is accepted but flagged as being either erroneous, missing or suspect. The error is dealt with by a subsequent procedure such as correction by special operators using VDU terminals.
- The data item is accepted, flagged and allowed to go through the DP system without further alteration. The error is corrected either by a subsequent error-correction run or during the next cycle of the routine. An example of the

latter is an erroneous entry into a supplier's account; this does not affect the actual situation as long as it is flagged to stop any action taking place before it is corrected.

Error messages

Detection of an error usually results in an error message being printed or displayed. The main point is that recipients of error messages should be enabled to understand fully their meanings.

Error messages may be either complete or coded. A complete message allows the recipient to act upon it without further information since the message itself provides all the required data. A coded message relies upon the recipient having a list of error codes together with explanations of the appropriate correction procedures. It is advisable to provide a brief annotation in addition to the error code so as to reduce the chance of the recipient looking up the wrong code.

When designing error detection procedures, it is advisable to avoid 'compounded' error messages. By this is meant a series of error messages appearing as a result of one only genuine error. For instance, a missing quantity results in the first error message, the batch total is then found to be incorrect, resulting in a second message, a third message appears announcing that the activity associated with the missing quantity has not been completed, and so on.

Dialogues

The use of terminals linked to a mainframe or minicomputer brings computing power much closer to the end-user. A logical step in this direction is for the end-user to converse directly with the computer; this is termed an interactive or a man—computer dialogue. A more complete definition of a dialogue is an interchange of messages and data between a person and a computer such that each relies upon the other in achieving the desired aim.

Ideally the dialogue would be in natural English or another natural language. There are, however, insurmountable problems with this, mainly because natural language relies heavily on colloquialisms and prior understanding of the subject matter of the dialogue. Even though there have been many attempts to utilize natural language, grammatical and syntactic variations and, of course, metaphors completely confuse a computer.

It is therefore necessary to adopt and adapt a dialogue that is the most suitable for the application and situation. The choice in this respect depends on two main criteria — the nature of the work, and the attributes of the dialogue user. The former covers a wide range — from occasional interrogations of file records to a continuous stream of multivarious transactions demanding rapid service. Dialogue users vary from casual users who need complete guidance in achieving their needs, to highly trained dedicated users who are capable of utilizing the dialogue with great expertise. It is obviously imperative that the dialogue provides the user with his precise requirements but also that it does so quickly, efficiently and with minimal effort on his part.

When designing a dialogue the main points to be borne in mind are as follows:

1. The user must never be left high and dry, i.e. he should always be aware of what to do next and when to do it. In this respect it should be made abundantly clear as to what responses are acceptable to the computer so that the user is not tempted to make up his own syntax. Similarly, user responses must not be assumed by default, e.g. if 'yes' or 'no' is required, the absence of 'yes' must not be interpreted as 'no'.

2. Errors on the user's part must be detected as far as is practicably possible, and he should not be allowed to proceed until the error is corrected.

3. All computer messages should be completely clear, i.e. without computer software jargon. In this respect the terminology employed should be consistent, e.g. terms such as 'modify', 'alter', 'change', 'update', that are intended to mean the same thing cause confusion if they differ between messages. It must also be apparent as to whether a message is a statement, a comment, a command or a question.

   If the computer's messages are inevitably too complex to display satisfactorily, they are best displayed as a code number so that the user can look up their meanings in a directory.

4. Any data or messages from the computer must remain on a VDU display for as long as they need to be referred to. It is no use instructing the user to make a choice or carry out a procedure if the necessary data has disappeared. Similarly, messages must be clearly seen, i.e. not hidden amongst other data. Windows are useful in these respects.

5. User messages or instructions to the computer should be acknowledged and, as far as possible, in such a way that the user receives confirmation of the correctness and completeness of his entry, e.g. the entry of an account number should be followed by the computer displaying the name of the account, i.e. a flashback check.

6. Incorporate a straightforward procedure for requesting hard copy of selected display data. If a local printer is used, remind the user to set it up. If the printer is at a distance, provide some indication as to when and how the hard copy will arrive.

There follows a number of dialogues that are practical propositions, either singly or in combination.

Query languages

Query languages are intended as a rapid means of interrogating databases, i.e. logical files, by the use of pseudo-English statements. The computer is enabled to pick out certain key words from the query and to use these to answer it.

> **EXAMPLE**
>
> 'DISPLAY products IN NUMERICAL ORDER OF product code THAT HAVE stock value GREATER THAN £10000'

The words in capitals are commands telling the computer what to do; the lower-case words refer to data items in the database.

This is a simple example, needing access to one or perhaps two files only. More complex queries would involve several files.

Query languages are non-procedural, i.e. the user specifies *what* is required rather than *how* to obtain it. The computer obviously merely detects the key words in order to achieve what is needed, and so in many cases it would not matter if the key words were not in exact order.

Query languages are generally specific to the particular type of database they interrogate, in this respect SQL has emerged as a standard for relational databases.

Mnemonic statements

A dialogue of this type employs a series of messages consisting of abbreviations, and/or other easily remembered words or codes i.e. mnemonics. The purpose behind this method is to make each message brief and informative but without being too difficult to compose or understand. A mnemonic dialogue demands that the user is trained to be conversant with the structure of and the mnemonics used in the messages. In practice, this means that the user is dedicated, i.e. using the dialogue frequently and as a main part of his occupation.

> **EXAMPLE**
>
> A typical message from an airline reservation clerk to a computer is:
>
> A 8SEP LON NYC 1500
>
> In this the 'A' is an action code meaning that the message is a request for the availability of seats on flights on the 8th September from London (LON) to New York (NYC) departing at about 3 p.m. (1500). The computer responds in similar vein, and so by an interchange of such messages, the customer's requirements are fulfilled.

The main point about a mnemonic statement dialogue is that the user must not be expected to remember too many mnemonics. If a large number is unavoidable, there should be some straightforward method of recalling and interpreting them, e.g. by means of a list that can be displayed when needed.

Menus

A menu selection dialogue requires the user to select one, or sometimes two, items from each of a succession of displayed lists (known as pages or frames). This type of dialogue is typified by the information systems available to the general public via domestic television, such as CEEFAX and ORACLE. The user indicates his choice of item by keying the number (action code) alongside, by pointer and mouse, by lightpen or by touchscreen, and this results in a new list appearing. This procedure continues until the page is displayed that contains the user's required information. The successive pages can be either hierarchical or independent.

Hierarchical means that each page after the first stems from its predecessor, e.g. a list of countries followed by the counties or states within the selected country, followed by towns within the selected county. Hierarchical menu selection may well necessitate the storage of a large number of pages if several levels are involved.

With independent menu selection each displayed list covers a set of items that are unrelated to those in the previous list. Consequently it is a good idea to display the lists concurrently, and if windows are available they can be scrolled independently. Generally a lesser number of pages have to be stored with independent than with hierarchical menu selection. Figures 7.9 and 7.10 depict hierarchical menus and independent menus respectively.

A useful variant of menus is the pull-down type. With these the procedure is to position the pointer over one of the several options along the top of the screen. This causes a menu to appear beneath the option, from which an item is selected by means of the pointer and mouse. When the pointer is positioned on a menu item, this switches into inverse video and is then selected by pressing the mouse button.

Menu selection is straightforward but is tedious for a dedicated user if the same lists have to be inspected repeatedly. This is alleviated by incorporating a shortcut such as direct page mode. Here the user is permitted to enter the number of the page he wishes to see, and the computer retrieves and displays this page directly. Direct page mode and conventional menu selection may be combined in the one dialogue, i.e. the user moves between the two methods as convenient.

Since menu selection is generally intended for casual users, it is important that the dialogue is 'user friendly', i.e. provides good guidance and control in leading the user towards his needs. In this respect a number of facilities can be included such as 'return to start' and 'return to previous page'. These enable the user to have another attempt if he becomes lost or makes a conscious mistake. Another facility is to provide a full list of page numbers with their headings or titles. This list could be available in various sequences, thus facilitating the use of direct page mode.

Directory searching

When there are a large number of items from which one is to be selected, the search can be narrowed down to the required item by displaying a series of lists in a similar manner to menu selection. Each list is in some logical arrangement,

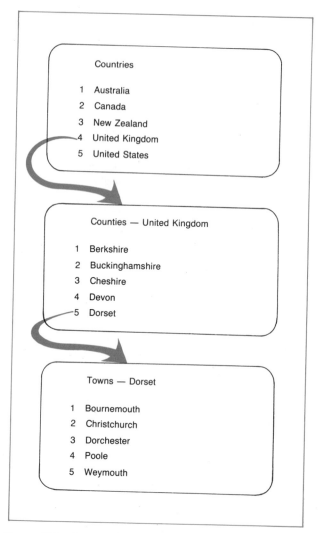

Figure 7.9 Hierarchical menus

e.g. alphabetical order, so that the required item or the one logically preceding it can be seen.

An instance of directory searching is where it is necessary to find the precise name and details of one of a large number of customers, many of whom have similar names. The search commences by entering the first few letters of the customer's name, whereupon a list is displayed of all names that start with these letters.

This allows the user to scrutinize the names and, hopefully, select the one for which details are required. If on seeing the customer's full name and address, the choice is perceived to have been incorrect, others can easily be tried.

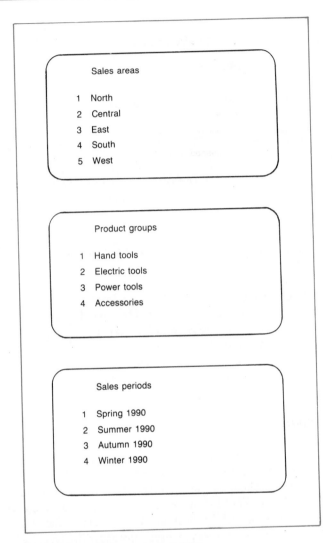

Figure 7.10 Independent menus

Form-filling (entry forms)

In this dialogue a set of attribute (data item) names is displayed, each having an adjacent blank box(es). The values of these attributes are entered from the keyboard and displayed immediately, thus allowing the user to check for correctness and completeness. Alternatively only one attribute is called for and displayed at a time.

Form-filling is a suitable method for repeatedly entering a large amount of data such as customer's remittances.

An example of a form for such a procedure is shown in Figure 7.11. As each

```
                    Customer's remittances

    Customer account no.        24835
    Customer's reference        359/165
    Date of remittance          18 12 91
    Amount   456.70
    Method of payment   CH
    _____
                    Methods of payment codes

      CA cash           CH cheque         CT credit transfer
```

Figure 7.11   Form filling

data item is keyed, the form is filled in and, at the same time, feasibility checks are imposed on it.

By having boxes, as shown, each data item is restricted in length to the size of its box. Other checks are as described earlier in this section.

On detecting an error, the screen is overlaid by a window giving details, thus enabling the user to make corrections. Windows can also be used to obtain help or further instructions in case of difficulty.

The lower portion of a form-filling screen often displays a list of possible entries, such as the methods of payment in this example.

Special keyboards

A special-purpose keyboard is designed or adapted for one particular application. The keys are labelled to show their meanings in terms of the dialogue's functions. So one key could be labelled 'cancel', another 'reserve', and so on.

Greater flexibility is achieved if the original keyboard is overlaid with a mat showing the keys' labels for each application. And, of course, the program needs to be capable of interpreting the key depressions accordingly.

7.6 Design of processing

The design of processing is largely a matter of interconnecting the subsystems of output, input and logical files so as to create a system that provides the requirements of each application. In most cases this also entails the design and creation of a database to hold the application's master data. In other cases the database already exists and the new system is designed to interface with it. It is also possible that the system needs to interface with software purchased from external suppliers, this applies particularly to the use of a database management system.

In most businesses the work falls into a number of applications. By and large, these are separate areas of responsibility and effort, generally by reason of the inherent departmentalization of most companies. There is no harm in designing an overall system in the form of applications provided the data in the database is not thereby replicated. The applications interface with one another at certain points in their logic and at certain points of time, this arises naturally through their use of the logical master files in the database.

A business application splits naturally into several routines (procedures).

Routines and jobs

A routine is a piece of DP work that produces some usable output, and is carried out as a series of related processing jobs on the computer. A routine is generally time-bounded by the arrival of source data and the production of the resultant information, especially documents. Routines vary in complexity from one organization to another but typically they relate to the applications as in the example.

EXAMPLE

Application	*Routines (procedures)*
Sales accounting	Order acceptance (daily) Credit control (daily) Invoicing (weekly) Statement preparation (monthly)
Payroll	Gross wage computations (weekly) Payslip printing (weekly) Payroll analysis (quarterly)
Production control	Job scheduling (daily) Labour planning (weekly) Materials requirements (monthly) Machine loading (monthly)

A routine usually comprises several separate jobs each of which is a continuous computer process involving one program, one main lot of input, and one main lot of output. This definition is a little dogmatic but is typical if not absolutely true. Routines are split into jobs simply because computers are often incapable of carrying out the complete routine in one go.

The main limiting factors in this respect are the following:

- the number of program instructions that the main store can hold at the one time;

- the availability of peripheral devices;
- the time relationships between jobs — these are normally under the control of external circumstances.

Routines and jobs both entail the carrying forward of data from one processing cycle to the next. This data is left stored on magnetic media so that the time taken to write and subsequently read it is minimal. With routines, disks or tapes are removed from the peripherals and held in a secure place between processing cycles. With jobs data is sometimes left in main store while a new program is loaded, e.g. order analysis figures accumulated during order acceptance are left stored for printing by a subsequent job.

Types of processes

The processes, jobs or runs used in conjunction with each other to form routines are mainly of the following types:

Data acceptance   This job validates, edits and totals the source data, and prints error messages and control totals. It also transfers the edited source data onto disk or tape so as to form a transaction file.

Sorting   If the transaction records are to be processed sequentially, the second job sorts them into the appropriate sequence.

Referencing   A further job is used to look up data from a master file(s), e.g. prices, descriptions, balances, and to apply these in some way to the transaction records. This may result in the creation of a transition file, e.g. holding priced transactions, but this is often omitted nowadays.

Updating   The master file records are updated by data from the transaction records, e.g. stock issues and receipts applied to stock balances.

Amendment   The master file is brought into a correct and up-to-date condition by the insertion of new records, deletion of obsolete records, and changes made to existing records. For instance, a record is inserted for each new product, the record is removed for each dead product, and alterations made to the prices of products.

File printing   Updated records are copied from the master file or are summarized or analysed before being printed, e.g. a list of the stock levels of all the materials.

Document printing   Master files and transaction files are used to print documents such as invoices, payslips, statements, etc. The output is frequently spooled (written) to an output file prior to being printed.

Diagramming the system

Flowcharting

A flowchart consists of interconnected symbols depicting the relationships of operations, logical files, processes, input/output, etc. Each symbol has an

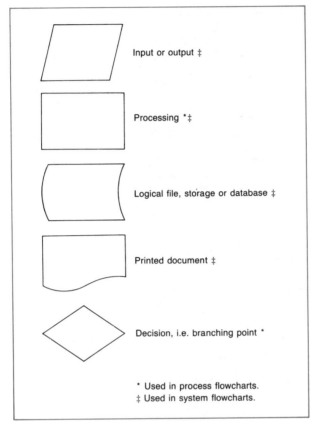

Figure 7.12 Reduced set of flowchart symbols

identifying reference which in some cases is linked to a narrative or other document.

The symbols shown in Figure 7.12 are drawn from those recommended by the ISO, BSI and NCC (see Reference 6.11). This reduced set has been chosen because the full set is now largely out of date, having been superseded by data flow diagrams and other methods.

Flowcharts are used at three main levels:

System (routine) flowcharts
The highest level represents the way in which the whole routine holds together, as in Figure 7.13. This is often referred to as either a system or a routine flowchart, and this example relates to the stock analysis routine described in Section 7.3.

It is probably better not to incorporate too many different types of symbols into a system flowchart but to stick to the four basic symbols.

The individual jobs or runs shown on a system flowchart need further definition and this brings us to the next level of flowchart — a job or run flowchart.

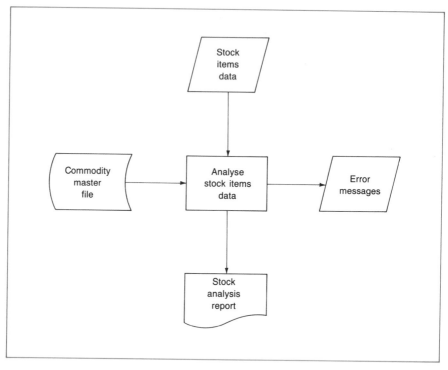

Figure 7.13 System flowchart of stock analysis routine

Process, job or run flowcharts
Figure 7.14 is an example of a process flowchart and applies to the stock analysis. This flowchart shows the processing in a single job or run, and the only symbols really needed are the processing symbol and the decision symbol. The main point is that each symbol must be explained in detail elsewhere since it is not possible to do this properly within the confines of the symbol outlines.

The philosophy of flowcharting is that all the necessary steps are incorporated but that the flowchart does not dictate the programming methodology.

Program flowcharts
These are used by the programmer to facilitate the writing of program instructions. This type of flowchart does not concern the systems analyst.

Data flow diagrams (DFDs)

DFDs are explained in Section 6.4 as applied to manual systems, they are also used to show the fundamental processes in a computer-based system. Bear in mind that a DFD is based on the flow of data between processes and data stores, and that three main symbols are involved (Figure 6.5).

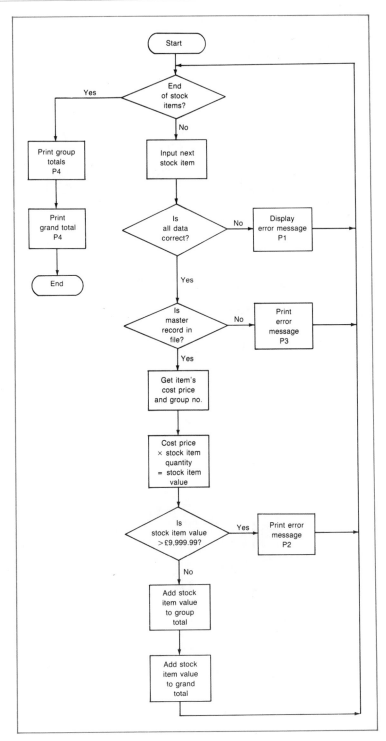

Figure 7.14 Process flowchart of stock analysis routine

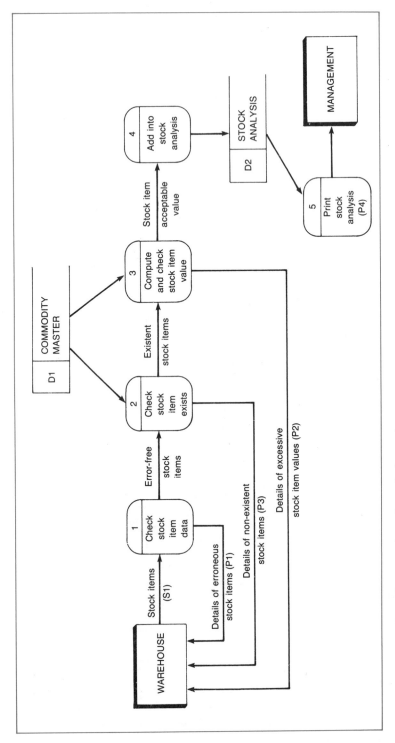

Figure 7.15 Data flow diagram of stock analysis routine

Figure 7.15 shows the DFD for the stock analysis example and, as is evident from this diagram, the annotations need to be amplified before being passed for programming; in this respect DFDs are similar to flowcharts.

Structure diagrams

The concept of a structure diagram (SD) is that it is composed of a number of modules each of which reports to a higher-level module, thus tying in with the principles of structured programming (Section 5.1). Each module should be as self-contained as possible, i.e. have the maximum binding and minimum coupling. As explained previously, binding means cohesiveness, that is to say, the module performs one clear-cut function, such as those depicted in Figure 7.16. Coupling means the interplay between modules, and by minimizing coupling, modules are independent from the program aspect.

A structure diagram is created as a hierarchical tree of modules and Figure 7.16 shows the stock analysis example split into modules in this way. The modules are executed from left to right and are shown in increasingly greater detail from top to bottom. Thus after completing a module the process normally goes back to the next higher level and then takes the next path to the right. The exceptions are the alternative modules (shown containing circles), only one of these is executed during the one processing cycle. When a module contains an asterisk, it is repeated as often as necessary before proceeding to the next module. This is the case for 'process stock item' in Figure 7.16 because of the large number of stock items, and similarly for the 'print group total' module.

Structure charts

Figures 7.17–7.19 depict, in increasing detail, another type of diagram known as a structure chart (SC). The principle is the same as described above but the final SC has more details and is, in effect, an amalgam of an SD and a DFD.

Referring to Figure 7.19, the arrows show movements of data and flags between the modules. Conceptually each module receives data and instructions from its higher-level module and passes results back to it. The higher-level module may pass the data either to its higher-level module or to another lower-level module for further processing. The modules are operated from left to right and those with connecting lines lying within the curved arrowed line are repeated as often as necessary; 'compute totals', for instance, is performed once for each stock item. At the end of the stock items, denoted by the flag ES, control passes back to the highest module (analyse stock) which then initiates the 'print report' module.

The diamond shapes denote alternative processes so that, for instance, either the error message P3 is printed or the stock item value is computed.

A convenient way of constructing an SD is to start with a broad outline showing

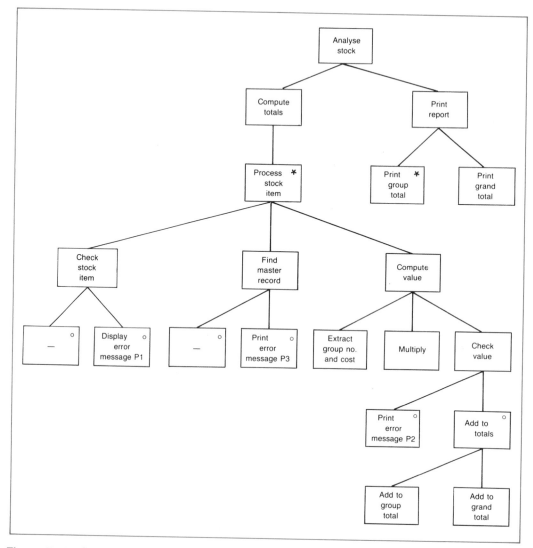

Figure 7.16 Structure diagram
Key: * repeated (iterative); ° alternative (selected); — do nothing.

just the main functions (Figure 7.17) and thereafter to amplify the modules into more modules working downwards (Figures 7.18 and 7.19).

This may have to be repeated several times until it is not worth while or indeed possible to amplify the modules further.

It is convenient and advantageous to abbreviate the data items and to create a list showing their definitive names and descriptions (Figure 7.20); this then forms the basis of a data dictionary.

DFDs and SDs are explained in greater depth in Reference 7.7.

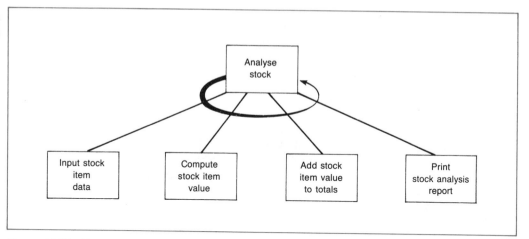

Figure 7.17 Structure chart — first stage

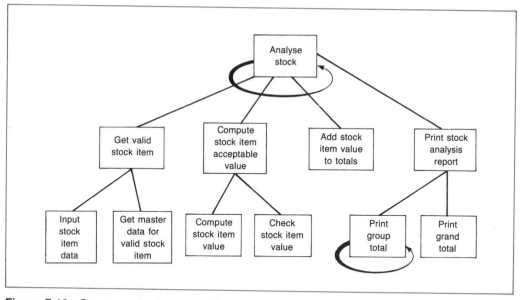

Figure 7.18 Structure chart — second stage

Pseudo-code

A number of similar methods have been devised to specify processes, these enjoy various names such as pseudo-code, action diagrams and structured English. An example is shown in Figure 7.21 from which it is apparent that there are strong similarities to structured programming. The names of the data items (in italics) and of the processes should conform to those in the data dictionary, thus eliminating any doubts as to their precise identification.

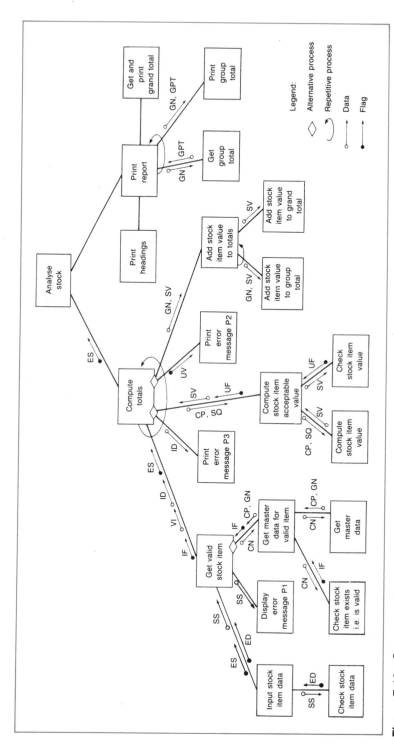

Figure 7.19 Structure chart — third and final stage

Abbreviation	Name	Description
CN	Commodity number	Identification of stock item's commodity
CP	Cost price	Cost price per unit of the commodity
ED	Erroneous stock item data flag	A designation indicating that the stock item data is erroneous or incomplete
ES	End of stock items flag	A designation to indicate the end of the stock items
GN	Group number	The group into which the commodity falls
GPT	Group total	The total cost value of the stock within a group
GT	Grand total	The total cost value of all the stock
IF	Invalid stock item flag	A designation indicating that the stock item is not in the master file
ID	Invalid stock item data	SN, CN, RN, SQ
RN	Rack number	The location of the stock item in the warehouse
SN	Serial number	The serial number pre-printed on the stock form
SQ	Stock item quantity	The quantity of the stock item in the warehouse
SS	Stock item source	SN, CN, RN, SQ
SV	Stock item value	The cost value of the stock item in the warehouse
UF	Unacceptable value flag	A designation indicating that the stock item's value is over the top limit
UV	Unacceptable value data	SN, CN, RN, SQ, CP, GN, SV
VI	Valid stock item	SN, CN, RN, SQ, CP, GN

Figure 7.20   Abbreviations used in Figure 7.19

```
ANALYSE STOCK
   DO COMPUTER-TOTALS
   DO PRINT-REPORT

COMPUTER-TOTALS
   REPEAT PROCESS-ITEM UNTIL all stock-items have been processed

PROCESS-ITEM
   GET next stock-item
   GET master-record in master-file
   IF master-record is found
      THEN DO COMPUTE-VALUE
   ELSE (master-record not found)
      SO print error-message-P3

COMPUTE-VALUE
   GET group-no and cost-price from master-record
   Stock-item-value = cost-price * stock-quantity
   IF stock-item-value is GT £9999.99
      THEN print error-message-P2
   ELSE (stock-item-value is LTE £9999.99)
      SO add stock-item-value to group-total
         add stock-item-value to grand-total

PRINT-REPORT
   print headings
   REPEAT print group-total UNTIL all group-totals have been printed
   print grand-total
```

Figure 7.21   Example of pseudo-code

Program specifications

The various methods described previously, such as DFDs, decision tables, structure charts and so on, do not always provide sufficient detail for the needs of programming. They are therefore supported by descriptive programming specifications into which all additional points are incorporated.

These specifications are particularly necessary for new programmers and for appendments to existent systems.

Although a programming specification generally covers the one program, this is not always the case. It sometimes turns out to be convenient to create two, or possibly more, programs from the one specification. This does not in itself affect the principle or contents of the specification.

The list below covers the main features of a programming specification but, of course, further points are added to suit particular circumstances.

- The job name, reference number and a brief explanation of the job's purpose.
- The contents and layouts of all input media, including the data items therein. If a DD is in existence the data items are specified by quoting their definitive names, otherwise full details as per Sections 4.4 and 6.4 are included.
- The contents and layouts of all output, both printed and displayed. This entails the use of print layout sheets as shown in Figure 7.6, and display layout sheets (Section 7.3).
- The feasibility and other checks to be imposed on input and at later stages of processing, and the consequent error-notification messages and error procedures.
- The calculations and logical processing such as accumulation of totals, updating of balances and arithmetic calculations. Any special quirks in the calculations are 'spelled out' by including actual examples.
- The storage and access modes of the relevant logical files. If, as is likely, a DBMS is in use, this is unnecessary.
- The meanings and significance of symbols, codes, etc., needed in the job, e.g. debit/credit symbols that entail alternative processing.

Top-down systems development

Top-down systems development is a general concept rather than a particular methodology. As the name suggests, it is an approach to systems development that takes an overall view of the organization's aims and activities. Each and every application possibly qualifying for computerization in the immediate or far future is taken into consideration. The main aim of this is to facilitate the integration of applications and routines, some of which may not be computerized for some time.

Top-down development ties in closely with prototyping and, in particular with staged and evolutionary prototyping (Section 6.9). It also connects with the creation of the database in that the contents of logical files are taken into account from the outset.

Figure 7.22 depicts in broad outline a top-down approach as applied to a fictitious company, Regis Jewellers Limited (RJL), described more fully in the case study of Chapter 9. For the moment it is sufficient to describe RJL as a firm of retail jewellers selling via a chain of branches. The firm buys from a number of suppliers and replenishes the branches through a central warehouse.

From Figure 7.22 it is seen that the two main functions of RJL are buying and selling with the obvious aim of profitability. The two secondary functions are accounting for stocks held and financial accounting, in particular the control of cash flow. These functions split into applications which in turn separate into routines and processing jobs (not shown in Figure 7.22). The red lines emphasize the interconnections between the routines, either through the DP procedures or other activities.

When a systems analyst undertakes a top-down development, it soon becomes apparent that other factors apart from DP enter into the organization's thinking. These are usually closely connected with each other and with the DP procedures. An instance of this is the 'Fashion demand forecasting' of RJL. This is inevitably a human activity supported by the computer-produced sales analyses but based mainly upon non-quantifiable considerations such as fashion trends and manufacturers' advertising campaigns.

This example should not be taken as a master plan for top-down systems development in all organizations. The large range of differing businesses and organizations inevitably necessitates various approaches. More levels than the four of the example are likely and, depending on the nature of the organization's aims and activities, the applications and routines have dissimilar priorities. An insurance company, for instance, would have minimal purchasing and stock activities but give a high priority to accounting and selling.

The principal advantages of top-down systems development are summarized below:

- easier integration and interfacing of applications and routines;
- lends itself to prototyping;
- project teams are able to interface their designs more satisfactorily;
- ensures the creation of a comprehensive database;
- encourages a structured (modular) approach to systems design.

7.7 Security and audit

Security and accuracy controls

Security and accuracy controls are necessary for the following reasons.

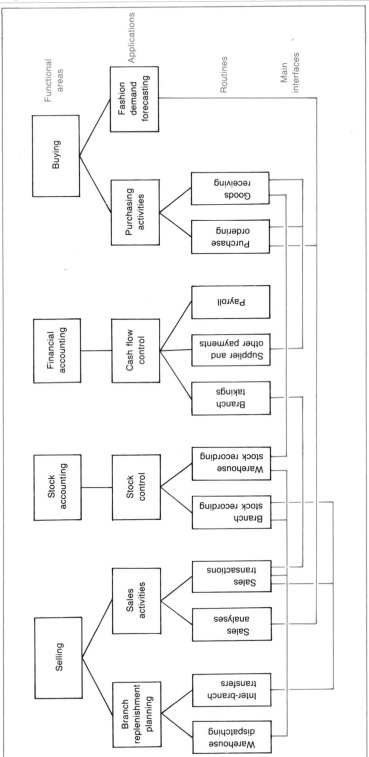

Figure 7.22 Top-down systems development in RJL

To detect and prevent terminal user errors
More users are involved in on-line systems than with batch-processing systems and so there is greater scope for errors to arise in the input data. On the other hand, the data is captured closer to its source, and so errors are corrected more easily.

To detect and prevent computer-room operator errors
These errors could be the loading of incorrect disk cartridges or tape reels.

To guard against hardware failure or program errors
The failure of the computer or of the transmission lines must not be allowed to cause the loss or duplication of data. A terminal user needs to be aware of which data has been accepted by the computer when a failure occurs, and how to proceed from then on. Similarly the operating system has to be capable of reconstructing records that have been lost or damaged.

To prevent fraud and abuse
There is always the possibility of fraudulent activities involving the computer and/or data where money or important information is entailed. A similar activity is so-called 'hacking', this is the theft of information by other users of a computer network. The hacker breaks into an organization's database and extracts information, often merely for the sake of so doing.

Abuse includes the overloading of the computer system by trivial demands upon it, e.g. frequent and unnecessary requests for complex information. Also coming within abuse is the unauthorized dissemination of private information.

To permit the auditing of the company's finances
It should be remembered that the obligations of the auditors are not changed by the computer system. The auditors' methods are different, however, and the controls should facilitate the methods adopted.

Security and accuracy methods

Physical security

The security measures employed for cash, etc., also apply to information. These include locks, safes, security officers and burglar alarms. Also involved are protection against wire tapping, and the identification of terminal users. Wire tapping is frustrated by the use of cryptography; terminal users are validated by using badges, passwords and interrogation questions.

Other aspects of physical security are protection against fire and flood. The latter is not usually a problem but it must be remembered that damage by water can be a consequence of fire-fighting.

The computer hardware itself should obviously be housed in a fire-protected area, and specialist advice obtained regarding this requirement. Back-up files are stored in fireproof and waterproof accommodation well away from the computer. In special circumstances the back-up files are held in a separate building in case of severe damage to the building housing the computer department.

Staff security

Employees who will have access to computers and data need to be screened in order to ensure that their interests are compatible with those of the organization. Those members of the DP staff who seem to have a grudge or who are under notice or resignation may need to be given special attention.

It is also important that all DP staff and users are obliged to take security seriously. This applies particularly to passwords, the use of which sometimes becomes very lax. Regular reissuing of passwords helps in this respect.

Batch control totals

Pre-prepared batch totals, counts and hash totals are applicable to remote job entry (RJE) as with conventional batch processing. They are unsuitable, however, for on-line work because the input messages originate from many terminals and in a random manner; pretotalling therefore is impossible. Post-control totals may, however, be created by the computer for each terminal and transmitted to the terminals at intervals for comparison with the locally prepared totals.

Message controls

These include check digits, the transmission of preknown values for checking against the corresponding value in the stored record, and feasibility checks. An example of preknown data is the input of the selling price along with the rest of the order. The computer then checks the input price against the stored price, mainly in order to ensure that the correct item is being looked up in the file.

Message serial numbers
Each message in an on-line system contains a serial number in order to ensure that none is lost without this being detected. After a breakdown, the terminal and the computer inform each other of the last serial received, and a correct restart can thus be achieved.

A more sophisticated method is where the computer allocates all the serial numbers and informs the terminals of each message's number. The terminal user knows that if he has received the serial number of an input message; it does not need to be retransmitted after a failure.

Message logging

A log is maintained on disk or tape to contain a copy of every input message on its receipt and at interemediate stages, together with its serial number. Other data can be inserted into the logged message such as the terminal number, time received, and data extracted from the master files. The log is available for reinput of messages after a failure has occurred.

Checkpoints

At intervals during processing, as determined by the computer's real-time clock, the status of the run is recorded on tape. These 'checkpoint tables' are reloaded after a breakdown and the supervisor program then decides which messages are capable of completion and which need to be retransmitted from the terminals. This is not a simple exercise because real-time messages are handled by a 'multithreading' procedure. Multithreading means that messages are processed a stage at a time in parallel, and the partially processed messages are held in queues between stages.

Bypass procedures

Whatever the nature of an on-line system, it must be capable of continuing to function when a hardware failure occurs. The level of service is generally degraded but this is better than a total break-off.

With a real-time banking system, in the event of a failure the clerk is allowed to accept cash and to allow withdrawals up to a certain predecided amount. To facilitate this, the computer transmits a portion of each day's closing balances to the branches during the night. A printout is thus available to provide some indication of the customer's financial status.

Another bypass procedure is the recording of transactions on magnetic medium at the terminal if it becomes cut off from the computer. On recovery, the data is transmitted rapidly to the computer.

Dumping (file reconstruction)

Each file is written to streamer tape (dumped) at intervals, and the message logs retained from the time of each dumping. If any records are lost or corrupted due to program or operating errors, the file is reconstructed from the dump and then updated by the logged messages.

Audit trails

The company's internal and external auditors are involved in a computer system during all stages of its development and use. A number of auditing techniques are available for these stages and must be integrated into the system. This is especially relevant to on-line systems. Further information is to be found in References 7.25−7.34 and below.

Audit considerations

It is the duty of an organization's auditors, internal and external, to make such tests and enquiries as are necessary to form an opinion as to the realiability of the records as a basis for the organization's accounts. The statutory responsibilities of the auditor are not diminished by the employment of a computer within the organization.

Nevertheless, the size of the computer and the sophistication and complexity of the system clearly have some effect on the auditor's approach to his tasks. The main difference between a manual system and a computer-based system is the lack of human readability of the records in the latter case. Another important aspect is that a computer operates from a stored program of instructions, the subtleties of which are not always immediately obvious to the non-programmer.

Audit trail
The above factors mean that an audit trail must be established. This is the means by which the details behind the summarized totals and analysis can be obtained. The auditor, having found a discrepancy in a total, wants to investigate the detail causing the discrepancy. And so the audit trail needs to be capable of being followed right through the system from source data to final output, and to provide readable evidence at each stage if required.

It is therefore desirable for the auditor to be involved with the DP system during its design stage. He is then in a position to make his requirements known and to determine how these are provided. This implies that the auditor needs a general understanding of DP systems, including hardware, programming, software and control methods.

Audit methodology

Control totals
The concept behind control totals is that each stage of processing generates control totals for carrying forward for checking against those of the next stage.

The purposes of control totals are to detect the following:

- the loss of documents or data;
- the accidental or intentional insertion of records or data;
- fraudulent alterations to data;
- manual, hardware and software errors occurring at any stage of processing.

The various types of control totals are explained under 'batching' in Section 7.5.

The sources of control totals are:

- the originating point of a batch of documents;
- the data preparation department;
- initial computer input;
- each stage of processing;
- computer output including batching of output documents.

Check digits
These are used in conjunction with auditing to detect errors, see Section 7.5.

File inspection
Any selected portion or all of a file has to be available in human readable form so that the auditor can examine the records if errors or fraud are suspected. This requirement is covered by audit packages but may need to be programmed specifically in certain cases.

Operation logs
Every job carried out on the computer is logged manually and/or by the operating system. The log notes the data volumes, times taken and storage devices that are loaded. This enables unauthorized use of the computer to be detected, for instance in order to perpetrate fraud or for private purposes.

Staff control
Only authorized staff are allowed to operate the computer and only during permissible working hours. Programmers are not to be allowed free access to the computer. Terminal operators must identify themselves; the computer then verifies that the terminal operator is entitled to the data requested. Several sophisticated methods of identification are now available (References 7.26 to 7.33).

Documentation
System and program documentation should be fully adequate for the auditor's needs (see Section 7.10).

Audit test data
Sets of input data are kept by the auditor together with the corresponding output results. Its purpose is for spot checking in order to detect unauthorized amendments to programs. This technique sometimes proves difficult in practice owing to authentic amendments to programs and files causing the output to be different from the auditor's version. In order to prevent an audit test from damaging file records, a copy is made of the file for audit test purposes.

Audit packages
In order to cope with the complexity of computers and DP systems, the auditor utilizes the computer itself, i.e. by means of an audit package.

The features of an audit package are as follows:

- extraction of selected file data by means of variable parameters;
- extraction of data by sampling;
- totalling of data items from records meeting certain criteria, e.g. total debit amounts of all foreign customers;
- computational functions to enable checks on extension, interest, discounts, etc.;
- subtotalling at certain points in a file;
- matching of files in the same sequence to detect omissions and replications (see Section 4.1);
- open-endedness to allow the auditor to extend the package to meet his further needs.

7.8 Computer job scheduling

An important aspect of systems design is the scheduling of the routines within the operational hours available. The use of an operating system in multiprogramming mode results in the actual jobs being loaded onto the computer for subsequent execution according to the dictates of the operating system. Nevertheless the systems analyst must schedule the jobs during the design stage in order to ensure they can be done within the times dictated by external factors. Allowance is also made for data preparation, ancillary operations, and reruns.

The factors taken into account in scheduling a routine are as follows:

- the times at which source data is available;
- the time taken for data preparation or entry;
- the time for each processing run;
- the time for handling and distributing stationery;
- the times by which output must be ready (deadlines).

Figure 7.23 is an elementary example of the scheduling of a number of jobs on the computer. Data preparation or key-to-disk entry and the handling of output stationery are also shown.

Several points are worth noting in this example:

- The data entry is staggered so that only one type of source data is dealt with at a time, although in some DP departments it is usual to mix the data preparation work. Much depends on the hardware used for data preparation or entry.
- A certain amount of computer processing is scheduled simultaneously, e.g. stock updating and invoice preparation. This is because the former demands input peripherals and the latter output peripherals.

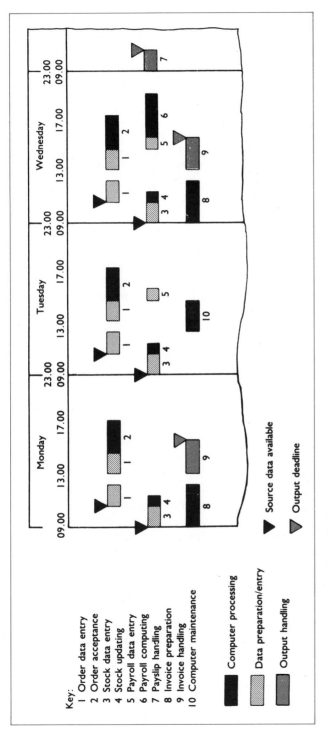

Figure 7.23 Computer job scheduling chart

- The handling of computer output and data entry are scheduled in only normal working hours (9 a.m.–1 p.m. and 2 p.m.–5 p.m.). The reality of this depends on whether the ancillary machine operators are prepared to work shifts or overtime.
- The computer and its operators work two shifts, i.e. from 9 a.m. to 11 p.m. in all.
- Scheduled computer maintenance is allowed for.

The activities in a routine may be scheduled either forward from a start point, i.e. when the source data becomes available, or backward, from a deadline, i.e. when the final output is needed. The latter tends to apply to jobs that must be completed by the deadline; the former to jobs that are less urgent.

The purpose of job scheduling during the system design stage is not to plan the work in detail but, as stated above, to make sure that the computer peripherals can handle volumes of input/output data within the working hours; and also that the data preparation or data entry facilities and the stationery handling facilities can cope. It could be that the eventual scheduling of jobs is different from the system design scheduling. This is of no consequence provided the selected computer configuration is able to handle the work load imposed upon it.

7.9 Costs and savings of new system

Estimating costs

In estimating the costs of a DP system, it is advisable to look forward over a period of five years or so. A lesser period does not allow the system to become fully effective, and beyond five years the situation is increasingly unpredictable.

The factors entering into the estimation of future costs include some of those listed below. The extent to which these are significant depends largely on how radical the change is to be. Changing from a completely manual system to a large mainframe necessitates more installation costs and personnel costs than moving to a microcomputer. Changing from one model of computer to another may attract only minimal costs.

Equipment costs – purchase, lease or rental

Processors, peripherals, terminals and communication equipment
Data preparation, capture and entry equipment
Ancillary machines, e.g. stationery handling
Air-conditioning equipment
Electric supply equipment – stabilizers and standby generators

Initial stocks of disk cartridges, diskettes and magnetic tapes
Racks, trolleys, trays, furniture, internal telephones etc.
Security equipment, e.g. alarm systems, safes etc.

Installation costs

Structural alterations to the existing building
Construction of a new building (unlikely but possible)
Demolition of an old building (unlikely but possible)
Removal and resiting of existing departments
Special floors, ceilings, walls and lighting, double glazing
Disposal of obsolete equipment (could be a negative cost).

Development costs

Software from computer manufacture and/or software houses
Consultant's fees
Changeover activities including file creation and system testing on time-hired
    computer.

Personnel costs

Salaries and allowances of all DP staff
Pension fund and charges of DP staff
Staff recruitment and relocation
Training, including course fees, accommodation and materials
Staff expenses, e.g. travelling, accommodation and meals
Redundancy payments.

Operating costs

Consumable materials, i.e. stationery, print ribbons
Floppy disk, disk cartridges and tapes – replacement or reconditioning
Maintenance of all equipment, especially computer hardware
Rent, rates, depreciation, maintenance and cleaning of DP department
    accommodation
Heating, electricity, data transmission and telephoning
Standby services
Insurance premiums including loss of profit through damage to the computer
    installation.

Each of the above costs is estimated for each of the five years from the start of the project and then totalled for each year. This is repeated for each system under consideration so that a table of comparable cost estimates is derived.

Estimating savings

Much of the savings of a new system is associated with eliminating or reducing the costs of the existing system, as discussed in Section 6.6. It is more difficult to estimate the savings from a system than its costs. Benefits from computer systems are often said to be 'intangible', nevertheless every effort should be made to put a monetary figure on an intangible benefit as otherwise it has dubious meaning.

Tangible savings include the following:

Equipment savings – replacement or rental

Obsolete computers, accounting machines, typewriters and other machines
Cabinets, racks, furniture and filing equipment.

Personnel savings

Salaries and allowances of redundant or transferred clerical and administrative staff
Pension fund, expenses and charges of above staff.

Operating savings

Consumable materials, i.e. stationery, ledger and stock cards
Maintenance of existing machines
Rent, rates, depreciation, maintenance and cleaning of redundant departments
Heating, electricity, telephone and insurance charges of above.

Capital allowances and taxes

These vary from time to time depending upon government policy, but may be significant in savings calculations.

Intangible savings include the following:

Planning information

The information needed for planning the company's activities should be available sooner and in a more accurate and comprehensive form. Much depends upon the nature and complexity of the activities.

EXAMPLES

Sales Statistical analyses and forecasts of sales, e.g. sales analysed according to customer, type of customer, salesman, area, country, product, product group, period, and any combinations of these heads.

Purchasing Suppliers' delivery promises versus actual deliveries, discount analysis, forward ordering and supplies availabilities.

Stock Forward stock requirements and valuation, stock holding costs.

Materials requirements More accurate and speedier determination of forward requirements of raw materials, bought-out components and tools

Production Forward machine loads, labour, plant and equipment requirements; detailed job scheduling and routeing, machine allocation, and rapid replanning of production

Cash flow Projected in and out movement of cash, and the net cash position in future periods

Investment appraisal Comparison of various projects from their long-term profitability prospects.

Control information

EXAMPLES

Debtors The more rapid collection of debts through more efficient invoicing, and the detection of incipient bad debts

Operating statements Quicker and more accurate preparation of all types of operational information, e.g. running profit/loss accounts

Stock control Optimum stock levels based on demand and stockholding costs.

Personnel

Less dependence on unreliable staff
Avoidance of complex training procedures for clerical staff
Minimal staff administration costs.

The estimated savings − tangible and intangible − are summated for each year and set against the corresponding costs. The net differences provide a basis for comparison with alternative systems by using investment appraisal techniques such as net present value in Section 6.6.

7.10 Systems documentation

The setting and maintenance of standards and documentation applies throughout the work of the systems analyst and programmer. These aims are particularly relevant to the designing of a system for a number of reasons:

- To facilitate designing the system by working to prescribed standards and having available clear descriptions of all the work covered so far. This implies that documentation must be on-going throughout the systems design and programming stages, and not left until all the work has been fully completed.
- To maintain a good level of communication between everyone concerned with the system, i.e. designers, programmers, operators and users. Some persons are obviously more deeply inolved with certain aspects than others but nevertheless they should all have access to whatever information is applicable to their involvement. This then allows for any misunderstandings or disagreements to surface before they become deeply entrenched in the system.
- To guard against subsequent loss of understanding of the system. This occurs only too easily when there is inadequate documentation and the originator of some work has left the company. It is sometimes difficult to understand one's own work let alone that of others after some time has elapsed. Ideally the standards, methods and documentation should be such that any qualified person can smoothly continue the work of a colleague who has left.

Aspects of systems documentation

The documentation of a system embraces the following:

Reports to management explaining the aims, costs, savings, and methods of the proposed system. These, especially methods, should be couched in terms that managers understand, it is counter-productive to 'blind them with science' by including unnecessary jargon. Where jargon cannot be avoided an explanation in clear English should be provided.

Instructions to users:

- The contents and layout of each document on which source data is recorded.
- The times and dates at which the various source data are to be available, either as documents or keyed into the system by the users.
- The procedures for notifying source data errors detected by the system and their correction by users.
- Details of batching and control totals associated with source data.
- Explanations of all outputs from the system to the users, these are mainly printed documents but also include VDU displays.
- The procedure for obtaining on-request output (Section 1.3) this includes

the actual information required and precisely when it is required, i.e. time and date or at a certain stage in the processing.
- The procedures for making on-line enquiries together with an explanation of the delays that might occur at unscheduled times.

Specifications for programmers covering the runs to be programmed.
Instructions for computer operating and control staff in relation to the running of operational jobs, acceptance of source data, usage of stored files, and the distribution of output.

Contents of a documented system

- A description of the purpose of each routine
- A flowchart or the equivalent for each routine
- Specifications of all processing runs
- Source data requirements and input procedures
- Contents of logical files and database requirements
- Layout and contents of all output prints and displays
- Operating instructions for the processing runs
- Systems amendment procedures
- All aspects of user participation.

See References 7.35–7.38 for details of documentation standards.

7.11   Systems development methodologies

In the early years of business data processing, i.e. the 1960s and 1970s, systems were generally developed along the lines suggested by the computer manufacturers. Their training courses and manuals tended to be orientated more towards programming than systems, but nevertheless what standards and methodologies there were stemmed largely from these sources.

The NCC and the BCS in the UK and other bodies elsewhere also entered into the scene by making recommendations for standards in the various aspects of systems development.

In spite of, or perhaps as a result of, the efforts of these various organizations, systems were developed and implemented in widely disparate ways. System efficiencies and acceptabilities differed enormously, and induced a considerable amount of replicated work.

The major weaknesses of the early systems were the following:

- Computer systems were speeded-up manual systems, quite often producing massive amounts of printout.

- Systems were inflexible in that it took an inordinate amount of systems/programming time and effort to make necessary alterations.
- Applications were directed towards the output of accounting/administrative documents, e.g. invoices, payslips, statements, etc., with little or no management information emanating from this work.
- Users were sceptical of computer systems, usually because they did not participate in the development of them.
- Users were apt to change their minds regarding the outputs wanted from computer systems, this was often because they had little idea of the computer's capabilities and systems staff had but little knowledge of business procedures and problems.
- Systems were often incomplete as they could not cope with exceptions, these were generally swept up by vestigial manual systems still operating in parallel.
- Documentation was often of a poor standard; as a result changes were difficult to implement and procedures were hard to operate. Even when the original documentation was acceptable, frequently it was not properly updated when changes were made.

In order to attempt to remedy these weaknesses, a wide range of organizations, especially consultancy firms, created a large number of methodologies. In this context a methodology means a philosophy incorporating sets of rules and recommendations covering procedures, structures, techniques, documentation, etc. From the hundreds of methodologies devised in the 1980s, two prominent ones, Information Engineering and SSADM, are described briefly in the ensuing pages. Other well-known methodologies are:

- JSD – Jackson Systems Development
- STRADIS – Structured Analysis and Design of Information Systems
- ETHICS – Effective Technical and Human Implementation of Computer-based Systems
- SSM – Soft Systems Methodology
- ISAC – Information Systems Work and Analysis of Changes
- Multiview

Information engineering

Information engineering (IE) is a methodology intended to support all aspects of a system's life cycle. Several versions have been developed although they are similar in content. IE is still evolving, especially as regards workbench and fourth-generation methodologies.

Essentially IE is a framework, as in Figure 7.24, supporting a variety of systems development techniques. These are not fundamental to IE and can therefore be replaced as new techniques emerge.

An underlying philosophy of IE is that data types rather than processes are the core of information systems. The reasoning behind this is that an organization's

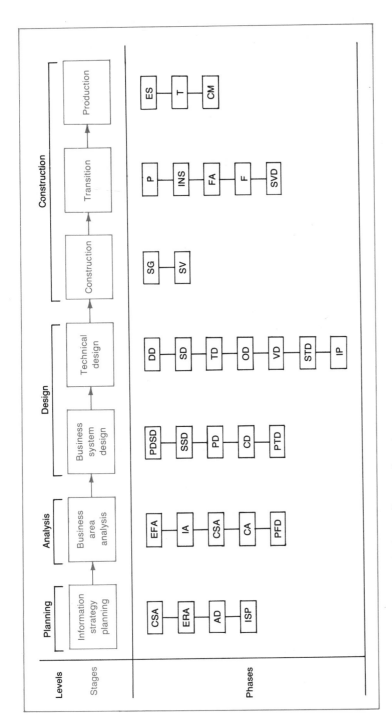

Figure 7.24 Framework of information engineering

data is more stable and permanent than its processes and so is a better base upon which to build an information system.

IE is diagram-orientated in the belief that diagrams convey understanding of the techniques more effectively. Each step aims towards producing fully definitive diagrams.

IE is a top-down approach to systems development with increasing detail as the steps are implemented. Progress is measured by the achievement of objectives at each phase.

As is seen from Figure 7.24, the framework consists of seven stages lying within four levels. Each stage is made up of between two and seven phases. The stages and phases are described briefly below.

Information strategy planning

This is an overview of the aims of the business, its main functions and information needs. The information strategy plan is documented in agreement between users and systems analysts.

Current situation analysis (CSA) An overview of the current postion including the efficacy of present procedures.

Executive requirements analysis (ERA) A survey of managers' aims, requirements, responsibilities and problems.

Architecture definition (AD) Identification of entity types, decomposition of functions, distribution analysis (geographical requirements), technical architecture (general technology direction), business systems architecture (ideal systems needed), information systems organization proposal.

Information strategy plan (ISP) Determination of business areas, business evaluation (plans for moving from present to desired situation), strategy plan (priorities and schedules).

Business area analysis

Business areas are treated individually in more detail and users involved.

Entity and function analysis (EFA) Analysis of entity types and relationships, analysis of processes.

Interaction analysis (IA) Data and functions relationships, entity life cycles, process logic, process actions.

Current systems analysis (CSA) Existing systems modelling, data flow modelling using canonical synthesis (see Glossary).

Confirmation (CA) Cross-checking the Current Systems Analysis for accuracy and completeness, examination of effect of changes.

Planning for design (PFD) Definition of design areas, evaluation of implementation steps, and planning design aims.

Business systems design

Facts gathered are used to create a logical design to meet the identified aims and requirements.

Preliminary data structure design (PDSD) An initial attempt at converting the entity model for the whole business to the structure of the proposed or existent DBMS.

System structure design (SSD) Definition of procedures and preparation of data flow diagrams.

Procedure design (PD) Examines the accesses required to entity types and control of user interaction, and charting of same.

Confirmation design (CD) Completeness by use of matrices, correctness according to IE rules and usability by prototyping are confirmed.

Planning for technical design (PTD) Definition of implementation areas and the preparation of technical design plans.

Technical design

The business systems identified previously are redesigned for computer operation so that the costs of construction and operation can be estimated.

Data design (DD) Preparation of data load matrices, refinement of database structure, design of data storage and files.

Software design (SD) Definition and design of programs, modules and test conditions.

Transition design (TD) Design of software and changeover procedures, planning of location implementation, definition of user training.

Operations design (OD) Design of security and contingency procedures, design of operating and performance monitoring, design of operations software.

Verification of design (VD) Benchmark testing and performance assessment.

System test design (STD) Definition of system tests and acceptance tests.

Implementation planning (IP) Review of costs and preparation of implementation plan.

Construction

System generation (SG) Construction of computing environment, construction of database/files, creation of modules and test data, integration tests, documentation.

System verification (SV) Creation of system test data and performance of system tests, creation of acceptance test data and performance of acceptance tests.

Transition

Preparation (P) Preparation of changeover schedules, training of users, installation of hardware.
Installation of new software (INS) Changeover and trial running.
Final acceptance (FA) Full changeover to new system.
Fanout (F) Installation of hardware at distant locations.
System variant development (SVD) Repetition of previous stages for locations requiring special facilities.

Production

This means the continuing operation of the system over its life, taking quality of service and amendments into account.

Evaluate system (ES) Measurement of benefits and costs, and comparison with design objectives.
Tune (T) Performance monitoring, software tuning, database reorganization.
Carry out maintenance (CM) Error correction and system modification as needed.

Structured systems analysis and design methodology (SSADM)

SSADM is an important methodology in the UK mainly owing to it being mandatory for systems development in the Civil Service. It was developed for this purpose partly by the government's Central Computer and Telecommunications Agency (CCTA).

SSADM is a data-driven methodology which gives systems developers a set of detailed rules and guidelines, these are contained in manuals published by the NCC and available for general use by other, non-government, organizations. (See References 7.10–7.13).

Systems maintenance is also covered; a set of procedures called 'Maintenance SSADM' is available for this purpose. Another variant, 'Micro SSADM', is available for small-scale applications.

SSADM is structured in three phases – feasibility study, systems analysis and systems design, as depicted in Figure 7.25. The first phase, the feasibility study, is optional to some extent. It is likely to be omitted for small projects or where the project forms part of a larger project that has already had a feasibility study carried out.

Each of the three phases is subdivided into a number of stages, which in turn are subdivided into a number of steps. The steps are made up of tasks. This hierarchical structure of SSADM results in a quite limited area of work at the

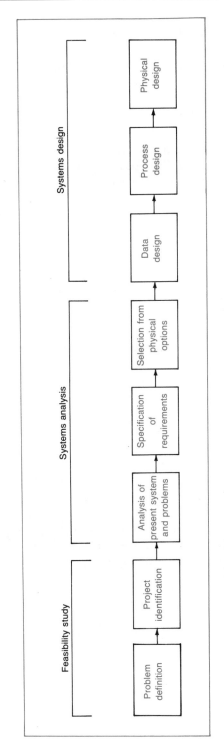

Figure 7.25 Framework of SSADM

lower levels, as can be imagined from the fact that there are about fifty steps and about 230 tasks in all.

There follows a brief description of each of the eight stages:

First stage — problem definition

The aim of this stage is to obtain a precise definition of the overall problem for resolution by the system to be developed. Overviews are created of the present systems and data structure, and current problems are identified.

Second stage — project identification

This stage aims to create a number of options for dealing with the problems identified in the first stage. The options are then evaluated and formalized for inclusion in the feasibility report.

Third stage — analysis of present system and problems

This stage entails analysing the existing system and documenting it in the form of data flow diagrams (DFDs) and logical data structures (LDSs).

Another goal is the creation of lists of the initial problems and of the requirements. This involves making a more refined identification of the problems found in the second stage.

Fourth stage — specification of requirements

In this stage the user requirements determined in the previous stage are defined more closely. A data structure is developed based on the LDSs created in the third stage. Audit, security and control aspects are defined and included to form the systems specification.

Fifth stage — selection from physical options

This stage involves the users and systems staff in selecting a suitable physical system. In most cases it is possible by this time to decide on the configuration of the hardware required and on the characteristics of the appropriate software. These requirements are related to the performance objectives, which are also defined in this stage.

Sixth stage — data design

Data structures for the proposed system are designed by combining the top-down view of the organization derived from the third stage with the bottom-up view of data groupings, i.e. composite logical data design.

Seventh stage — process design

This stage is carried out in conjunction with the data design stage, in particular it utilizes the composite logical data design. The logical processing associated with enquiries and updating is defined (all processes are seen as these). Following this the logical design is validated by means of a quality assurance review before proceeding with the physical design.

Eighth stage — physical design

The logical design is translated into programs and the database contents. The data dictionary is updated and the design tuned to meet performance objectives. Programs and system are tested. Operating instructions are created. Implementation plan is drawn up and the manual procedures are defined.

See References 7.10–7.13 for further information on SSADM.

7.12 Exercises

Exercise 7.1 Entity relationships

Develop an entity-relationship diagram containing the data processing entities — users, data items, programs, files and records. The diagram should reflect your knowledge and experience of the entities. Incorporate further entities into your diagram as appropriate.

Give a short description of a report that could be obtained from such a database. Define who could use each report and for what purpose.

(BCS part II, Option C1, April 1986)

Exercise 7.2 Screen dialogues

Describe the types of screen dialogue that might be suitable for:

(a) A senior manager consulting a system infrequently to obtain summarized information.

(b) A sales office entry clerk entering orders into an on-line order processing system.

(CACA level 2, Sys. an. & des., June 1988)

Exercise 7.3 Job costing

On the basis of the situation and activities described below prepare an output analysis chart along the lines of Fig. 7.5.

At the end of each week job progress forms are received from the factory. Each of these holds the following data:

- Job number, week number, material code and the corresponding quantity used for the job, employee number and the hours worked in the week.
- Each material has a standard cost up to £99.99, and is coded with picture AA999.
- The employees each have a normal rate and an overtime rate depending on their trade and grade.
- The current jobs are numbered from 1 to 999, and the weeks from 1 to 53.
- The quantity of a material used on a job in a week is not more than 800 units, and is measured to the nearest tenth.
- The employees are numbered from 1,000 upwards, the highest number being 4,500. The hours worked are recorded to the nearest quarter below. The normal and overtime rates are expressed in pence per hour, the maximum is 350 pence per hour.
- There are forty trades (picture AA) with up to six grades each (coded 1–6).

It is required to prepare a job cost summary each week. This is to show for each job (in job number sequence):

(a) the material cost this week and to date;
(b) the labour cost this week and to date;
(c) the total (material + labour) cost this week and to date.

No total exceeds £5,000 expressed to the nearest penny.

Exercise 7.4 Sales orders

Harvey Agricultural Ltd is a cattle-food merchant with a manual accounting system in which sales orders and invoicing are carried out as follows:

1. Orders are received by the sales order/invoicing department, mainly by telephone.
2. On receipt, an official order form is prepared and passed to the sales ledger clerk to be vetted for creditworthiness of the customer.

3. From there it is passed to the despatch department to prepare prenumbered despatch documents and assemble the goods for despatch.
4. The despatch department then prepares a delivery schedule for delivering the various orders by its own transport. After delivery, a copy of each delivery note, signed by the customer, is returned to the despatch department for matching with the original.
5. The despatch department accounts for all despatch note numbers and passes executed notes to the sales order/invoicing department for invoice typing.
6. The invoicing department despatches top copy invoices direct to the customers and the second copies go to the ledger clerk for entry in the sales journal and posting to the sales ledger.

Requirements

(a) Prepare an overview manual procedures flowchart showing, in outline, the activities of the various departments described above and the movement of documents.
(b) Compare and contrast the way the operations depicted in the flowchart are carried out manually with the way they would be carried out in a computerised order entry and invoicing system with remote terminals in each of the departments involved.
(c) Comment on the ways in which you consider that a computerised system would provide greater control over the transaction cycle.

(ICAEW PE1, Aud, sys. DP, Nov. 1988)

Exercise 7.5 Customer's orders

A company supplies frames to the building trade. The complete frames have five components, each of which is available separately. The frames are available in ten different heights and twelve different widths. Orders are received for separate components and complete frames, the latter orders only being met if all five components for that frame are in stock. If a given size frame is not available the customer is usually prepared to accept the frame having the next larger or smaller height or width. Prices vary according to height and width.

Describe, using appropriate diagrams, the following aspects of a computer program to determine how a customer's order may be satisfied:

(a) the method of allocating complete frames and components to customers' orders,
(b) the data structures used, and
(c) the invoicing.

How would you modify the data structures to include stock reorder levels and quantities?

(BCS part I, Gen. paper II, April 1986)

Exercise 7.6 Sales order entry

Your organization is a medium-sized wholesale company supplying a wide range of medical products to hospitals, health centres and pharmacies. Orders are taken by sales people on field visits, by postal requisition from customers and by requests over the telephone.

A medium-sized computer system with adequate on-line access is in use. Describe how you would see the organization and operation of the sales order entry system and its associated procedures. (Flowcharts and procedural diagrams may be used in your answer.)

(ICSA part 4, Man. sys., June 1987)

Exercise 7.7 Seat reservation system

A travel organization specializes in charter flights. The seats aboard their aircraft have the following attributes:

(i) row number
(ii) seat number
(iii) window, aisle or centre
(iv) non-smoking or smoking.

Customers are allowed to reserve seats by specifying:

either (a) the number of adjacent seats required and non-smoking or smoking
  or (b) a combination of attributes (iii) and (iv), e.g. window, non-smoking.

Reservations are processed on a 'first come, first served' basis.

(a) By means of an appropriate diagram, or otherwise, describe a computer program that will input a customer's choice, select the best fit to that choice and output boarding cards detailing the seat allocation.
(b) Describe in detail all data structures used.

(BCS part I, Gen. paper I, April 1987)

Exercise 7.8 Library system

Prepare a specification of the files, input, processing and output of a computer system which you consider would be suitable for use by a public library to control its stock of books and to provide lending records relating to them.

(ICAEW PE1, Aud. sys. DP, Nov. 1987)

Exercise 7.9 Loan accounting

A finance company uses a manual accounting system to handle its 1,000 loan agreements. It is planned to expand these to 5,000 agreements over the next two years. A decision has therefore been taken to install a computerized loan ledger to ensure controlled growth.

The loans, sometimes secured, are repayable by either twelve or twenty-four equal monthly instalments. One borrower may have several loan agreements. Because the capital element of each repayment increases with time, the respective elements of each repayment are scheduled on each loan ledger account at the outset. All loan repayment instalments are made by standing order direct to the loan company's bank account.

Requirements

(a) Describe the features and capabilities you would be looking for in selecting suitable software for the above system.
(b) State the data fields which you consider should go to make up a loan agreement record in the new computer loan ledger.

(ICAEW, PE1, Aud., sys. & DP, May 1988)

7.13 Outline solutions to exercises

Solution 7.1

Refer to Figure 7.26 and Table 7.3.

Table 7.3

Report	*Used by*	*Purpose*
List of files	User	Checking existence
File contents	User	Applications development
File contents	Programmer	Program writing
List of programs	Programmer	Control of software
Program statements	Programmer	Program updating
Data items in database	Database administrator	Control of database
List of computer users	DP manager	Computer job costing

Solution 7.2

(a) Menu dialogue using WIMPS: the menus should be short and the items therein highlighted on selection. Refer to 'Menus' in Section 7.5 for further details.
(b) Form-filling as described in Section 7.5.

Solution 7.3

Refer to Figure 7.27.

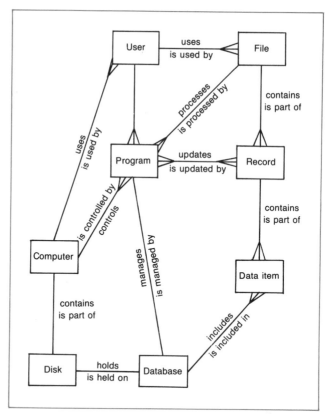

Figure 7.26 Entity relationship diagram for Exercise 7.1

Solution 7.4

(a) Refer to Figure 7.28.

(b) Orders entered directly into system via terminals and stored in file, official order forms are unnecessary since these are simulated on the screen.

The computer vets orders automatically as it can deduce customer's creditworthines from data in the stored sales ledger.

Computer prints dispatch documents for dispatch department, and stores a record of each set.

Delivery schedule prepared as at present.

Signed delivery notes are used for ticking-off the stored dispatch documents simply by entering their serial numbers.

Computer now has a record of executed deliveries and corresponding orders. From these the invoices are prepared automatically using (i) a file of cattle food prices and, (ii) a file of customers' names and addresses.

Details are posted to the sales ledger file concurrently with invoicing.

(c) Avoidance of errors in human transcription, typing and calculating.

No fear of documents being mislaid.

Control figures are determined more easily.

Ref. no.	Data item	Picture	J (Job progress form)	FI (Material file)	F2 (Employee file)	F3 (Trade/grade file)	F4 (Job costs file)	PI (Job costs summary)
1	Job No.	999	✓				✓	F4
2	week No.	99	✓					J
3	material code	AA999	✓	✓				
4	material qty.	999.9	✓					
5	Employee No.	9999	✓		✓			
6	Hours worked	99.99	✓					
7	Trade code	AA			✓	✓		
8	Grade no.	9			✓	✓		
9	Normal rate	999				✓		
10	Overtime rate	999				✓		
11	material std. cost	99.99		✓				
12	Material cost this week	9999.99						c 4.11
13	Labour cost this week	9999.99						c 6,9,10
14	Total cost this week	9999.99						c 12.13
15	Material cost to date	9999.99					c 12.15	c 12.15
16	Labour cost to date	9999.99					c 13.16	c 13.16
17	Total cost to date	9999.99						c 15.16

Figure 7.27 Output analysis chart of Exercise 7.3

Vetting of customer's credit worthiness is absolute, i.e. not prone to misunderstandings.

The higher speed of the sales orders cycle minimizes the chance of confusion, especially as caused by human frailties.

Solution 7.5

This question would involve a complex and lengthy solution if answered taking alternatives into account, a simplified solution therefore follows below.

(a) If order for component:

Enter component no., order no., order quantity, customer no.

If unallocated stock $\geq$ order quantity

subtract order quantity from unallocated stock, add order quantity to allocated stock, invoice quantity = order quantity.

If unallocated stock < order quantity

outstanding order quantity = order quantity − unallocated stock,

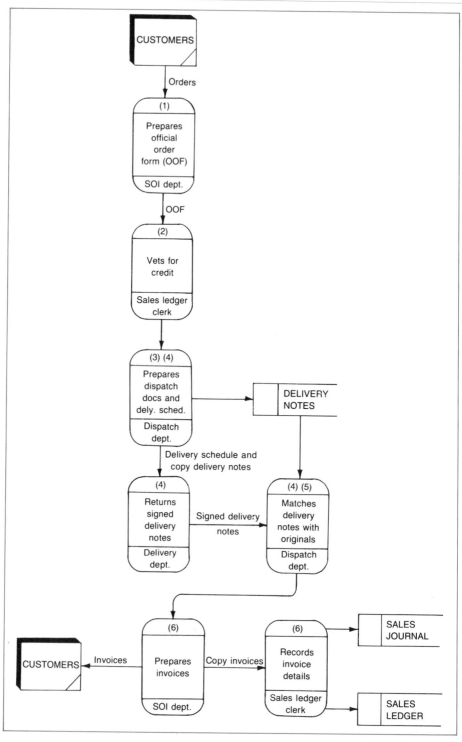

Figure 7.28 Sales orders procedures of Exercise 7.4

invoice quantity = unallocated stock, add invoice quantity to allocated stock, put outstanding order quantity into outstanding order record, make unallocated stock zero.

If order for frame:

Enter frame no., order no., order quantity, customer no.

Breakdown frame order into its five components, i.e. component requirement = frame order quantity × component quantity per unit frame.

Process each component as per component order.

(b) Component stock and price file (frame file similar)

Component no. and description

Allocated stock

Unallocated stock

Reorder level

Reorder quantity

Price per unit

Frame constituents file

Frame no.

Component no. ⎱ for each of five components

Quantity per frame ⎰

Invoicing file (outstanding orders file similar)

Customer no.

Order no.

Date of order

Frame/component no.

Invoice quantity

(c) Read invoice record

Look up customer name and address, print headings on invoice.

For each item:

Look up price and extend by invoice quantity = invoice item value

Print item line and add item value to invoice value.

After last item:

Print invoice value. Calculate discount, carriage, VAT and print along with net amount.

Solution 7.6

General points

Pharmaceutical/medical products are extensive in number and hence an early problem is identifying the customer's precise requirement. The products are obviously code-numbered but nevertheless measures must be taken to minimize errors. Possibilities are:

OMR order forms (negates on-line entry, however);

product lists on screen for selection by mouse and pointer, touch-screen or action codes;

validation checks such as echo checks, range checks and probability checks;

check digits

Procedure (see Figure 7.29)

Each order item validated against product master file.

Order quantity compared with unallocated stock (similarly to Solution 7.5) and

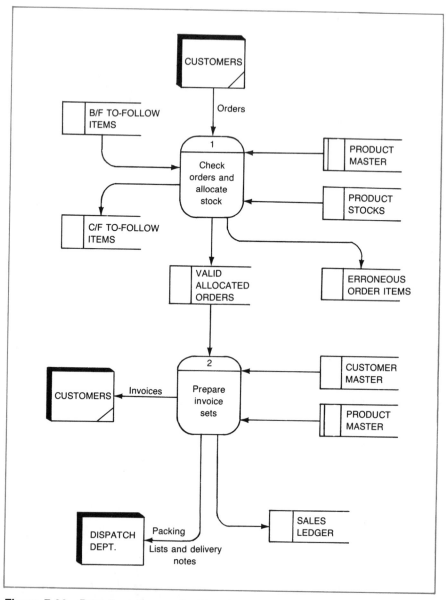

Figure 7.29 Data flow diagram for Exercise 7.6

recorded in invoice and to-follow files.

Shortages are held in to-follow file until next cycle when they receive priority (by which time more stock may have arrived).

Invoice set is prepared prior to dispatch as quantities are known to be available, i.e. packing list and delivery note.

During the invoicing run, the sales ledger is updated for subsequent use for statements and accounting.

Solution 7.7

1. Refer to Figures 7.30–7.33, these relate to the chosen flight. Figures 7.30 and 7.31 are conventional flowcharts for the two alternative types of reservations. Figure 7.31 is segregated into subroutines as indicated by the coloured boxes. Figure 7.32 depicts the interrelationships of the subroutines and lists the constituent modules. Figure 7.33 shows the processing within each of the modules.

2. Seat availability file:
   Flight number
   Row number
   Seat number (in row)
   Seat type (window, aisle or centre)
   Status (reserved, earmarked or unreserved)

   Row area file:
   Flight number
   Row number
   Area (smoking or non-smoking)

   Individual requirement:
   Seat type
   Area
   Flight number

   Block requirement:
   Flight number
   Area
   Number of seats

   Boarding cards:
   Flight number
   Date of flight
   Boarding time
   Airport
   Row number
   Seat number(s)

Solution 7.8

General points

The library would be computerized and have machine-readable, i.e. bar-coded, books and members' tickets (plastic cards). Each book would have a Book Identification Number (BIN), each publication, edition of a book, would have an International Standard Book Number (ISBN) and a Classification Code, i.e. subject of the contents.

The BIN of a book is printed in a label stuck inside the front cover in the form of a bar code. This gives complete identification of the individual copy itself not just of the edition of the book, since this is the purpose of the ISBN.

Each member of the library would have a ticket on which is printed his member number in bar-code form. These are used merely for borrowing books and are not handed over at this time but retained by the member. Control over the number of books in the hands of a member at a time could be by the computer checking at each take-out time but this would be unusual and so is not included here. Members can reserve a book for future borrowing.

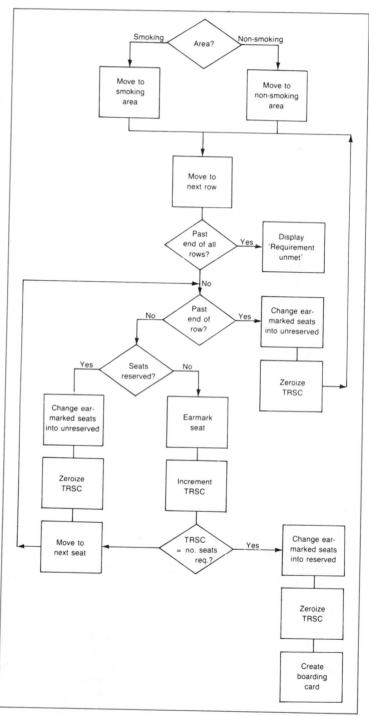

Figure 7.30 Process flowchart for Exercise 7.7

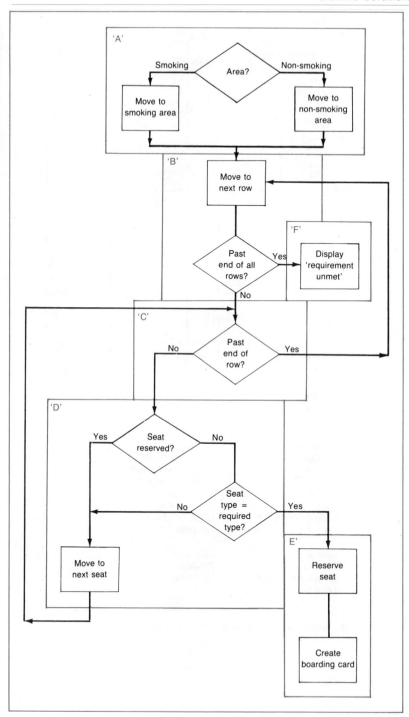

Figure 7.31 Process flowchart for Exercise 7.7 segregated into subroutines (Red letters are subroutine names.)

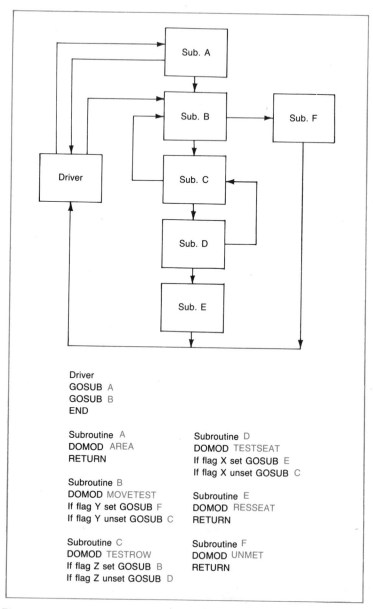

Figure 7.32 Structure of subroutines in Exercise 7.7

The four types of procedures considered here are acquisitions, loans, returns, disposals and reservations.

Logical files
Book master file (BMF):
    BIN
    ISBN

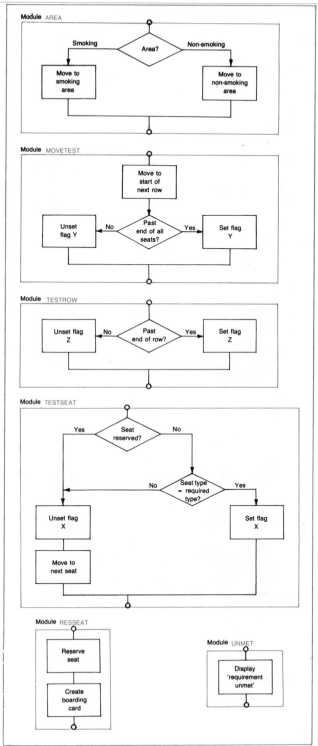

Figure 7.33 Modules in Exercise 7.7

Author name
Title
Classification code
Date of acquisition
Member master file (MMF):
Member number
Name and address
Date joined
Ticket number (for reference only)
Loans file (LF):
BIN
Member number
Date due for return
Reservations file (RF):
Member number
BIN
Date reserved
Loans analysis file (LAF):
BIN
Number of loans this year to date
Number of loans last year
Number of loans pre-last year
Inputs
Acquisition – all data items in BMF
Loan – member no., BIN, date due (automatic)
Return – BIN
Disposal – BIN
Reservation – member no., BIN, date reserved (automatic)
Processing
Acquisition – create new record in BMF
Loan – create record in LF, update LAF, delete record from RF if present
Return – delete record from LF, check whether in RF
Disposal – delete record from BMF
Reservaton – create record in RF
Outputs
Overdue loand list (for reminders)
Reservations available list (for notifications)
Stocktaking list (in classification code or any other order)
Loans analyses (according to ISBN/BIN, classification code/BIN)

Solution 7.9

(a) The software must be capable of the following:
  • accepting and checking loan repayments transmitted from the borrowers' banks via EFT;
  • updating the loan records in the loan ledger with repayments and new loan agreements;
  • providing control totals and audit figures;

- searching for a specific record, e.g. by using the loan account number, bank account number, borrower's name, etc.;
- searching for records of a certain type, e.g. overdue accounts, large loans, unsecured loans, etc.;
- producing reports showing various lists, tabulations and analyses based on the current loan situation;
- analysing the cash input flow over the next twenty-four months so as to assist with decisions regarding the future pattern of loans.

(b) The following data items would form the records in the loan ledger. It is probable that even if a DBMS is not used, there would be several files, e.g. a loan file, a repayments file, and a name and address file.

- Loan account number.
- Borrower's name and address.
- Secured/unsecured designation.
- Number of instalments.
- Date of agreement, i.e. state of loan.
- Borrower's bank account number.
- Initial capital element of loan.
- Initial interest element of loan.
- Current capital element outstanding.
- Current interest element outstanding.

Also for each repayment:

- Date of repayment.
- Amount repaid.
- Transaction number.

7.14 References and further reading

Systems design and methodologies

7.1 Hawryszkiewycz, I., *Introduction to Systems Analysis and Design* (Prentice Hall, 1988).

7.2 Page-Jones, M., *The Practical Guide to Structured Systems Design* (Prentice-Hall, 1988).

7.3 Aktas, Z., *Structured Analysis and Design of Information Systems* (Prentice Hall, 1987).

7.4 Cornes, R., *Business Systems Design and Development* (Prentice Hall, 1990).

7.5 Kendall, K.E. and Kendall, J.E., *Systems Analysis and Design* (Prentice Hall, 1987).

7.6 Avison, D.E. and Fitzgerald, G., *Information Systems Development* (Blackwell, 1988).

7.7 Gane, C. and Sarson, T., *Structured Systems Analysis* (Prentice Hall, 1979).

7.8 Yourdon, E., *Modern Structured Analysis* (Prentice Hall, 1989).

7.9 Yourdon, E., *Managing the Structured Techniques* (Prentice Hall, 1989).

7.10 Downs, E., Clare, P. and Coe, I., *Structured Systems Analysis and Design Methods* (Prentice Hall, 1987).

7.11 Anderson, N.E., *et al.*, *Professional Systems Development: Experience, Ideas and Action* (Prentice Hall, 1989).

7.12 Davis, W.S., *Systems Analysis and Design: A Structured Approach* (Addison Wesley, 1985).

7.13 Layzell, P.J. and Loucopoulos, P., *Systems Analysis and Development* (Chartwell-Bratt, 1986).

7.14 Longworth, G. and Nicholls, D., *SSADM Manual – Vol. 1* (NCC, 1987).

7.15 Longworth, G. and Nicholls, D., *SSADM Manual – Vol. 2* (NCC, 1987).

7.16 Martin, J. and McClure, J.L., *Action Diagrams: Clearly Structured Specifications, Programs and Procedures* (Prentice Hall, 1989).

7.17 Martin, J. and McClure, J.L., *Structured Techniques: A Basis for CASE* (Prentice Hall, 1988).

7.18 Sutcliffe, A., *Jackson System Development* (Prentice Hall, 1988).

7.19 Martin, J. and Leben, J., *Strategic Information Planning Methodologies* (Prentice Hall, 1989).

Database design

7.20 Remenyi, D. and Dalby, J., *dBASE II and III* (Pitman, 1986).

7.21 Barden, R.A., *DP Back-up Procedures* (NCC, 1986).

7.22 Hanson, O., *Design of Computer Data Files* (Pitman, 1988).

7.23 Howe, D.R., *Data Analysis for Database Design* (Arnold, 1983).

7.24 Hook, C., *Data Protection Implications for Systems Design* (NCC, 1989).

Security and audit

7.25 Chambers, A.D. and Court, J.M., *Computer Auditing* (Pitman, 1988).

7.26 Hoyt, D., *Computer Security Handbook* (Macmillan, 1988).

7.27 Cooper, A.J., *Computer and Communications Security* (Macmillan, 1988).

7.28 Baskerville, R., *Designing Information Systems Security* (John Wiley, 1988).

7.29 Schwitzer, J.A., *Computer Business and Security: The New Role for Security* (Butterworth, 1987).

7.30 Ellison, J.R. and Pritchard, J.A.T., *Security in Office Systems* (NCC, 1987).

7.31 Douglas, I.J. and Olson, P.J., *Audit and Control of Computer Networks* (NCC, 1986).

7.32 Doswell, D. and Simons, G.L. *Fraud and Abuse of IT Systems* (NCC, 1986).

7.33 Wood, M.B., *Guidelines for Physical Computer Security* (NCC, 1986).

7.34 Watne, D.A. and Turney, P.B., *Auditing EDP Systems* (Prentice Hall, 1987).

Systems documentation

7.35 Denton, L. and Atlas, M., *Designing, Writing and Producing Computer Documentation* (Macmillan, 1988).

7.36 *Student Notes on NCC DP Documentation Standards* (NCC, 1987).

7.37 Pakin and Assoc., *Documentation Development Methodology* (Prentice Hall, 1984).

7.38 Foehr, T. and Cross, T.B., *The Soft Side of Software: A Management Approach to Computer Documentation* (John Wiley, 1986).

7.39 Price, J., *How to Write a Computer Manual* (Addison Wesley, 1984).

Systems implementation

8.1 DP staff

As with other departments, DP departments' structures and staff complements vary from company to company. The size of this department has a general relationship to the size of the company but also reflects the complexity of the company's operations. Whereas a mail-order company with a huge turnover may have a quite small DP department owing to the relative simplicity of its operations, a manufacturing company may need a larger DP department because of its complex production control activities.

Most DP departments are organized on some sort of hierarchical basis but perhaps not in quite the rigidly structured fashion shown in Figure 8.1. In broad terms, a largish DP department is subdivided into systems, programming and operations. The dividing line between systems and programming is not so clear as between the latter pair, and, as mentioned in Section 6.1, the two functions are sometimes merged into one.

It is also possible that systems are seen as a function outside the orbit of the DP department, perhaps as a department in its own right or part of a management services function. Another possibility is where the systems analysts are on the staff of user departments, either on a temporary basis or permanently. This arrangement has the advantage of keeping the systems analysts close to actual user department activities.

It is likely that the programmers work as a closely knit group; this is useful in that they can assist one another especially in the early days of new software. The danger is that they become a closed society impervious to outside influence and then no longer see themselves as true servants of the company. Another problem that sometimes arises is the career structure of programmers. As more packaged software becomes available, there is a lessening demand for application programmers. This means that some programmers should be retrained into systems work for their continued careers. As explained in Section 6.1, this is not always a straightforward matter.

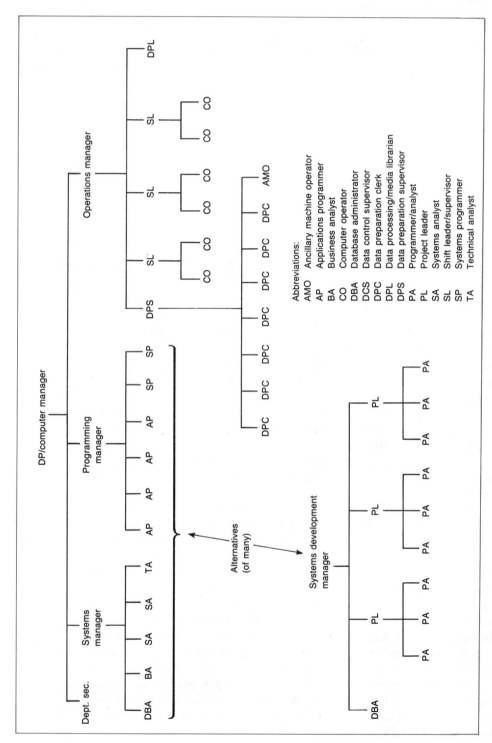

Figure 8.1 Data processing department organization

Operations covers two main aspects — mainframe operators and data preparation operators. The former also have limited career prospects with the levelling off of the numbers of mainframes. A similar problem arises as with programmers, i.e. how can they be retrained for other work? It does not necessarily follow that a high level of skill at mainframe operating makes a person suitable for retraining as a programmer or systems analyst.

The continuing fluidity of the DP scene has not yet allowed the careers of DP staff to settle into the formalized and qualification-based structure of other professions such as accountants. There follows below a brief description of the duties of the various kinds of DP staff.

Management services manager

An organization with a management services department is usually quite large, consequently the management services manager is a high-level position. Management services are normally taken to include DP in all its aspects, O&M, OR and special services such as investment, insurance and legal.

There are some management services departments that do not incorporate DP, and others that include systems but not programming and operations.

DP manager/computer manager

These titles are somewhat ambiguous. In one organization this person is in charge of systems work, programming and the day-to-day running of the computer. In another, he or she may merely be in charge of the operational aspects of DP. Administrative ability is needed for either arrangement.

Business/information analyst

This post entails working with the end-users of a DP system in order to define their information requirements. A good knowledge of business and manufacturing procedures is desirable as the business analyst is often the prime instigator of new systems.

Systems analyst/designer (technical analyst)

This person requires more technical knowledge than the business analyst, and is sometimes a specialist in areas such as real-time systems, data capture or data transmissions (see Section 6.1).

Applications programmer

This person writes computer programs for use in business (or scientific) applications, also tests, documents and maintains application programs. An increasing proportion of applications programmers' time is spent on familiarizing themselves and others with purchased applications software.

Programmer/analyst

Does both of the previous two jobs, as explained in Section 6.1.

Systems programmer

This job differs from the above in that a systems programmer designs and writes computer software programs such as operating systems. This person is normally employed only by larger user organizations, computer manufacturers or software houses.

Database administrator

This person controls the database, and as such is the sole adjudicator regarding modifications to the database's structure. He or she need not, however, be concerned with the actual contents of the database as this arises naturally from the activities of the user departments.

Computer operator

Operates the mainframe, this work mostly consisting of the loading and unloading of tape reels, disk cartridges, input media and output stationery; also simple maintenance, e.g. cleaning tape heads. Operators are also concerned with maintaining contact with online and batch users. This is necessary in order to deal with contingencies such as erroneous source data and late results due to operational problems such as hardware breakdown and overloading of terminal facilities.

Shift leader

The senior operator in charge of the computer operations for the shift (around eight hours).

Chief operator/operations manager

This is the most senior operator or administrator in charge of the above two groups of staff, and possibly the data entry clerks and ancillary machine operators also.

DP librarian/data controller

This is an administrative job in a larger DP department. The DP librarian logs work on and off the computer, and is in charge of the tape reels, disk cartridges, input media and documents before and after these have been through the computer room. This function may be split into the two posts of DP librarian and data controller in the larger DP departments.

Data entry/preparation clerk

This is a keystation operator who transcribes source data into computer-sensible form.

Ancillary machine operator

This person operates the stationery handling machines and may also be a computer operator or a data entry clerk at other times.

8.2 System testing

Before a DP routine is brought into operation it must obviously be tested thoroughly so that all errors are eliminated. There are two stages to this: (1) the testing of individual programs by their programmers, and (2) the testing of the overall routine or group of routines.

Program testing is the responsibility of the programmers, and is normally a straightforward procedure provided the systems analyst's specification is correct and has been adhered to.

With a structured program the modules are checked individually before being progressively combined to form the whole program. Groups of modules are often checked in combination if they follow a logical sequence of processing. The main aspect of testing structured programs is the coupling of interfacing modules.

As an added check that the program specification has been fully understood, the systems analyst also prepares a set of input data together with the corresponding output.

Program testing

The precise steps in program testing depend to some extent on the software support for the program, i.e. the level of sophistication of the DBMS, the compiler and the other associated software. The main aspects are, however, as follows:

- feasibility and validity checks on the input data;
- correct interpretation of symbols, e.g. debit/credit;
- branching and looping brought about by program decisions and modifications;
- confusion due to the occurrence of meaningless values, e.g. negative amounts of stock-in-hand;
- logical file addressing and searching, involving the DBMS if used;
- capacity of storage areas and buffers;
- contents of carried-forward records;
- contents and layout of printed and displayed output;
- batch control totals;
- interfacing with other programs, software, database and operating systems;
- documentation and handover after final testing.

Routine testing

The testing of routines entails the interfacing with users and the external situation in general.

The main aspects of testing a routine (system) are as follows:

- interfacing of runs within a routine;
- compilation and continuity of control totals;
- error-correction procedures including user involvement;
- user requests for amendments and output;
- timing of runs and routines for the data volumes to be actually handled;
- output preparation and distribution;
- audit requirements;
- logical and physical file housekeeping and control.

Test data

The usual procedure in testing is to create artificial data for the initial tests, and to use live data for later testing.

The main points are as follows:

- both the artificial and the live data should be representative of reality;
- the results from live data can sometimes be compared with the previous system's results, any discrepancies must be completely reconciled;
- logical files are usually needed to test fully the programs and routines;
- data generating techniques are useful for simulating large volumes of input data and file records;
- in the final trial run of the complete routine, a set of input data is passed through to the resultant output and/or file updating stage;
- test data should include known incorrect data in order to test the validation and control procedures.

8.3 Database creation

The designing and creation of a database is beyond the scope of this text. What we are concerned with here is the creation of the logical files needed for the complete system. These files almost certainly become part of a database but this does not affect the work involved in the initial stages.

The initial sources of the logical files are source documents, semi-automated data, e.g. embossed plates, and magnetic media if converting from another computer system. Possibly all of these are involved, and consequently, it is sometimes the case that the creation of the logical files is more difficult than the subsequent routines.

The data items needed to create logical records may have to be acquired from different departments or from data held in dispersed locations. An example of the former problem is a product master file in which the constituents of the products are derived from material specifications held in the production control department, whereas the current stock comes from the stock control department, and the manufacturing costs from the costing department. An example of data acquired from dispersed locations is the gathering together of stock levels from a large number of a company's retail branches in order to create a central stock file.

It is quite usual for various data sets to be amalgamated to form a logical file, such as described in Section 4.1 (merging). The important questions in this regard are:

- Do the data items from the different sources correspond one-to-one when being merged into one record? This is important as otherwise certain resultant records will be incomplete.
- Are the code numbers of the corresponding entities on different data sets exactly the same? If there are even marginal differences, this can cause great difficulty during file creation.
- Does any data conflict between data sets? For instance, individual costs might not add up to the total cost derived from another source.
- Is there any duplication of supposedly unique entity data records, or is the same code number used for two or more different entities?
- If data is to be transferred from another computer's database, have all the interface problems been found and dealt with?

Further points in file creation;

- During the period in which a file is being created, transactions and amendments applicable to the file need to be frozen. They are then applied to it before bringing the file into operation.

    It is a good idea to create files during non-working periods if possible, e.g. at night or during a weekend or holiday.
- Errors, omissions and conflict should be expected. Planned procedures for dealing with these contingencies must therefore be made beforehand.
- Complete or partial proof listing of file data derived from manual procedures is generally necessary to ensure accuracy and completeness.
- Control totals are necessary if any manual procedures are involved in the creation processes (Section 7.5).

8.4 Changeover procedures

It is likely nowadays that changing over to a new system entails either (1) moving from one computer system to another, or (2) transferring from a manual system to a computer already in operation on other work.

The former case has the advantage that a substantial part of the system is already planned and only the amendments/additions are truly new. And even though changes have been made, it is usually possible to make a quantified comparison of the two sets of results.

The situation in case (2) is fundamentally the same as when introducing a computer for the first time, except that the DP staff are familiar with the existing hardware and operational software. This is obviously safer than when changing over to a completely new computer.

When the new system has been thoroughly tested, the files or database created, and the hardware installed, it is possible to change over from the old to the new system. The method adopted for changing over depends on the particular applications and the company's *modus operandi*. There is no universal best method, only that which most suits the particular situation and circumstances at the time of the changeover.

Preparations for changeover are made over a period of time and include the activities described in the previous pages.

Fundamentally, there are four changeover methods, as shown in Figure 8.2 and described below.

Direct changeover

With direct changeover, the old system ceases abruptly and is replaced immediately by the new system. The changeover is best done at a weekend or

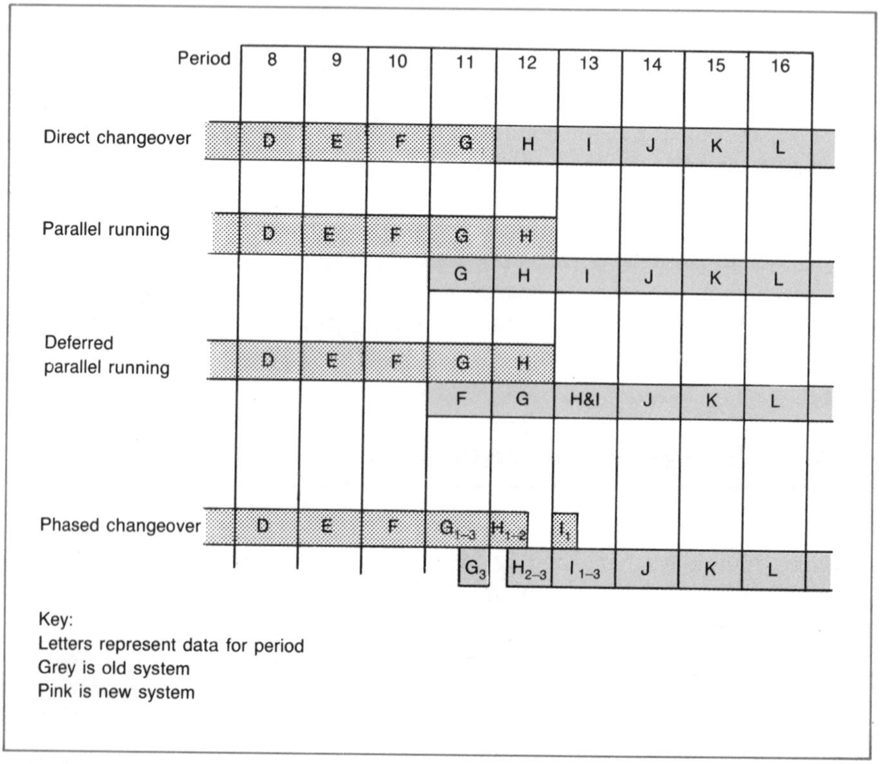

Period	8	9	10	11	12	13	14	15	16
Direct changeover	D	E	F	G	H	I	J	K	L
Parallel running	D	E	F	G	H				
				G	H	I	J	K	L
Deferred parallel running	D	E	F	G	H				
				F	G	H&I	J	K	L
Phased changeover	D	E	F	G_{1-3}	H_{1-2}	I_1			
					G_3	H_{2-3}	I_{1-3}	J	K	L

Key:
Letters represent data for period
Grey is old system
Pink is new system

Figure 8.2 Changeover procedures

during a holiday period so that it is fitted into a natural break in the stream of work. The main hazard with direct changeover is the possibility that the new system is not entirely correct or complete. This problem is aggravated by the absence of results from the old system to compare with those from the new system once changeover has occurred.

Also if the new results are incorrect, it is difficult to make corrections to the system and, at the same time, keep it operational.

Certain applications do not lend themselves to any viable method except direct changeover. This is true of on-line and real-time systems because these cannot normally have the old system running simultaneously with the new system.

Direct changeover is an efficient method in so far as it minimizes the duplication of work but demands careful planning, testing and attention to operational detail if it is to be completely successful.

Parallel running

With this method the old and new systems are run concurrently for a few periods. This means that the two sets of results can be compared for similarity immediately if this is intended to be the case. If it turns out that there are discrepancies not easily reconciled, the old system continues until things are put right.

If the changeover is from one type of computer to another, as is likely to be the situation nowadays, parallel running should present few problems. The input data is held on a compatible medium, e.g. magnetic tape, and fed into both systems almost concurrently. This assumes that the old computer can remain *in situ* for the period of parallel running.

When the results are not intended to be exactly alike, it is nevertheless usually possible to check the new results against the old by making reconciliations manually.

The major drawback of parallel running is the duplication of effort imposed upon the user department staff as it is likely that the same persons have to run both the old system and the new system during the periods of parallel running. This problem is much less severe with computer-to-computer changeover.

A variant of parallel running (deferred parallel running) involves rerunning the data from the previous period whilst the old system continues with the current data. Also known as pilot running, this method has the advantage of allowing more time for arranging the source data and checking the results. When the new system is proved to be fully correct, a double cycle of the work, i.e. two periods worth, is done in order to catch up, and the old system ceases.

The disadvantage of deferred parallel running is the necessity to carry out the double cycle of work.

Phased changeover

Phased changeover is similar to parallel running except that at the start only a portion of the data is run in parallel, e.g. only certain customer accounts from a sales accounting system. The portion taken into the new system increases each period and, after the final portion has been run in parallel, the old system is abandoned.

This method has the weakness of delaying the full implementation of the new system if several periods are taken.

A situation for which phased changeover is often suitable is where a number of branches of the company are undergoing changeover. Starting with one or just a few branches, an increasing number are changed over each successive period.

Prototype changeover

Referring to Section 6.9, it is apparent that three of the categories of prototyping – pilot, staged and evolutionary – entail parallel running and/or phased changeover. Pilot prototyping, for instance, has strong similarities to phased changeover. Staged prototyping might necessitate parallel running if the new system is an enhancement of the old system.

Changeover planning

It is evident from the foregoing explanations that a considerable number of activities is involved in the changeover procedure. In a large system these may run into hundreds, and so the systems analyst needs a logical method for scheduling and controlling the project so that the precise progress achieved at any time is clearly known.

The two main methods for project control are bar charts and network analysis. These techniques are applicable to any project involving numerous activities, e.g. systems analysis, as well as to changeover planning.

Bar charts

Otherwise known as a Gantt chart, a bar chart consists of a list of activities on a chart marked off in time periods. Each activity is entered initially as a horizontal line denoting its duration and scheduled periods. As and when progress is made, these lines (bars) are annotated to show the achievement to date.

The major weakness of bar charts is that they fail to demonstrate the dependence of one activity upon another, nor do they facilitate the planning of resources and costs. Nevertheless they are convenient for small projects and can be managed entirely by hand. An improvement is the GASP chart, which allows activity dependencies to be shown.

Network analysis

Also known as 'critical path method', this technique can cope with a large number of activities, especially if a computer package is used. It is a powerful management tool, and in its more advanced form (known as PERT) incorporates resource allocation and cost planning.

In utilizing network analysis for changeover planning, a list is drawn up incorporating all the activities in the changeover procedure together with their estimated times, resources needed and the activities that immediately precede them.

From this information a network diagram is constructed based upon the logical relationships of the activities. By utilizing the network diagram it is straightforward to compute the span of dates during which each activity must be performed if the changeover is to be completed in the minimum time. We can also find the 'critical' activities, i.e. those with no spare time, these determine the overall time of the changeover.

It is also possible to obtain a picture of the amounts of resources (programmers, systems analysts, etc.) needed during each period of the changeover, and thereby to allocate the staff accordingly. The resource requirements can be converted into costs so as to give a pattern of accumulating costs throughout the changeover.

Network analysis also caters for progressing the changeover so that when activities are completed, partially completed, amended, inserted or deleted, the remaining activities can be quickly rescheduled. Regular updating of the changeover in this way provides a means of continuous monitoring so that the completion date and the resource requirements are predicted well beforehand.

Readers requiring more information on network analysis are directed to References 8.5 and 8.6.

8.5 System presentation

Part of a systems analyst's work is to present and explain a proposed or actual new system. This may need to be repeated several times through the life cycle of system development. In the early stages of the system development the proposals are tentative and somewhat intangible, and so engender many questions from management and user staff. Even when there is already a computer-based DP system in operation, proposals regarding a new system cause some degree of apprehension, if not suspicion.

The systems analyst needs to propose his ideas and system enthusiastically, confidently and clearly. In answering questions and dealing with objections, he must not talk down to nor allow a confrontation to build up with his questioners. Neither should he allow himself to be drawn into situations that are really management's responsibility, e.g. redundancy policy.

One of the main points is that the systems analyst makes it clear that he fully understands the problem and that his proposals are intended to help the user rather than for the sake of change or using new technology. The prospective users should be left with the feeling that they are fortunate to be able to work with the new system. It seems to be a fact of life that whereas engineers, technicians and scientists are pleased to use new equipment and methods, business staff are in general not so. The more they can be persuaded that they are also entrepreneurs, the better.

The type of audience must be taken into account in the presentation. Top managers usually have little technical knowledge but are interested in information for decision-making. It is advisable to keep presentations to management quite short but polished and with effectual visual aids. Prospective users of the system are interested in the aspects relating to their work. The presentation to users is therefore more technical and may include some operational details.

Communication with users

Steering committee
This body (Section 1.5), formed in the stages, acts as the focus for maintaining communication between the systems analysts, the user departments and, later, the DP department. It is a convenient link for organizing the activities described below.

Discussion meetings
Formal and informal meetings between the systems analysts and the user staff, including trade union representatives, are a good means of maintaining communication.

The formal meetings should have a prepublished agenda so that all the participants are well acquainted with the discussion points. The informal meetings are a good opportunity for the user staff to ask questions and make suggestions. They also tie in with prototyping in that prototypes are intended as a basis for discussion. By the time the final prototype has been agreed, it is inevitable that users are well acquainted with the proposed system.

The use of project teams also facilitates communication as the project team members are in close touch with the staff of their own departments.

Training courses
Courses for user staff may be held either internally, at a training school or at a local college. They fall into two categories — general informative and specific training. The former can be attended by a wide range of user staff, perhaps on a voluntary basis in some cases. The specific training courses are aimed mainly towards staff who will be performing certain operational tasks such as using terminals, entering marks on documents (OMR) and filling in source documents.

Magazine articles
Articles in the staff magazine are best if of a general informative nature rather than technical. They are made more interesting by the inclusion of photographs of the proposed hardware.

Visits

In the early stages certain staff are taken on visits to other companies using similar methods to those proposed.

Later this can be extended to allow user groups to visit the company's own computer department at prearranged times. Although these visits may not convey much information, they often arouse interest and make visitors aware that people as well as machines are involved in DP.

Methods of presentation

Before giving a formal lecture, or even an informal talk, it is important to prepare the material so that it is presented clearly and logically. Very few people are capable of giving off-the-cuff talks of a good standard.

The lecturer may make use of the following audio and visual aids.

Microphone

It is normally not necessary to use amplification equipment, unless the audience is large (several hundreds) or the speaker's voice is weak. Nevertheless it is important that everyone can hear the speaker, and so he should project his voice and speak clearly. If amplification equipment is utilized, it requires installing professionally otherwise it may do more harm than good.

Tape recordings

Although these enable a word-perfect talk to be presented, they are lifeless and cannot answer questions. They are sometimes used in conjunction with slides in the form of proprietary presentations, as mentioned below.

Slides

Slides are available on loan or hire from computer manufacturers. They are useful for showing pictures of hardware and diagrams depicting systems generally. For particular purposes slides involve a lot of preparatory work and are not usually worth the trouble of making unless they are used repeatedly.

Overhead projectors

These are effective for showing fairly complex diagrams through the use of pre-prepared transparencies. The transparencies may be laid over one another to emphasize comparisons or a build-up of ideas. Another approach is to use a continuous transparency that is 'scrolled' across the projector.

An advantage of overhead projectors is that they can be used in normal lighting, although bright sunlight is best avoided. A skilled user can write or draw on the transparency as he talks, but beware of attempting this without practice.

Microcomputers

The presentation of information by means of a microcomputer's visual display is effective provided the information is clear and understandable to the audience.

The display must be capable of being seen by everyone present and so either a large screen display or multiple linked microcomputers are used.

The demonstration should relate to the audience's responsibilities and is improved by encouraging hands-on interaction by certain members of the audience. These are best chosen beforehand as complete novices can make an awful mess of things.

On the whole, graphical displays are more effective than sets of figures to a general audience.

Graphical techniques are briefly described below.

Films

Films are good for presenting a general background and they are usually professionally produced. They are available on hire from film libraries such as the National Film Library.

Films are likely to be too mundane to be of interest to organizations that have employed computers previously.

Flip charts

Good if well prepared, portable and flexible in use. Need some practice if the material is to be created (using a felt pen) at the time.

Blackboard and chalk

A flexible method but needs care and is dusty. Portable blackboards are not usually large enough.

Whiteboard

A whiteboard is best used in conjunction with a dry marker as this is most easily erased.

Diagrammatic techniques

A number of techniques make a good impact upon readers or on an audience, i.e.

- *Histograms* – blocks representing amounts.
- *Line charts* – vertical or horizontal lines representing quantities.
- *Bar charts* – similar to line charts, but often used to represent time periods on a graph.
- *Graphs* – different scales and intercepts are used to emphasize the details but a graph should not be misleading.
- *Pie charts* – circles divided into sectors to illustrate proportions of the whole.
- *Pictograms (ideographs)* – different sizes or numbers of pictures of objects represent a quantity.

The above presentations can be displayed in colour on a screen by software such as spreadsheets (Section 5.4). This method gives life to the presentation and relates to the use of a microcomputer as described above.

Report writing

A report is a written and, possibly, a diagrammatic presentation of a policy, situation or plan. The following points are worth noting:

- A report is not, *per se*, the end aim of the report writer. The report merely serves as an aid in achieving an objective.
- The person requesting a report should give an indication of its intended purpose. This helps the report writer in presenting the facts and suggestions in the most suitable manner.
- Follow a logical approach, e.g. introduction, sectionalized main body, conclusions, summary and appendices. An index is useful if the report is extensive.
- The writer should present the facts and suggestions in an unbiased way, and must not omit any relevant information.
- Present quantitative data rather than qualitative explanations but beware of swamping the reader with masses of figures. Summarized figures in the main text with detailed figures in the appendices are beneficial.
- Keep to correct but not stilted grammar, avoid verbosity, jargon, and tautologies. Refer to a dictionary if you are at all uncertain of a word's precise meaning, and a thesaurus for word ideas.

8.6 System appraisal and maintenance

The implementation of a DP system, even though it is fully correct and complete, is not the end of the matter. Systems are ongoing so need to be reappraised continually and regularly maintained in order to keep them efficient and up to date.

Shortly after the changeover to the new system, appraisal is required to ensure that actual performance is close to that predicted during the design stage. There is always the possibility that certain operational factors were overlooked during the design stage. Similarly, circumstances could have changed between the dates of the systems investigation and its implementation, since this might be a year or two.

The particular factors entering into the immediate appraisal of a system are the following:

- *Throughput speed* from the capture of source data to the delivery of output.

How does this actually compare with the estimated times for various data volumes?

- *Storage space* occupied by the logical files. Has this turned out to be greater than allowed for and if so, what are the reasons and consequences?
- *Errors, exceptions and queries* arising in the system. These can be expected to be higher at first than later, but are they disproportionately high for the amount of data? If so, why is this?
- *Date capture, preparation and ancillary operations.* Are the costs of these in line with estimates? Alternatively, are the throughput times as low as estimated?
- *Response time.* Is this as short as was envisaged for each type of input message and for a given traffic level? Has the peak level of traffic caused the response time to increase above an acceptable level?

The subsequent reappraisal and system maintenance also includes the following factors:

- *Cost/benefit.* Is this still at an acceptable level in general terms? That is to say, are the end-users satisfied with the information they received or has it become irrelevant, confusing or no longer in the most suitable form?
- *Source data.* Has the pattern and/or amount changed to the extent that it is worthwhile to reconsider the methodology?
- *Technology.* Have hardware developments made the existing computer and associated equipment obsolete to the extent of seriously affecting the efficiency of the system as compared with that possible with more modern hardware?
- *Legislation.* What are the effects of impending legislation such as in regard to tax, social security, privacy, databanks and information disclosure?
- *Patching.* Has the existing software, especially application programs, been patched, i.e. amended, to the extent of jeopardizing its efficiency?

8.7 DP resources

DP bureaux (computer service bureaux)

Certain DP work is carried out by computer service bureaux, most of which accept jobs of a general nature. A few bureaux specialize in their services, e.g. data preparation, COM services and specialized applications.

There are three basic types of service bureaux, as below.

Batch processing (batchwork)

The bureau collects or receives the client's source data, either in documentary or computer-compatible form, runs the jobs, and returns the output and source data to the client. Master files are usually retained by the bureau for use during the next run of the client's work.

Batchwork is relatively inexpensive but is a slow procedure owing mainly to the time taken for collection and delivery. This time lag is of no consequence with some applications, the main considerations being economy, reliability and the user company's non-operational involvement. The bureau often operates in conjunction with a security and/or delivery company. This arrangement could, for example, involve the processing of payroll data by the bureau followed by the security firm collecting the cash from the bank, making up the cash envelopes, and delivering these to the factory for distribution to the workforce.

Remote job entry (RJE)

With RJE the client has a terminal in his premises linked to the bureau's computer, generally via public telephone lines. When a job is ready for processing he dials the computer, inputs the job information followed by the data, and then starts the program. The results are either transmitted to the client's terminal or sent by other means in the form of printed documents. As most business jobs involve a large amount of input and output, the client needs powerful terminal equipment if the results are transmitted.

Time-sharing

This is similar to RJE in that the client uses a terminal and shares the computer with other users. It is most suitable for jobs with little input/output but considerable computation or file enquiry needs. It is particularly advantageous for dedicated applications, such as stockbroking, financial analysis and technical problems. Dialogues (Section 7.5) are often employed, and the programs are held on-line by the computer.

Bureau selection

In choosing and using a DP bureau, the following factors need to be taken into account:

- Is the bureau staff familiar with the type of work that the client wants done? This includes the data preparation and output handling in most cases.
- Precisely who does what? Where does the client's responsibility end and the bureau's start? The bureau's service may, on the one hand, be a 'facilities management' operation, i.e. a completed DP service; on the other hand, the bureau merely processes the prepared data as received and returns the output to the client uninspected.
- Can the turnaround or response time be maintained at peak load periods? This depends largely on the bureau's reserve of computing power.
- What are the bureau's stand-by arrangements in case of an extended period of hardware failure?
- Who owns the programs and are they portable? These points are relevant if the client is likely to install his own computer at a later date.
- What are the contractual terms of the service, including the quotation or estimate of charges for the work?

Software houses

A software house is a company supplying products such as applications and systems software, the former either as packages or in bespoke form. To a lesser extent services such as programming and systems analysis are provided, especially in an advisory capacity. There are many variations in the services offered, and many software houses specialize in certain areas of work and applications. By so doing they are able to build up a depth of experience beyond that of the ordinary computer user.

Large organizations may be able to afford the services of a software house without concern, but a small company needs to be particularly clear as to what it will be charged and precisely what it is getting.

Consultancy firms

A business consultant usually works at quite a high level, giving advice to top management and broad systems. Some companies of professional accountants also provide consultancy service or will recommend suitable consultants. The main point is to ensure that the consultancy firm has practical experience of solving problems similar to those of its client. This is more evident if the consultancy firm is a subsidiary of a company that has actually implemented the system being purveyed.

As with bureaux and software houses, the terms of contract should be agreed at the outset.

Finance houses

These are merchant banks or finance companies, and provide the capital to assist prospective computer users in financing the hardware. Few companies are able to purchase a computer from their own funds, and others do not wish to do so.

There are four main methods of acquiring a computer:

- *Outright purchase* by means of a loan from a finance house.
- *Renting* from the computer manufacturer.
- *Leasing* from a finance house after this has purchased the client's choice of computer from the manufacturer. At the end of the leasing period, the lessee chooses either to renew the lease, probably on different terms; to enter into a fresh contract for new equipment; or to end the agreement.
- *Industrial hire purchase* by which the user hires the computer for an agreed period, after which it becomes his property.

The relative advantages of the above methods depend partly upon the taxation legislation in force at the time in the country of contract.

Training establishments

Training establishments operate under a variety of titles but are essentially in business to provide concentrated training in DP subjects. The courses last from one or two days to up to a few weeks, and are orientated towards topics such as systems skills, user staff appreciation, management appreciation, programming, computer operating, real-time applications and database understanding.

Computer manufacturers also run courses; these tend to be either appreciation or programming courses, and have a natural bias towards their own hardware.

Computer manufacturers

The services offered by the manufacturers are:

Equipment maintenance

Scheduled (regular) and unscheduled (repair) maintenance is usually carried out by the manufacturers' engineers. The important issues from the customer's point of view are: (1) the availability and skill of the maintenance engineers; (2) the availability of spare parts; and (3) the standby arrangements that can be made with local users of similar hardware in case of an extended period of breakdown.

Third-party maintenance is becoming popular with large-scale computer users. This means that only the one maintenance firm is responsible for perhaps several different makes of computers and associated equipment.

Training

As mentioned above, various courses are run by the manufacturers and may be charged for in relation to the hardware purchased.

Software

The software produced by the manufacturers is charged for separately from their hardware, i.e. unbundled. This puts the manufacturers in direct competition with software houses.

8.8 Data Protection Act, 1984

There follows below an outline of the main aspects of the 1984 Data Protection Act as applicable to the United Kingdom. This synopsis is not a definitive guide to the Act but is merely a broad description of its requirements.

● A user must register with the Data Protection Registrar if data is held concerning individual identifiable persons and the data is to be automatically processed, e.g. if held on computer database files.

- Exceptions to this are (1) data regarding employees that is solely for the purpose of processing wages or pensions, (2) data for accounting purposes, e.g. purchase ledger.
- The user must comply with the principles of the Act, and with requirements made by the Registrar arising from suspected breaches of the principles.
- Personal data can be used for only the purposes stated on registration, and should not exceed what is required for these purposes.
- Personal data must be protected against unauthorized disclosure and alterations.
- Persons have a right of access to data concerning them, and to have corrections made where necessary.

It is apparent from the above that many computer-based records come within the Act. These would include any files that contained data not strictly within the exceptions. Thus a payroll file that also included personal data not needed for the payroll itself would have to be registered. All personnel files must be registered as they inevitably hold private information. So must files about customers and suppliers if they contain historical data no longer really necessary for current accounting.

8.9 Exercises

Exercise 8.1 DP department organization

Draw up an organization chart for the operations function in a large centralized data processing department. Describe the principal responsibilities of each job holder.

(BCS part I, Option C, April 1986)

Exercise 8.2 DP staff

Explain the work and responsibilities of the following:

(a) analysts:
(b) programmers; and
(c) operators.

(ICSA part 2, Inf. sys., June 1987)

Exercise 8.3 System testing

A sales ledger system is under development, and is intended to include batch data entry and on-line enquiry facilities. The design specification has been accepted and implementation is under way. To date, all program specifications, user documentation, screen and forms design have been completed, and the appropriate hardware installed. However, before changeover begins it is the system analyst's responsibility to test the component parts of the system, both individually and collectively.

List the various tests on inputs, outputs, files, clerical and computer procedures which would be carried out prior to changeover.

(CACA level 2, Sys. an. & des., June 1988)

Exercise 8.4 Systems documentation

The documentation of a computer-based system should contain all the information relevant to the application.

Describe the nature of the information pertinent to:

(i) the systems analyst;
(ii) the programmer;
(iii) the user.

Discuss the importance of maintaining the documentation.

(BCS part I, Gen. paper II, April 1987)

Exercise 8.5 File conversion

Examine the procedures and controls which should form part of the file conversion aspects of systems implementation.

(ICSA part 4, Man. sys., Dec. 1988)

Exercise 8.6 Systems documentation

'However efficient the processing and well satisfied the users, a system cannot be considered adequate unless it is documented to a very high standard.'

(a) Why is so much emphasis placed on the quality of system documentation?
(b) For each of the following, state the purpose and briefly describe four issues which should be included in the specification or manual.
    (i) Program specification
    (ii) Computer operations manual
    (iii) User manual
    (iv) System changes manual

(CACA level 2, Sys. an. & des., Dec. 1987)

Exercise 8.7 Data Protection Act

The Data Protection Act 1984 has had an effect on almost every organization and individual using computers, indeed the CIMA has published a 'Practical Guide' to the Act. Many accountants have become alarmed at the publicity received by the Act and the implications of installing a new computer. You have been requested to give advice on a number of points relating to the interpretation of the Act.

You are required:

1. to state *three* major requirements of the Act;
2. to state *four* data protection principles contained in the Act relating to the processing of personal data;
3. with reference to an organization with which you are familiar, to
   (a) state *two* exemptions which might apply.
   (b) describe *four* files and systems which might need to be registered.

(CIMA, stage 2, Inf. tech. man., May 1988)

8.10 Outline solutions to exercises

Solution 8.1

Refer to Figure 8.1 and Section 8.1.

Solution 8.2

(a) Refer to Chapters 6–8.
(b) Refer to Chapter 5 and Section 8.1.
(c) Refer to Section 8.1.

Solution 8.3

Refer to Section 8.2. This section may be enhanced by mention of the following:
checks on customer details, e.g. names and addresses;
checks and controls on opening balances in sales ledger;
checks on batching and control-totalling of input, especially customers' payments;
checks on the accuracy and completeness of sales statements.

Solution 8.4

Refer to Section 7.10.
  (i) Documents associated with the investigation and design of the system, these include the various charts and diagrams described in Chapters 6 and 7.
 (ii) Information passed from the systems analyst initially, such as the program specifications (Section 7.6), these need considerable augmentation by the programmer's own documentation. The main purpose of this is to enable himself and other programmers, existing and future, to follow through the steps in the program when making changes.

(iii) Instructions to users are listed in Section 7.10. These could well be amplified by further information emanating from the users' experience of the system.

Solution 8.5

Refer to Section 8.3.

Solution 8.6

Refer to Section 7.10.
(a) To facilitate making changes to the system at a later date.
To allow the users to operate the system with the minimum of trouble, particularly in its early stages.
To enable any errors (bugs) detected subsequently to be rectified quickly.
To facilitate auditing of the system and auditing in general.
(b) (i) Input specification, file contents, processing specification, output contents and layouts − as per Section 7.6.
   (ii) Security arrangements − checkpoints, spooling, backup files, physical security, passwords.
   Control section − release of disks and tapes, handover of output, receipt of input media.
   Operations − disk and tape loading, operating system messages, error messages, printer stationery and set up.
   Job scheduling − times of start and completion of computer jobs.
   (iii) Refer to 'Instructions to users' in Section 7.10.
   (iv) Details of changes, authorization for changes, target dates for completion, test data and test results covering changes to system.

Solution 8.7

Refer to Section 8.8.

8.11   References and further reading

8.1 Harris, S., *People and Communication* (NCC, 1987).
8.2 Singer, L.M., *Written Communications for MIS/DP Professionals* (Macmillan, 1986).
8.3 Abbott, J., *Unit and Integration Testing Manual* (NCC, 1988).
8.4 Perry, W.E., *A Structured Approach to Systems Testing* (Prentice Hall, 1984).
8.5 Battersby, A., *Network Analysis for Planning and Scheduling* (Macmillan, 1970).
8.6 Wall, A.J., *Project Planning and Control Using Micros* (NCC, 1988).
8.7 Brodie, A., *Computer Buyer's Handbook* (NCC, 1988).
8.8 Edwards, C. and Savage, N., *Information Technology and the Law* (Macmillan, 1986).

9 Case study – stock control and sales analysis

This case study expounds the application of a microcomputer to a hypothetical business. It is based upon an actual situation but simplified somewhat in order to keep within the bounds of comprehension for study purposes. The aims of the case study are to demonstrate the activities arising in a practical business and to relate these to the methodologies described in the previous chapters.

Figure 9.1 lists the abbreviations used throughout the case study.

9.1 Background to Regis Jewellers Limited

Regis Jewellers Limited (RJL) is a retail company selling a wide range of middle-price jewellery and associated articles. It has ten outlets (branches) located within a limited geographical area and these are replenished from a central warehouse. The articles sold are purchased centrally from a number of manufacturers and importers, sometimes in bulk quantities.

Since jewellery is essentially a fashion trade, there is no deliberate policy to maintain continuing availablility of any particular article. A certain type of wristwatch, for instance, may be stocked and thus available for sale at one point of time but not necessarily available at a later date. In this respect RJL's stock control differs from many others because it does not involve the automatic reordering of particular articles.

RJL's stock is for the most part held in its branches and, in fact, many articles are permanently displayed in the windows. Thus the warehouse stock is kept to a minimum, especially as regards the expensive articles such as rings and watches.

The warehouse acts as a distribution point under the direction of the stock control department. Its principal functions are the packing and dispatch of goods to the branches on a daily basis.

Abbreviation	Name
AMU	Actual markup
AN	Article number
ASP	Actual selling price
ASV	Actual selling value
BN	Branch number
BRL	Branch replenishment list
BRN	Branch return note
DD	Date dispatched
DR	Date received
GRL	Goods received list
IBT	Inter-branch transfer
MU	Markup
PDF	Price discrepancy form
PP	Purchase price
PV	Purchase value
RF	Received from
RJL	Regis Jewellers Limited
RMU	Recommended markup
RSP	Recommended selling price
SCD	Stock control department
SP	Selling price
TAMU	Total actual markup
TASV	Total actual selling value
TPV	Total purchase value
TRMU	Total recommended markup
TRSV	Total recommended selling value
VAT	Value added tax

Figure 9.1 Abbreviations used in the case study

Two other important departments in RJL are the buying department and the stock control department (SCD). The former is responsible for placing orders with suppliers at an economic price and checking their receipt via its goods-receiving section (GRS). It is also responsible for deciding each article's recommended selling price (RSP). This price is based largely on two factors — current fashion and ongoing demand. Fashion articles are usually in a lower price bracket and have a rapid turnover, their markup (selling price less purchase price) can therefore be relatively small. Ongoing articles have a steady but lower demand and thus necessitate a higher markup to compensate for being held longer in stock.

The SCD is responsible for planning the distribution of articles between branches. Replenishment is effected according to the recent sales of branches and the consequent need to maintain suitable levels of branch stocks. These decisions call for human knowledge and judgement of external circumstances and are therefore not, as such, amenable to computerization.

The SCD also handles requests from branches for particular articles demanded by customers. A request is met by searching through the stocklists of the warehouse and branches in order to locate the requirement. If the article is in another branch, an inter-branch transfer (IBT) is initiated. IBTs are effected for only the more expensive articles as otherwise the cost of transfer might nullify the markup.

It must be remembered that in the jewellery trade ready availability of goods is of paramount importance. This is because customers are often capricious in their requirements, and because competition is severe. RJL therefore aims to hold a wide range in each branch, and to cover this by ensuring that articles are quickly available from other branches.

In regard to the RSPs, a branch manager has some discretion to sell at a lower price. Price reductions generally apply only to slow-moving articles, and may be at the suggestion of the buying department when it is realized that certain articles have been dormant for some considerable time. Price reductions are closely monitored by the audit section.

9.2   System investigation

Management's aims

- To have available in every branch, or to provide at short notice, a wide range of jewellery in current demand.
- To make accurate forecasts of future demands based, among other factors, on the patterns of recent sales.
- To minimize the amount of dormant stock, i.e. articles no longer attractive to customers.
- To ensure that every article can be accounted for from its receipt from the supplier to its sale to a customer.

Facts Found

Goods sold

The quantities of articles held in stock amount to about 1,000 in the warehouse and 8,000 in the branches on average. The articles are mostly individual, i.e. different from each other, or in small batches. Exceptions are the low-priced articles such as watchstraps, but nevertheless every article has its own unique article number.

An article number consists of five numeric digits, this arrangement allows for a long period before reallocation of a number is necessary.

For the purposes of sales analysis and stock handling it is convenient to segregate articles into nine categories.

Categories of articles

Table 9.1 shows the categories of the articles.

The first digit of the article number denotes the category of the article. In the case of watches, the second digit denotes the manufacturer. Watches differ from other articles in that the customers are aware of the manufacturers' names and often ask for a particular make. By using the second digit in this way, it is straightforward to analyse sales according to manufacturer.

Table 9.1

Category no.	Description
1	Rings
2	Watches
3	Necklets and pendants
4	Bracelets and bangles
5	Earrings and hair adornments
6	Brooches, cufflinks and tie slides
7	Clocks and barometers
8	Gold and silver ornaments
9	Other articles

Price ranges

Jewellery encompasses a wide range of prices — from a few pounds for a watchstrap up to thousands for a jewelled watch or a gold ornament. It is of importance to RJL's management to know the overall pattern of sales according to price and also the price distribution between branches, i.e. which branches can sell expensive articles and which must stick to the lower-priced.

For the purpose of these analyses it is satisfactory to have the five price ranges as shown in Table 9.2.

Table 9.2

Price range no.	Range of selling prices
1	Less than £10
2	£ 10 to £ 99.99
3	£ 100 to £499.99
4	£ 500 to £999.99
5	£1000 or over

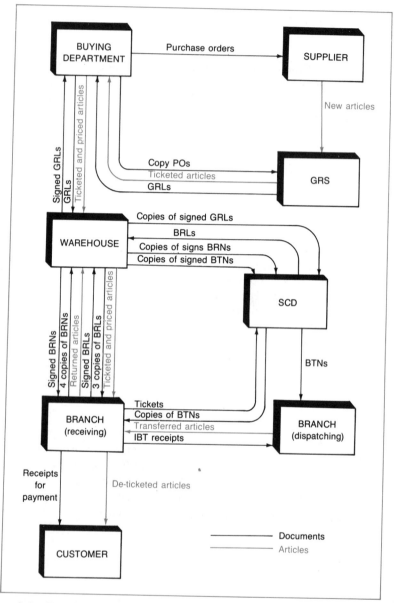

Figure 9.2 Data flow diagram of manual system. NB: Copies of all movement documents and signed receipts are also sent to the audit section (not shown).

Present procedures

This explanation should be read in conjunction with Figure 9.2.

1. Purchase orders (POs) are sent by the buying department to the suppliers, with copies to the goods receiving section (GRS) (part of the buying department).

2. On arrival from suppliers, the articles are checked in the GRS against the copy PO. Any discrepancies are notified to the buying department for reconciling with the supplier.

3. For each article an article number is extracted from a list (one list per category) and written onto a small tag or a self-adhesive label (henceforth referred to as a ticket). This ticket is then attached to the article and is not removed until the article is sold. From this time onwards this article number is the definitive identification of the article.

4. A goods received list (GRL) is made out each day showing details of all articles received. For each article is listed its article number, a brief description, purchase price and supplier.

5. The ticketed articles together with a copy of the GRL are passed to the buying department.

6. The buying department checks the articles for acceptability and enters the recommended selling price (RSP) onto the GRL and the article's ticket.

7. The articles are then passed to the warehouse together with two copies of the priced GRL, one of which is signed by the warehouse staff as a receipt. The audit section (part of the accounts department) and the stock control department (SCD) each receive a copy of the GRL.

8. The GRLs act as warehouse stocklists for the SCD, and are used to decide on branch replenishments in conjunction with the returned tickets (see below).

9. The branch replenishment lists (BRLs) are passed to the warehouse where articles are packed and dispatched to the branches. Each package is accompanied by three further copies of the BRL – one for the branch, one to be signed as a receipt for the warehouse and one for the audit section. The latter also receives a copy of the BRL directly from the warehouse. Any discrepancies between a BRL and its accompanying articles are reported to the audit section. The BRL retained by the branch forms a supplement to its stocklist.

10. When an article is sold its ticket is removed and these are sent daily to the SCD to represent sales. The tickets and the retained copies of BRLs enable the SCD to maintain records of branch stocks. Each sale should also be recorded on the branch's BRL so as to maintain an up-to-date stocklist, this is sometimes overlooked at busy times.

11. As mentioned earlier a branch manager has a limited discretion to sell at a lower price than the RSP. When this occurs, the actual selling price (ASP) is entered on the ticket before return, and also on the BRL. It is also necessary to notify the audit section by means of a price discrepancy form (PDF). This is also obligatory if an article is accidentally sold at a wrong price.

12. When the SCD decides on an inter-branch transfer (IBT), a branch transfer note (BTN) is sent to the two branches concerned. On receipt of a BTN, the sending branch dispatches the article to the receiving branch along with a copy

of the BTN to be returned as a receipt. The audit section is also sent copies of BTNs.

13. Occasionally it is necessary to return an article from a branch to the warehouse owing to it being faulty or damaged. In this event a branch return note (BRN) is made out in sextuplicate. Four copies go with the returned article — one for the warehouse, one to be returned as a signed receipt, and one signed copy each to the SCD and the audit section. The latter also receives a BRN directly from the branch (the fifth copy), and the branch retains the sixth copy.

Weaknesses of the present procedures

As is evident from the above explanation, a large amount of form-filling, photocopying and interchange of documents is involved. These activities are inherent to the jewellery trade mainly due to the need to keep track of the whereabouts of every article at all times. Without this precaution losses through carelessness and pilfering could be enormous.

In spite of this high volume of paperwork, it is still not possible to analyse sales quickly enough — or even at all. The best that is achieved are spasmodic analyses of certain categories and branches; and even this entails considerable tedious searching through BRLs, with consequent errors and delays.

Another weakness is in the updating of the BRLs held in the SCD. This work is time-consuming and prone to mistakes owing to the large number of BRLs involved. It should be borne in mind that some articles remain unsold for a long time, resulting in a backlog of BRLs. This is because a BRL is not archived until all the articles thereon have been sold.

Yet a further problem is in dealing with requests from branches for specific demands from customers. As explained above, this is catered for by inter-branch transfers, but before an IBT can be initiated the SCD has to search through its BRLs to find a suitable article. This again is a time-consuming activity as there are hundreds of BRLs in existence at any time. In fact it is doubtful whether IBTs are really economic except for high-priced articles.

9.3 System design

General points

- Decisions regarding purchasing, branch replenishments and inter-branch transfers are to remain essentially as at present. That is to say, based on manual decisions but supported by a database held in microcomputer storage.
- Details of all movements and transactions are to be entered into a

microcomputer system in order to maintain up-to-date stock and sales statistics.

- The microcomputer system is to be employed to prepare a set of information reports such as sales analyses and stock figures for use by management and other staff.
- Existing documents are to be continued as the means of data capture for the microcomputer system. This is to include article tickets exactly as at present.
- The present article numbering system is to be continued without change.
- All movements are to be double-entered into the system, e.g. a dispatch from the warehouse and the corresponding receipt by the branch. In this way an audit trail is established for every article during its life in the firm.
- The daily total of each branch's sales is to be computed by the system for reconciliation against the actual daily takings banked, i.e. a branch cash account.

Figures 9.3 to 9.5 list the data items pertaining to the files and processes.

Logical files (data stores)

The three main logical files (henceforth referred to simply as files) are F2, F3 and F4. Between them these files hold a continuous record of all articles from receipt from suppliers until sold to customers. Every movement of articles is

Data item	Layout (picture)	Bytes	Min.	Max.	Remarks
Actual markup	9999.99	6	0.50	1000.00	
Actual selling price	9999.99	6	2.00	4000.00	
Article number	99999	5	100000	99999	
Branch name	A(10)	10			Abbreviated if necessary
Branch number	99	2	1	10	
Category number	9	1	1	9	1st digit art. no.
Dates (all)	99.99.99	6			Format DD.MM.YY
Description	X(18)	18			Abbreviated if necessary
Manufacturer name	A(9)	9			Abbreviated if necessary
Manufacturer number	9	1	1	9	2nd digit art. no. (watches)
Price range number	9	1	1	5	
Purchase price	9999.99	6	1.50	3000.00	
Quantities (all)	9999	4	0	9999	
Recommended markup	9999.99	6	0.50	1000.00	
Rec. selling price	9999.99	6	2.00	4000.00	
Status	9999.99	1	1	5	
Totals (all)	99999.99	7	0	99999.99	
Values (all)	99999.99	7	0	99999.99	

Figure 9.3 Data dictionary of main data items

Ref.	Transaction/movement	From	Article no.	Branch no.	Description	Purchase price	RSP/ASP	Other branch no.	Date received	Date dispatched	Date sold
										Data items →	
T1	Warehouse receipt from buying dept. (receipt)	GRL	✓		✓	✓	✓		✓		
T2	Warehouse dispatch to branch (replenishment)	BRL	✓	✓						✓	
T3	Warehouse receipt from branch (return)	Signed BRN	✓	✓					✓		
T4	Branch receipt from warehouse (replenishment)	Signed BRL	✓	✓					✓		
T5	Branch dispatch to other branch (transfer-out)	BTN	✓	✓				✓		✓	
T6	Branch dispatch to warehouse (return)	BRN	✓	✓						✓	
T7	Branch receipt from other branch (transfer-in)	Signed BTN	✓	✓					✓	✓	
T8	Branch sale to customer (sale)	Ticket	✓	✓			✓				✓

Figure 9.4 Data items in transactions and movements (data usage chart)

Sources of data items:
T denotes transaction as no.
F denotes file as no.
I means input
C means calculated

Ref.	Document or display Name	Article no.	Branch no.	Description	RSP	ASP	Price difference	Purchase price	Rec. markup	Actual markup	Date received	Date dispatched	Date sold	Other branch no.	Status
R1	Warehouse receipts from branches (returns)	T3	T3	F1							T3				
R2(a)	Receipts not on BRL	T4	T4	F1							T4				
R2(b)	Sales not in F3	T8	T8	F1									T8		
R2(c)	Dispatches not in F2	T2	T2	F1								T2			
R3	Sales price discrepancies (see Fig. 9.23)	T8	T8	F1	F1	T8	C	F1	C	C			T8		
R4	Branch dispatches (transfers-out)	T5	T5	F1								T5		T5	
R5	Branch receipts (transfers-in)	T7	T7	F1							T7			T7	
R6	Branch dispatches to warehouse (returns)	T6	T6	F1								T6			
R7	Responses to enquiries	F2/F3	I	F1	F1									F3	F2/F3
R8–13	Documents shown in Figs 9.24–9.28	Sources of data items evident from Figs 9.8–9.12													

Figure 9.5 Data items in documents and displays output analysis chart

recorded as a dispatch, a receipt or a sale. For example, when an article is transferred from the warehouse to a branch, this is recorded in F2 (warehouse stock file) as being in transit and then later in F3 (branch stocks file) as being in the branch's stock.

F1   Prices and descriptions file

This file holds one record per live article. The record is created when the article reaches the warehouse, and is eventually deleted after it has been sold. The data items per record are as follows:

Article number
Description
Purchase price
Recommended selling price

F2   Warehouse stock file

This file contains one record for each article that is in the warehouse or in transit to a branch. The record is deleted when the article has been received by the branch. The data items per record are as follows:

Article number
Status (1 = in warehouse, 2 = in transit)
Date received into warehouse
Date dispatched to branch ⎱ blank until dispatched
Branch number (receiving) ⎰

F3   Branch stocks file

This file holds one record for each article that is in a branch or in transit to the warehouse or another branch. The record is deleted when the article has been sold or received back into the warehouse. The data items per record are as follows:

Article number
Branch number
Date received by branch
Status (3 = in branch, 4 = in transit to another branch, 5 = in transit to
    warehouse)
Branch number received from (0 = warehouse)
Date dispatched (if status = 4 or 5)
Branch number dispatched to (if status = 4)

F4   Branch sales file

This file has one record for each article sold and the record remains in existence for some time afterwards. The data items in the record are as follows:

Article number

Branch number (selling)
Date sold
Actual selling price

F5 *Cumulative sales file*

This file contains a record for each combination of branch and category, i.e. 10 branches × 9 categories = 90 records. Within each record are the total sales for each of the previous 10 weeks of trading. Since this is an ongoing file, the number of records remains at 90 but the relevant weeks change incrementally. The data items are as follows:

Branch number
Category number
Actual selling value $\Big\}$
Purchase value   repeated for each of the 10 weeks
Total quantity sold

Estimate of storage required

Table 9.3 shows the estimate of the storage required. Allowing for 700,000 bytes and several versions of the files, this is easily accommodated on a hard disk — or even on a few floppy disks.

Table 9.3

File	Max. records	Bytes per record*	Storage (bytes)
F1	9,000	35	315,000
F2	1,000	20	20,000
F3	8,000	23	184,000
F4	7,200	19	136,800
F5	90	163	14,670
		Total	670,470

Note: * Assuming one byte per digit; this could be less in some systems.

Estimate of input keying

Table 9.4 shows the estimate of the input keying. Say 60,000 key depressions per day at an average of 10,000 per hour means six hours work per day.

Table 9.4

Transaction	No. per day	Keys per transaction	Key depressions per day
T1	600	41	24,600
T2	600	13	7,800
T3	15	13	195
T4	600	13	7,800
T5	20	15	300
T6	15	13	195
T7	20	15	300
T8	600	19	11,400
		Total	52,590

Although this amount could be keyed into one microcomputer, it is safer to have two linked to the one hard disk. This allows for overloads and security against breakdown.

Estimate of output printing

Table 9.5 shows the estimate of the output printing. The other documents, not listed in Table 9.5, are too short to be worth taking into account. Allowing for 10,000 lines per day, this would take about three hours on a medium-speed serial printer. Thus two printers provide ample safeguard against overloads and breakdowns.

Table 9.5

Document	Lines per day
R8 Warehouse stocklist	1,000
R9 Branch stocklist	8,000
R10 Sales report	600
Total	9,600

Process (job) specifications

Process P1

The input to process P1 are the warehouse receipts (T1) used to enter new articles into files F1 and F2, at the same time checking for errors and creating control totals.

1. Check that article is not already in F1, see (7) below.
2. Check that article is not already in F2, see (7) below.
3. Create record in F1.
4. Create record in F2 with status = 1.
5. Count articles in the day's batch to form a control total.
6. Summate RSPs in the day's batch to form control total.
7. If either of the checks is not satisfied, an error message is displayed and the transaction is ignored.

The above procedures are depicted in Figures 9.6 and 9.14–9.18.

Processes P2–P9

The steps in these processes are evident from Figures 9.7–9.13. In the interests of brevity only selected details of processing are included, see Figures 9.19–9.28.

9.4 Exercises

Exercise 9.1 Order processing/inventory control

An order processing and inventory control system produces the following: commodity picking list, dispatch note, stock replenishment report and sales analysis.

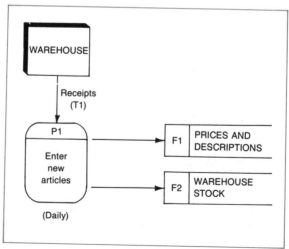

Figure 9.6 Data flow diagram of the new article routine

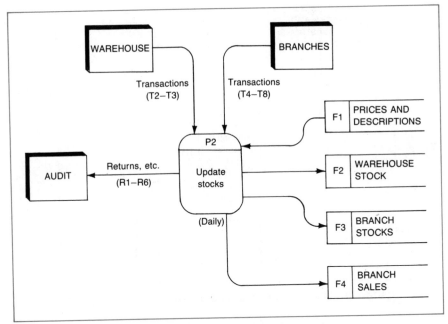

Figure 9.7 Data flow diagram of the stock updating routine

Required:

(a) State the purpose of each of the above reports.
(b) List the data items which each report will contain and indicate the
    source of each such item (i.e. whether it is from a master file (M),
    input (I) or processing activity (P), giving the names of the relevant files
    or inputs).

(CACA level 2, Sys. an. & des., June 1987)

Exercise 9.2 File contents and organization

You have been asked by your manager to provide details of the file layouts
(i.e. what each record would contain) for both a payroll master file and a
stock master file.

The payroll file is for all employees in the company and is updated on a
monthly basis. However, the stock file is updated as orders are placed by
customers and as new stock is received, thus ensuring that the data is as up
to date as possible.

Identify what information would be stored on each of the files, what file
organization would be most appropriate, and why, and finally what methods
you would recommend for making security backup copies of the files.

(ICSA part 2, Inf. sys., Dec. 1988)

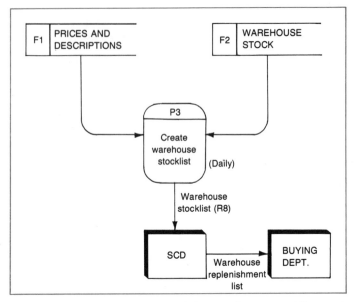

Figure 9.8　Data flow diagram of the warehouse stocklist routine

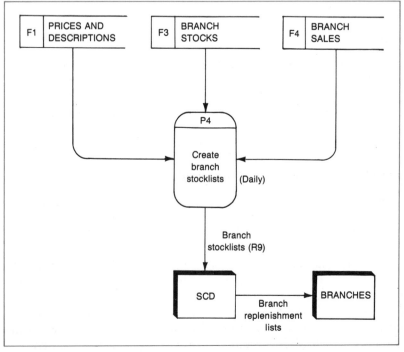

Figure 9.9　Data flow diagram of the branch replenishments routine

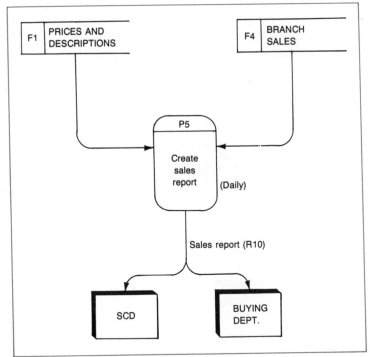

Figure 9.10 Data flow diagram of the sales reporting routine

Exercise 9.3 Computer configuration/staff training

A company based at a single location handles the letting of 2,500 holiday properties, 1,000 of which are overseas. The local properties are let for 45 weeks per year on average, whilst the overseas properties are let for 49 weeks per year. Approximately 50 per cent of bookings for the local properties are for 2 weeks and 50 per cent for 1 week, whereas 75 per cent of bookings for overseas properties are for 2 weeks and 25 per cent for 1 week.

The company keeps records of its customers for the past three years and mails catalogues to them at the start of each season. Fifty per cent of bookings are made by existing customers; 90 per cent of bookings are made in the 12-week period December–February. The company wishes to install a computer system to handle all bookings, the invoicing and a catalogue mailing list.

(a) Describe the characteristics of a suitable computer system and give reasons for your choice.

(b) Derive an estimate for the cost of the system chosen in (a).

(c) Describe the scope of the training programme that would be necessary if the present staff were used to operate the new system.

(BCS part I, Gen. paper II, April 1987)

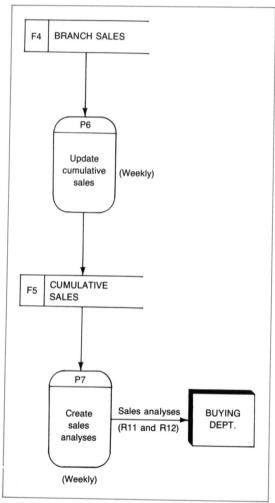

Figure 9.11 Data flow diagram of the sales updating and analysis routine

Exercise 9.4 Holiday booking system

A holiday booking system is split between local offices, dealing directly with customers, and a Head Office dealing with bulk arrangements with hotels, airlines, etc. Enquiries concerning holiday availability, and subsequent bookings, are made on-line from the local offices to a common centralized file, held at the Head Office. Customer details are held locally.

Describe the data structures needed

(a) for the centralized holiday file, and
(b) for the local customer files.

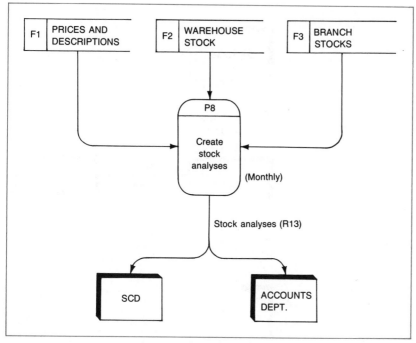

Figure 9.12 Data flow diagram of the stock analysis routine

Outline, using a suitable diagram, the main processing logic for making holiday enquiries and reservations.

(BCS part I, Option C, April 1987)

Exercise 9.5 Retail business

Your organization is a national based retail chain operating from about one hundred branches but with central buying and merchandise functions. Retail branches are small sales units employing up to ten sales staff. Sales are all on a cash/credit card basis and goods for sale are received direct from suppliers.

Given the use of computer-based systems, how would you see the operation of the sales, goods acquisition and stock control systems?

(ICSA part 4, Man. sys., Dec., 1986)

Scenario concerning PISCES

The following scenario is referred to in exercises 9.6–9.8.

1. The Professional Institute of Systems Competence and Software Engineering, known as PISCES, is an association founded in the late 1960s and has a total UK membership of 20,000.

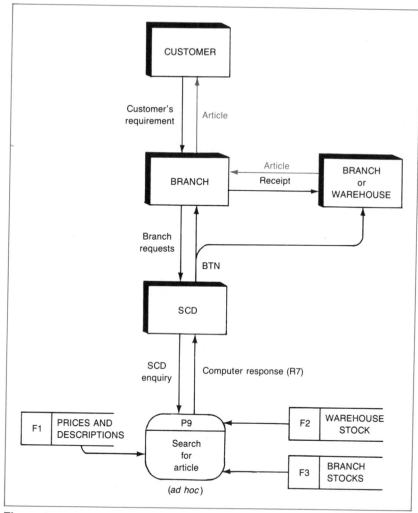

Figure 9.13 Data flow diagram of the customer requirement routine

2. Each member is allocated to one of the fifty geographical branches which have the responsibility of running meetings in their locality. The branches are allocated a budget for this purpose, and receive delegated responsibility for publicizing their branch meetings and attempting to recruit new members. The branch meetings are open and publicized to non-members.

3. The branches vary in size from 200 to 1,200 members and also in the geographical region served. The largest branch, numerically, is Inner London and the largest, geographically, covers six counties in the south-west of England.

Is article's record in F1?	Y	—	N	—
Is article's record in F2?	—	Y	N	—
End of transactions?	—	—	—	Y
Display error message	X	X		
Ignore transaction	X	X		
Create record in F1			X	
Create record in F2			X	
Add to control totals			X	
Display control totals				X

Figure 9.14   Decision table of process P1

4. The Headquarters uses a Computer Bureau to maintain membership lists and to produce printed labels for distribution of publications, notices of general meetings and other selective mailshots.
5. The Bureau has facilities for producing labels for the members of any specified branch, but Branch Secretaries find the lists to be inaccurate, out-dated and inflexible in that they have demands to include on their lists a number of non-members, local organizations and members of adjacent branches who attend their meetings.
6. A number of branches produce their own newsletters, others simply mail all their members with details of branch meetings.
7. Branches are encouraged to run courses and seminars with fees charged to participants. These can be as varied as awareness talks for students and non-members to 'state of the art' seminars for specialists and advanced practitioners. Many of these functions give rise to the need for the production of handout materials.
8. Several Branch Secretaries use their personal microcomputers to carry out the branch administration. Others have, over a number of years, maintained branch mailing lists on their companies' computers.
9. One branch has been sponsored by a computer manufacturer with a two-year loan of a powerful microcomuter which it finds invaluable for its work. It has approached the headquarters secretariat for permission to purchase the computer at the end of the loan period. There is, however, a certain amount of concern being expressed that the company which has loaned the machine has a very small share of the market and the machine does not run the most popular application packages but implements so-called clones.
10. With the falling prices and improved capacities and performance of computers, a number of branches have at various times put in varied

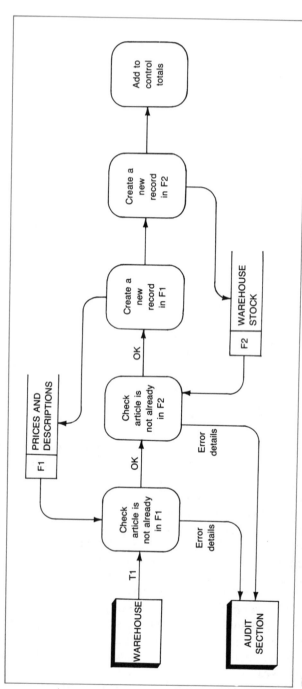

Figure 9.15 Data flow diagram of process P1

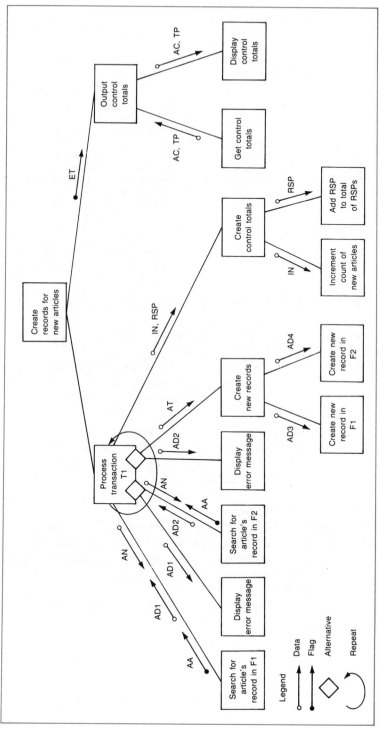

Figure 9.16 Structure chart of process P1 (See Figure 9.17 for abbreviations.)

Abbreviation	Name	Description
AA	Article absent flag	Denotes record is not in F1
AC	Article count	A count of the number of articles
AD1	Data items from F1	AN, PP, RSP, DE (if already in F1)
AD2	Data items from F2	AN, ST, DR (if already in F2)
AD3	Data items to F1	AN, PP, RSP, DE
AD4	Data items to F2	AN, ST, DR
AN	Article number	Unique identification of article
AT	Data items from T1	AN, DE, PP, RSP, DR, ST
DE	Description	Brief description of article
DR	Date received	When received by warehouse
ET	End of transactions flag	Denotes all transactions have been processed
TN	Increment of one	One is added to article count
PP	Purchase price	
RSP	Recommended selling price	
ST	Status	Denotes whereabouts of article
TP	Total of RSPs	Total of all RSPs in day's batch

Figure 9.17 Abbreviations used in structure chart of process P1

requests for the purchase of microcomputers but, despite increasing pressure, none has yet been approved.

11. In response to these developments a small working party has been set up consisting of representatives from a number of different branches, some enthusiastic to the purchase of computers and others who have expressed doubts on this being a valid use of members' money.

12. Before convening the first meeting of the working party, the Chairman discovered that there were plans going ahead to conduct a feasibility study into the purchase of a computer system for head office. This would be used for all the mailing activities currently operated from the Bureau and would maintain all membership records and process all the examination entries and results.

13. The Treasurer has pointed out that many branches, as a result of running courses and seminars, have sufficient funds in their own accounts to purchase computers independently of headquarters' funding and many branches have members employed by, or with close links to suppliers or manufacturers.

14. The Secretary of the largest branch has offered to use his own computer but has requested permission to use branch funds to purchase a laser printer.

(CIMA, stage 2, Inf. tech. man., Nov. 1988)

Exercise 9.6 General points

This question is to be answered with reference to the material presented in the scenario concerning PISCES.

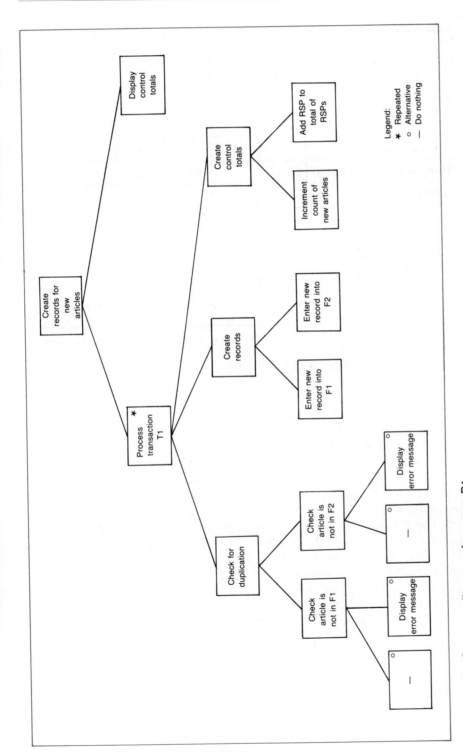

Figure 9.18 Structure diagram of process P1

Type of transaction	T2	T3	T4	T5	T6	T7	T8
Check record is not in	F3	F2	F3	—	F2	—	—
Check record is in	F2	F3	F2	F3	F3	F3	F3
Check status is	1	5	2	3	3	4	3
Make/change status	2	1	3	4	5	3	—
Insert into record	BN, DD	—	—	BN, DD	DD	DR, RF	—
Check in record	—	—	—	BN	—	BN	—
Change in record	—	—	—	—	—	BN	—
Delete from record	—	—	—	—	—	BN, BN	—
Delete record from	—	F3	F2	—	—	—	F3
Insert new record in	—	F2	F3	—	—	—	F4
Insert in new record	—	AN, DR	AN, BN DR, RF	—	—	—	AN, BN DS, ASP

Abbreviations: AN, article no.; BN, branch no.; DR, date received; DD, date dispatched; RF, received from; ASP, actual selling price.

Figure 9.19 Decision table of process P2

You are required to:

(a) Explain the use of the term 'clone', list and justify briefly *three* reasons why the branches should be constrained to purchase identical models.

(b) Justify *two* distinct reasons why it might be preferable for each branch to have the freedom to act independently of others in the purchase.

(c) List *three* types of standard program package which might be useful for branches and explain briefly how they might benefit the Branch Secretary.

(d) List the items of hardware, indicating capacity speed and type of device, which might be necessary for each branch to possess in order to carry out the required tasks.

(e) Explain what is meant by a laser printer, giving an indication of its speed and quality of print.

(f) Explain what is meant by desktop publishing in the context of the use of microcomputers.

(g) Comment critically on the problems of using members' companies' computers for the maintenance of branch membership and mailing lists.

(CIMA, stage 2, Inf. tech. man., Nov. 1988)

Exercise 9.7 Implementation of computer system

This question is to be answered with reference to the material presented in the scenario concerning PISCES.

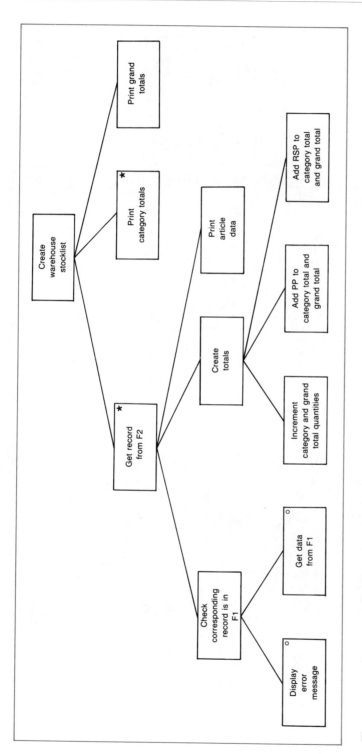

Figure 9.20 Structure diagram of process P3

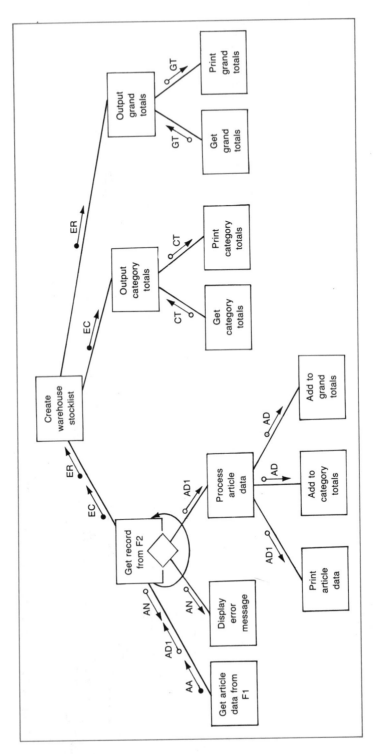

Figure 9.21 Structure chart of process P3 (See Figure 9.22 for abbreviations and Fig. 9.16 for legend.)

Abbreviation	Name	Description
AD	Article data	PP, RSP, IN
CPV	Category purchase value	Sum of PPs of articles in category
CQ	Category quantity	Quantity, i.e. count, of articles in category
CRSV	Category recommended selling value	Sum of RSPs of articles in category
CT	Category totals	CQ, CPV, CRSV
EC	End of category flag	Denotes end of articles in category
ER	End of records flag	Denotes end of records in F2
GPV	Grand purchase value	Sum of PPs of all articles in warehouse stock
GQ	Grand quantity	Quantity, i.e. count, of all articles in warehouse stock
GRSV	Grand recommended selling value	Sum of RSPs of all articles in warehouse stock
GT	Grand totals	GQ, GPV, GRSV
IN	Increment of one	One is added to article count

Other abbreviations are as shown in Figure 9.17.

Figure 9.22 Abbreviations used in structure chart of process P3

```
                    SALES PRICE DISCREPANCIES on 11.12.89

ART.NO.    DESCRIPTION      BR.    RSP      ASP      DIFF.     PP      RMU     AMU

13720  18CT.TOPAZ/DIAMD.    5   1200.00   950.00   250.00   800.00   400.00  150.00
13806  9CT.PINK TOURMLN.    4     52.00    45.00     7.00    30.00    22.00   15.00
25397  MENS PULSAR GOLD     5     65.00    60.00     5.00    40.00    25.00   20.00
26651  LADIES SEIKO GOLD    2     99.50    89.50    10.00    60.50    39.00   29.00
34619  9CT.CULT.PEARL       7     62.50    49.00    13.50    40.00    22.50    9.00
50938  18CT.DIAMOND         2    545.00   495.00    50.00   400.00   145.00   95.00

          TOTALS                2024.00  1688.50   335.50  1370.50   653.50  318.00
```

Figure 9.23 Specimen of price discrepancy list (R3)

```
                  WAREHOUSE STOCKLIST as at 15.12.89

ARTICLE    DESCRIPTION        DATE       PUR.      R.S.    STATUS    DATE
 NO.                        RECEIVED    PRICE     PRICE              DESPD.

12805    22CT.PLAIN         18.11.89    28.00     37.50    Stock
12986    18CT.PLAIN         23.11.89    21.50     28.75    Stock
13140    18CT.SING.DIAMOND  26.11.89    42.30     56.70    To br.5   11.12.89
13402    22CT.PATTERNED     30.11.89    33.40     43.25    Stock
13955    PLAT.PLAIN         12.12.89    32.00     42.00    To br.2   13.12.89

CATEGORY 1 QTY.   236    CATGY.1 VALUES 2714.50  3609.15


21274    ROLEX GOLD         21.11.89   486.00    649.95    Stock
21499    OMEGA S.S.         28.11.89   175.00    237.50    Stock


TOTAL QUANTITY    2683    TOTAL VALUES 25264.85 36897.70
```

Figure 9.24 Specimen of warehouse stocklist (R8) (R9 is similar.)

```
┌─────────────────────────────────────────────────────────────────────┐
│               SALES REPORT  -  POOLE for 11.12.89                     │
├─────────────────────────────────────────────────────────────────────┤
│                                                                       │
│   ARTICLE      DESCRIPTION         R.S.      A.S.     ACTUAL    PRICE  │
│   NO.                              PRICE     PRICE    MARK-UP   REDUCT.│
│                                                                       │
│   12738        18CT.TWIN DIAMOND   46.80     46.80    12.40           │
│   12742        22CT.PLAIN          35.75     33.90     7.45     1.85   │
│   12755        18CT.SING.DIAMOND   65.30     65.30    18.50           │
│   12769        PLAT.PATTERNED      98.50     98.50    23.75           │
│   12803        18CT.PLAIN          29.00     24.90     4.10           │
│      |            |                  |         |         |            │
│      |            |                  |         |         |            │
│      |            |                  |         |         |            │
│      |            |                  |         |         |            │
│                                                                       │
│   BRANCH QUANTITY   54      BRANCH VALUES   891.50   236.80    28.25   │
└─────────────────────────────────────────────────────────────────────┘
```

Figure 9.25 Specimen of sales report (R10)

```
┌─────────────────────────────────────────────────────────────────────────────────────┐
│               SALES ANALYSIS by BRANCH & CATEGORY at week 24                          │
│                                                                                       │
│  BRANCH  CAT.        ---------------------- WEEK NUMBER ----------------------        │
│                       15    16    17    18    19    20    21    22    23    24         │
│                                                                                       │
│  POOLE    1    TASV  1217  1306  1415  1321  1195  1206  1272  1440  1266  1225        │
│  POOLE    1    TAMU   303   329   350   335   289   317   325   358   325   309        │
│                                                                                       │
│  POOLE    2    TASV  2517  2293  2128  2003  1805  1895  1640  1932  1700  1613        │
│  POOLE    2    TAMU   618   576   527   501   423   475   426   488   425   401        │
│    |      |      |     |     |     |     |     |     |     |     |     |     |          │
│    |      |      |     |     |     |     |     |     |     |     |     |     |          │
│    |      |      |     |     |     |     |     |     |     |     |     |     |          │
│  POOLE  BRANCH TASV  4715  4301  4471  4997  4614  4004  4102  4350  4245  4133        │
│  POOLE  BRANCH TAMU  1246  1182  1102  1281  1180  1106  1285  1197  1019  1171        │
│                                                                                       │
│                                                                                       │
│      GRAND TASV 46311 45032 44990 43216 45004 44867 45242 46334 45297 44168           │
│      GRAND TAMU 11605 11234 11266 10859 11065 11279 11426 11637 11305 11004           │
└─────────────────────────────────────────────────────────────────────────────────────┘
```

Figure 9.26 Specimen of sales analysis (R11)

Despite the skills possessed by the members of PISCES, the headquarters staff have no experience of the regular use of a major computer application. Therefore you have been called to advise the Secretary General on a number of matters concerning implementation.

You are required:

(a) To list *six* main stages in the installation and implementation of a computer system.

(b) Given that there are three different strategies which can be adopted for the actual changeover to a new computer system (direct changeover, parallel running and pilot running), to provide a brief explanation of *each*, with direct reference to a possible new installation of a computer system at the headquarters designed to maintain membership records, giving an advantage and a disadvantage of each strategy.

WATCH SALES ANALYSIS by MANUFACTURER at week 24

		15	16	17	18	WEEK NUMBER 19	20	21	22	23	24
ROLEX	£	1352	1300	1270	1505	6450	2000	1260	0	3450	550
OMEGA	£	1160	1200	3500	1140	850	2000	750	1450	2600	1500
TISSOT	£	976	1000	2300	1750	2900	1160	390	1400	2240	1870
LONGINES	£	1250	3450	760	1100	1340	450	1200	1600	2300	560
TOTALS	£	12550	13700	14800	20100	17300	19000	18570	13400	11900	12600

Figure 9.27 Specimen of sales analysis (R12)

STOCK ANALYSIS by BRANCH & CATEGORY at week 24

BRANCH	CAT.	QUANTITY	TPV	TRSV	TRMU
POOLE	1	53	723.50	952.80	229.30
POOLE	2	28	1286.75	1614.60	327.85
POOLE	3	60	681.00	897.75	216.75
POOLE	4	25	213.56	284.08	70.52
POOLE	5	18	150.20	202.60	52.40
POOLE	TOTALS	283	3201.90	4303.35	1101.45
	GRAND TOTALS	2998	34215.30	45796.15	11580.85

Figure 9.28 Specimen of stock analysis (R13)

(c) With reference to the proposal to use the computer for the administration of examinations, to describe briefly *two* problems which would be peculiar to this specific application.

(CIMA, stage 2, Inf. tech. man., Nov. 1988)

Exercise 9.8 Systems investigation

This question is to be answered with reference to the material presented in the scenario concerning PISCES.

Fact finding is a most important stage in the systems development cycle. You are required to

(a) List all the stages of the systems development cycle.
(b) Describe *four* different methods of fact finding and justify *one* principal advantage and *one* principal disadvantage of *each*.
(c) Describe briefly the *three* main skills required by a systems analyst and state, with reasons, which you consider to be the most important.

(CIMA, stage 2, Inf. tech. man., Nov. 1988)

9.5 Outline solutions to exercises

Solution 9.1

(a) Commodity picking list
Used in selecting and packing the items in a customer's order. Ideally the picking list is in a sequence that minimizes the effort entailed in picking.

Dispatch note
A note sent to a customer listing the items dispatched against a particular order from the customer. Also known as a delivery note, it enables the customer to check the contents of a delivery. A signed copy is sometimes returned as a receipt.

Stock replenishment report
A list showing the items that have fallen to or below the reorder level. It is normally used by the purchasing department as a basis for placing replenishment orders with suppliers or with the factory.

Sales analysis
A wide range of sales analysis reports are produced. These are for two main purposes: (a) to help in forecasting future sales demand, and (b) to monitor current sales achievements. The former analyses tend to concentrate on products and sales patterns over time, the latter on sales areas and representatives.

(b) Commodity picking list

Customer no.	(I)	Order
Order no.	(I)	Order
Commodity code	(I)	Order
Commodity description	(M)	Stock file
Shelf no.	(M)	Stock file
Quantity	(I)	Order

Dispatch note

Customer no.	(I)	Order
Customer name & address	(M)	Customer file
Order no.	(I)	Order
Commodity code	(I)	Order
Commodity description	(M)	Stock file
Quantity sent	(I)/(P)	Order or processing
Date sent	(P)	Processing

Stock replenishment report

Commodity code	(M)	Stock file
Commodity description	(M)	Stock file
Quantity required	(P)	Processing
Supplier no.	(M)	Supplier file
Supplier name & address	(M)	Supplier file

Sales analysis

Below is one of many possible analyses.

	(P)/(I)	Processing or selected
Period no.	(P)/(I)	Processing or selected
Commodity code	(M)	Sales history file
Commodity description	(M)	Sales history file
Sales value this period	(M)	Sales history file
Sales value year-to-date	(M)	Sales history file
Sales value this period last year	(M)	Sales history file
Sales value last year	(M)	Sales history file

Note: Commodity description is also shown in the stock file, although this infers redundancy, if a DBMS is employed this would not be the case. The stock file could also be read during sales analysis processing to avoid this redundancy.

Solution 9.2

Payroll master file

One record per employee containing:

Employee no. & name, department/location no., tax code, NI no., annual gross salary, pay year-to-date, tax year-to-date, superannuation (pension) contribution year-to-date, NI contribution year-to-date, SSP contribution year-to-date, tax paid other employment, all other deductions per month (separately), all other deductions year-to-date, bank account no.

File organization

The most suitable file organization is sequential in employee number within department/location number sequence. This is the sequence in which the payslips are printed and distributed.

Security backup

During each monthly payroll processing cycle a backup copy of the payroll file is created using the principle of grandfather/father/son (Section 4.2) if on tape or by regular dumping to tape or another disk if on disk.

Stock master file

One record per commodity containing:

Commodity no., commodity description, reorder level, reorder quantity, allocated stock-in-hand, unallocated stock-in-hand, supplier no., shelf/rack no.

File organization

In as much as the stock file is updated frequently but randomly, a suitable organization is indexed-sequential. This allows rapid updating by random transactions and yet fast printouts in commodity code sequence. If the volatility of the file is low, binary searching is also feasible.

Security backup

Since this file is on disk, it should be dumped to tape or another disk or at least to another area of the disk at regular intervals of time and/or after a certain amount of updating.

Solution 9.3

(a) The characteristics of a suitable computer system are as follows:

Number of terminals

Local properties let for an average of $1\frac{1}{2}$ weeks per booking, i.e. 30 bookings p.a.
Overseas properties let for an average of $1\frac{3}{4}$ weeks per booking, i.e. 28 bookings p.a.
1,500 local properties × 30 bookings p.a. = 45,000 bookings p.a.,
1,000 overseas properties × 28 bookings p.a. = 28,000 bookings p.a., giving a total of 73,000 bookings p.a.
During the twelve-week period bookings amount to 90 per cent, i.e. 65,700, this is an average of 5,625 bookings per week, and if we allow for the peak to be 50 per cent more than average, there will be 8,438, say 9,000 per week.
The booking office will be open for about fifty hours per week, giving an average of 180 bookings per hour. This will also peak and allowance has to be made for enquiries that do not result in bookings, thus 300 transactions per peak hour is not untoward.
A transaction takes about three minutes of terminal time, this means that the number of terminals needed is 300 × 3 ÷ 60, which is 15.

Mailing list file

Since there are 73,000 bookings p.a. and records are kept for the past three years, there are around 190,000 customers on the mailing list (this reduced number makes allowance for repeated bookings in successive years).
Thus 190,000 catalogues have to be mailed at the start of each season. Each customer needs a name and address on the mailing list file, resulting in a record of about 70 bytes and a total storage requirement of 190,000 × 70 = 13.3 megabytes.

Bookings file

Each booking consists of a customer no. (6 bytes), property no. (4 bytes), start week no. (2 bytes) and no. of weeks (1 byte). Because this is numeric data it would be possible to occupy less than the sum of these, if we assume 10 bytes per record, the file will need 73,000 × 10 = 0.73 megabytes.

Property lettings file

This file contains a slot for each week for each property, into which is inserted the customer no. when a booking is made. Thus the number of slots is 2,500 properties × 49 weeks = 122,500, assuming 6 bytes for each, the file occupies 0.735 megabytes.
Total storage required is 13.3 + 0.73 + 0.735 = 14.765 megabytes, say 15 for files and 5 for other data and programs, i.e. 20 megabytes.

Printing requirements

Catalogue mailing: 190,000 envelopes × 5 lines = 950,000 lines p.a.
Invoicing: 73,000 invoices × 8 lines = 584,000 lines p.a.
The main problem is the catalogue mailing as this needs to be done in two weeks, i.e. say fifty hours of computer time. This rate of print output demands a line printer capable of 400 l.p.m.

(b) The purchase price of a minicomputer with a 400 l.p.m. printer, a disk drive and linked to fifteen terminals lies in the region of £30,000 at 1989 prices.

(c) The foremost aspect of staff training is terminal operation, i.e. using a keyboard and a dialogue-based screen. Given a suitable dialogue, training should not be difficult with an application as straightforward as this. Fewer staff need to be trained to operate the printer and the removable disk, if purchased.

Solution 9.4

(a) Centralized holiday files
Hotels file

> Hotel ref. no.
> Single rooms vacant }
> Double rooms vacant } for each week of the holiday season
> First local airport
> Second local airport

Note: A local airport is the nearest to the hotel accepting flights from/to the UK. If it is the intention to reserve the actual room during the booking procedure, then additional storage is necessary.

Flights file

> Flight no.
> Date of flight
> Outward/return
> Departure airport
> Arrival airport
> No. of seats vacant

(b) Local customer files
> Customer name and address
> Start week of booking
> No. of weeks booked
> Hotel ref. no.
> Outward flight no.
> Return flight no.

Refer to Fig. 9.29 for the main processing logic.

Solution 9.5

This situation has many similarities to the case study of Regis Jewellers Ltd. in this chapter. The main point of difference is that in this case the goods from suppliers are received directly by the branches. This means that the stock control system must keep records of the branch stocks (as in the case study) and branches inform the system of sales (again as case study).

 Thus the answer to this question could be closely based on the case study.

Solution 9.6

(a) See glossary for 'clone'. Identical models allow:
 Compatibility in hardware, software and operations between branches, thus giving simplicity, accuracy and security in data transfers, probably via floppy disks.

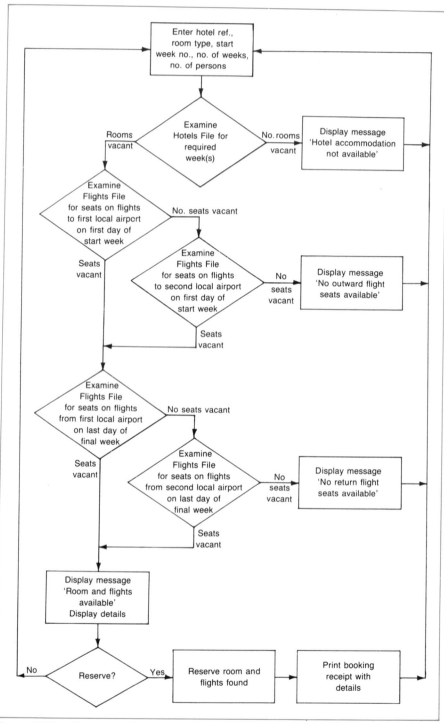

Figure 9.29 Flowchart of enquiries and reservations for Exercise 9.4

Staff training and use experience can be shared between branches.
Price discounts on bulk purchases of hardware and software.
(b) Independent purchasing allows:
Build up of experience of various hardware and software so improving second-round purchasing decisions.
Particular requirements of branches to be met, especially *vis-à-vis* applications software.
(c) Word processing for membership correspondence:
Desktop publishing for newsletters.
DBMS for membership records.
(d) Microcomputer with 500 kilobyte memory, floppy disk drive, monochrome screen, dot-matrix printer (100 c.p.s.) and perhaps a hard disk.
(e) Refer to Section 3.11.
(f) Refer to Section 2.6.
(g) Very undesirable on the grounds of security, legality and practicality. See Data Protection Act in Section 8.8.

Solution 9.7

(a) (i)   Physical installation of hardware – not onerous with a microcomputer.
    (ii) Testing software (Section 8.2).
    (iii) Creation of files/database (Section 8.3).
    (iv) User staff training/briefing (Section 8.5).
    (v)   Changeover procedures (Section 8.4).
    (vi) System appraisal (Section 8.6).
(b) Refer to Section 8.4.
(c) Examination administration in the full sense is complex and tedious from both the manual and computer aspects. It is improbable that using a microcomputer would help except for the more straightforward tasks such as printing name and address labels for examinees.
    The numbers of examinees are unlikely to be sufficient to justify the expenditure on software/programming for examination administration.

Solution 9.8

(a) Refer to Section 7.1.
(b) Refer to Section 6.8.
(c) Refer to Section 6.1.

9.6 Further reading

9.1 McConn, C.E., *Business Computer Studies: Design, Programming and Maintenance with Case Studies* (Prentice Hall, 1989).
9.2 Huff, K., *Developing and Using Microcomputer Business systems* (West Ed. Pub. 1987).
9.3 Wetherbe, J.C., *Cases in Structured Systems Design* (West Ed. Pub., 1988).

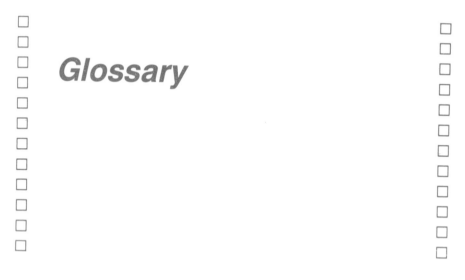

Glossary

The terms and acronyms in this glossary are included either to supplement the text or to act as reminders of textual material. They are not included in the index in most cases.

3GL See third-generation language

ACM (Association for Computing Machinery) An American professional society dedicated to the furtherance of computing.

Ada A programming language for real-time and process control applications.

AFIPS (American Federation of Information Processing Societies) A federation of American professional computing societies.

ALGOL (ALGOrithmic Language) A high-level programming language for mathematical problems, unsuitable for business.

algorithm A set of computational and/or logical steps for converting a data item's value into another value, e.g. a code number into a storage address.

Alvey A US fifth-generation project.

analogue computer A computer that uses physical entities to represent data, e.g. an electric voltage. Analogue computers are not used for business data processing.

ANSI American National Standards Institute.

APL (A Programming Language) A high-level language that is particularly effective for preparing programs involving the processing of arrays.

ASCII (American Standard Code for Information Interchange) A code representing alphanumeric characters, symbols and control codes. Consists of seven bits interpretable by different computer systems.

ASIS American Society for Information Science.

associated storage See content addressing.

ATM (automated teller machine) A more sophisticated type of cash dispenser catering for credit transactions, transfers between accounts and complex enquiries.

Backmann diagram A diagrammatic representation using special symbols of the interconnections between records in a database.

baud The rate of change per second of a signal level, equivalent to bits per second if there are only two signal levels.

BCD See binary coded decimal.

BCS (British Computer Society) A British professional society dedicated to the furtherance of computing.

benchmark test A program(s) and data designed to determine the performance of and comparison between different models of computers. See Whetstone rating.

binary A numbering system to the base 2, thus using only the digits 0 and 1 (bits).

binary coded and decimal A coding arrangement using 4 bits to represent each decimal digit in a number, e.g. 47 is 0100 0111.

bit The digit 0 or 1 as used in a binary numbering system.

bit-mapped See memory mapped.

boot The initial start-up procedures of a computer. Cold boot means starting from a switched-off state; warm boot is restarting from a neutral state omitting the initial procedures. Derived from 'bootstrap' meaning a computer's ability to start without a program in main store.

bootstrap See boot.

BOS (business operating system) A 16-bit multi-user operating system for microcomputers.

BSI British Standards Institute.

bubble chart A diagram depicting entities and their attributes in the form of ellipses joined by lines.

bucket Synonymous with 'block'.

buffer An area in main store for holding data awaiting processing or transfer to an ouptut peripheral, known as input and output buffers respectively.

bug An error in a program or data.

Bureaufax The international facsimile service operated by British Telecom.

bus A path (circuit) in a computer along which data, programs and control are moved. Also a channel for transmitting data in a data communications network.

CACA/ACCA The Chartered Association of Certified Accountants.

CAD/CAM (computer-aided design/computer-aided manufacturing) The employment of a computer for designing manufactured artefacts and for controlling the process of manufacturing. CAD entails the extensive use of visual display in conjunction with light pens, etc. CAM is the on-line, real-time control of production processes and is closely associated with robotics. These topics are not covered in this book.

CAFS *See* content addressing.

Cambridge ring A LAN system which utilizes 'slots' for passing data through the network, known as empty slot access/protocol. Each slot holds forty bits of which sixteen are for data and the rest for addressing and control purposes.

canonical model A representation of the inherent properties and structure of data independently of any hardware or software using it.

canonical synthesis A technique for collating all the data identified in an organization, e.g. reports, forms, screens, etc., into a coherent structure, i.e. the entity model; entails drawing bubble charts.

CASE (computer-aided software engineering) Various techniques built into a package for alleviating the work of a systems analyst. Also known as workbench technology. CASE also stands for computer-aided support environment.

CCD (charge-coupled device memory) An array of tiny metal squares each capable of holding an electric charge and thus enabling a large amount of data to be stored in a small volume. This method is volatile and therefore data is lost when switched off. CCD has not been adopted to any extent.

CCITT (Consultative Committee on International Telegraphy and Telephony) An organization making recommendations for international telecommunications.

CCTA (Central Computer and Telecommunications Agency) The standards and purchasing authority of the UK government for computers and telecommunications.

channel A path along which data or programs are moved. Also a track of magnetically stored data on a disk or tape.

CHILL A high-level programming language.

chip A wafer of silicon on which is contained a complete electronic circuit intended to fulfil a particular function, e.g. memory or part of a microprocessor.

CIMA The Chartered Institute of Management Accountants.

CIPFA The Chartered Institute of Public Finance and Accountancy.

circuit A set of interconnected electronic components for performing a certain function.

CISC (complex instruction set computer) The type of microprocessor currently used in most microcomputers. These are capable of handling large instruction sets and powerful instructions. Each CISC instruction is often interpreted into several micro-instructions within the chip itself. *See also* RISC.

clock frequency *See* clock rate.

clock rate The rate at which electrical pulses are generated in a computer in order to represent data. Clock rate is a measure of a computer's processing speed.

clone Hardware or software that mimics or functions in the same way as other hardware or software so that there is no apparent difference.

cluster controller A device controlling the data passing to and from a number of terminals. Data from a distant source is addressed to the cluster controller and readdressed by it to the terminal, and vice versa.

CMOS (complementary metal-oxide semiconductor) A type of chip used for the main storage (memory) of most computers. One such chip holds a million bits in an area of less than a square centimetre.

CODASYL (Conference on Data Systems Languages) An organization responsible for co-ordinating the development of high-level languages, e.g. COBOL, and database management systems.

COMAL (Common Algorithmic Language) A high-level language incorporating the notational style of BASIC and the control structures of Pascal.

command An instruction to a computer that is obeyed immediately instead of awaiting the execution of a program.

compaction *See* data compression.

compression *See* data compression.

concurrency A computer's ability to perform several jobs simultaneously and to switch between them.

conferencing A system that enables participants at a distance from each other to take part in a mutual discussion. Video conferencing permits participants to both see and hear one another, audio conferencing is hearing only, and medicated conferencing includes the recording of messages so that absentees can catch up on return to the conference.

console A terminal comprising a VDU and perhaps a serial printer for use by a computer operator in loading jobs and programs, receiving messages and inputting commands.

content addressing The concept whereby data is stored and accessed based on its content value(s) rather than its key value. Also termed CAFS (content-addressable file store) and associative storage.

conversational mode Alternate message and data passed between a computer and a user at a terminal such that each responds to the other.

CORAL a high-level programming language.

core store Immediate access storage consisting of small rings of magnetic material that can represent a 0 or a 1. Core store is now obsolete.

CRT (cathode ray tube) Sometimes used synonomously for VDU, although strictly speaking a CRT and a VDU are not the same. A CRT is merely a vacuum tube as in a television set.

CSA (Computing Service Association) A British association representing the interests of computer service bureaux and software houses, and dedicated to maintaining high standards in services and products.

cybernetics The theory of communication and control in all types of systems.

cycle stealing The utilization of some of the computer's electronic operating cycles for data transfer purposes external to the processor without significantly affecting the latter.

databank A set of data for use by a number of organizations. This term has largely fallen into disuse in favour of 'database'.

data compression (data compaction) Methods of reducing the storage space required by data, e.g. by removing spaces and encoding common values of data items.

data description language (DDL) A computer language for informing the DBMS regarding data structures used.

data encyclopaedia Similar to a data dictionary but holding information re processes (Section 4.4).

Data Language/One (DL/1) A language devised by IBM for specifying logical and physical data structures.

data management system (DMS) A scaled-down DBMS for controlling data in existent files used by only a few applications.

Data Processing Management Association (DPMA) An American professional association dedicated to the promotion of business data processing.

Datel A generic name for British Telecom's data transmission services.

dBase IV A relational database management system.

DDL *See* data description language.

debug To detect and remove errors from a program.

diagnostic routine Software for detecting errors in software and malfunctions in hardware.

direct memory access (DMA) The transfer of data between main store and backing storage without involving the CPU. Not to be confused with 'direct access'.

directory A list of all files, programs and documents held on a disk, available via the DBMS or operating system.

disk operating system (DOS) An operating system held on disk for immediate transfer into main store on startup.

DL/1 *See* Data Language One.

DMA *See* direct memory access.

DMS *See* data management system.

domain A set of data items of the same type forming a flat file.

dragging Moving an image on a screen by means of a mouse and pointer.

DTE (data terminal equipment) Any piece of hardware with an interface to a data communication system.

duplicated configuration Two similar computers used in conjunction in the one system for backup and security purposes.

Easywriter A comprehensive word processing package capable of interaction with ASCII programs.

EBCDIC (Extended Binary Coded Decimal Interchange Code) A code representing alphanumeric characters, symbols and control codes. Consists of eight bits interpretable by different computer systems.

EBNF (extended Backus–Naur form) The rules for defining the semantics of a program written in a language such as Pascal.

ECMA (European Computer Manufacturers Association)

EDP (electronic data processing) The same as data processing.

EISA See Extended Industry Standard Architecture.

embedded Held in the data itself rather than in a separate index or directory, e.g. a pointer to a related data item held in a record.

emulation The imitation of one device or system by another. Emulation may be achieved either by hardware or software and allows programs written for one type of computer to be executed by another type.

ESPRIT (European Strategic Programme for Research in Information Technology) A European fifth-generation project.

Ethernet A LAN system using CSMA-CD in which devices are linked to each other by interface units easily attachable to a coaxial cable. The cable is up to 2,500 metres long, and as many as 100 devices, situated up to 50 metres from the cable, can be linked.

ETHICS (Effective Technical and Human Implementation of Computer-based Systems) A systems development methodology.

Euronet A European data communications network.

expansion card A slot-in card holding additional chips for enhancing a microcomputer's processor or memory.

Extended Industry Standard Architecture A 32-bit bus standard.

facilities management Management and operation of all activities involved in providing a comprehensive DP service by a computer bureau for a client.

fail soft An orderly close down of a system or a failure that does not cause an immediate catastrophe.

FIFO (first-in first-out) Also known as a queue, this means that the first item or message to arrive in a system or in memory is the first to be dealt with, i.e. serviced or processed. See also LIFO.

firmware Software that is permanently resident in ROM.

flat file See relation.

FORTRAN (Formula Translator) A high-level language used mainly for scientific and engineering applications. Well known versions include FORTRAN IV and FORTRAN 77.

fuzzy theory A scientific approach to dealing with inaccurate data and indistinct situations.

gb See gigabyte.

gigabyte (gb) One thousand megabytes (2^{30} bytes).

graph plotter A device controlled by a computer and used for printing graphs and line diagrams in one or more colours. Rarely used in business as yet.

graphics The display of graphical, diagrammatic or pictorial output from a computer. In business generally coloured graphs and charts.

hacking The unauthorized intrusion into a computer system with a view to stealing, altering or damaging data or programs.

handshaking A start-up procedure to check that two DTEs or networks conform to the same protocol.

hard wired A circuit not incorporating software, i.e. micro-instructions. See also circuit.

hertz One hertz is one cycle per second.

heuristic A term applicable to any method or process that is based on trial and error, rules of thumb or intuitive decisions.

housekeeping Computer operations not specifically connected with an application but contributing to the overall efficiency of the computer's usage, e.g. redistributing stored files.

Huffman code A method of code numbering entities or data such that those with the highest probability of occurring have the shortest code numbers, thus minimizing storage and transmission requirements.

IAS (immediate access store/storage) Now called main store/storage or memory.

ICA/ICAEW The Institute of Chartered Accountants in England and Wales.

icon A shape on a VDU screen symbolizing a possible function or procedure of the computer, e.g. a filing tray symbolizing the storing of data.

ICON A programming language for string and list processing.

ICOT (Institute for New Generation Computer Technology) A Japanese organization set up to run the fifth-generation project.

ICSA The Institute of Chartered Secretaries and Administrators.

IDPM (Institute of Data Processing Management) A British professional society devoted to the furtherance of DP in business.

IEEE (Institute of Electrical and Electronic Engineers) A British professional society devoted to the furtherance of high standards in electrical and electronic engineering.

IEF (information engineering facility) A software system comprising a database management system and an application code generator.

IFIP (International Federation for Information Processing) A multinational federation of professional societies concerned with computing, DP and information.

image recording The recording of documents, diagrams, signatures, etc., in digitized form, thus permitting their processing and analysis, e.g. automatic recognition of peoples' signatures.

information theory A mathematical theory concerning the communication of signals, i.e. information, between two points. Also covers the 'value' of a piece of information based on its rarity.

INGRES A relational database management system.

installation A particular computer and its associated equipment at a certain location.

Integrated Services Data Network *See* ISDN.

integrity Maintenance of error-free and accurate data through the detection and removal of errors.

interface Circuitry enabling two devices to interchange data. A serial interface passes data as a single stream of bits, a parallel interface passes several streams, e.g. eight, simultaneously. Interfaces are nowadays standardized so that a variety of devices can be attached together, e.g. RS232C.

ISAC (Information Systems Work and Analysis of Changes) A systems development methodology.

IRDS (Information Resource Dictionary System) A standard for data dictionaries developed by ANSI.

ISDN (Integrated Services Data Network) A network designed for data transmission and capable of carrying all types of traffic.

ISO International Standards Organization.

job control language Control commands entered by a computer operator to describe a computer job to the operating system.

JSD (Jackson Systems Development) A systems development methodology.

kb *See* kilobyte.

kilobyte (kb) A kilobyte is strictly 1024 (2^{10}) bytes, although k is usually taken to mean a thousand.

KWIC (keyword in context) An alphabetic list in which each item appears once for each keyword in its title.

LCD (liquid crystal diode) A small tube of crystalline substance that alters its polarity and so becomes more visible when an electrical voltage is applied to it.

LDST *See* Logical data structuring technique

LED (light emitting diode) A small vacuum tube that glows red when an electric current is passed through it.

LIFO (last-in first-out) Otherwise known as a stack, this means that the last item, message or whatever to arrive in a system or in memory is the first to be dealt with, i.e. serviced or processed. *See also* FIFO.

LISP (LIST Processing) A programming language for handling data structures in the form of lists or strings such as in compilers; also used in artificial intelligence problems.

list Data items each of which is connected to the next by an address pointer (see 'chains' in Section 4.3).

load-sharing Two or more processors sharing a load of work, generally on-line processing, on an equal footing.

lockout Prevention of more than one user simultaneously changing data in a file or record.

Logical data structuring technique (LDST) A term used in SSADM to cover the modelling and charting of entity relationships. Similar to entity modelling.

log in/out, logout/off Procedure for gaining access to or exiting from a computer.

LOGO A language based on graphics for use in education.

LOTUS 1-2-3 A popular and sophisticated spreadsheet program offering the means of controlling a multiplicity of spreadsheets.

LSI (large scale integration) The solid-state technology of microchips where a large amount of electronic circuitry is compressed onto a small chip of silicon. VLSI (very large-scale integration) is an extension of this.

magnetic bubble memory Tiny bubbles of magnetism circulating in magnetic fields to represent data. Although non-volatile, its long access time has resulted in limited use.

magnetic ledger card (MLC) A card printed on one side and carrying the equivalent magnetic data on the other. Used with visible record computers (VRCs), now obsolete.

magneto-optical reading The detection of magnetic spots by optical methods.

main store/storage Storage giving immediate access to data and programs, and into which program instructions are transferred before execution. Memory is a synonymous term, mainly used with microcomputers.

mb *See* megabyte.

MCA (micro-channel architecture) A 32-bit bus standard.

megabyte (mb) A megabyte is actually 1,048,576 (2^{20}) bytes, although M is usually taken to mean a million.

memory *See* main store.

memory-mapped An exact replica in main storage of the pixels forming a display on a screen, also known as 'bit-mapped'.

Mercury A data and speech transmission service utilizing a fibre optic network interfaced to microwave and satellite transmission systems.

MERISE A French methodology similar to SSADM.

microchip A silicon chip (thin wafer) holding a minute electronic circuit capable of performing certain computing functions.

microsecond (μs) One millionth of a second (10^{-6} seconds).

migration The storage of data such that the more frequently used data is held in more accessible areas, and vice versa.

millisecond (ms) One thousandth of a second (10^{-3} seconds).

mips (millions of instructions per second) A measure of the speed at which processors operate. The power of the instruction set must also be taken into account when assessing a processor's capability.

MODULA A high-level programming language.

modulation The process whereby an electromagnetic or an electric current is modified in order to carry information, i.e. by varying their amplitude frequency or phase.

monitor A CRT and circuitry specifically designed for displaying computer output. Usually capable of the high-quality display of coloured graphics.

MOS Metal oxide semiconductor.

ms *See* millisecond.

MTBF (mean time between failures) The average time that a piece of hardware or a computer system is required and available for use between successive breakdowns. MTBF is a measure of reliability of equipment.

multithreading The processing of messages, generally real-time, in parallel through a thread of program modules.

Multiview A systems development methodology.

nanosecond (ns) One thousand-millionth of a second (10^{-9} seconds).

Nassi−Schneiderman (N−S) chart A diagram consisting of several adjoining areas of three types − processes, decisions and iterations − for depicting a process. Each area contains a brief description of a step in the process.

NBS (National Bureau of Standards) An American equivalent of the British Standards Institute.

NCC (National Computing Centre) A British government sponsored body dedicated to providing advisory services, conferences, training and publications associated with computing.

NLQ (near letter quality) A high standard of printing, often from a superior dot-matrix printer or a daisywheel printer.

node A point in a network at which there is a junction of transmission lines.

ns *See* nanosecond.

object-orientated DBMS A new method of structuring a DBMS that is claimed to have advantages over relational DBMSs.

OCCAM A computer language devised for

concurrent programming and intended for use with transputer-based computers.

octal A number system to the base 8, e.g. 237 in octal is 159 in decimal
$(2 \times 8^2 + 3 \times 8^1 + 7 \times 8^0)$.

octet A set of eight related bits of data, similar to a byte.

ODA (open document architecture) A data interchange standard (ISO 8613) for the electronic transmission of documents and conforming to OSI architecture.

OEM (original equipment manufacturer) A manufacturer who buys equipment from other manufacturers and builds it into the end product for sale to customers.

off-line Not directly linked to a computer. Sometimes also implying away from a computer system's mainstream activities.

ORACLE A relational database management system.

OS/2 An operating system from IBM and Microsoft designed to replace MS-DOS by being much more user-friendly.

PABX (private automatic branch exchange) A telephone exchange internal to one organization.

PAD (packet assembler/disassembler) A facility enabling DTE not conforming to X25 to be linked to an X25 PSS. *See also* 'protocol converter'.

Page description language (PDL) A high-level language for specifying the layouts of pages printed by laser printers. These may include both text and graphics as in desktop publishing.

palette The range of colours available on a VDU for text and graphics displays.

paper tape A long strip of paper punched with machine-readable holes representing data. Paper tape is now obsolete.

parameter A value which can be altered, used to control a certain piece of processing within a program, e.g. a tax rate in a payroll program.

PC Personal computer.

PDL *See* page description language.

picosecond (ps) One million-millionth of a second (10^{-12} seconds).

PILOT A special-purpose programming language for developing software for computer-assisted learning (CAL).

plug compatible Capable of interchange without any hardware or software alteration.

polymorphism The concept of making up a required configuration by linking units drawn from sets of duplicated units. This gives great

flexibility and hence a high level of reliability since only one unit of each pair needs to be operational for the whole configuration to be operational.

port A point for input or output on a processor, a port is normally capable of accepting a variety of devices via a standard interface.

portability The extent to which software can be run on different computers.

PROLOG A descriptive programming language used mainly for research into artificial intelligence and in education.

protocol converter Software enabling DTE not conforming to X25 to be linked to an X25 PSS. *See also* 'PAD'.

ps *See* picosecond.

PSS (Packet Switching System) *See* switchstream service.

pulse rate *See* clock rate.

punched card A machine-readable card through which holes are punched to represent data, one card represents one entity or activity. Punched cards are now obsolete.

punched tape *See* paper tape.

queue *See* FIFO.

Quickbuild A fourth-generation language from ICL with an interface to SSADM.

RACE (Research in Advanced Communications in Europe) A research programme devised by the EEC to develop integrated high-speed communication systems, and to assess the feasibilities of related products and services.

real-time clock An electronic clock built into a computer to indicate the time of day and to measure elapsed time.

re-entrant Capable of being shared by several jobs or programs at the same time, e.g. a subroutine.

relation A flat, i.e. two-dimensional, file of normalized data items.

resilience The ability of a computer system to remain operational despite various failures.

RISC (reduced instruction set computer) This type of microprocessor has only a small hard-wired instruction set (about one-fifth of the size of most CISC microprocessors). Although cheaper and faster than CISC, each instruction achieves less.

RS232/RS232C Standard interfaces in common use, especially for microcomputers.

reverse Polish notation An arrangement of numbers or data items followed by the operators that are applied to them, for an example see FORTH in Section 5.2.

SAA (systems application architecture) A standard interface for all IBM computers (mainframes, minicomputers and microcomputers).

satellite transmission The transmission of information, including computer data, over long distances by means of radio beams retransmitted from satellites in stationary orbits above the earth.

schema A map of the overall structure of a database. A schema could include a DDL to define all the occurrences of data items, records, sets, etc.

self-checking number A number containing a check digit.

shell A protective data structure encapsulating information being transmitted over communication lines. The sender needs to specify only the recipient's name and company.

silicon chip *See* chip.

SNA (systems network architecture) A set of formats and protocols designed by IBM for transmitting data in a communications network system. Similar to X25 to which it can be interfaced.

SNOBOL A high-level programming language.

solid-state *See* LSI.

SQL (structured query language) A standard database language and interface for use with microcomputer relational databases.

SSADM (Structured Systems Analysis and Design Method) The UK government's standard method for the systems analysis and design of an information technology project.

SSM (Soft Systems Methodology) A systems development methodology.

stack *See* LIFO.

stepwise refinement The repeated breaking down of a procedure into smaller procedures until they can be easily programmed, probably in a structured language such as Pascal.

STRADIS (Structured Analysis and Design of Information Systems) A systems development methodology.

SUPERCALC 5 A sophisticated spreadsheet program incorporating financial functions, data searching and high-resolution graphical presentation.

Switchstream Service British Telecom's PSS, formerly called Packet Switching System. Kilostream and Megastream are faster versions.

syntax The rules governing the structure of statements or instructions in a source language.

tally roll A long strip of paper upon which figures are printed, sometimes in OCR font or subsequent automatic input to a computer.

Telenet An American data communications network.

telesoftware Transmission of computer software over telephone lines, and particularly computer programs downloaded from a central computer to many microcomputers.

Teletex A European high-speed public electronic mail service. Not to be confused with Teletext.

third-generation language (3GL) A high-level programming language such as COBOL or Pascal, i.e. one level below fourth-generation languages.

top-down A broad term meaning the development of a system or preparation of a computer program such that the overall design is completed and tested first. When this 'skeleton' is working, further modules are interfaced to it.

traffic The data, voice, video, etc., carried by a line or a network.

transaction processing The entering and processing of a string of transactions all of which pertain to the entity specified in previously entered header data.

transparency The transmission of data via equipment that has no effect on the data as finally received. Two modems, for instance, one modulating and the other demodulating the transmitted data, are transparent to the receiver.

transputer A RISC 32-bit microprocessor for executing the instructions of the OCCAM language. Transputer is also a more general term meaning any device capable of transforming movement into electricity.

tuple A group of related data items in a database, often called a 'record'.

turnkey operation The designing and implementation of a DP system by an external organization, e.g. a consultancy firm, with minimal involvement by the user company.

Tymnet An American data communication network.

unified database A database incorporating both text and images intended for desktop publishing.

UCSD An operating system allied to structured programming languages such as Pascal.

μs *See* microsecond.

V24 A recommendation of the CCITT regarding

the interfacing between terminals and modems, forms part of X25.

VANS (value added network services) A service supplied by a VAN operating company whereby a user can simply plug into an interface in order to send or receive data over worldwide networks and thereby obtain access to a wide range of information and services.

VDM (Vienna Development Method) A language for creating formal systems specifications.

virtual circuit The apparent connection together of two nodes (points) in a network. There is no complete electrical connection at any time.

virtual storage A technique that facilitates programming by allowing the programmer to proceed as if he has an unlimited amount of main storage at his disposal.

virus Latent patches of program intended to cause errors and corruption of data. These are introduced deliberately and are often capable of passing to other linked systems.

visible record computer (VRC) A manually operated accounting machine holding a stored program thus enabling it to take over from the operator at certain times, now obsolete.

VLSI See LSI.

volatile storage Storage that loses its contents when the power is cut off, e.g. solid state storage.

volume Originally any demountable storage unit such as a magnetic disk cartridge. Also refers to any storage device accessible by using one or more read/write mechanisms.

Von Neumann architecture The concept of treating program instructions in the same way as data in a computer. The program instructions are executed serially and held in storage and, most importantly, are alterable rather than in a fixed format. Von Neumann architecture has been utilized in all digital computers since the late 1940s.

walkthrough A procedure for checking the correctness of a system during the course of its development. The walkthrough is carried out by a team, each member of which has specific tasks. Problems and errors found during walkthroughs are documented for subsequent correction.

wand A hand-held device for optically reading bar codes on goods, labels and shelves.

Warrier–Orr diagram A diagram made up of brief descriptions of the steps in a process linked by brackets and laid out in a hierarchical format.

Whetstone rating A standard benchmark of computer performance based on a mix of instructions simulating the user's requirements.

wide area network A communications network covering a widespread geographical area and generally utilizing microwave links and communication satellites.

WIMP Windows, icons, menus and pointer *or* windows, icons, mouse and pull-down (or pop-up) menus.

WordPerfect A comprehensive word processing program offering the means of creating, editing and printing documents. It includes checking spelling, footnotes and text merging.

Wordstar A screen-orientated word processing program with a high level of performance and flexibility. It is used to create and edit documents of a wide range of size and complexity.

workbench *See* CASE.

workstation A point through which a user has access to remote storage and also performs local computing. Typically, a microcomputer linked into a LAN.

WORM (write once, read many) Optical disks holding archival records and analogue information such as signatures, X-rays and photographic images.

writing tablet A device for converting handwritten impressions into coded characters and positional coordinates for input to a computer. This enables it to be used for capturing small amounts of data and for the automatic recognition of signatures.

X25 A recommendation of the CCITT regarding the protocol for the data transfer between terminals and PSSs.

X75 Similar to X25 but for interconnected PSSs (internetworking).

X400 The electronic mail protocol within OSI.

Z A language for creating formal systems specifications.

Further reading

G1 Anderson, R.G., *A Concise Dictionary of Data Processing and Computer Terms* (Pitman, 1985).

G2 Disney, C., *Information Technology Dictionary* (Pitman, 1986).

G3 Steer, M., *Business Studies Dictionary* (Pitman, 1986).

G4 Longley, D. and Shain, M., *Macmillan Dictionary of Information Technology* (Macmillan, 1988).

G5 Longley, D. and Shain, M., *Data and Computer Security: A Dictionary of Terms and Concepts* (Macmillan, 1987).

G6 Longley, D. and Shain, M., *Macmillan Dictionary of Personal Computing and Communications* (Macmillan, 1986).

G7 *Dictionary of Computing* (OUP, 1986).

G8 Scott, J. and Rogers, I., *First Dictionary of Microcomputing* (Arnold, 1987).

G9 Rosenberg, J.M., *Dictionary of Computers, Information Processing and Telecommunications* (Wiley, 1987).

G10 Sippl, C.J., *Macmillan Dictionary of Microcomputing* (Macmillan, 1985).

G11 Sippl, C.J., *Macmillan Dictionary of Data Communications* (Macmillan, 1985).

G12 *McGraw-Hill Dictionary of Computers* (McGraw-Hill, 1985).

G13 Lynch, D., *Information Technology of Acronyms and Abbreviations* (Chartwell-Bratt, 1988).

G14 Illingworth, V., *Minidictionary of Computing* (OUP, 1986).

Index